Politics and
Government in Israel

Politics and Government in Israel

The Maturation of a Modern State

Second Edition

Gregory S. Mahler

ROWMAN & LITTLEFIELD PUBLISHERS, INC.
Lanham • Boulder • New York • Toronto • Plymouth, UK

Published by Rowman & Littlefield Publishers, Inc.
A wholly owned subsidiary of The Rowman & Littlefield Publishing Group, Inc.
4501 Forbes Boulevard, Suite 200, Lanham, Maryland 20706
http://www.rowmanlittlefield.com

Estover Road, Plymouth PL6 7PY, United Kingdom

British Library Cataloguing in Publication Information Available

Library of Congress Cataloging-in-Publication Data
Mahler, Gregory S., 1950–
  Politics and government in Israel : the maturation of a modern state / Gregory S.
Mahler. — 2nd ed.
      p. cm.
  Includes bibliographical references and index.
  ISBN 978-0-7425-6827-3 (cloth : alk. paper) — ISBN 978-0-7425-6828-0
(pbk. : alk. paper) — ISBN 978-0-7425-6829-7 (electronic)
  1. Israel—Politics and government—20th century. 2. Israel—Social conditions—
20th century. I. Title.
  JQ1830.A91M34 2011
  320.95694—dc22
                                    2010037872

♾™ The paper used in this publication meets the minimum requirements of
American National Standard for Information Sciences—Permanence of Paper for
Printed Library Materials, ANSI/NISO Z39.48-1992. Printed in the United States of
America

Contents

Boxes, Figures, Maps, Photos, and Tables

BOXES

FIGURES

MAPS

PHOTOS

TABLES

Preface

It has been a pleasure to again work with the good people at Rowman & Littlefield on the second edition of this project. The study of Israeli politics has interested me for my entire professional life—my doctoral research was done in Israel's parliament in Jerusalem shortly after the 1973 war—and I have been active in research in the field since that time. Having the opportunity to write an introductory textbook is both rewarding and challenging. The reward comes from being able to discuss issues that I believe are important and from being able to feel that I may be contributing in a small way to student interest in the topic. The challenge, of course, comes from trying to decide what goes into the book. This is true not only in terms of major topics, but also in terms of detail. The chapter on historical background in this volume is but a small fraction of the size of other volumes devoted exclusively to that subject, and someone will certainly be dissatisfied that something has been omitted from the discussion or that I appear to be following one line of interpretation rather than another. That is, indeed, unfortunate, but in the many decisions about what to include and what to omit, those determinations had to be made.

It is probably inevitable that some will be unhappy with particular aspects of this book, critical either that I have omitted or included certain facts or that I have drawn some of the conclusions presented here. Unfortunately, I think that any volume dealing with a large number of essentially controversial subjects, as this one does, faces this dilemma; I simply do not see any way around the problem. If we are to discuss controversial material—and, indeed, a fundamental commitment to this type of discussion and inquiry is central to our academic mission—then this is a risk we must face. I can only say here that I have endeavored to present a balanced picture.

The completion of a book manuscript gives an author the opportunity to acknowledge publicly the assistance and encouragement received in the course of his work. Many of my colleagues in the Association for Israel Studies were very enthusiastic about earlier books that I have written on this topic and encouraged me to undertake this project. Their suggestions about what should and should not be included were very helpful indeed. I want to thank the anonymous reviewers contacted by Rowman & Littlefield for their very helpful suggestions in the earlier stages of this manuscript, and for their suggestions of ways that a second edition might improve upon the first. My colleagues Mark Tessler at the University of Michigan, Ken Stein at Emory University, and Reuven Hazan at Hebrew University have offered special encouragement in the past, and for this I am in their debt.

Susan McEachern and Carrie Broadwell-Tkach at Rowman & Littlefield have been supportive as I've worked on the second edition project. I also want to thank Jeremy Rehwaldt-Alexander, my copyeditor at Rowman & Littlefield, for trying to make my writing more clear. None of these people, of course, is responsible for the shortcomings that may be found in these pages, and I alone am accountable for any errors of content or omission in this manuscript, as well as its conclusions.

As I have done in many settings in the past, I want to acknowledge the role of my wife, Marjorie, who first introduced me to the streets of Jerusalem and to the study of Israel. As we have returned to Jerusalem over the years, with our daughters and by ourselves, our wonderful experiences have been shared experiences. This book, accordingly, should be shared with her too.

Introduction

The Study of Israel in Comparative Context

WHAT DO WE STUDY?

The study of politics has long attracted those interested in the world around them. Indeed, political science as a discipline can be traced back to at least the time of Plato (c. 427–347 B.C.) and Aristotle (384–322 B.C.). Aristotle is often referred to as the first "real" political scientist because of his study of many of the political systems that he found in the world at his time. His comparisons of constitutions and power structures contributed many words to our political vocabulary today—words such as "politics," "democracy," "oligarchy," and "aristocracy."[1] Since the time of Plato and Aristotle—and before it—observers have sought to understand both the social and political institutions of the state, as well as the state's behavior, as a way of understanding a significant part of the world around them.

When we talk about politics, we mean a variety of different things. For many, the word suggests very clear ideas: political campaigns, voting in elections, streets full of demonstrators, or military action. For others it might suggest more subtle political influence by lobbyists, overt political manipulation by the political elite, or a long and painfully drawn-out process of policy decision making by those in a position to make decisions. Those who are familiar with formal political institutions may think of constitutions, legislatures, executives, courts, political parties, and interest groups. In short, the term *politics* will mean different things to different people.

An example will show the broad range of perceptions that can be associated with political terms. When I was involved in my first research project in Jerusalem in 1975, focusing on Israel's parliament, the Knesset,[2] I asked members of the Knesset about their first political memories.[3] The responses

1

ranged profoundly from those who associated politics with elections, to those who associated politics with demonstrations, to those who associated politics with their parents being killed in the Holocaust.

This demonstrates that the study of politics must include a wide range of topics, from the most obvious formal political institutions (like constitutions, legislatures, bureaucracies, and the like) to far more subtle factors (like culture, religion, and the impact of history), and that we cannot walk into an analysis of a culture or a political system with a preset perception of what is important to study. Knowing how often elections must take place or how many members there are in a national legislature will tell us something about a nation, but to understand fully how and why political policy is made, we need to know much more than this.

To understand Israeli politics, we must look at the broad political environment. We want to understand patterns of interactions among individuals and groups in Israeli society.[4] This kind of study focuses upon those interactions that involve power, or authority. The "classical" political scientist David Easton referred to *politics* as dealing with the "authoritative allocation of values for a society," the process by which the social goals and standards binding upon members of a society are set.[5] Thus, the study of politics may involve the study of legislatures, the study of voting, the study of political parties, the study of the role of a minority group in a political system, the study of power, more generally the study of how public policy is made, or all of these—and more.

Why do we study politics at all? What are we looking for? As suggested above, the range of subjects for our inquiry is extraordinarily broad. In the Israeli context we might be trying to learn about the relationship between religion and the state; similarly, we might be interested in understanding why some individuals have power and others don't. We might want to understand how social policy is made or why a given election is won by one political party rather than another.

In short, there are many different reasons for studying political behavior, and there are many different aspects of political behavior to study. One thing, however, is clear: political science is only one of the social sciences concerned with helping us to understand the complex world around us. The others, including economics, psychology, sociology, and anthropology, also study the same general types of social phenomena that we study.

HOW DO WE STUDY POLITICS?

One of the key decisions that we have to address at a very early stage involves how we will approach our study of politics. One approach is the case study approach, in which we focus upon one case, or subject, or nation—here the nation is Israel—and we study the political institutions and behavior of that nation. This is done without explicit comparison with other nations or other case studies. The advantage of this approach is that we study our case in much greater detail and come to understand the various components of our case far more thoroughly than we might if we used the alternative approach.

The alternative approach is called the comparative approach. We know what the term *compare* suggests; it involves terms of relativity, like *bigger, stronger, freer, more stable, less democratic,* and so on. A comparative approach to a political study, then, involves no more and no less than a search for similarities and differences between political phenomena, including political institutions (such as legislatures, political parties, or political interest groups), political behavior (such as voting, demonstrating, or reading political pamphlets), or political ideas (such as Zionism, socialism, liberalism, conservatism, or Marxism).

Using this approach we continuously compare and contrast Israeli political institutions and Israeli political behavior with the political institutions and political behavior of other nations. The advantage of this approach is that it permits us to appreciate more fully some of the special characteristics of Israeli politics, or to appreciate more fully the consequences of some of the characteristics of Israeli politics.

The fact that in 2010 Israel—with a population of over 7.5 million at the time—had twelve political parties represented in its national legislature (and well more than that number seeking seats in the 2009 election for Knesset membership) takes on greater significance when we realize that the United States, with more than 308 million people, had two major parties represented in its national legislature. Israel's "constitutional" government has no written constitution. Israeli political institutions may be said to operate relatively smoothly when they are viewed in isolation; when they are viewed from a comparative perspective, we may say that they operate more smoothly than those of Italy but less smoothly than those of Canada, and we may then seek to understand why this is so. The value of the comparative method is that it enables us to appreciate relative performance, and it often permits us to view and appreciate characteristics of a political system that we simply would not see if we were viewing that system in isolation.

The problem with a consistent comparative approach, of course, is that we have to compare all aspects of Israeli politics with all comparable aspects in other countries, and thereby a substantial proportion of this book would not be focused on Israel at all, but rather would be showing comparable political institutions or political behaviors in the United States, Britain, Italy, Japan, Jordan, or any number of other nations. This would help us appreciate those structures and behaviors to be found in Israel, but would also distract us from our study of Israel.

My solution in this volume is to offer an approach that is primarily a case study approach, but in some instances, where appropriate and effective, I draw in some comparative "threads" for perspective. This might be referred to as a case study analysis from a comparative perspective. We are primarily interested in understanding Israeli political history, Israeli political institutions, Israeli political behavior, and Israeli foreign policy. On occasion, however, some characteristics of Israel's history, institutions, or behavior will be so special that we will compare them with those of Britain, the United States, Italy, or other political systems in order that we might fully appreciate the significance of what we are studying.[6]

STUDYING POLITICAL INSTITUTIONS AND BEHAVIOR

Why are we undertaking the particular comparison that we are undertaking? What kind of objects do we want to study? As indicated earlier, the subjects of comparative political inquiry are as disparate and varied as one might imagine. Generally, it can be suggested that there are three broad categories of subjects to examine in the comparative study of politics: government structures, political behavior, and public policy. When we study Israeli government and politics, we seek to understand all three of these areas.

The first general approach focuses on the governmental institutions themselves. This type of study may focus on legislatures, executives, courts, constitutions, legal systems, bureaucracies, and perhaps even political parties. By studying the institutions of a regime, it is argued, we can understand how it behaves and how political decisions are made. One obvious example of this in the Israeli context involves the electoral system: the fact that Israel has a specific type of electoral system—involving proportional representation elections—means that there will be a large number of political parties. This invariably means that there will have to be coalition governments (since no single party can win control of a majority of seats in the Knesset, the parliament). This, in turn, means that prime ministers are not as free to exercise autonomy in the construction of policy because they consistently have to be worried about maintaining their political base of power.

A second general thrust of study is oriented toward political behavior. Studies of this type may focus upon voting behavior, political stability, political elites, leaders in politics, party behavior, and so on. The central ideas of this approach involve the assumption that if one understands how people behave in a political system—and this includes all people, both the leaders and the led—then one will develop an understanding about the political system within which that behavior takes place. Much has been made of the *ein breirah* ("no alternative") psychology of politics in Israel. Israeli citizens find themselves in a very difficult environment, and this environment and Israelis' resulting political behavior lead to certain consequences for the political system.

In studies of public policy, the focus of attention is on the result of what governments do. These studies will invariably pay some attention to the related questions of how governments act, how they do what they do, why they act, and which stimuli help the governments in question decide to act as they do when they do. There are a number of very fundamental issues in Israeli society that serve to divide the public, perhaps more than in just about any other democratic society. We can find "normal" policy disagreements over government economic policy—the traditional "left" and "right" of political systems—but in addition to these, we also find fundamental disagreements in the world of Israeli policy over the relationship between religion and the state, over questions dealing with Zionism and the state, and over questions dealing with national posture vis-à-vis the Palestinians and the question of a Palestinian state (as distinct from general questions dealing with national security, which can be found in all political settings). These policy debates, as well as others, are often the subject of study.

In addition to these three very broad categories, we need to understand the context within which the nation exists, its environment and its setting. We need to understand some of the most fundamental characteristics of the state, too. This includes discussion of the state's very creation and existence: how it came into being, how easily it has survived, and how likely it is to survive into the future. Political borders can (and do) change, as a result either of war or of agreement between parties involved, or, perhaps, as a result of both. National security is a key variable here.

We also need to appreciate the ideological underpinnings of the regime. The notion of Zionism at the turn of the twentieth century was based on the idea that there was a "nation" of Jewish people that were "stateless" in a number of nation-states around the world and that a Jewish state was needed for them to call their home. This Zionist concept subsequently gave birth to the state of Israel.[7] It is indeed ironic that in a very similar manner today, Palestinians are claiming the need for a state of their own, independent of Israel, Jordan, Egypt, Saudi Arabia, and other Middle Eastern states.[8]

STUDYING ISRAELI GOVERNMENT AND POLITICS

Although the modern state of Israel is just over six decades old, since its establishment it has played a role on the world's political stage far greater than its size alone would suggest. This has led to a significant increase in the number of students interested in studying both the domestic and international environment in which the Israeli political system operates. Despite a corresponding proliferation of scholarship, however, only a few textbooks are designed to introduce the world of Israeli politics.

In order to study Israeli politics, one has to do three things. First, one simply must appreciate the historical background and social context within which the state came into existence. Second, one must master the intricacies of the significant political structures and patterns of political behavior that exist in the political system. Finally, one must understand the external environment within which the political system operates. This book attempts to help the student to do all three of these; many other books focus on one or two, but not all three.

Although the study of relevant history and context is important for appreciating the political environment of any nation, it is especially so in the Israeli case, if for no other reason than the fact that some continue to challenge the very legitimacy of the state. Since the student is in no position to understand or evaluate the validity of those challenges without an appreciation of the historical record, it is important that any study of Israel devote some attention to the historical background, to understanding the general claims of the Israelis (and others) to the territory of the state in question, and to understanding what was promised to whom by the British and what happened during and after World War II. Chapter 1 presents a brief discussion of the historical roots of the contemporary Israeli political system, including the antecedents of the contemporary Palestinian crisis. Prestate political evolution is discussed, as are the political machinations that led to a British withdrawal from the region at the end of World War II. The impact of World War II and the Holocaust are discussed and lead to an examination of the transition to statehood from 1945 to 1948.

Beyond this, there are a number of other "background" topics that are especially important in the study of Israeli politics and, therefore, should be discussed. Chapter 2 focuses on Zionism, religion, and the domestic political environment within which Israeli politics operate. While it is true that all national political structures are influenced by the context within which they operate, there are some unique characteristics of Israeli society that go beyond the "normal" range of issues. Zionism is one of these characteristics. The relationship between religion and politics in the state is another. The debate in Israel over the relationship between religious orthodoxy and the more secular part of the population is often highly politicized. And, of course, while Israel is known as "the Jewish State," the fact is that nearly one Israeli in five is *not* Jewish, and this has political implications for the state as well. What should be the relationship between one "kind" of Israeli and another? For that matter, given the different groups within the Jewish population, what should be the relationship between one "kind" of Jew and another? After being introduced, albeit briefly, to the questions and problems raised by these subjects, the student is better prepared to undertake a direct examination of the overtly "political" characteristics of the Israeli polity.

Chapter 3 features discussion of other contextual variables, such as social (including gender) and economic variables, which are often translated into political variables, including the identity of non-Jews (e.g., who are "Israeli Arabs"?) and different kinds of Jews (e.g., what is the significance of the differences between Sephardic and Ashkenazic Jews?). Issues related to immigration and emigration, social class, education, and the like also are discussed. Some of the very important issues in the polity relate to Israeli Arabs—Arab citizens of Israel, as distinct from Arab residents of the Occupied Territories. How are Israeli Arabs treated in the Israeli political world? Do they have the same status and rights as Israeli Jews? Following this discussion, Israel's economic identity and characteristics are evaluated and discussed.

With that accomplished, the second major dimension of study in Israeli politics involves the more "traditional" aspects of the political system, the significant political structures, governmental institutions, and patterns of political behavior that exist in the political system. Included are such topics as constitutionalism, the general structure of parliamentary government, the character and behavior of political parties and interest groups, the electoral system and voting behavior, the traditional political structures of the Knesset, the prime minister and cabinet, the bureaucracy, and the judiciary. An appreciation of the political structures and behavior found in a regime makes up the core of any "area studies" political science course, and this is no less true for Israel than for any other state.

Chapter 4 examines the constitutional system and Israel's version of parliamentary government. Not all constitutional settings are alike, and Israel's constitutional system is unique in the world. Israel has an "unwritten" parliamentary constitution that differs significantly from those of other parliamentary nations. This chapter examines Israel's decision to have an "unwritten" constitution, with a related decision to write a constitution over time. It also discusses the basic structures of Israel's constitution, the role of the courts in Israeli politics, and the impact of the courts on the evolution of the Israeli constitutional system. Finally, it analyzes the implications of Israel's unique version of a "parliamentary" structure and attempts to interpret the significance of Israeli idiosyncrasies in this regard.

Within the parliamentary world, the relationship between the prime minister and the parliament—the Knesset—is key. Chapter 5 discusses the prime minister's relationship with the Knesset and the operation of both the legislative and executive branches of government today. This chapter also covers the setting and organization of the Knesset, how legislation is passed, and the role of individual members of the Knesset (MKs). After the Knesset's organization has been explained, the nature of coalition politics is examined, and the unusual but highly significant role of coalition government in Israel is analyzed in order to understand why Israeli governments act the way that they do.

The building blocks of Israeli democracy are Israel's political parties, and they are discussed in chapter 6. Israel was described nearly fifty years ago as a *parteienstaat* ("party-state"), and the role of political parties in the day-to-day operation of the polity has not diminished. This chapter examines how political parties are organized in Israel, their key issues, and how they differ from each other. Following a thorough discussion of the parties, the focus shifts to interest groups, another very important structure in the contemporary Israeli democratic arena.

While familiarity with parties and interest groups is of great importance to understanding how Israeli politics operates, the fact is that parties and interest groups cannot be understood without knowledge of the "rules of the game," how they are expected (and permitted) to behave in the polity. Israel's proportional representation electoral system for Knesset elections (and, relatively recently, the addition of a direct election for the prime minister, followed less than a decade later by a return to the original model of elections) has rendered elections in Israel consistently problematic. Chapter 7 also discusses key factors influencing election outcomes and examines trends in recent elections to understand the significance of the electoral framework for Israeli voting behavior and Israeli politics more generally construed.

Other formal political structures of the Israeli polity also need to be examined, and they are discussed in chapter 8. The bureaucracy and local government are significant in the day-to-day operation of politics in Israel, in the context of an understanding of unitary politics in Israel. Judicial institutions are unique as a result of the religion-and-politics debates discussed in chapter 2, and this is the point at which further discussion of the role of religion in Israeli politics takes place. Religious courts influence the daily lives of many Israelis, and this chapter examines their roles. Finally, the political role of the much-discussed Israeli Defense Forces is analyzed. The military's role in politics has changed considerably over the last fifty years, and many of the legends of the military's role are simply that, legends. The military is still highly significant in the political arena—quite apart from its role in the strategic arena—and an understanding of its structure and organization is of importance for a complete mastery of the material presented in this book. The chapter also keeps the particular status of Arab Israelis as an active dimension of discussion and analysis.

The third and last major dimension of study of Israeli politics involves recognition of the external environment and foreign policy. Foreign policy is an integral component of any country's political system, and this is particularly true for Israel. There are several reasons for this, the most important being the continued state of hostility that has existed between Israel and some of its Arab neighbors, and the hostile geopolitical atmosphere in which it has had to operate since its creation. The study of Israeli foreign policy thus encompasses, among other important topics, an examination of the geopolitical and strategic contexts within which foreign policy decisions are made, the history of Israeli and Arab foreign policies, military strategy and tactics, and the evolving definition of what constitutes "national security." Chapter 9 briefly examines each of these issues with an eye toward more fully understanding both the context within which Israeli foreign policy is made and the strategic considerations that constantly preoccupy decision makers. This chapter examines the legacy of warfare experienced in this region and analyzes the strategic considerations that have contributed to Israeli foreign policy over the last five decades. The issue of military security has traditionally been paramount in Israeli politics, and this chapter traces the history of Israeli military operations. In a parallel manner, this chapter also examines the political, diplomatic, economic, and cultural factors that have been significant in the Israeli foreign policy setting over the last fifty years.

The conflict that has existed between Israelis and Palestinians for well over half a century is confusing, and chapter 10 seeks to clarify it somewhat. Labels used in discussion of the Middle East conflict are not value-free, and for some observers there are significant emotional attachments involved in these discussions. This chapter discusses both the historical and the contemporary significance of concepts in the equation, concepts such as *Occupied Territories* or even *Eretz Israel*. The term *West Bank* is rooted in history, as are terms like *Palestinian* and *Zionist*, and before a student can fully understand the nature of current debate, she must understand the history and current meaning of the terms involved. In this chapter the student also meets a more substantial discussion of the term *Palestinian* to understand the historical and contemporary meaning of that label. Beyond this, the importance of Jerusalem to the various actors in the debate is also discussed.

The final chapter of this book discusses the elusive, frustrating, sometimes partially successful, yet ultimately (so far) unreachable goal of peace in the Middle East. This chapter discusses long-term Israeli plans, policies related to building settlements, and issues of military governance, as well as issues related to Palestinian nationalism, the Middle East political arena, and questions of national security for Israel with increased Palestinian sovereignty. This chapter also includes a historical discussion of the peace process itself and of events leading up to the Camp David Peace Agreement and the peace treaty between Israel and Egypt in 1979. Key events since that time, from Oslo and Madrid to Camp David (again) and Annapolis, are also described. The chapter ends with a discussion of prospects for peace in the future.

It is not the assumption of this volume that a student who has worked his or her way through these pages will know everything that there is to know about contemporary Israeli politics. Even the most cursory glance at the brief suggested reading sections at the end of each chapter will indicate how truly massive the relevant literature is. The purpose of this volume is not to develop comprehensive expertise, but to raise consciousness and familiarity; not to provide all of the answers, but to introduce many of the questions; not to decide which side is right and which side is wrong, but to show that sincere and reasonable individuals may, in fact, disagree over what the "facts" are, and, correspondingly, may draw different conclusions from the same presentation.

I

THE POLITICAL SETTING

1

History and the Creation of Israel

This chapter presents a discussion of the historical roots of the contemporary Israeli political system. This includes domestic Israeli politics, Israel's foreign relations generally construed, and the antecedents of the contemporary Palestinian crisis. After briefly referring to very early events related to Jewish communities inside and outside of *Eretz Israel*, a fuller discussion of the emergence of Zionism from 1830 to 1917 is presented.[1] Subsequent sections of the chapter focus on the growth of the *Yishuv* from 1880 to 1939 and the Balfour Declaration and British Mandate Period from 1917 to 1947. It also discusses the impact of World War II and the Holocaust and examines the transition to statehood from 1945 to 1948. This chapter includes a number of maps to show the several proposed partitions of Palestine, as well as the 1949 armistice lines. Woven into this historical analysis is a discussion of the non-Jewish Palestinian population in the region and how the growth and development of the Jewish and Zionist population affected those individuals and led to conflicts between Palestinians and Israelis in future years.

The study of the history of any country is often an important prerequisite for a complete understanding of how and why its political system has developed as it has. This statement is nowhere truer than in the case of Israel. While it might be argued that one could understand the operation of the American political system without a complete exposure to the history and

---

The fortified palace Massada that was built by Herod the Great between 37 and 31 B.C., which was the site of a siege of Jewish Zealots by the Roman Army in 66 A.D., during the First Jewish-Roman War

thought of preindependence America, this simply is not true for the study of the Israeli political system; for example, an understanding of the current tensions between Israel and the Palestinian population requires a historical context within which to evaluate them. Modern Israel is a nation conceived in an era of crisis, a nation whose idea evolved during times of struggle and hardship, and a nation born during an epoch of horror, tragedy, and violence. Israel's very existence was challenged from the moment its independence was declared, and this challenge has been continued by most of its neighbors to this very day.

How has modern Israel come to be located where it is? What were the factors that led to the movement commonly referred to as Zionism? What did the supporters of this movement do to achieve their political ends? What were the antecedents of the Israeli-Palestinian conflict? These are each short and straightforward questions, but their answers are neither short nor straightforward. The issues involved are quite complex and, to make matters worse for the interested and conscientious student, not all of the "facts" are agreed upon by those studying these, and related, considerations.

Our purpose in this chapter is to identify some of the major issues necessary for a general understanding of the historical context from which modern Israel emerged. A single chapter cannot, of course, present a comprehensive discussion of all, or even most, of the issues involved. Indeed, the 1996 edition of one of the definitive political histories of Israel—Howard Sachar's *A History of Israel: From the Rise of Zionism to Our Time* (Alfred A. Knopf)—is more than one thousand pages in length! Rather, this chapter seeks to present enough information so that the concerned student can appreciate how truly complex the issues are and, in so doing, can comprehend the linkage that exists between modern Israel and its past. Beyond this, the student must turn to specialized and more detailed resources in his or her quest for a richer understanding of modern Israel.

This chapter discusses several different periods of Jewish and Israeli history. We begin with a necessarily brief discussion of some of the ancient and historically distant roots of contemporary Israel. The development of the concept of Zionism is, of course, crucial in this process, and we briefly trace its origins and evolution from a political current that began in nineteenth-century Europe to a much more fully developed movement that led to the establishment of the state of Israel in 1948.

We do not focus our attention on the Israeli-Palestinian conflict and the Middle East peace process until this book's final chapter. However, it is important that we understand how this conflict developed, and that goes back to the earliest days of the establishment of Israel. Although Zionism is certainly a complex phenomenon, the interaction of Zionists with the very complex political, economic, and social situation they found in Palestine in the early part of the twentieth century served to turn a complicated and sensitive situation into a conflictual one. As we progress through the subjects covered in this volume, we regularly keep an eye on the related Palestinian agenda to endeavor to understand better how today's conflict developed and what the relevant positions are in that conflict. We also must understand one of the essential characteristics of historical analysis: it can be affected by perspective and by the passage of time. The "standard" histories of the Middle East and of the creation of the state of Israel are being reexamined today and reinterpreted, so much debate today is not between individuals who have studied history and individuals who have not studied history, but instead between individuals who have studied history from one perspective and individuals who have studied it from another.[2]

Following World War I, Britain was entrusted with a mandate over Palestine, and throughout the interwar period exercised a significant influence on the region as a whole. This chapter therefore seeks to show how the most important political activities of this period contributed to the establishment of the state of Israel, as well as the manner in which World War II and the Holocaust were significant in emphasizing the immediacy of that end. Finally, it documents the actual transition from Mandatory Palestine to independent Israel in the years after World War II.

It must be recalled, however, that the land upon which modern Israel was established was *not* empty when the Zionists began to organize systematic waves of migration to Palestine. As we trace the historical roots of the development of the state of Israel, we cannot forget to note where appropriate the nature and the history of the indigenous population in Palestine and the impact of the growth of the Zionist and Jewish population upon the non-Jewish and non-Zionist people already living on that land.[3] This would become later, of course, the basis of an ongoing tragedy as Palestinian nationalism would conflict with Israeli security concerns and desires for control over much of the land on the West Bank of the Jordan River.

HISTORICAL ROOTS OF CONTEMPORARY ISRAEL

We do not begin our discussion of modern Israel by referring to biblical or religious sources, although such a start would be possible and might even be considered necessary by some. There would be, however, several substantive problems for any contemporary social scientist who wanted to base his or her analysis upon such sources, including the fact that the information itself is fragmentary, incomplete, and not always consistent. For example, in the Bible the number of years that the Hebrews "sojourned in Egypt" is given in one account as 400, in another as 430, and elsewhere as simply four generations.[4] Territorial descriptions are likewise approximate and inadequate in providing bases for current political claims. The size of *Eretz*

Israel is described at one point as running "from the river of Egypt [the Nile] into the great river, the river Euphrates."[5] Elsewhere those dimensions are different, leaving the student in a quandary about what the "real" boundaries of the territory were.[6] In a sense, of course, it is not fair to expect that biblical passages should meet standards of detail and exactness required of contemporary historical sources. That was not the purpose of their creation, nor is that the reason they have stayed as visible and significant as they have over the centuries.

It is only with the appearance of the Romans that we begin to find more accurate and detailed histories. We know, for example, that Alexander the Great conquered *Eretz Israel* in 332 B.C. and that after his death *Eretz Israel* was merely one part of the empire caught up in the wars of his successors.[7] We also know from a variety of sources that, over a long period of time, there was virtually constant instability in this part of the world. Around 167 B.C. a significant Jewish uprising against the Romans took place in *Eretz Israel*.[8] After the assassination of Caesar in 44 B.C., Judea—the name given to *Eretz Israel* by the Romans—was caught up in the tensions of its civil war. What became known as the Great Revolt against the Romans in 66 A.D. led to a massive retaliation against the Jews. The historian Josephus stated that during the battle of Jerusalem more than a million Jews were killed by the Romans; his contemporary, Tacitus, placed the number killed at six hundred thousand.[9] Whatever the precise figure, it is at this point that we first witness the disappearance of the Jews from this part of the world and the development of the Diaspora, the creation of Jewish communities outside *Eretz Israel*. Indeed, following the Great Revolt, the Romans began a concerted series of anti-Jewish acts, ranging from physical expulsion to prohibitions against the existence of synagogues. In 135 A.D. the Roman emperor Hadrian officially changed the name of Judea to Syria Palestina so that maps would not contain official references to Jews.[10]

From the end of the Roman period (approximately 600 A.D.) to the advent of the Great Crusades (beginning in 1095) a period of Arab domination of Syria Palestina took place. During this five-hundred-year interval, there was apparently little European interest in what would be called the Holy Land. A very small Jewish community continued to exist in what would come to be known as Israel, but it was apparently both politically and economically insignificant. The Crusades themselves extended from approximately 1095 through 1291.[11] Beginning during the tenure of Pope Urban II in 1095, the Roman Catholic Church made a series of efforts to rescue the Holy Land from "the infidels" and recover it for Christendom. Several individual Crusades took place, while some groups of Christian pilgrims from Europe actually reached the Holy Land. But by the end of the thirteenth century, the Crusaders disappeared from the area, and it once again fell under the total rule of Islamic states.

During the fourteenth and fifteenth centuries, many Jews whose ancestors had sought refuge in Europe from Roman persecution began returning to what had by now become known simply as Palestine. Their continued sense of cultural isolation, as well as their feelings of vulnerability as a result of the Crusades, prompted them to move back to their "traditional" home. To some extent it also reflected, for the most part, the amicable relations between Palestine's Jewish minority and the Arab majority.[12] From approximately 1517 until 1917, then, Palestine was controlled by a number of different Turkish dynasties.[13] Forces at work between the European powers and their Jewish minorities ultimately upset this image of religious coexistence.

THE EMERGENCE OF ZIONISM, 1830–1917

The concept of Zionism emerged during the nineteenth century as the rationale for the creation of a Jewish state.[14] The term derives from the word "Zion," which early in Jewish history was taken to be synonymous with Jerusalem.[15] According to estimates at the time, the total population of *Eretz Israel* by 1800 was less than three hundred thousand. The Jewish population itself was a small minority, probably not exceeding five thousand, along with a somewhat larger Christian population of approximately twenty-five thousand.[16] Prior to the nineteenth century, then, the overwhelming majority of the world's Jews had no contact at all with Palestine.

By the mid-1800s a number of missionary organizations had increased their presence in Jerusalem. To some extent this expanded activity was encouraged by political considerations of the major European powers. Governments declared themselves "protectors" of specific religious groups in the Holy Land and used this as their basis for establishing a significant presence in Jerusalem. For example, Russia sought to protect the Greek and Russian Orthodox believers, France the Roman Catholics, Britain the Protestants, and so on.[17] Because Jews lacked a government patron, some individuals came to play more prominent roles. Sir Moses Montefiore, a British Zionist, was among the first to intervene in support of the establishment of a Jewish state in Palestine. In 1838 Montefiore negotiated with Mohammed Ali, the viceroy of Egypt (who at that time also ruled modern-day Syria and Palestine), over a charter for land in *Eretz Israel* where Jews might live without interference. From 1831 to 1840 Mohammed Ali of Egypt occupied Palestine, and Egypt was the power that controlled Palestine and Jerusalem. But Montefiore was unsuccessful in his endeavors, primarily because of Ali's overthrow in 1841 and the restoration of Ottoman-Turkish rule.[18]

Another of the early roots of Zionism can be traced to Rabbi Judah Alkalai, author of an 1839 work entitled *Derchai Noam* ("Pleasant Paths"), which suggested that Jewish colonies needed to be established in the Holy

Land as a condition for the return of the Messiah. By the time of his death in 1878, Alkalai had organized groups of followers and had himself moved to Palestine to work for increased Jewish settlement there.[19] One of Alkalai's followers was Simon Herzl, the grandfather of Theodor Herzl (about whom we shall hear much more shortly). Indeed, by the mid-1860s an active Jewish community known as the *Yishuv* had developed in Palestine.[20]

In 1860 the first Jewish community outside the walls of the Old City of Jerusalem was built. By 1870 that community had established an agricultural college called *Mikveh Israel*, adjacent to the Arab city of Jaffa (on the outskirts of modern Tel Aviv). And in 1878 the *Yishuv* established Petah Tikva, today a town of more than one hundred thousand people near Tel Aviv. The reasons for this renewed, even urgent, interest in Palestine are not difficult to detect.

During this period historical events were occurring in Europe that accelerated Jewish out-migration. In the early 1880s Tsar Alexander III of Russia issued a series of anti-Jewish decrees, which drove hundreds of thousands of Jews out of their villages. Between 1881 and 1914 an estimated 2.6 million Jews left Russia and the surrounding territories.[21] Among them was Leo Pinsker. After emigrating from Russia in 1881, he published the following year his *Autoemancipation*. In it he asserted that world Jewry needed a national homeland if it was ever to receive any respect from other nations. Pinsker's general thesis was that Jews were vulnerable without a territory of their own. As he put it, "There is something unnatural about a people without a territory."[22] In 1884 he became the leader of *Hovevi Zion* ("Lovers of Zion"), a group that actively encouraged Russian emigration to Palestine. Between 1882 and 1903 about twenty-five thousand Jews immigrated to Palestine, many motivated by the *Hovevi Zion* movement in Russia, and a number of *Hovevi Zion* organizations were created there.[23]

Another powerful and wealthy backer of Jewish settlement in Palestine was the French Baron Edmond de Rothschild. Although Rothschild was not directly linked with other movements such as the *Hovevi Zion* organization, he was aware of their existence and shared many of their goals. Between 1884 and 1900 Rothschild invested enormous sums in Palestine, acquiring property and assisting communities of Jews there.[24]

But certainly the single most significant figure in the growth of Zionism during the nineteenth century was Theodor Herzl.[25] Born in 1860 in Budapest and reared in a Liberal (Reform) Jewish tradition, Herzl studied law at the University of Vienna, where he developed an interest in culture and literature, writing a number of plays and essays. While at the university he also became especially sensitive to "the Jewish Question" and the increasing frequency of anti-Semitic incidents in Europe. In 1896 he published his book *Der Judenstaat* ("The Jewish State") with the subtitle "An Attempt at a Modern Solution to the Jewish Question."[26] As Herzl put it: "The idea which I have developed in this pamphlet is an ancient one. It is the restoration of the Jewish state. . . . I shall do no more than suggest what cogs and wheels comprise the machinery I propose, trusting that better mechanics than myself will be found to carry the work out. . . . The world needs the Jewish state; therefore it will arise."[27]

His central contention was that Europe's hatred for its Jewish population was unavoidable and that Jews were going to be victimized and persecuted as long as they remained a vulnerable and unassimilated minority: "We have sincerely tried to merge with the national communities in which we live, seeking only to preserve the faith of our fathers. It is not permitted us."[28] The only solution to the problems faced by Jews of the day, Herzl wrote, was the establishment of a Jewish homeland.

Photo 1.1.   Theodor Herzl, regarded as the founder of Zionism, is found throughout Israeli society, including on currency.

During this time the "institutionalization" of Zionism became increasingly visible. In August 1897, the First Zionist Congress met in Basle, Switzerland. Zionism by now clearly responded to several needs. First, more and more Jews were becoming disillusioned with events in "modern" and "sophisticated" Europe that demonstrated that discrimination against Jews as Jews was not a thing of the past. One prominent and infamous example was the Dreyfus Affair in France.[29] Second, the continuing pattern of anti-Jewish persecution in Russia and eastern Europe convinced many that there was no future for them there either.

Zionism as a national movement, therefore, had two distinct, yet interrelated, goals. First, it sought to carry out the return of Jews to the land, to a resurgence of agricultural activities, and to a revival of Jewish national life—socially, culturally, economically, and politically. Second, it sought to acquire a publicly recognized, legally secure home for the Jews, where they would be free from European-style persecution.[30] Indeed, the official articulation of the Basle Program stated that "the aim of Zionism is to create for the Jewish people a home in Palestine secured by public law."[31] And it was in Basle that Herzl himself had opened his speech with the words, "We are here to lay the foundation stone of the house which is to shelter the Jewish nation." In his diary[32] he later wrote, "If I were to sum up the Basle Congress in one word—which I shall not do openly—it would be this: 'At Basle I created the Jewish State.'"[33]

In 1898, at the meeting of the Second Zionist Congress, a resolution was passed sanctioning efforts to obtain a legal charter for Jewish settlement in Palestine. Herzl initially tried to work through Kaiser Wilhelm II, since Germany had influence with the Ottoman Empire, which at the time controlled the region. But the Ottoman sultan opposed the idea, and the kaiser would not support Zionism over the objections of his ally.

Herzl's attention shifted in 1903 when British colonial secretary Neville Chamberlain (the future architect of Britain's "appeasement" policy toward Germany) indicated that there might be a possibility for the Zionists to receive a land grant in British East Africa in what today encompasses Uganda and Kenya. Herzl preferred land in Palestine, but he was a pragmatist and felt that any territory was preferable to no territory. When the Sixth Zionist Congress met in 1903, therefore, a map of East Africa was hung on the dais, rather than one of Palestine. After a heated debate Herzl managed to push through a proposal to consider British East Africa as a possible Jewish homeland, although the vote was not overwhelming, 255 to 177, with 100 abstentions.[34] While the Zionists fought among themselves over the acceptability of the idea, the British decided against it, and by early 1904 the East Africa option was dead. Ironically, so too was Herzl, who died that same year at the age of forty-four.[35]

By this point two main camps can be identified within the Zionist movement: the "cultural" Zionists and the "political" Zionists. The "cultural Zionists" were more concerned with the issues of Jewish and Hebrew culture, language, arts, religion, and identity in general than they were with the establishment of a political state. "Political Zionists," on the other hand, saw the need for a physical territory for the Jews as paramount. Herzl's attitude toward British East Africa was an excellent example of this position, advocating as it did the need for a Jewish state as the number-one priority, wherever it might be geographically.

GROWTH OF THE *YISHUV*, 1880–1939

As the Zionist movement grew, more and more Jews migrated to Palestine, expanding existing Jewish communities and developing new ones. In 1909 the first kibbutz, Degania, was founded on the south shore of Lake Kinneret, the Sea of Galilee. In 1909 Tel Aviv was founded outside the Arab city of Jaffa. The Jewish presence in Palestine, in fact, had continually grown from about five thousand early in the nineteenth century to eighty-five thousand by 1914. In the early years of the twentieth century, the population of Palestine diminished, largely as a result of Turkish action, and by 1917 the Jewish population of Palestine was only about fifty-five thousand.[36] The term *Yishuv*, as mentioned earlier, refers to the actual Jewish community in Palestine, primarily a direct result of immigration.[37]

When we talk about "a Jewish community in Palestine," however, we cannot talk as if we were discussing a Jewish community in an empty, unsettled, and undeveloped land. There were people in Palestine at the start of the twentieth century who were not Jewish, and they composed the vast majority of the population there at the time. In 1914, Jewish ownership made up something less than 2 percent of the total land in Palestine,[38] and in 1918 Jews made up only 8.5 percent of the total population of Palestine.[39] As Jewish immigration to Palestine continued, and regardless of the enthusiasm and good intentions (from their perspective) of the Zionist settlers, the non-Jewish population of Palestine became increasingly unhappy with the growth of the Jewish population and, more generally, with the pattern of immigration.

This immigration did not happen in a random pattern.[40] There was a discernable sequence of *waves* of immigration, referred to as *aliyot* (plural of *aliya*, "ascent" or "going up"), that took place over several decades. The first *aliya* was made up primarily of Russians who arrived between 1882 and 1903. Between twenty and thirty thousand Jews are reported to have landed in Palestine during this period, to a large degree as a reaction to and consequence of growing anti-Semitism in Russia.[41]

The second *aliya* took place during the first years of the 1900s, largely as a result of the failure of the 1905 Russian Revolution.[42] These immigrants were more ideological, espousing "socialist Zionism," and were especially interested in the theme of Jewish labor for Jewish land. It was this wave of immigrants that established the first kibbutzim, then, as now, seen as symbols of socialism and Zionism. By 1914 there were eighty-five thousand Jews in Palestine.[43]

The third wave of immigration occurred between 1919 and 1923. This group came from eastern Europe, again primarily from Russia, and these immigrants are said to have migrated to a substantial degree because of economic conditions in their homelands. Like the second wave of immigrants, this group was ideologically committed to Zionism and Palestine. Roughly thirty-five thousand new immigrants arrived during this period.

The fourth *aliya* (1925–1929) consisted of an increased proportion of immigrants from Poland, again as a result of economic conditions in eastern Europe. As one author later put it, "If the third aliya was Russian and ideological, the fourth was Polish and middle class."[44] By 1929 the Jewish population of Palestine had reached nearly 160,000.[45]

The fifth *aliya* is usually considered to have taken place between 1933 and 1936, this time largely as a response to Hitler's 1933 rise to power in Germany. During this period nearly 164,000 Jews migrated to Palestine, and the rate of immigration was increasing. In fact, in 1935 alone more than sixty-six thousand Jews immigrated.[46] By the spring of 1936, the *Yishuv* totaled nearly four hundred thousand, or almost 30 percent of the total population.[47]

By the time of independence in 1948, the *Yishuv*—the Jewish community in Palestine—had changed its character significantly from that of 1880. The Jewish population was significantly larger than it had been in earlier years, and its makeup had been altered as well: western European Jews were now a majority of the Jewish population. By the time the Mandate was terminated in 1948, the Jewish population in Palestine had increased substantially through immigration, from about 65,000 in 1919 (less than 10 percent of the population) to nearly 650,000 (more than 80 percent of the population).[48]

Mark Tessler notes that it is difficult to characterize in a few words the Arab response to Zionism in the years before World War I and that "the record does not lend itself to simple generalization." He writes, "On the one hand, there were instances of dialogue, cooperation, and a recognition of mutual interests. On the other, there was indifference, followed by suspicion and, eventually, active mutual antagonism."[49]

In far greater detail than is possible here, Tessler chronicles the history of the Arab—especially the Palestinian Arab—response to increasing Zionist activity, showing the gradual, yet increasing, concern during the years of the second and third *aliyot* about the possibility that Zionism might turn into an active threat to a political future for Palestine. The Palestinian newspaper *Filastin* dealt directly with issues related to the growing impact of Zionism, and in 1913 the newspaper ran a campaign to establish a "Palestinian Patriotic Society" of Arab notables to purchase state land before it was purchased by the Zionists.[50] Tessler writes,

> While it is essential to take note of the significant increase in both political activity and opposition to Zionism among Palestinian Arabs in the years before the war, the magnitude of these two interrelated trends should not be exaggerated. . . . Leadership continued to be vested in a small number of wealthy and extended Muslim families. . . . Although a few of their sons had become involved in nationalist politics abroad, these powerful clans had little reason to seek radical change. Having fared well under Ottoman domination, most remained loyal to the empire and sought no more than constitutional reform and greater local autonomy.[51]

While opposition to Zionism was clearly beginning to form in the years before World War I, it was not universal, and while there were clearly critics of increased Zionism in Palestine, there were also Palestinian notables who were not opposed to the Zionist presence, some believing that Zionist immigration could contribute to the economic well-being of the area.[52]

THE BALFOUR DECLARATION
AND THE BRITISH MANDATE PERIOD, 1917–1947

The assassination of Austrian archduke Franz Ferdinand on June 28, 1914, precipitated World War I, which would last until 1918. The war made the Suez Canal—built from 1859 to 1869 by France and acquired by Britain in 1875—and its adjacent territory strategically important to the British. By extension, the regions near the canal became strategically important as well. This was especially true because Turkey was a part of the German-Austro-Hungarian alliance, and the British were very concerned about any allies of the Germans getting too close to the canal.

In October 1915, the British high commissioner in Egypt, Sir Henry McMahon, wrote to Emir Abdullah, the eldest son of Hussein, the Hashemite sherif (governor) of Mecca (and the great-grandfather of modern-day King Abdullah of Jordan). He indicated that Britain was prepared "to recognize and support the independence of the Arabs in all the regions within the limits demanded by the sherif (Syria, Arabia, Mesopotamia) with the exception of those portions of Syria lying to the west of Damascus," if the Hashemite Arabs would join the Allied war effort against the Ottoman Empire.[53] Spurred on by this invitation, the Arabs began a revolt against the Ottomans in 1916, led by Emir Faisal (Hussein's second son) and aided by legendary British officer T. E. Lawrence (a.k.a. "Lawrence of Arabia").[54]

According to Tessler, when the war was over, "there emerged a disagreement about whether Britain had intended that Palestine be excluded from the area specified by the Husayn-McMahon Agreement." Apparently the British indicated to Hussein (spelled Husayn by Tessler) that the reference to "west of Damascus" was meant to calm concerns of the French, who had aspirations to control present-day Lebanon, and did not indicate that the area that would become known as Palestine would be included in the "west of Damascus" delimitation. Tessler notes,

> this interpretation was consistent with the facts of geography. Palestine was regarded as southern, not western, Syria; and the territory lying directly west of Damascus, Homs, Hama, and Aleppo is all north of Palestine. Thus the Arabs were convinced, with reason, that they had received a promise of British support for their independence in Palestine, as well as elsewhere.[55]

While the Arabs were fighting against the Turks, representatives of the British and French governments met to negotiate their respective postwar spheres of influence in the Arab world, in essence dividing up the spoils of war in advance of the war's end. The British representative, Sir Mark Sykes, and the French representative, Charles François Georges-Picot, met in January 1916. Although the war was by no means over, they decided without consulting any Arab ruler on the shape of the postwar map of the Middle East. Most of Syria and Lebanon would be under French influence; most of Jordan and Iraq would be under British influence; most of current-day Israel would be ruled by a "joint allied condominium" for religious and political reasons.[56] As Britain's wartime position strengthened, while France's weakened, London changed its mind about the "joint condominium" plan. In 1917 Prime Minister David Lloyd-George instructed his ambassador in Paris to notify the French that Britain was expanding its postwar claim and that the French would simply have to accept a British protectorate over all of Palestine after the war, since Palestine was a "strategic buffer to Egypt."[57]

Indeed, the entire history of the period between the Balfour Declaration and the Sykes-Picot agreement illustrates that British actions were continually steered by British perception of the strategic value of Palestine. The record during this period is a consistent one of the British playing the Zionist forces against the Arab forces and, correspondingly, the Arabs against the Zionists, using the demands of one to offset the demands of the other. While it is very clear that the basic responsibility for the conflict in Palestine belonged to the Arabs and the Zionists, it is also true that there were a number of occasions when Britain found this conflict convenient to its Middle East strategy.[58] This theme would reoccur for as long as the British were a presence in Palestine.

In 1917, with the outcome of the war still in doubt, America not yet a belligerent, the Russian monarchy overthrown, and the eastern front collapsing, the British hoped that the support of Jews throughout the world would aid in their war efforts. There was also more than a little concern that if the British failed to act to attract world Jewry to their side, the Kaiser would. (German relations with world Jewry were clearly very different in World War I than in World War II.) The Kaiser was, apparently, considering an expression of his own of support for Zionist goals. The British government, accordingly, issued its own portentous proclamation echoing Herzl's original objectives, despite the fact that many British Jews were intensely anti-Zionist because they feared that if Zionist goals were endorsed by the British government, they might be pressured to leave Britain and move to Palestine.[59] On November 2, 1917, in a letter to Lord Rothschild, president of the British Zionist Federation, British foreign secretary Arthur James Balfour wrote,

> Dear Lord Rothschild: I have much pleasure in conveying to you, on behalf of His Majesty's Government, the following declaration of sympathy with Jewish Zionist aspirations which has been submitted to, and approved by, the Cabinet: "His Majesty's Government view with favour the establishment in Palestine of a national home for the Jewish people, and will use their best endeavours to facilitate the achievement of this object, it being clearly understood that nothing shall be done which may prejudice the civil and religious rights of existing non-Jewish communities in Palestine, or the rights and political status enjoyed by Jews in any other country." I should be grateful if you would bring this declaration to the knowledge of the Zionist federation.[60]

It is interesting to note that the original draft of the document (July 1917) had suggested the "reconstitution of Palestine as the National Home of the Jewish People." The final version of the plan, however, merely suggested establishing in Palestine "a national home" for the Jewish people, something that might be geographically much smaller. The alteration was made after the British cabinet as a whole would not agree to the broad mandate as originally proposed. The Balfour Declaration, as it has since become known, was thus left as a more vague and general declaration of support.[61]

Almost a year later, in November 1918, following a great deal of internal negotiation and debate, the Zionist leadership offered the Lloyd-George government its own alternative "interpretation" of the Balfour Declaration.[62] To wit: "The establishment of a National Home for the Jewish People . . . is understood to mean that the country of Palestine should be placed under such political, economic, and moral conditions as will favour the increase of the Jewish population, so that in accordance with the principle of democracy it may ultimately develop into a Jewish Commonwealth."[63] This was a stronger position than the British were willing to take, however, and London refused to commit itself to this counterproposal.

Because of their concern about British intentions and about London's interpretation of the admittedly ambiguous Balfour Declaration, some Zionist leaders sought to establish direct links and work cooperatively with Arab leaders in Palestine. In January 1919, Chaim Weizmann, a Zionist leader, and Emir Faisal, leader of the previously cited 1916 Arab revolt against the Turks, signed a formal pact in London. As noted in its preamble:

> His royal highness the Emir Feisal, representing and acting on behalf of the Arab Kingdom of Hejaz, and Dr. Chaim Weizmann, representing and acting on behalf of the Zionist Organization, mindful of the racial kinship and ancient bonds existing between the Arabs and the Jewish people, and realising that the surest means of working out the consummation of their national aspirations is through the closest possible collaboration in the development of the Arab State and Palestine, and being desirous further of confirming the good understanding which exists between them, have agreed upon the following articles.[64]

The most important articles for our purposes here were those guaranteeing Jews the right to free immigration into Palestine and legal settlement on the land. These articles were accompanied by a reciprocal assurance that Arab tenant farmers would be safeguarded on their own plots of land and assisted in economic development, and that freedom of religion and of worship would be protected in Palestine and that Muslim holy sites would remain under Muslim control. Arab nationalists, however, subsequently repudiated this agreement. They argued that Faisal was "gravely out of touch with local Arab sentiment."[65] This disagreement among the Arabs certainly contributed to Britain's ability to manipulate its Palestine policy to its own ends, rather than to the ends of those living there.

There was, in fact, disagreement between the British and Arab leaders about exactly what had been promised in the McMahon letter, too. The Arabs believed that only the areas west of Syria would be excluded from their soon-to-be independent state; the British argued that areas west and south of Syria were to be excluded, meaning that Palestine west of the Jordan River would not be included in the new state. Thus, while "the Arabs were convinced, with reason, that they had received a promise of British support for their independence in Palestine, as well as elsewhere," the British took a different view.[66]

Historians have suggested that ultimately "both the Zionists and the Arabs were used by Britain for its own purposes." Weizmann's goals were supported by Britain because they would permit Britain to continue to exercise military control over Palestine; their concerns for the principles of Zionism were of no significance. On the other hand, the British were willing to support the Arabs as long as it was convenient to hold the French interests in the region in check.[67]

Although Britain assumed de facto (practical) mandatory control over Palestine with the Ottoman Empire's defeat in 1918, it was not until April 1920 that the Supreme Council of the Paris Peace Conference awarded Britain a *de jure* (legal) mandate.[68] During the years from 1920 to 1922, tensions between the Arab and Jewish populations in Palestine increased, with both sides re-senting the British presence. A case in point for the latter surfaced in 1922 when Colonial Secretary Winston Churchill issued an official White Paper offering a more restrictive interpretation of the Balfour Declaration:

> Phrases have been used such as that Palestine is to become "as Jewish as England is English." His Majesty's Government regard any such expectation as impracticable and have no such aim in view. . . . [W]hen it is asked what is meant by the development of a Jewish National Home in Palestine, it may be answered that it is not the imposition of a Jewish nationality upon the inhabitants of Palestine as a whole, but the further development of the existing Jewish community . . . in order that it may become a center in which the Jewish people as a whole may take . . . an interest and a pride. . . . But in order that this community should have the best prospects of free development . . . it is essential that it should know that it is in Palestine as of right, and not on sufferance.[69]

The Churchill White Paper concluded that Palestine as a whole would not become the Jewish national home and introduced the concept of "economic absorptive capacity" into regulations governing Jewish immigration. Unlimited Jewish immigration would no longer be permitted, and Jewish immigrants henceforth would have to demonstrate that their presence in Palestine would be of an economic benefit to the land.

Tessler shows that the key dimension of "economic absorptive capacity" as a source of conflict in Mandatory Palestine was the purchase of land by the Zionists. The magnitude of Zionist land ownership, however, is often exaggerated, as table 1.1 shows.

As mentioned earlier, in July 1922 the fledgling League of Nations formally awarded Britain the mandatory power over Palestine that it had in effect possessed since the end of the war. The Mandate contained the text of the Balfour Declaration regarding the establishment in Palestine of a national home for the Jewish people that would extend to both sides of the Jordan River, and

Table 1.1   Jewish Land Ownership in Palestine, 1900–1947

Year	Dunams Held by Jewish Owners	Jewish Ownership as Percentage of Total Land
1900	218,000	0.84
1914	418,000	1.61
1927	865,000	3.33
1936	1,231,000	4.73
1947	1,734,000	6.67

Source: Mark Tessler, *A History of the Israeli-Palestinian Conflict* (Bloomington: Indiana University Press, 1994), p. 174.
Note: One dunam measures approximately one-fourth of an acre. Total land area of Mandatory Palestine exceeded 26,000,000 dunams.

recognized the "historical connection of the Jewish people with Palestine" and the "grounds for reconstituting their national home in that country."[70]

Immediately upon receiving mandatory power, however, Britain proceeded to partition Palestine into two territories divided by the Jordan River: one called Palestine, and the other Transjordan (see map 1.1). Jews were prohibited from settling to the east of the river. The Mandate for Palestine[71] was nonetheless important for several reasons, among them the fact that it formally recognized both Zionist claims and the Zionist movement itself.[72] It was, however, sufficiently vague in its wording to serve as the basis of much debate and disagreement.

During the 1920s and early 1930s, Palestine was "run like a British crown colony."[73] The British high commissioner during this period, a Jew by the name of Sir Herbert Samuel, sought to do what he could to calm the anger of the Arab residents over continued and substantial Jewish immigration.[74] Despite his efforts, significant civil unrest continually plagued relations between the Jewish and Arab communities, and there were periodic intense outbreaks of violence between the two communities.

In November 1936 a royal commission of inquiry known as the Peel Commission (after its chairman, William Robert Wellesley Peel, Earl of Peel) was sent on a fact-finding mission to Palestine by the British government. Its subsequent report of July 1937 addressed the problems directly. It found that many of the grievances of the Palestinians were reasonable and that the "disturbances" of 1920, 1921, 1929, and 1933 were related to and based on the issues of Arab desire for national independence, on one hand, and conflict between Arab nationalism and Zionist goals, on the other. It found that "an irrepressible conflict has arisen between two national communities within the bounds of one small country. . . . About 1,000,000 Arabs are in strife, open or latent, with some 400,000 Jews. There is no common ground between them."[75] It concluded that the claims of the Arabs and the Jews were essentially "irreconcilable" and that since the situation was a "fundamental conflict of right with right," the only solution was to partition Palestine.[76] The partition plan suggested the creation of a Jewish state in one part of Palestine and an Arab state made up of Transjordan and the rest of Palestine, with a British zone of control around the city of Jerusalem (see map 1.2).

Reaction to the Peel Report was mixed. Some Zionists opposed a Jewish state smaller than that of the entirety of 1922 Palestine, while others urged acceptance of the plan on the grounds that at least it was a concrete proposal for a real state. The Arab leadership rejected the commission's proposals totally. After more violence (this time primarily Arab), another royal commission—the Palestine Partition Commission—was dispatched in 1938. When the Woodhead Report (named after Sir John Woodhead, the commission chair) was issued on November 9, 1938, it declared that the Peel Report had been unrealistic and its proposed partition lines unreason-

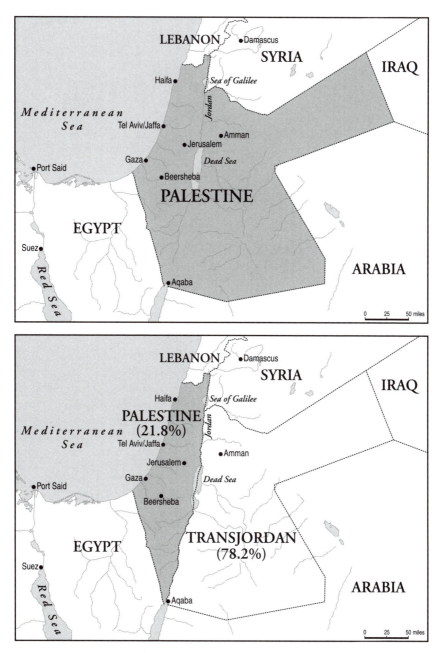

Map 1.1. The First Partition of Palestine, 1920 and 1922

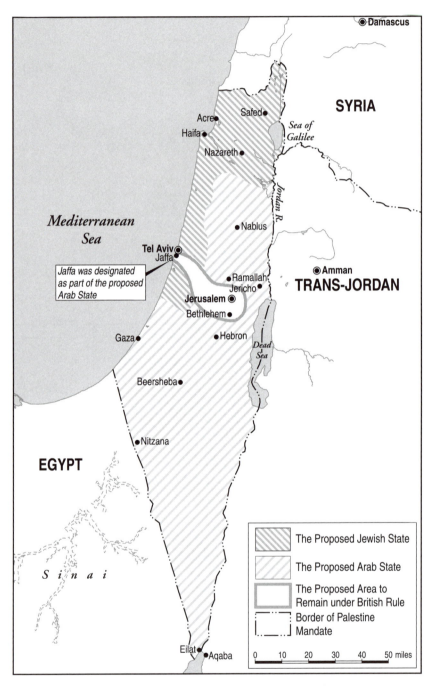

Map 1.2.   The Peel Commission Partition Recommendation, 1937

able.[77] A new partition plan, creating a much larger Arab state and a much smaller Jewish state, was proposed (see map 1.3). This time the Zionists objected most strongly, noting that the Jewish state to be created under the Woodhead Report would be less than one-twentieth the size of West Palestine and less than one-hundredth the size of the original Mandate territory.[78] Arab nationalists, for their part, opposed any plan that would establish any Jewish state.

By February 1939, the imminence of another war with Germany once again raised concerns in Britain about the political status of the Middle East. Colonial Secretary Malcolm MacDonald met with both Zionist and Arab leaders and asserted that the British government had no choice but to look at the Middle East from a strategic perspective. "His Majesty's Government was left with no choice but to ensure that the Arab governments were not tempted to accept support from hostile powers. If it came to a choice between Arab and Jewish support, MacDonald explained, Jewish help, however valuable, represented no compensation to Britain for the loss of Arab and Moslem goodwill."[79] In brief, the Arabs were strategically important to Britain and needed to be placated. The Jews were not.

The outgrowth of this sentiment came in May with yet another White Paper. This White Paper declared that the authors of the original mandate "could not have intended that Palestine should be converted into a Jewish state against the will of the Arab population of the country,"[80] and announced that within ten years it would organize an independent unitary Palestinian state—in addition to the Jordanian state already created—and would then gradually transfer political power to it. The plan said that "the state should be one in which Arabs and Jews share in government in such a way as to insure that the essential interests of each community are safeguarded."[81]

The British also established a new quota for future Jewish immigration to Palestine at ten thousand per year for the following five years, plus a one-time allotment of twenty-five thousand refugees. Once this five-year total of seventy-five thousand was reached, no additional immigrants would be admitted without Arab consent. Effective immediately, all sale of land to Jews was prohibited.

Although the British government's 1939 White Paper passed the House of Commons by a vote of 268 to 179 (with 110 members of Parliament [MPs] abstaining), the new policy generated opposition in both London and Geneva. Winston Churchill, for one, now condemned the government's action:

> This pledge of a home of refugees, of an asylum, was not made to the Jews of Palestine . . . but to the Jews outside Palestine, to that vast, unhappy mass of scattered persecuted wandering Jews whose intense, unchanging, unconquerable desire has been for a national Home. . . . That is the pledge which was given, and that is the pledge which we are now asked to break.[82]

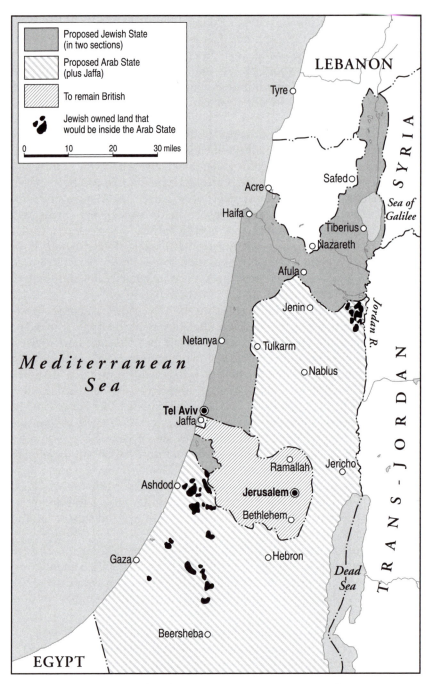

Map 1.3.   The Woodhead Commission Partition Recommendation, 1938

The League of Nations Mandates Commission likewise declared that "the policy set out in the White Paper was not in accordance with the interpretation which, in agreement with the Mandatory Power and the Council, the Commission had placed upon the Palestine Mandate."[83] In the opinion of the League, Britain, in its most recent decisions in relation to its Palestine policy, had reneged on its commitment to the League and to the Zionist movement to support the principles of the Balfour Declaration and the needs of the Jewish people. The advent of World War II, however, rendered the commission's position moot and relegated the question of Palestine to the back burner of Britain's priorities, where it remained until 1947 when the British announced their intention to leave the area, and the British handed over the Palestine conflict to the United Nations.

WORLD WAR II AND THE HOLOCAUST

The Holocaust, certainly the darkest experience in the history of the Jewish people, is a subject to which a text of this nature cannot possibly do justice. Indeed, a definitive work on the subject takes up three substantial volumes of more than twelve hundred pages![84] The often-quoted figure of six million Jews killed between 1939 and 1945 (and we should not forget that nearly the same number of non-Jewish east Europeans were also killed) represented almost 90 percent of all Jews in those parts of Europe occupied by the Germans and close to one-third of world Jewry.[85]

Much attention has also been paid to the issue of whether or not the Western powers knew about the full magnitude of the Holocaust. It is probably true that at the outset of the war there existed substantial disbelief over rumors circulating about atrocities and exterminations in some of the German camps. Yet there is clear evidence that within a relatively short period the Allied nations did, in fact, know what was happening in these camps and opted—for a variety of reasons—not to set the destruction of these camps as a top military or political priority.[86]

Certainly one consequence of the Holocaust was its mobilization of many Zionist groups all over the world to intensify their efforts to convince the British to expand Jewish immigration quotas to Palestine and assist Jewish transit there.[87] Another related and important aspect was the fact that the Holocaust was instrumental in weakening or eliminating opposition to Zionism in most non-Arab countries. Public sentiment outside of Palestine, both Jewish and non-Jewish alike, had often been pointedly unenthusiastic about the idea of Zionism in the period prior to World War II. However, once the horror and the enormity of the Holocaust became known, many changed their views and openly supported the idea of a homeland for the Jewish people.

An ironic and even tragic problem for the Jewish refugees, however, was the fact that while many Western powers were appalled at what the Germans had done, they were not prepared to encourage increased Jewish resettlement in their own countries. When the war ended in 1945, it is reported that American president Harry S. Truman asked British prime minister Clement Atlee to "open up" immigration to Palestine as a humanitarian gesture. In response Atlee told Truman that if he was so concerned about the plight of Jewish refugees, he should increase quotas for admission to the United States.[88]

Their dispute further underscored two essential lessons that came out of the Holocaust for Jews, lessons that are still discussed as important in Israel today and that have a direct impact on contemporary Israeli policy making, both domestic and foreign. These two lessons are, first, that nothing is ever "too horrible to happen," and, second, that Israel must never again be in a position in which it must depend upon others for its very survival. A brief comment on each of these lessons is in order here.

As rumors of the Holocaust started appearing in Germany, across Europe, and around the world, one of the most common reactions was, "That can't be! That is simply too horrible to happen. People just wouldn't do something like that in the modern, civilized world." We know today, of course, that the Holocaust was not too horrible to happen; it did happen. Jews at the time—and subsequently Israelis as well as other Jews around the world—drew from this event the lesson that one simply cannot assume that a given act may be, indeed, too horrible to happen. There may, in fact, be people in the world willing to commit acts that we believe to be inhumane. This belief, obviously, has consistently carried enormous implications for Israeli foreign policy, as we shall subsequently observe.

The other lesson frequently invoked by Israelis is that much of the Holocaust happened because the Jews of Europe were dependent upon someone else—Britain, the United States, and others—to protect them. The inference is that Jews must always be prepared to protect themselves—and that Israel must be prepared to protect itself; they cannot permit a situation in which they are dependent upon another actor to defend them, because when the time comes, that other party may be unable or may actually decline to do so. This, too, has produced direct foreign policy implications for the Israeli political system, implications that we return to later in this book.

TRANSITION TO STATEHOOD, 1945–1948

As World War II drew to a close, more and more pressure was brought to bear on Britain to amend its earlier policies and reinstate permission for Jewish refugees to emigrate to Palestine. Nevertheless, the British government continued to follow the policies outlined in its 1939 White Paper. Despite Britain's best efforts to prevent other governments from selling boats or generally assisting Jewish refugees, however, the flow toward Palestine continued. The unintended result of Britain's policy of no more immigration was that illegal immigration to Palestine actually increased, and within a few years a significant number of new Jewish refugees had successfully settled there.[89]

International Zionist organizations were also continuing to be active in response to the British White Paper of 1939. In the United States one of the most visible such activities involved a meeting that took place at New York City's Biltmore Hotel in May 1942 that became known as the Biltmore Conference. Zionist leaders from many nations participated, and more than five hundred delegates promoted an active agenda to support Jewish settlers in Palestine.

In Palestine itself the violence escalated, with the British tending to blame the Zionists for most of the problems that arose. The *Haganah* (the Jewish Defense Force) became more active, as did the *Irgun* (the shortened name of the *Irgun Zvi Leumi*—the National Military Organization) and *Lehi* (the name comes from the initials of the words for the Fighters for the Freedom of Israel) organizations. The latter two organizations were clearly viewed by the British as terrorist organizations, and the British made every possible effort to destroy them.[90] In 1944, for example, the *Irgun* was linked to several bombings in Jerusalem, Haifa, and Tel Aviv. Their targets were usually British governmental offices and officials.[91] This battle between Britain and the indigenous terrorist organizations continued until the British withdrawal in 1948.[92]

In 1946 the violence further increased after the British decided to establish "relocation camps" for Jewish refugees on the Mediterranean island of Cyprus. All illegal Jewish immigrants seized in or en route to Palestine were sent to Cyprus for repatriation. Perhaps the most dramatic illustration of this occurred in 1947 when the ship *Exodus* arrived in Haifa with nearly four thousand refugees on board.[93] The British would not permit them to disembark in Palestine, insisting instead that the ship return to its French port of origin. Eventually, after France would not cooperate with Britain, the British government actually sent the refugees back to their occupation zone in Germany.[94]

Examples like the *Exodus* failed, not surprisingly, to win the British much sympathy. Rather, they resulted in a worldwide increase in support for the plight of Jewish refugees. In 1946 an Anglo-American commission of inquiry was established to investigate the refugee problem and in May it recommended that one hundred thousand Jews be permitted to immigrate to Palestine immediately. In response to this plan, the British government proposed the so-called Morrison Plan (named after Herbert Morrison, the commission's chair), which would convert the Mandate for Palestine into a "trusteeship," divide the country into Jewish and Arab provinces, and create separate districts for Jerusalem and the Negev. The British would retain control over police, defense, foreign relations, customs courts, prisons, harbors and railways, aviation, communications, and other essential services.[95]

The Morrison Plan accepted the admission of another one hundred thousand Jews to Palestine as had been advocated by the Anglo-American commission. After this one-time exception, the principle of "economic absorptive capacity" would again be the basis of Palestine's immigration policy. The United States would be responsible for both the logistics and the costs of this undertaking. However, neither the recommendations of the Anglo-American commission nor the Morrison Plan was accepted due to both Arab and Jewish opposition.[96] At this point, the British government decided to transfer the problem to the infant United Nations[97] and requested a special session for this purpose on April 2, 1947.[98]

In response, the United Nations created a Special Committee on Palestine (UNSCOP), composed of Australia, Canada, Czechoslovakia, Guatemala, India, Iran, the Netherlands, Peru, Sweden, Uruguay, and Yugoslavia. After many hearings and much debate, the committee recommended termination of Britain's Mandate, and partition of Palestine into independent Arab and Jewish states, along much the same lines as recommended by the Peel Commission a decade earlier (see map 1.4).[99] There was apparently some debate as to the exact nature of the partition. Seven of the eleven nations on the committee recommended partition into two states, with Jerusalem remaining an international trusteeship of the United Nations, while three (India, Iran, and Yugoslavia) favored a federal-type arrangement of separate Jewish and Arab provinces. This minority group argued that outright partition would not be fair to the Arab population of Palestine. Australia remained neutral in this discussion.[100]

Debate on the UNSCOP report lasted two months. Britain opposed any kind of partition and the Arab states opposed anything other than a single Arab state in Palestine. In November 1947, however, the United Nations voted by a margin of thirty-three to thirteen, with Britain abstaining, to accept the UNSCOP's recommendation. Jews in the *Yishuv*, as well as Zionists outside of Palestine, generally supported the recommendations of UNSCOP. Arab governments opposed the recommendations.[101]

UN General Assembly Resolution 181 had several components:

1. Termination of the Mandate and British withdrawal by no later than August 1, 1948
2. Establishment of a Jewish state, an Arab state, and a special region for the city of Jerusalem, administered by the United Nations
3. Cooperation by the two new states in economics, transportation, currency, customs, and a variety of other respects

Map 1.4.   The United Nations Partition Recommendation, 1947

4. Formation of a Palestine Commission of five states to promote peace in the region and the effective operation of the partition plan.[102]

The official termination date of the British Mandate was to be May 15, 1948, but since May 15 was also the Jewish Sabbath, leaders of the newly created Zionist National Council met on the afternoon of May 14, 1948, and declared the state of Israel's independence. The first three countries to recognize Israel were the United States (on May 14),[103] Guatemala (on May 15), and the Soviet Union (on May 18).[104] Within eight hours of its declaration of independence, however, Israel was simultaneously attacked by seven Arab armies.

The War of Independence was eventually to last more than eight months, with two intervening truce periods (from June 11 to July 8 and again from July 18 to October 15).[105] On November 16, 1948, the UN Security Council ordered the parties concerned to enter into an armistice. A cease-fire was signed by Israel and Transjordan on November 30. On December 13 the parliament of Transjordan annexed nearly twenty-two hundred square miles of the Arab state territory not occupied by Israel and declared its union with Transjordan, despite angry reactions from both Syria and Egypt (see map 1.5).[106]

A cease-fire with Egypt was agreed to the following January (1949). By that time all of the fighting had stopped. Israel had gained almost twenty-five hundred square miles of territory that under the original UNSCOP partition plan would have gone to Arab states, while Jordan and Egypt divided up the rest. Several different armistices were subsequently signed with Egypt (February 1949), Lebanon (March 1949), Transjordan (April 1949), and Syria (July 1949).[107] It was only with the signing of the Camp David Treaty, fully thirty years later, that, for the first time, an armistice agreement was replaced by an actual peace treaty with Egypt. Israel still remains technically at war with many of its other neighbors, and the "peace" shared with many of its neighbors today is often referred to as a distinctly "cold" peace. During the 1948 fighting, hundreds of thousands of Palestinian Arabs fled from the new state of Israel.[108] We consider these nearly 650,000 refugees and their descendants regularly in our analysis in this volume.[109]

THE PALESTINIANS

As we have previously noted, a heterogeneous population already lived in Palestine when Zionist leaders called for a relocation of the world's Jewish population there.[110] Some of this population was Jewish, but most of it was not. The non-Jewish population of Palestine, estimated to be almost 95 percent of the population in 1882, had by 1948 fallen to

Map 1.5. Armistice Lines, 1949

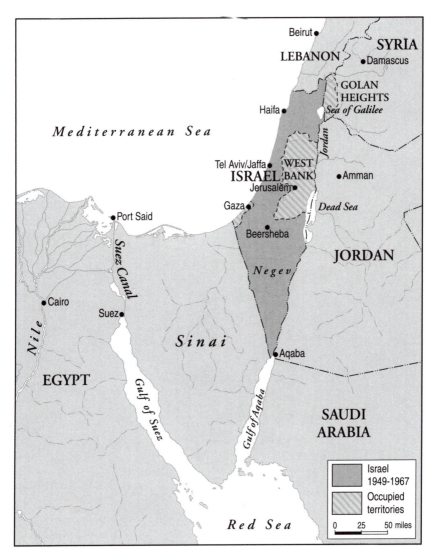

Map 1.6.   Israel's Borders, 2010

less than 20 percent as a result of the substantial emigration of non-Jews during the period leading up to and during the War of Independence (see table 1.2).

The Palestinians are the descendants of two distinct historical peoples, the Canaanites and the Philistines, and as such have a long and identifiable history in the Middle East.[111] While the key ingredients of Palestinian nationalism are not the focus of our study here, it is important to note that

Table 1.2 Non-Jewish Populations in Palestine, 1882–2008

Year	Jewish Population	Non-Jewish Population	Total
1882	24,000 (5.3%)	426,000 (94.7%)	450,000
1918	56,000 (8.5%)	600,000 (91.5%)	656,000
1935	355,000 (27.1%)	953,000 (72.9%)	1,308,000
1948	650,000 (80.6%)	156,000 (19.4%)	806,000
1967	2,384,000 (85.8%)	393,000 (14.2%)	2,777,000
1985	3,517,200 (82.4%)	749,000 (17.6%)	4,266,200
1990	3,946,700 (81.9%)	875,000 (18.1%)	4,821,700
1995	4,522,300 (80.6%)	1,090,000 (19.4%)	5,612,300
2000	4,955,400 (77.8%)	1,413,900 (22.2%)	6,369,300
2005	5,313,800 (76%)	1,676,900 (24%)	6,990,700
2008	5,569,200 (75.6%)	1,804,800 (24.4%)	7,374,000

Sources: Adapted from Michael Wolffsohn, *Israel: Polity, Society and Economy 1882–1986* (Atlantic Highlands, N.J.: Humanities Press International, 1987), p. 121; Central Bureau of Statistics, *Statistical Abstract of Israel, 2009* (Jerusalem: Central Bureau of Statistics, 2009), p. 86, Table 2.1, "The Population by Population Group," www.cbs.gov.il/shnaton60/st02_01.pdf, accessed January 2010.

the Palestinian desire for independence has a long history and should not be seen as only a product of anti-Israeli or anti-Jewish sentiment.[112] Also, we cannot overstate the importance of the fact that there were Palestinians on the land declared to be *Eretz Israel*.[113] Currents of Palestinian nationalism predated the state of Israel and existed under Ottoman and British rule; Palestinian nationalist-based action can be seen to have taken place in each of these eras, as shown in table 1.3.[114]

The Palestinians were a physical presence through the various stages of Jewish immigration. According to one source, "before the war of 1948, Palestinians owned about 87.5 percent of the total area of Palestine . . . while Jews owned 6.6 percent of the total lands. The remaining 5.9 percent was 'state land' as classified by the British Mandate."[115] By the end of the war, Israel controlled 77.4 percent of the land, and there were 726,000 Palestinian refugees located outside of the armistice lines (Israel's borders) and approximately 32,000 refugees inside the armistice lines.[116]

As more Zionists moved to Palestine, more of the native non-Jewish population there began to oppose the pattern of Jewish immigration, and we have already seen the pattern of violence and demonstrations that resulted in various royal commissions being created through the 1920s and 1930s.[117] In 1921 the Palestinians sent a delegation to London to explain their case against the Balfour Declaration. A second delegation was sent to London in 1930 to press the British to end Jewish immigration to and land acquisition in Palestine. In 1939, in a conference attended by both Palestinian and Zionist delegations, the British

Table 1.3   Palestinian Revolts, 1909–1938

Year	Revolt
1909–1911	*Al-Arabia Fatah*, an alliance of Palestinians, Syrians, Lebanese, and Egyptians, demanding Arab rights in the Ottoman Empire.
1913	Arab Nationalist Congress meets in Paris to demand autonomy for the Arab provinces.
1916	Revolt against Ottomans for independence and political federation of Arab countries.
1920	Anti-Zionist riot in Jerusalem.
1921 (May)	Anti-Zionist revolt in Jaffa protesting Jewish mass immigration.
1921 (November)	Anti-Zionist demonstrations in Jerusalem.
1929	Riot dealing with the rights of Jews to worship at the Wailing Wall ("Wailing Wall riots"), which followed a demonstration by Zionists trying to change the status quo regarding their access to the Wall. Palestinian riots also broke out in the Jewish Quarter in Hebron.
1933	Riots in Jaffa and Jerusalem protesting Jewish immigration and British pro-Zionist policy.
1936	"Great Rebellion" protesting Zionist influence.
1937–1938	"Great Rebellion," phase two, in response to the partition plan.

Source: Derived from Palestinian Academic Society for the Study of International Affairs, *Datebook, 1996* (Jerusalem: PASSIA, 1996), p. 188.

sought a settlement acceptable to both parties regarding immigration; the conference was concluded with no satisfactory outcome, and shortly thereafter the British issued their White Paper restricting Jewish immigration and land buying.[118] Ultimately, of course, the British decided to relinquish their Mandate in 1947 and the United Nations decided in 1947 to partition Palestine.[119]

The Palestinians refer to the Israeli War of Independence as *Al-Naqba* ("the Catastrophe"). From their perspective it was the United Nations Partition Plan of 1947 (UN Resolution 181) that caused the War of 1948 by partitioning Palestine. They argue that the plan created a Jewish state with just over 56 percent of the land at a time when Jews owned less than 7 percent and made up about one-third of the population.[120]

This, then, was the setting at the time of the creation of the modern state of Israel. The fact that Israel was established in a space where land and resources were contested has meant that this dimension of Israel's existence has been a consistent source of tension with its neighbors. All new states must address a large number of problems—sometimes all at the same time—in their early years. We have seen here that Israel had at least one additional level of concern to address beyond normal demands and crises: the claim that it was illegitimately occupying someone else's territory.

HISTORY AND THE CREATION OF ISRAEL

This chapter began with the statement that knowledge of any society's history is always an important prerequisite for a complete understanding of its political system. It should now be clear to the new student of Israeli politics why this is so. Not only was Israel born out of disaster, despair, and conflict, but many aspects of the "birth" itself are subject to dispute. It has not been our intention here to side authoritatively with one or the other viewpoint in the debate, for there are various sets of "facts" on both sides that one can invoke. The important lesson for the student to recognize is that there *are* different sets of "facts" and that it is possible, if not desirable, to evaluate both sides of the debate before taking a position.

The emergence of Zionism as a political movement was a result of religious, historical, and political variables, and its appearance on the scene in Palestine was one of those factors that shape the history of society. Had Theodor Herzl been able to convince the World Zionist Congress to accept the British offer of land in East Africa, the history of the Middle East might, in fact, have been considerably different from the history we know today, although one set of tension-related variables (Palestinian nationalism) might have been traded for another (East African nationalism). Herzl was unsuccessful, however, and Zionism continued to focus on Palestine. The rest, as they say, is history.

The community of Jews in Palestine, the *Yishuv*, grew dramatically over a period of several decades as a result of economic, political, and religious factors. The presence of the *Yishuv* not only encouraged subsequent waves of immigrants to move to Palestine, but set the scene for an increased level of conflict in Palestine between the new immigrants and a native population that did not approve of the greatly increased Jewish presence in the land. And, we must recall, there was a native population prior to the Jewish immigration to Palestine. This fact, and it is an undisputed fact, sets the groundwork for a good deal of historical literature and much current political tension. The question of who was on the land first is essentially an academic one, because the answer to the question may depend upon how we define kinship systems and what "the land" means. The fact is that, at the end of the day, the dilemma that the British faced in trying to respond to two mutually contradictory sets of demands has endured for more than a half century.

The British were charged with the responsibility of overseeing a peaceful outcome of the whole process. From their appearance on the scene during World War I through their ultimate departure in 1948, they attempted to control the political environment in a way that would please all of the various segments of the population. Commitments made in the McMahon Letter of 1916 and the Balfour Declaration of 1917 set the stage for a seemingly inevitable and irresolvable conflict. The Peel Commission acknowledged this in 1937 when it declared that a conflict of "right with right" existed. Both groups had legitimate and mutually incompatible claims. Completely satisfying each was impossible, and in the end the British decided that they could not give all involved parties what they demanded. This tension, which the British alone were not able to resolve, led to the eventual abdication of the Mandate to the United Nations.

The horror of World War II, combined with the intensity of feeling emerging from the Holocaust, increased the Jewish demands for statehood. In the end the United Nations authorized a partition of Palestine as the best conceivable outcome. Ultimately, of course, a peaceful resolution to the problem could not be achieved. A painful and inconclusive war followed before the first round of fighting stopped. We say *first* round, of course, because the fighting resumed in 1956, 1967, 1969, and 1973, and there still is not a stable peace in this region.

There existed a native non-Jewish population in Palestine at the time of the British Mandate, and that population has grown since. It has also not been assimilated by either the state of Israel or any other neighboring state. The spirit of nationalism that has reared its head throughout the Americas, Africa, Asia, and eastern and western Europe has also appeared in the Palestinian people, and this nationalism, combined with a strong sense of identity, has led to conflict and suffering that have simply refused to go away. This is something to which we will return in the tenth chapter of this volume.

This chapter has sought to convey a sense of the major issues central to the birth of the modern state of Israel. It is important to realize that we have only just scratched the surface; there remains much more to present and discuss. However, because the focus of this text is on Israeli politics, not Israeli history, we must leave those endeavors to others.[121]

FOR FURTHER READING

Chertoff, Mordechai, ed. *Zionism: A Basic Reader*. New York: Herzl, 1975.

Karsh, Efraim, and Inari Karsh. *Empires of the Sand: The Struggle for Mastery in the Middle East, 1789–1923*. Cambridge, Mass.: Harvard University Press, 1999.

Kimmerling, Baruch. *The Palestinian People: A History*. Cambridge, Mass.: Harvard University Press, 2003.

Morris, Benny. *Making Israel*. Ann Arbor: University of Michigan Press, 2007.

Sachar, Howard. *A History of Israel: From the Rise of Zionism to Our Time*. New York: Alfred A. Knopf, 1981.

Shapira, Anita. *Israeli Historical Revisionism: From Left to Right*. Portland, Ore.: Frank Cass, 2003.

Shlaim, Avi. *Israel and Palestine: Reappraisals, Revisions, Refutations*. London: Verso, 2009.

Smith, Charles D. *Palestine and the Arab-Israeli Conflict*. Boston: St. Martin's, 2007.

Tessler, Mark. *A History of the Israeli-Palestinian Conflict*. Bloomington: Indiana University Press, 1994.

Troen, S. Ilan. *Imagining Zion: Dreams, Designs, and Realities in a Century of Jewish Settlement*. New Haven, Conn.: Yale University Press, 2003.

Williamson, H. G. M. *Understanding the History of Ancient Israel*. New York: Oxford University Press, 2007.

2

Zionism, Religion, and the Domestic Political Environment

The Israeli political world exists in a very special setting. While it is true that all national politics are influenced by the context within which they operate, there are some unique characteristics of Israeli society that go beyond the "normal" range of issues. Zionism is one of these characteristics, and this chapter discusses the concept of Zionism and its impact in Israel. Following this, the chapter turns to the relationship between religion and politics in the state, discussing the debate over the relationship between religious orthodoxy in Israel and the more secular part of the population. What should the relationship be between religion and the state? While Israel is known as "the Jewish state," what is the significance of having several different religious communities in Israel? What should be the relationship between one "kind" of Jew and another? These questions have received much attention in modern Israeli politics and, indeed, have continued to receive highly visible attention in social and political debates in very recent times.

We noted in chapter 1 that one of Israel's fundamental goals has been that advocated by the original Zionists: a Jewish majority in a Jewish state. But what are the applications and implications of this? We have already seen instances in which terms that may appear on the surface to have clear and unambiguous meanings are not, upon closer examination, as clear and

---

The juxtaposition of the Dome of the Rock (sacred to Muslims) above the Western Wall (sacred to Jews) is symbolic of tension in the Middle East.

unambiguous as we had thought. This is very much the case in discussion of concepts such as Zionism, broader discussions of the nature of Judaism, or in the relationship between religion and politics generally.

This chapter begins with the premise that not all individuals who are Jewish share exactly the same beliefs. It also follows that the political orientations of all Jews may not be the same; that is, the relationship between religion and politics may reflect many of the differences between different segments of the Jewish population as a whole. This is, in fact, the case in contemporary Israeli politics.

Our task in this chapter is to examine in greater detail some of the fundamental concepts that have already been introduced in order to understand more fully those aspects of them that perhaps differ from the way we imagined. Here we become familiar with the concept of Zionism and its historical context. We need to understand the use of the concept in the contemporary political context, something that may not be the same as that initial context might have implied. How exactly is the concept of Zionism used today? Could it be interpreted differently than it was at the turn of the century?

Similarly, although students may come to the study of Israeli politics with a general understanding that Israel is a "Jewish state," certain a priori assumptions included in this understanding need to be examined. Not all members of the Jewish population of Israel are alike; they differ in a number of respects. We may approach the study of Israeli politics with an awareness that Israeli Jews may be politically different from Israeli non-Jews, but we also need to be aware that some Israeli Jews are different from other Israeli Jews. The distinction between the Ashkenazic and the Sephardic Jews (the former coming primarily from what today is western Europe and the latter coming from what today is primarily the Middle East and North Africa) is politically important. So too are differences between Orthodox Jews and Conservative Jews and between Conservative Jews and Reform Jews. Hasidic Jews are different from all of these groups, and so on.[1] Before we can feel confident that we understand sufficiently all of the nonpolitical dimensions of Israeli society, we must spend some time discussing these religious and ideological characteristics of Israeli life.

THE CONCEPT OF ZIONISM

As was mentioned in chapter 1, the core of Zionism originally contained two objectives. First, it sought to promote the return of Jews to the land of Israel and the revival of Jewish society, culture, language, and other institutions. Second, it sought to establish a publicly recognized, legally secure home for the Jews in Palestine, their "historic homeland," where they would make up a Jewish majority in a Jewish state and thus be able to guarantee future generations freedom from persecution.[2] In this sense, Zionism has been succinctly defined as "the Jewish people's movement of national liberation,"[3] and the creation of the state of Israel in 1948 was really the climax of the Zionist movement.[4] Although Zionism may well be a movement of "Jewish nationalism" or "Jewish national liberation," it has been suggested by others that it is much more complex than conventional national independence movements and ideologies.[5] It evolved outside of the territory toward which it was directed, and the target of the movement, the Jewish population, was scattered all over the world rather than concentrated in one geographic area. Such factors were bound to leave their imprint.

While these two major principles were the core of classical Zionism in its most simple formulation, it is useful to examine Zionism as it exists in today's world. Have its central principles changed over the last hundred years? Have recent geopolitical or military events altered the substance or general nature of Zionism? Has Zionism in Israel today become what some have called a "civil religion"?[6] It is to these questions that we turn our attention.

The Zionist movement has aimed since the creation of the state in 1948 to encourage immigration from a variety of sources. Israel's population in 2008 was indicated by the government of Israel to be 7,374,000—a substantial proportion of which, as we shall see shortly, resulted from immigration. Indeed, in the eight years between 2000 and 2008, the population of Israel increased by 1,004,700 people: 750,913 of this number resulted from a natural increase, and 253,787 resulted from immigration.[7]

Over three million Jews have migrated to Israel since 1948. Israel has become home for Jews from all over the world. As the data in table 2.1 show, immigrants from Europe and America have accounted for just less than 70 percent of immigrants since the establishment of the state, and those from Asia and Africa have accounted for just more than 30 percent of the immigrants in that period of time.[8] Some Arab nations, such as Egypt, Morocco, Libya, and Syria, have seen virtually their entire Jewish populations depart since 1948. One of the most dramatic such instances was Operation Magic Carpet, which transported 110,000 Jews from Iraq to Israel over the course of a single year. In 1949–1950 the Jewish population of Yemen was about forty-five thousand; most were moved to Israel in one massive immigration wave, and today there remain only about eight hundred Jews.[9]

The issue of Jews from the former Soviet Union has long been an important one for Israel. November 1917 saw two important historical events take place: on November 2, Lord Balfour sent his letter to Lord Rothschild declaring British sympathy with the Zionist movement, and on November 7, the Bolsheviks took power in Russia. Zionism came to be seen as counterrevolutionary, and many Jews tried to leave the Soviet Union throughout its history.[10] In recent years the question of Russian immigration has become

Table 2.1   Sources of Israeli Immigration

	Number	Percentage of Total Immigrants	Percentage of Total Population
Total Population of Israel, 2008	7,374,000	—	—
Total Immigration, 1948–2008	3,044,109	—	41.3
From Asia	432,076	14.2	5.9
From Africa	503,126	16.5	6.8
From Europe	1,827,359	60.0	24.8
From America/ Oceania	249,958	8.2	3.4
Not Known	31,590	1.0	0.4

Sources: Adapted from Michael Wolffsohn, *Israel: Polity, Society and Economy 1882–1986* (Atlantic Highlands, N.J.: Humanities Press International, 1987), p. 121; Central Bureau of Statistics, *Statistical Abstract of Israel, 2009* (Jerusalem: Central Bureau of Statistics, 2009), p. 234, Table 4.2, "Immigrants by Period of Immigration and Last Continent of Residence," www.cbs.gov.il/shnaton60/st04_02.pdf, accessed January 2010.

an extremely visible one in Israel after the former Soviet government started to permit more Jewish emigration, including emigration of Jews to Israel. Of a total Israeli population of more than 7.3 million people in 2008, more than 1.1 million had immigrated from the former Soviet Union, including almost 800,000 in the period from 1990 to 1999. This was more than 15 percent of Israel's total population![11]

With all of this immigration, however, Israel in 2009 still was home to just about 40 percent of world Jewry. As figure 2.1 indicates, the proportion of the world's Jewish population that is Israeli has increased significantly over the years, but it is still a minority of the total Jewish population.

One dimension of the immigration question that has received a good deal of attention over the years is immigration to Israel from the United States. The absolute numbers have not been impressive; in 2008 Israeli government figures showed that 2,022 individuals immigrated to Israel from the United States, out of a total of 13,699 immigrants.[12] According to a study commissioned by the American Jewish Committee, "barely 17 percent of American Jews have ever given the idea [of immigration to Israel] any serious thought at all," and "American Jewry has given Israel a smaller proportion of its population than any other major Diaspora community."[13]

American Jews have never seen immigration to Israel as holding as high a priority in terms of their support for the state. In fact, some have noted, since the 1920s most American Zionist organizations have emphasized financial and political support for Israel rather than emigration from the United States to Israel, very likely because they knew that American Jews were not likely to emigrate in significant numbers.[14]

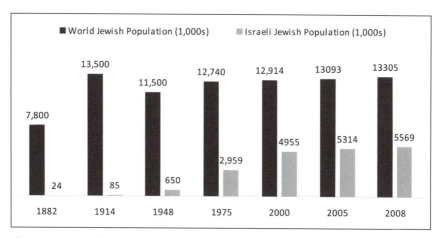

Figure 2.1. Jewish Population in the World and in Israel
Source: Government of Israel, *Central Bureau of Statistics, Statistical Abstract of Israel, 2009*, Table 2.27, "Jewish Population in the World and in Israel," p. 163, www.cbs.gov .il/shnaton60/st02_27.pdf, accessed January 2010.

One offshoot of contemporary Zionism is an emphasis on expanded patterns of Jewish settlement. That is, these people accept the model of the "Jewish people in a Jewish land" advocated by *classical Zionism*. But their belief is that the "Jewish land" over which Israel had control when the fighting stopped in 1949 was insufficient. Perhaps one of the best examples of this viewpoint is the group known as *Gush Emunim* ("Bloc of the Faithful"), the purpose of which is to effect immediate, massive Judaization of Judea and Samaria[15] through the establishment of hundreds of settlements, promoting a revival of Zionism as an ideological and cultural movement.[16]

A more mainstream current of traditional Zionist philosophy is referred to as *socialist Zionism*, which focuses less on geographic boundaries than on how Jewish communities are to be operated. Socialist Zionism is based on a pioneering concept of social behavior that involves asceticism, voluntarism, collective orientation, and egalitarianism. Central to this are the twin emphases on idealism and collective materialism.[17] This socialist Zionist philosophy was very significant in Israel's early years, especially among founders of the state such as David Ben-Gurion, Golda Meir, and Levi Eshkol. The dominance of this philosophy helped to explain why their political party, the Mapai Party, dominated Israeli politics for nearly thirty years.[18] Changing migration and demographic patterns, in turn, help to explain why Mapai's position eroded over the years, a topic to which we shall return in a later chapter in this book.

The idea of *revisionist Zionism*, usually identified with Vladimir Jabotinsky (1880–1944), emphasized national redemption in place of social redemption, stressing the need to attain sovereignty. There was greater emphasis on the role of the military, and although revisionists believed in an "equalitarian distribution of resources at the level of basic human needs, or a limited welfare state," they also believed in a strong free enterprise system.[19] *Neorevisionism*, which appeared after the creation of the state of Israel in 1948, continues to emphasize the importance of reestablishing the *Malchut Israel* ("Kingdom of Israel") in the whole of Mandatory Palestine. It also advocates taking a strong and even militant stand against the Arab powers of the region.[20] This interpretation of Zionism has been most influential on a significant block of recent Israeli political leaders, including Menachem Begin, Yitzhak Shamir, and Ariel Sharon.

Yet a fourth offshoot of the traditional interpretation of Zionism is *religious Zionism*. Motivated by the same nationalistic goals as "regular" Zionism, it seeks to revive traditional Judaism with appropriate Jewish religious values and make it an integral part of the state. Its goals go beyond simply reviving Jewish *political* independence; it seeks to revive *Jewish* political independence.[21] This has provided its own set of conflicts in Israel, some of which we will cover later in this chapter when we discuss Judaism and the interplay of religion and politics in contemporary domestic Israeli political issues.

The interplay of religion and Zionism and religious Zionism has also proven to be significant in further complicating Israeli-Palestinian issues. Not only are the "normal" issues on the agenda—negotiations concerning a cease-fire, a prolonged peace treaty, and an independent state for the Palestinians—but so too are issues that would not appear elsewhere: What is the relationship between the West Bank and biblical Judea and Samaria? Do the territories that were occupied in 1967 include land that biblically is Jewish land? Religious Zionism and religious nationalism have added into the mix of concerns to be resolved a number of issues that are not conventionally matters for international relations.[22]

The interaction of religion and Zionism has led to some interesting, if not paradoxical, confrontations. A relatively small segment of very religious Jews, for example, has argued that the very idea of a Jewish state is blasphemous. Perhaps the best known of the groups advancing this position is the *Neturei Karta* ("Guardians of the City"), who contend that the establishment of a secular state was an "act of rebellion against God" because Jews are "enjoined to wait for God to reestablish a Jewish state." They conclude, therefore, that "Zionism is the great heresy of modern Judaism" and that the Holocaust, in fact, "was God's punishment for the Zionist heresy, inflicted on the Jewish people for abandoning their true religion and substituting secular nationalism."[23]

Most religious Jews, however, do not see an inherent contradiction between Judaism and Zionism. Indeed, in 1967, for example, the (Sephardic) chief rabbi of Israel went so far as to issue the equivalent of a policy paper prohibiting on religious grounds any evacuation of Judea and Samaria.[24] Even one of the mainstream "religious" parties, *Mizrachi*, is an avowedly religious Zionist organization, having constituted itself as a separate party within the World Zionist Organization as early as 1902.[25]

Many Zionists of today do see a need to separate or compartmentalize the concept of Zionism from the question of religion in the state. Some argue that religious Zionism is a noble goal and support the coexistence of religion and Zionism, but argue that this does not imply that religion and Zionism are related. Their goals are different and should not be merged or synthesized. One of the best-known contemporary Zionists of this persuasion is the late scientist and philosopher Yeshayahu Leibowitz (who died in August 1994 at the age of ninety-one). Leibowitz might have been best known as a political critic who called for the complete separation of religion and the state, who declared that his Zionism was based upon "being fed up with being ruled by Gentiles," rather than having a direct link with religious doctrine. He further contended that "Zionism is the desire of Jews for political independence in their own land" and "has nothing to do with the cultural, historical, or spiritual essence of Judaism. Hence the State of Israel cannot and ought not concern itself with the problems of Judaism."[26] As might be guessed, the compartmentalized notion of Zionism is not acceptable to most religious Zionists.

As ideas have evolved, new dimensions of tension have developed. One of the questions to appear in recent years has dealt with the sociocultural relationship between Israel and the United States, trends in contemporary American Judaism,[27] and the impact of American culture on Israeli culture.[28] There is, clearly, a Jewish dimension to this discussion, and discussion regularly takes place dealing with the impact of American life and American ideas about Judaism and Zionism on values and attitudes that are central to Israeli, Jewish, and Zionist values, as illustrated in box 2.1.[29]

The general label "new Zionism" has been placed upon a variety of ideas that can be described as being a rather "loosely knit belief system which combines secular and religious elements . . . [combining] some broad historiographical strands which deal with the meaning of anti-Semitism and the Holocaust."[30] It is difficult to be specific as to exactly what would and would not be included in all of the variations of new Zionism. They would undoubtedly entail some discussion of Jewish identity, Jewish land, and Jewish vulnerability without a Jewish state, but the exact balance of these three themes would vary.[31]

The political manifestations and interaction of these contending notions of Zionism have been blamed for many of the tensions at work in the Middle East today. As tersely put by one critic, "My proposition is that the

Box 1.1. The Americanization of Israel?

Behold the great paradox of classical Zionist ideology. The more we are like all the nations, the less we resemble ourselves. "The Return to Zion is coupled with a metamorphosis of the Jew into a new man," wrote Amnon Rubinstein, today Israel's education minister, in his important book *The Zionist Dream Revisited* (1984). "The Jew would become a *goy* in the double meaning that this word has in Hebrew, signifying both 'gentile' and 'nation.'" If Americanization and Westernization are inexorably engulfing the globe, if the pleasures of a homogenized consumer culture of rollerblades and McDonald's, of faxes and laptops, of home shopping via cable TV (slated to arrive this summer) are as irresistible to Israelis as to anyone else, what becomes of tradition, Judaism, self-sacrifice—of Zionism itself?

. . .

Obviously we are still a long way from losing our distinctive national character. We live proudly by a Jewish clock. Our kids still go to school on Sundays and get off on Purim and Shavuot. Serious Hebrew-language fiction and drama continue to find a wide audience. The fastest-growing sectors of our population, the ultra-Orthodox and the Arabs, are the least Westernized. Orthodox rabbinic authorities still control Jewish marriage, divorce, burial, and conversion, and though there are a few chinks in the wall—mild advances in religious pluralism are another index of creeping Americanization—the so-called religious "status quo" agreement negotiated at the dawn of Israeli statehood is unlikely to be overturned anytime soon.

Zionist values, codified in Israeli law, remain the basis of our civic culture; it may be argued that they are the secular equivalent of religious mitzvot and act as a brake on self-indulgence. Israelis serve bravely in the army, absorb wave after wave of immigrants, and ante up high taxes to pay for it all. For now, at least: It is worth noting that there's been a slight drift downward in the percentage of Israelis serving in the armed forces; that there is widespread talk of tightening the Law of Return; and that when Prime Minister Rabin tried to impose a tax on stock-market profits the outcry was so shrill you'd have thought our very survival was at stake. It's surely symbolic of something that the state-run Israel Broadcasting Authority is marking Yom Ha'atzma'ut, our sacred Independence day, by sponsoring a nationwide scavenger hunt wherein Israelis will follow clues in search of six hidden treasures.

Will crass Americanization eventually swamp our consciousness and wreck our noblest values? I think not, and dearly hope not. I for one didn't follow my grandparents eastward to live in a pint-sized clone of a vanilla suburban dream. On the other hand, I genuinely relish taking my kids to the world's first kosher Burger King in the Jerusalem Mall, so they grow up knowing that french fries are supposed to be bronzed and crisp, not the color and consistency of flaccid lokshen.

Source: Stuart Schoffman, "The Americanization of Israel," *Jerusalem Report* (May 18, 1995): CD-ROM.

fundamental problem in the Arab-Israeli conflict is the Zionist character of the State of Israel."[32] The thrust of the argument is that the root cause of conflict in the Middle East is not the Muslim-Jewish religious division, but rather the tension caused by substantial Jewish immigration and eventual majority status in a land previously inhabited by an Arab majority.

Today, the Arab world generally continues to reject the Israeli nation planted in its midst. "The Arabs see Israel not only as an unwanted transplant but as a spreading malignancy that threatens their very existence. The Israelis see the Arabs surrounding them as an eternal menace, eternally rejecting them: 'The Arabs will never make peace.'"[33]

Most Israelis see Zionism as a philosophy of nationalism and protection for an otherwise vulnerable Jewish minority whose only salvation is a Jewish state with a Jewish majority. Over the years a number of variations on this general theme have arisen, stressing culture, economic policy, national security, and so on. It is clear, however, that whatever the variation, the concept of Zionism has been, and continues to be, critical to the state of Israel by providing, despite its permutations, a sense of identity, continuity, and purpose to an otherwise disparate population.

THE RELIGIOUS COMMUNITIES OF ISRAEL

One of the most common misperceptions of Israel held by students new to the subject is the assumption that Israel is a Jewish state, therefore all Israelis must be Jewish. The visibility of Israeli Arabs has been low, but contemporary political tension has made their presence more visible.[34] In fact, as we have already indicated, more than 24 percent of the population, according to 2009 census data, is non-Jewish, and most of this group is Muslim. Of the 1.5 million individuals classified as belonging to a religious group other than Jewish, roughly 10 percent are Christians, 81 percent are Muslims, and 8 percent are Druze (see table 2.2).[35] There are very small communities of Greek Catholic, Greek Orthodox, Armenian, Protestant, and Maronite followers as well.[36]

The 1948 Declaration of Independence guaranteed freedom of religion to all citizens. The individual religious communities are free to exercise their own faith and administer their own internal affairs. Each major community has its own religious courts and the Ministry of Religious Affairs, which is responsible for overseeing the needs of all religious communities in Israel, respects their jurisdictional authority, including primary responsibility for religious questions, along with personal matters that may be regulated by the religious communities, such as marriage and divorce. Indeed, one of the ironies in Israel is that the Christian and Muslim communities are provided greater degrees of freedom and self-regulation than are some Jewish communities. Specifically, some Reform Jewish leaders argue that they are subject to greater regulation by the Orthodox Jewish community in Israel than are the non-Jewish sects.[37]

Table 2.2   Israel's Population and Religious Communities, 2008

	Number	Percentage of Total
Population, 2008	7,374,000	—
Population group		
Jewish, "non-Arab Christians," and those not classified by religion	5,569,200	75.5
Arab	1,487,600	20.2
Other	317,100	4.3
Religion		
Jewish	5,569,200	75.5
Muslim	1,240,000	16.8
Christian	153,100	2.1
Druze	121,900	1.7

Source: Government of Israel, Central Bureau of Statistics, *Statistical Abstract of Israel, 2009* (Jerusalem: Government of Israel, 2009), Table 2.1, "Population, by Population Group," p. 85, www.cbs.gov.il/shnaton60/st02_01.pdf, and Table 2.2, "Population, by Religion," p. 87, www.cbs.gov.il/shnaton60/st02_02.pdf, accessed January 2010.

JUDAISM IN ISRAEL

Just as it is a mistake to assume that all Israelis are Jews, so too is it a mistake to assume that all Israeli Jews are alike. In fact, there are several different trends in Judaism today, and in many cases the tensions that exist between them are greater and perceived as more threatening than the tensions that might exist between Jews and non-Jews in Israel.[38] This is largely because the various Jewish sects see themselves as competing with each other for influence over the same population, rather than being fearful that the existing non-Jewish communities in Israel will successfully recruit from the Jewish population.[39]

Judaism, unlike various Christian sects, can be referred to as nondenominational.[40] That is, the same general prayer book is used in religious services throughout the world. However, there are differences in the way various groups of Jews *practice* their religion. Three major branches of Judaism exist today: Orthodox, Conservative (or Traditional), and Progressive (or Reform). The Orthodox group tends to be most rigorous in following Jewish religious law, called *halacha*. This often implies interpreting religious laws literally and placing the importance of such law above the conveniences of day-to-day life.[41] Conservative Judaism also argues that *halacha* should govern one's life, but is more flexible about accepting adaptations of *halacha* and is more receptive to making "reasonable" accommodations. Reform Judaism allows and encourages even more adaptation and modification of *halacha* to respect different individual patterns of living. Reform Jews tend to place greatest emphasis on Jewish ethics, rather than specific religious

Photo 2.1. The Dome of the Rock is an iconic symbol of the importance of Jerusalem to Muslims worldwide.

edicts, and argue that there should be greater freedom for Jews to decide for themselves how strictly they will follow *halacha*.[42]

What has happened within the Jewish community is that disagreements over interpretation and application developed among these different groups. In the past, Orthodox leaders have condemned Reform Jews as not being "real" Jews, suggesting that the Reform wing has so adapted Judaism to be "relevant" to the contemporary world that it has lost a portion of the essence of its theology.[43] Their basic argument has been that both Conservative and Reform Judaism "were responses to Judaism's minority status in a Christian setting, and that they therefore have no place in a Jewish state."[44] When Reform Judaism decided that women could serve as part of the *minyan*,[45] Orthodox Judaism decided that the Reformers had deviated so far from traditional interpretations of *halacha* that Reform Judaism could no longer be accepted as "real" Judaism.

A very important structure in this intra-Judaic tension has been the position of the chief rabbi. Sephardic and Ashkenazic Jews each have their own national chief rabbis in Israel,[46] and each of these groups has its own chief rabbi in most major cities in Israel.[47] The chief rabbinate as an institution has played a significant role over the years in the maintenance of Jewish orthodoxy in Israel, and therefore the chief rabbis have had much political, as well as religious, influence.

The national chief rabbis are the official spokesmen of Judaism in Israel, and each chief rabbi serves as the head of a significant bureaucracy.[48] This bureaucracy is significant for the average Israeli for many reasons, not the least of which is that it supervises laws dealing with *kashrut* (dietary laws) and marriages and divorces. Chief rabbis serve single ten-year terms in office and are elected by 150-member electoral boards consisting of rabbis from local religious councils and public figures. Originally, the chief rabbinate was designed to be an authority "issuing halachic rulings to mediate between the demands of tradition and a modern state." Increasingly in recent years, however, the chief rabbis have been closer to ultraorthodox positions on issues than to religious Zionist positions. This has pleased the ultraorthodox in Israel's population, but has not been such good news for the rest of the population—the vast majority.[49]

One example of a particularly divisive issue concerns the role of women on (Jewish) religious councils. An Orthodox woman who was a member of the city of Yeroham's local council as a representative of the Labor Party was proposed by the council to be one of its candidates for membership on the religious council, the body that provides religious support services, enters into contracts, and holds property on behalf of the religious community in its district. The minister for religious affairs and the local rabbinate opposed her nomination. She appealed to the Supreme Court of Israel on the grounds that opposition to her holding the position was gender-related, referring to "a letter addressed to her on May 6, 1986, by the responsible official in the Ministry for Religious Affairs, in which she was told in plain language it was impossible for a woman to be a member of a religious council."[50] The Supreme Court ruled that since the sole duty of the council was to supply support services for religious activities and not to give *halachic* or authoritative religious rulings, the only permissible criteria for membership on a council could be (a) that a person must be religious, or at least not antireligious, and (b) that a person must represent a body or community having some religious interest. The person need not have qualifications in law or *halacha*. On those grounds, the Court overturned the actions of the Ministry of Religious Affairs and ordered the woman be given her position on the religious council, because excluding a person from membership on a council by virtue of her gender alone violated Israeli law.

This kind of conflict has resulted in tension between various sects that is often more divisive than that between Jews and non-Jews. The Ministry of Religious Affairs, controlled by Orthodox Jewish religious political parties almost continually since 1948, has essentially given non-Jewish religious groups a free hand in their internal governance.[51] However, the ministry has been much more restrictive in its dealings with the Reform community in Israel, limiting its ability to build synagogues and requiring that all marriages, divorces, and births be registered in accordance with Orthodox, rather than Conservative or Reform, religious law.[52] Indeed, even rabbis are affected by this policy: Orthodox leaders do not recognize the legitimacy of Conservative and Reform rabbis as rabbis. Also, Conservative and Reform synagogues receive less state support than Orthodox ones.[53]

That there is tension between Jewish groups in Israeli society is readily apparent to all who live there. The former mayor of Jerusalem, Teddy Kollek, observed at one time in the not-very-distant past that "the growing abyss between secular and Orthodox Jews is much more dangerous than [Palestinian Authority President] Arafat's ambitions regarding the city."[54] This observation was clearly made at a time and in a context that was far away from the *intifada* and violence of recent years, but Kollek's point is clear: the myth of Jewish unanimity is just that, a myth. The division between Jewish groups is apparent in a wide range of business, social, and economic dimensions of life there. The (often self-imposed) "separate but equal" status of the religious Orthodox extends to divisions in the Israeli armed forces and to the kibbutz movement as well.[55]

The very question "Who is a Jew?" has proven an exceptionally divisive and contentious issue in Israeli politics since independence.[56] This deceptively simple question is asking which set of rules will decide what constitutes "Jewishness."[57] Will conversions, marriages, and divorces be undertaken according to Orthodox rules as defined by *halacha* or according to the rules of any of the major Jewish groups? The answer, more often than not, has been that the Orthodox rules are the rules recognized by the state.

In 1986 the Israeli Supreme Court ruled in favor of a new immigrant from the United States who had challenged the Ministry of the Interior's labeling her a "convert to Judaism" on her identity papers. The immigrant, Shoshana Miller, was converted to Judaism as a Reform Jew in the United States. The Reform movement is not authorized to conduct conversions in Israel, but Ms. Miller claimed that since she had been converted in the United States, she entered Israel "as a Jew." The three-judge Supreme Court panel ruled that although the Population Registry is allowed to specify religious affiliation on an immigrant's identity card, it is not authorized to include "any other details, such as how people achieved their status." The Court ruled that doing so might "undermine the unity of the Jewish people" and added that "such differentiation runs contrary to the spirit of Judaism."[58] Thus, the "unity of the Jewish people" has been perceived to be threatened by the "Who is a Jew?" question.[59]

In recent years this general question has surfaced again and again in Israeli politics. The issue of "Who is a Jew?" and the nature of religious-political interaction became highly visible during the coalition-formation period immediately following the 1988 Knesset elections. At that time the Orthodox parties appeared to be the key to the formation of a majority coalition either for Yitzhak Shamir and his Likud Party or for Shimon Peres and his Labor Party. Their demands, as we chronicle in far more detail later in this volume, all focused on the principle of turning state policy in a more Orthodox direction. The Orthodox parties have struggled to have the government recognize only Orthodox marriages, divorces, and conversions, while the Reform and Conservative groups have argued that they, too, should be recognized as "officially" Jewish movements. An editorial at the time criticized the Orthodox opinion:

> The Orthodox and *haredi* [ultraorthodox] insistence on placing outside the law Jews whom they consider halachically impure is threatening the unity of the Jewish people. . . . Prime Minister Yitzhak Shamir played the innocent when he told a delegation of the British United Israel Appeal that "we have no intention of intervening in the internal affairs of our fellow Jews abroad. We are not questioning the legitimacy of any Jew outside Israel." The amendment to the Law of Return, or the "conversion law," which our Orthodox spiritual warriors are demanding, cannot be interpreted in any way other than placing into question the Jewish legitimacy of those whom Shamir condescends to include in the category "our fellow Jews." It is only out of respect for Shamir that we say "playing the innocent" rather than accusing him of insensitivity or of outright, conscious wickedness.[60]

In 1998 the "Who is a Jew?" question surfaced again very visibly with the report of the Neeman Commission. In January 1998 the Druckman Committee report was handed down; it was concerned with the issue of the conversion of infants adopted abroad by Israeli families.[61] This was a specific variation of the very volatile issue of adult conversions in different Jewish movements—whether the Orthodox powers in Israel would recognize Reform and Conservative conversions from abroad—and the public waited with great interest for the Neeman Commission report to be handed down a month later.

In an editorial that did a very good job of summarizing the tensions involved in the conflict, the *Jerusalem Post* observed that

> The Neeman Commission began as a mechanism to defuse a looming legal and legislative battle royale between American Jews and Israel's religious establishment. Reform and Conservative Jews wielded the Supreme Court, while the Orthodox religious parties seemed poised for victory in the Knesset. At this last moment before either agreement or collapse, both sides should realize that there will be no winners if this historic opportunity is missed, and no losers if it succeeds.

The basic conflict arises from the fact that there are two radically different realities in Israel, the Jewish state, and in America, home to the world's largest Jewish community. The American reality is of Jewish pluralism and of the separation between church and state, which has become as much of a Jewish cultural value as it is an American one. The Israeli reality is one where both pluralism and separation between state and religion are considered almost unnatural, even anathema.

> Given the strong opposition of these paradigms, it is perhaps a wonder that they have not come into open conflict more often. There was, of course, the fight over "who is a Jew" before, when the religious parties tried to amend the criteria for citizenship under the Law of Return to include only those who are Jewish according to Halacha. But since then an uneasy truce has prevailed—until now.[62]

The final report of the Neeman Commission recommended that conversions in Israel would be conducted exclusively by rabbinical courts attached to the Chief Rabbinate—a victory for the Orthodox disputants—and that other conversions (conversions of a non-Orthodox nature) would not be conducted, or if they were conducted, they would not be recognized by the state. The process of conversion itself, however, would be placed in the hands of a "tripartite body" made up of rabbis representing the three main movements in Judaism—Orthodox, Conservative, and Reform. The Orthodox movement won a significant part of the battle before the Neeman Commission by virtue of the commission's accepting the principle that only Orthodox conversions would be done in Israel, a fact Orthodoxy's two major rivals recognized. However, the Conservative and Reform movements won significant victories from the commission because, for the first time, the state of Israel and the Orthodox institutions of the state officially recognized the existence of the Reform and Conservative movements and recognized them to be a part of the religious life of international Jewry.[63]

The fact that the support of the Orthodox religious political parties has been absolutely necessary for governments to stay in power has meant over the years that more often than not the Government has sided with the Orthodox in these questions. As things turned out in the case of the 1988 election, both Likud and Labor found the demands of the religious parties—that the Law of Return be amended so that only Orthodox converts to Judaism would be recognized as "real" Jews eligible for immigration under that law—so distasteful that they joined together in another national unity government, something they both had pledged during the campaign they would not do, in order to avoid the necessity of yielding to the Orthodox demands.

A 2009 public opinion survey found that a minority of Israelis felt that only Orthodox conversions should be recognized by the state. "Nearly 60 percent of the public felt that the State should abolish the ultra-Orthodox monopoly on conversion to Judaism and recognize additional types of conversions." This included support for "all types—including civil" of conversion (27 percent), "Orthodox, Reform, and Conservative" conversion (32 percent), as well as "only Orthodox" conversions (41 percent).[64]

The issues have not gone away, however, and the "Who is a Jew?" question has continued to have real consequences for Israeli citizens and would-be citizens. To take one example, in a relatively recent policy decision, the Chief Rabbinate, which controls marriages and divorces involving Jews in Israel, has announced that "all new immigrants—from any country—who made aliya since 1990 must prove they are Jewish before a special rabbinical court if they want to be married by the rabbinate."[65] According to the regulations set down by the Chief Rabbinate, in any case where a couple coming to register for marriage includes a new immigrant (who arrived after 1990), the registrar should direct the new immigrant to the nearest conversion commission for clarification of Jewishness. The form issued by the special rabbinical court states, "You are invited to appear before a rabbinical court for the purpose of clarifying Jewishness." It asks the prospective spouse to bring his or her original birth certificate, that of his or her mother and other maternal relatives, his or her parents' marriage certificate, family photographs, and "any document certifying Jewishness." It is important, the form states, to arrive with one's parents and, especially, one's mother.[66]

RELIGION AND POLITICS—JEWISH ISSUES

It should come as no surprise that the general societal tensions that surround religion and politics—and here we confine our comments to the tensions felt between Jewish groups in Israeli society—often focus on specific questions of public policy. Questions of public policy, after all, are illustrations of how the government puts its values into operation; one might expect attitudes related to the proper relationship between religion and politics to become apparent in questions dealing with public policy.[67]

Among the most intensely felt attitudes in the Israeli political world are those dealing with interactions between religion and politics, the former being among the most private values an individual can hold, the latter by definition requiring public articulation and behavior and, in fact, leading to the imposition of one citizen's opinions upon another.[68]

Reflecting the heterogeneity of Judaism itself is the broad range of differences within Israeli public opinion about what the relationship between religion and politics should be. This has been a source of tension in Israel since the creation of the state, and it continues to be a source of tension today. In a very well-studied survey done a quarter-century ago, in 1981, the populace was clearly split on whether the Government should "see to it that public life is conducted in accordance with Jewish religious tradition." A depiction of the distribution of public opinion would reflect an almost evenly divided population in a roughly symmetrical distribution similar to that shown in table 2.3.

Table 2.3   Religion and Politics

"Should the Government see to it that public life is conducted in accordance with Jewish religious tradition?"

Definitely	27%
Probably	23%
Probably not	23%
Definitely not	26%

Source: Adapted from Asher Arian, *Politics in Israel* (Chatham, N.J.: Chatham House, 1985), p. 217.

This pattern has changed very little over the last several decades. The problem is that, despite the symmetry of the relationship illustrated in table 2.3, the policy relationship is not so symmetrical. Nonreligious Jews should not be surprised, one observer has written, "that while they respect the Orthodox and their needs, such consideration is not always mutual. 'Live and let live,' pleads the non-Orthodox Israeli Jew, not grasping that this is a secular concept at total odds with pure religious faith."[69] In other words, "whereas even the most anti-religious Jew respects the fact that the religious Jew has inviolable boundaries of behaviour beyond which he cannot go, such as eating non-kosher food or desecrating the Sabbath, religious leaders tend to assert that such limits do not exist on the other side."[70] This belief on the part of the religious leaders—that nonreligious Jews have no finite limits on their behavior—prompts them to want to use the instruments of the state to legislate these limits. And, of course, the values used to determine these limits come from religious orthodoxy.

And that is key. The major plank of the political ideology of the Orthodox groups is to have the state of Israel organize its public life in accordance with Jewish religious law, *halacha.*

Religion is a central issue in Jewish political life. It is crucial because of the broad consensus within the Jewish population that Israel should be a Jewish state. The conflict is over the *degree* to which legislation and civil life in Israel should reflect the norms and decisions of established [Orthodox] religious authorities. The Knesset has passed legislation regarding some of these matters. For example, (1) the 1950 Law of Return assuring the right of every Jew to immigrate to Israel; (2) the 1952 Law of Citizenship granting citizenship to every Jew, his or her spouse, children, and grandchildren; (3) the 1953 law establishing sole jurisdiction to the Orthodox rabbinical courts regarding marriage and divorce among Jews; (4) a 1951 law making the Jewish Sabbath an official rest day for Jews and requiring a permit to employ a Jew on the rest day; (5) the 1962 law prohibiting the raising of pigs in Israel except in areas in which there is a concentrated Christian population; (6) the 1986 law prohibiting Jews from displaying leavened food for sale during the days of Passover; and (7) the 1990 law allowing local authorities to regulate whether enterprises involved in entertainment [movies and theaters] will be allowed to operate on the Sabbath and holy days.[71]

Although the public is divided on what the Government's role should be in seeing that daily life is conducted according to Jewish religious tradition, it is clear that what are referred to as "secular" Jews today are not happy about having significant dimensions of their lives regulated by the Orthodox. There are real differences in attitudes on separation of religion and state and the value of freedom of religion and conscience between the Orthodox and the secular. In a 2009 public opinion research project, data showed much public unhappiness with the political power of the religiously orthodox (see table 2.4).

> Despite freedom of religion being pronounced as a fundamental right in Israel's Declaration of Independence, many compromises have been made granting exclusive powers to ultra-Orthodox religious institutions. As a result, a broad range of civil affairs, including education, marriage and divorce, public transportation, welfare and military service, are strongly influenced by ultra-Orthodox religious leaders.[72]

This pattern of disagreement about the appropriate role of the state in enforcing religious values is repeated in applied settings, too. Data from a

Table 2.4   Attitudes on Freedom of Religion and Conscience among Jews

"Should the State ensure freedom of religion and conscience?"

	Total	Religious Observance			
		Ultraorthodox	Observant	Traditional	Secular
Strongly Agree	60%	21%	35%	53%	76%
Moderately Agree	23%	26%	30%	28%	18%
Slightly Agree or Disagree	17%	53%	35%	18%	6%

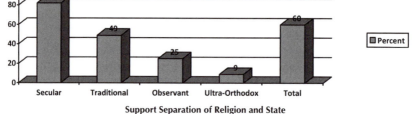

Support Separation of Religion and State

Source: Shahar Ilan, ed., "Preliminary Public Opinion Research for the 'Religion and State Index' Project," p. 3–4, *Hiddush*—For Religious Freedom and Equality, www.hiddush.org/UploadFiles/file/ReligionStateIndexResearchReport2009.pdf, accessed January 2010.

2009 public opinion study show significant Orthodox-secular differences on a number of specific questions about government policy, as indicated in table 2.5.

Despite the fact that a vast majority of the population is not Orthodox in its observation of Jewish religious law, there have been few sustained efforts to decrease the degree to which Jewish religion is reflected in the law of the state. Judaism is reflected in the practices of the state in a number of ways. National holidays are Jewish holidays, not Christian or Muslim, although members of those communities are certainly permitted to practice their religions freely. Public transportation does not run on the Jewish Sabbath, movie theaters are closed, and most restaurants are closed from sunset Friday until sunset Saturday and do not reopen until the Sabbath is officially declared over.[73] In 1982 a major conflict developed regarding El Al, the national airline. The religious parties wanted the airline to be grounded on the Sabbath, since it was owned and supported by the Government.[74] The airline protested, arguing that it would lose too much business. After much debate and a near toppling of the Government, the authorities gave in to the demands of the religious parties and ceased the Sabbath operations of El Al.

The issue of permitting El Al to fly on the Sabbath has not gone away over the years. The management of the national airline has argued that by not flying on the Sabbath it loses a tremendous amount of money.

Table 2.5   Israeli Jewish Religious Practice and Belief

Support Public Transportation on Saturdays (full or limited service):

	Full service	Limited service	Total
Secular	32%	52%	84%
Traditional	10%	41%	51%
Observant	5%	24%	29%
Ultraorthodox	0%	15%	15%

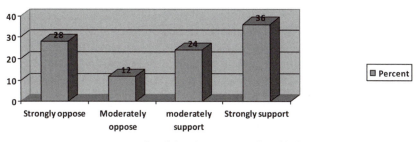

Operation of Shopping Centers on the Sabbath

Source: Shahar Ilan, ed., "Preliminary Public Opinion Research for the 'Religion and State Index' Project," pp. 6–7, *Hiddush*—For Religious Freedom and Equality, www.hiddush.org/UploadFiles/file/ReligionStateIndexResearchReport2009.pdf, accessed January 2010.

Indeed, in 2001 the issue of privatizing El Al—having the Government sell it to a group of private interests that would run it as a private company— again came to the foreground. The decision was made that the minister of transportation would be permitted to submit to the Ministerial Com- mittee on Privatization a proposal to convert El Al from a national busi- ness to a private concern. The key issue, of course, was that if it became a private concern, it would be permitted to fly on the Sabbath. The conflict continued over the years, as a result of El Al needing increasing govern- ment subsidies to continue to not fly on the Sabbath; in 2004 El Al was, finally, privatized, and discussion continued about whether that would provide the cover for increased operation on the Sabbath. Because of pres- sure from Orthodox constituencies, however—which make up between 20 and 30 percent of its market—even the privatized El Al has refrained from flying on the Sabbath.[75]

The relationship between the Government and religion is made more complex by the various meanings of Jewishness. Israelis are split over these matters. Arian has observed, "it is fascinating to note the different patterns over time in the distribution of answers to questions regarding personal religious behavior on the one hand, and the role of religion in public life on the other." Despite enormous change across most of Israel's existence, the rate of those responding that they observe "all" or "most" of Jewish religious law is amazingly stable at 25 to 30 percent; the other responses provided were "some" and "none." These numbers are consistent with the estimate that about a quarter of Israeli Jews are observant in an Orthodox sense, including 6 to 10 percent *haredi*, or ultraorthodox; that about 40 percent are determinedly secular; and that the rest are somewhere between those poles.[76]

One team of scholars has suggested that there are three levels of interac- tion between the state and religion in Israel: the symbolic, the institutional, and the legislative.[77] On the symbolic level are the many images of Jewish religious tradition that appear in Israeli life. The seven-branched cande- labra, or *menorah*, is the official symbol of Israel and appears on stamps, money, and other official contexts. On the institutional level, we can iden- tify a number of different types of religious institutions that are funded by the state or have official governmental status. The Ministry of Religious Affairs underwrites a number of them, and the Government has tradition- ally respected an Orthodox monopoly in this regard.[78] In terms of religious legislation, there exist numerous acts of cooperation. There is a wide body of Sabbath law closing cinemas and regulating hotel and restaurant behav- ior, bus lines, and so on. This kind of legislation includes rules governing marriages and divorces, and even includes laws governing pig farming.

Some observers have suggested that the call for the separation of religion and state in Israel has never had broad public support for four reasons.[79]

Photo 2.2.   The menorah is the official emblem of the State of Israel. The Knesset Menorah was donated to the Knesset by members of the British Parliament in 1956.

1. *Politics:* Religious parties have been significant in government coalitions, and the suggestion for separation wasn't politically viable.
2. *Symbolism:* Most Israelis support the idea of Israel as a Jewish state. While there are debates about what the term *Jewish state* means, some dimension of religion appears to be part of that definition for a substantial proportion of the population.
3. *Habit:* Most Israelis are used to the Jewish nature of Israel, such as having the Sabbath on Saturday.
4. *Principle:* The call for the separation of religion and the state is foreign to most of Jewish history and the history of the Middle East.

There are several reasons why the vast non-Orthodox majority has never been able or inclined to push for the separation of church and state. First and foremost is politics. All Israeli governments since independence have been coalition governments that customarily include religious party representation.[80] This means that the major parties have been forced to depend upon the religious parties for their support in order to stay in power, and the religious parties have demanded in return for this support the maintenance of the status quo with respect to the role of religion in the state.[81]

An additional reason for this lack of separation between religion and the state has been the feeling on the part of many non-Orthodox Jewish Israelis that while they might not be Orthodox themselves, it is appropriate for the state to be at least sympathetic to Orthodoxy. After all, if the Orthodox population cannot receive governmental support in Israel, where can it ever expect to? This explains the almost contradictory data presented in tables 2.3 and 2.4. There are clearly many individuals who do not personally observe Jewish religious law (77 percent indicate that they observe Jewish religious law "only somewhat" or "not at all"), but who feel that it may be appropriate for the state to promote the following of Jewish religious law (50 percent indicate that the state should "definitely" or "probably" see to it that public life is conducted in accordance with Jewish religious tradition).

In more recent years, especially since 1977 when the Government of Menachem Begin came to power with the assistance of *Agudat Israel*, an ultraorthodox religious party, highly contentious and controversial religious policy issues have been introduced more frequently into the political agenda.[82] For example, in the 1981 coalition agreement, *Agudat Israel* convinced the Government to take positions on the following:

1. Strengthening government policy against abortion
2. Strengthening the protection of Jewish gravesites against the activities of archaeologists, road builders, or property developers
3. Strengthening policy against autopsies
4. Facilitating the excuse of women from military services
5. Strengthening policy forbidding work on the Sabbath and religious holidays
6. Applying religious law to the state's determination of who is a Jew and insisting that only conversions carried out by Orthodox rabbis will be recognized
7. Opposing the activities of Christian missionaries
8. Strengthening regulations against the production or sale of nonkosher food
9. Forbidding swearing in the name of God in court proceedings[83]

Again in 1988, following the elections for the Knesset, the ability of the Orthodox religious parties to play a crucial role in the creation of a government coalition gave them great leverage in forcing the Government to promise more Orthodox interpretations of social policy, although the religious parties were so unrelenting in their demands that they ended up alienating the other significant actors in the coalition-formation process. Although a more detailed analysis of the role of the Orthodox religious parties in the coalition-formation period is presented later in this volume, it is enough to note here that the religious parties were significant and that their demands upon Mr. Shamir, the prime minister designate, were strong enough to force him to form a coalition with Shimon Peres, leader of the Labor Party and his chief opponent for political leadership in Israel, rather than join with them, as was his initial inclination.

ISRAEL'S NON-JEWISH COMMUNITIES

As noted earlier in this chapter, around 75 percent of Israel's population is classified as Jewish. We noted in chapter 1 that Israeli Arabs have full legal and political rights in Israel, and these rights extend to their religious identity.[84] The Declaration of the Establishment of the State of Israel (1948) guaranteed freedom of religion for all citizens of Israel. The law guaranteed that each religious community would be able to

> exercise its faith, to observe its holidays and weekly day of rest and to adminis-
> ter its internal affairs. Each has its own religious council and courts, recognized
> by law and with jurisdiction over all religious affairs and matters of personal
> status such as marriage and divorce. Each has its own unique places of wor-
> ship, with traditional rituals and special architectural features developed over
> the centuries.[85]

The state of Israel recognizes a number of non-Jewish religions, including Christianity, Islam, Druze, and Bahaism; within the Christian religion the state formally recognizes the following denominations: Greek Orthodox, Greek Catholic, Latin (Roman Catholic), Armenian Orthodox, Armenian Catholic, Maronite, Syrian Orthodox, Syrian Catholic, Chaldaic (Catholic), and Evangelical Episcopal (Anglican).[86] Muslim Arabs make up nearly three-quarters of the Arab-Israeli sector, and most of these are Sunni Muslims.

Ironically, many of the challenges and tensions that exist between Jewish Israelis and their government do not exist between Muslim and Christian Israelis and the Israeli government. (This is not to suggest that Muslim and Christian Israelis do not experience tensions with the Israeli government for other reasons—perhaps because of their criticism of the Israeli government over its policy regarding the Palestinians, for example—but is to suggest that religion is not the primary cause of tensions.) This is so because, as we have already seen, the major governmental actor in these issues—the Ministry of Religious Affairs—is run by Orthodox Jewish interests, and its primary concerns involve Jewish issues; it is therefore inclined to give Christian and Muslim interests a substantial degree of autonomy. Muslim and Christian interests have access to Ministry of Religious Affairs funding, as do Jewish groups, and have authority to regulate their own practice in terms of marriage, divorce, and matters of policy connected closely with religious principles.

It should be noted here that many Israeli Muslims and Israeli Christians believe that the Israeli government does discriminate against them, a view shared by others outside of Israel. According to the U.S. Department of State's *Annual Report on International Religious Freedom for 1999: Israel*, while the Israeli government "generally respects" freedom of worship, "The overwhelming majority of non-Jewish citizens are Arabs and they are subject to various forms of discrimination. It is not clear that whatever discrepancies exist in the treatment of various communities in Israeli society are based on religion *per se*."[87]

The government does not provide Israeli Arabs, who constitute around 25 percent of the population, with the same quality of education, housing, employment opportunities, and social services as it does Israeli Jews. In addition, government spending and financial support are proportionally far lower in predominantly non-Jewish areas than in Jewish areas. According to the press, a 1998 Ministry of the Interior report noted that non-Jewish communities receive significantly less government financial support than their Jewish counterparts. Israeli-Arab organizations have challenged the Government's "Master Plan for the Northern Areas of Israel," which listed as priority goals increasing Galilee's Jewish population and blocking the territorial contiguity of Arab villages and towns, on the grounds that it discriminates against Arab citizens.[88]

ZIONISM, RELIGION, AND THE STATE

We began this chapter by noting that while one of the fundamental goals of Israeli founders was the establishment of a Jewish majority in a Jewish state, there have obviously been problems with its realization. Often, terms whose meanings appear clear and unambiguous on the surface may not be, upon closer examination, as clear and unambiguous as we had thought. Terms such as *Zionism* and *Judaism*, therefore, must be looked at more carefully in this light. Not all Zionists are cast from the same mold, for there have been, and clearly remain, quite significant differences among Zionists. Zionism can variously have a cultural, economic, military, or religious interpretation, to name but a few of the possible variations of the term. Although we offer no definitive positions on whether one or another of these is more correct, it is the case that as students of Israeli politics, we must be careful to understand our own and others' assumptions.

Similarly, we saw that the phrase "to be a Jew" means different things to different people. Some might interpret Jewishness as an ethnic or historical label. For others, it has very rigorous and strict behavioral implications. Views having to do with the relationship between a Jewish state and the Jewish religion vary considerably, from the ultraorthodox who wish to institutionalize theopolitics to those who desire a complete and strict separation of the two.[89]

Our task here was not to evaluate these positions or to suggest either that some views of Zionism are more correct than others or that certain relationships between religion and politics are more valid or more legitimate. Rather, the goal of this chapter has been to impress upon the student that the political world in Israel is complicated even more than it might otherwise be by the existence of these sources of potential political division. Not only does Israel have the "normal" political issues that must be addressed by any state, such as economics, foreign policy, social welfarism, and the like, but it also has to address such questions as "Who is a Jew?" "What should the Government do to promote or restrict the role of religious orthodoxy in the state?" and the like. Later, we see that these issues surface over and over again as political rather than exclusively religious issues.

FOR FURTHER READING

Avnery, Uri. *Israel without Zionism: A Plan for Peace in the Middle East.* New York: Collier Books, 1971.

Cohen, Asher, and Bernard Susser. *Israel and the Politics of Jewish Identity: The Secular-Religious Impasse.* Baltimore: Johns Hopkins University Press, 2000.

Cohen, Mitchell. *Zion and State: Nation, Class, and the Shaping of Modern Israel.* New York: Columbia University Press, 1992.

Dieckhoff, Alain. *Invention of a Nation: Zionist Thought and the Making of Modern Israel.* New York: Columbia University Press, 2002.

Dowty, Alan. *The Jewish State: A Century Later.* Berkeley: University of California Press, 2001.

Halpern, Ben, and Jehuda Reinharz. *Zionism and the Creation of a New Society.* New York: Oxford University Press, 1998.

Kaplan, Eran. *The Jewish Radical Right: Revisionist Zionism and Its Ideological Legacy.* Madison: University of Wisconsin Press, 2005.

Lederhendler, Eli. *Who Owns Judaism? Public Religion and Private Faith in America and Israel.* New York: Oxford University Press, 2001.

Lee, Robert Deemer. *Religion and Politics in the Middle East: Identity, Ideology, Institutions, and Atttitudes.* Boulder, Colo.: Westview, 2010.

Lehmann, David, and Batia Siebzehner. *Remaking Israeli Judaism: The Challenge of Shas.* New York: Oxford University Press, 2006.

Rebhun, Uzi, and Chaim Waxman. *Jews in Israel: Contemporary Social and Cultural Patterns.* Hanover, N.H.: University Press of New England, 2004.

Rotenstreich, Nathan. *Zionism: Past and Present.* Albany: State University of New York Press, 2007.

Rubinstein, Amnon. *From Herzl to Rabin: The Changing Image of Zionism.* New York: Holmes and Meier, 2000.

Sharkansky, Ira. *The Politics of Religion and the Religion of Politics: Looking at Israel.* Lanham, Md.: Lexington Books, 2000.

Sofer, Sasson and Dorothea Shefer-Vanson. *Zionism and the Foundations of Israeli Diplomacy.* New York: Cambridge University Press, 1998.

3

The Social and Economic
Context of Politics

Just as the Israeli religious context influences the operation of politics, so do social, cultural, and economic factors. Social (including gender) and economic factors can be translated into political variables, including issues regarding the identity of non-Jews (e.g., Who are Israeli Arabs?) and Jews (e.g., What is the significance of the Sephardic/Ashkenazic debate?), issues related to some of the immigration and emigration tensions raised earlier, and issues related to social class and education. Also of significance is the debate over Israeli Arabs in Israel. How are Israeli Arabs (i.e., non-Jewish Israelis) treated in Israeli society? How prepared is Israel to grant Israeli Arabs full civil and social—as distinct from legal—rights?

Although this is a study of the Israeli political system, an understanding—or at least an awareness—of the cultural and economic dimensions of Israeli society, along with its history, is needed for a more complete appreciation of political phenomena there. As discussed in this and later chapters, social, cultural, and economic factors can be directly translated into political variables. For example, in this chapter we examine the concept of ethnicity. In our subsequent discussion of political parties, it will become apparent that many political parties have made special efforts to appeal to specific ethnic groups, to claim to be "the party" of Israelis from certain ethnic backgrounds. Thus, it is clear that social and cultural factors, such as

Israeli society is quite diverse and illustrates the blending of the modern with the traditional.

being an Israeli citizen with an ethnic background from Russia, as distinct from being an Israeli citizen with an ethnic background from France, can make a difference in the political world.

The fact that Israel's population is as heterogeneous as it is, that not all Israelis are Jewish, and that not all Jewish Israelis come from the same ethnic, geographic, or religious background has significant implications for Israeli society and, consequently, for Israeli politics. Although the Israeli-Arab conflict has been of paramount significance over the last four decades as a source of concern and anxiety in the lives of Israeli citizens, it is nevertheless the case that the kinds of issues described here, issues such as ethnic group membership, degree of religious orthodoxy, social class, education and culture, and governmental economic policies, are all regular sources of significant tension in the Israeli political arena.

PEOPLES OF ISRAEL

While the majority of Israel's (2008) population of 7,374,000 is native-born, this has taken many years to achieve.[1] One of the most obvious characteristics of Israel is the remarkable heterogeneity of its population, with substantial communities coming from a wide range of national and ethnic origins.[2] The various communities constituting the country have maintained many of their national characteristics, thereby making Israeli society extremely diverse.[3] Of relevance here is the fact that not all of Israel's population is Jewish and not all Jews in Israel have identical Jewish backgrounds. In other words, to say that Israel has a Jewish majority is correct, but to assume that all Jews are alike in social and cultural characteristics or that they all approve of other Jews' religious practice or degree of religiousness is not. The implications of this for the overall political process can be both invigorating and divisive.

As we noted earlier, Israel has a substantial non-Jewish population,[4] including Christians, Muslims, and Druze (followers of a religion that is an outgrowth of Islam, but which contains elements of Judaism and Christianity).[5] Nearly 10 percent of the Arab population is Bedouin, and a substantial portion of this group still live as nomads in Israel's southern deserts.[6] This diversity—especially the balance between the Jewish and non-Jewish population segments—is the source of much discussion and debate in official policy-making circles. One of the central tenets of Zionism, as we noted in chapter 1, was the goal of creating and sustaining a Jewish majority in a Jewish state, and the concept of *majority* is key here.

The reader will recall that the reason for the development of this Jewish-majority-in-a-Jewish-state goal was the idea that in a democracy, it is the majority that makes policy, and we have seen that historically the majority may either forget about or consciously decide to ignore the interests of a minority. Thus, Zionists reached the conclusion that one of the best ways for Jewish minorities in a number of different political settings to protect themselves was to come together in a Jewish state in which they themselves would make up a majority of the state's population. They could then use that majority status in a democratic context to be certain that the state's policies would be aware of and sympathetic to Jewish goals. Accordingly, then, the inescapable fact is not lost on the political leadership that the nearly 25 percent of Israel's current population that is *not* Jewish is increasing at a rate greater than the natural rate of increase for the Jewish population; therefore, in the future the proportion of Israel's non-Jewish population can be expected to increase even more (see table 3.1).[7]

Beyond this, of course, is the issue of the status of the Palestinians in the Occupied Territories. Should the more than four million Palestinians in the West Bank and Gaza Strip—who are not included in the nearly 25 percent non-Jewish population figure—ever become Israeli citizens, the religious proportions of the population would change even more dramatically, raising the possibility that in the relatively near future, Israel would no longer have a Jewish majority, a completely unacceptable eventuality to traditional ideas of Zionism and, correspondingly, to a substantial segment of Israel's population.

As one scholar noted many years ago,

> The fact that Israeli Arabs have one of the world's highest birth rates has increased their number by 400 percent since 1948, from about 10 percent of the population to over 15. Some demographers estimate that Israeli Arabs will

Table 3.1   Population in the West Bank and the Gaza Strip

	Total	*West Bank*	*Gaza Strip*
1997 Census	2,895,683		
1998 Census	3,005,719		
1999 Census	3,119,936		
2000 Census	3,238,493		
2009 (est.)	4,013,126	2,461,267 (61.3%)	1,551,859 (38.7%)

Birth Rates (2009, est.)	
West Bank	2.1 percent
Gaza	3.4 percent
Israel	1.7 percent

Source: Palestinian Central Bureau of Statistics, "Population, Housing, and Establishment Census, 1997," as reported in the *Palestinian Academic Society for the Study of International Affairs Diary, 2000* (Jerusalem: PASSIA, 2000), p. 250; U.S. Central Intelligence Agency, *World Factbook*, https://www.cia.gov/library/publications/the-world-factbook/region/region_mde.html, accessed January 2010.

equal the number of Israeli Jews within a century. Socioeconomic, cultural, linguistic, and political differences between Israeli Jews and Israeli Arabs have increasingly politicized the issue and raised serious questions about the future of Israel as a Jewish State.[8]

It should be noted in passing that members of the various Arab communities are not required to serve in the Israel Defense Force (IDF), although they are permitted to volunteer. The only exception has been male members of the Druze community, who have been required to serve in the armed forces since 1950, at the request of their community leaders.[9]

Arab-Israeli citizens who do not serve in the military face special social challenges: they cannot receive security clearances and are therefore not able to work in companies with defense contracts or that work in security-related fields, which provide jobs for a significant share of the Israeli workforce.

> Those not subject to the draft also have less access than other citizens to those social and economic benefits for which military service is a prerequisite or an advantage, such as housing, new-household subsidies, and government- or security-related industrial employment. [However,] under a 1994 government policy decision, the social security child allowance for parents who did not serve in the military and did not attend a yeshiva (including Arabs) was increased to equal the allowance of those who had done so.[10]

ASHKENAZIM AND SEPHARDIM

Perhaps the central dimension along which Israeli (Jewish) society and culture can be, and often has been, divided concerns the ethnic communities of Israel's Jewish populations. Simply put, these communities can be categorized into two groups based upon their geographic roots.[11] One group, the Ashkenazic Jews (or Ashkenazim), looks to Europe for its ethnic roots. These are Jews who immigrated to Israel (or Palestine) from such countries as Britain, France, Germany, Austria, Hungary, Russia, Poland, and Lithuania, to name but a few. The label "Ashkenazic" also applies to immigrants from North and South America. Many Ashkenazic Jews historically used Yiddish as a second language in the communities in which they resided.

The other group, Sephardic Jews (or Sephardim), includes Jews with Mediterranean roots, coming from ethnic communities in the Middle East and even Africa.[12] Sephardic Jews have lived in the Middle East since their expulsion from Spain in 1492.[13] It is important to note that not all non-Western Jews are Sephardic. Many Sephardic Jews had as a common second language a tongue called Ladino. Many non-Western Jews, especially those coming from some Middle Eastern and African areas, have very little in common with either the Ashkenazic or the Sephardic cultures. These Jews are sometimes referred to as Oriental Jews and might include immigrants from Persia, India, and even China.

The two major groups are not equal in size: about 85 percent of the more than fourteen million Jews in the world are Ashkenazic, while only about 15 percent are Sephardic. On the other hand, while a mere 10 percent of all Ashkenazic Jews in the world live in Israel, nearly two-thirds of all Sephardic Jews do. Thus, Sephardim today make up a majority of Israel's Jewish population.[14]

The Ashkenazic-Sephardic distinction is an important one because it has been a significant source of tension in Israeli society over the years.[15] The Sephardic and Ashkenazic Jews each have their own chief rabbi—something that was mentioned earlier—and their own separate synagogues. Although they differ very little in terms of religious substance and laws, they do differ in cultural and social practice, dress, music, architecture, and so on.[16] One does not need to look far to find manifestations of this division.

An illustration of how relatively insignificant issues can sometimes assume significant proportions took place in 1975 and involved grass growing out of the holy Western Wall in Jerusalem. The Ashkenazic chief rabbi, Rabbi Shlomo Goren, announced that since grass growing between the huge rocks making up the Western Wall would eventually cause the wall to crumble, all Jews had an obligation to pick the grass as it grew. The Sephardic chief rabbi, Rabbi Ovadia Yosef, announced that the grass symbolized the quest for life, and thus the grass should be permitted to grow and be protected.[17] This, of course, resulted in tension, and occasionally physical violence, between the two groups of Jews. Not wishing to antagonize either group, the Government of the day took no position on the issue.

There have also been social barriers between Ashkenazic and Sephardic Jews over the years. Often they have been a function of education, with Western or European—Ashkenazic—Jews having more education than their Sephardic counterparts.[18] One result of this gap was that Ashkenazic Jews held a disproportionately greater number of high-paying jobs in the Israeli economy and in the government bureaucracy.[19] Until Menachem Begin came to power in 1977, the Ashkenazim had systematically dominated the political elite in Israel.[20] One of the most significant political changes in Israeli politics brought about by the Begin Government was a recognition of the Sephardim and their political leverage.

IMMIGRATION AND EMIGRATION

As we noted earlier, one of the central notions of Zionism is the "ingathering of the exiles," the idea of the importance of Jews moving to Israel and thereby creating a Jewish majority in a Jewish state. This has meant that immigration has been a significant and meaningful component of the social planning of Israeli governments since before independence, despite the considerable budgetary demands this has sometimes created.[21] The Law of Return (1950) asserted the right of all Jews to "return" to Israel and be automatically granted citizenship. Since then, hundreds of thousands of Jews have used this law as the basis for such a claim. Israel's first prime minister, David Ben-Gurion, noted that "this law lays down not that the State accords the right of settlement to Jews abroad but that this right is inherent in every Jew by virtue of his being a Jew if it but be his will to take part in settling the land. This right preceded the State of Israel; it is that which built the State."[22]

The policy laid down in the Law of Return has been successful. As we pointed out in table 1.2 dealing with non-Jewish populations in Palestine, while Israel's Jewish population was about 680,000 in 1948, the 2009 *Statistical Abstract of Israel* indicates it as more than 5.5 million (see table 3.2).[23] This increase has resulted from both natural increase and continued immigration from the free world, eastern Europe, and, despite restrictions, Islamic lands and the Soviet Union.[24]

The largest single wave of immigration came immediately after independence. In 1949 alone there were almost 250,000 immigrants. During this period there were substantial numbers of immigrants from displaced persons camps in Europe, as well as survivors of the Nazi concentration camps. A significant bloc came from eastern Europe as well, especially Poland and the Soviet Union. This left the population in Israel and its political leadership heavily dominated by Ashkenazic Jews.

The great increase in the Sephardic immigrant population of the early 1950s followed that of the Ashkenazim. Immigrants during the 1950s began arriving from Asia and North Africa, resulting in substantial Moroccan, Iraqi, and Yemeni communities in Israel.[25] To take just one example, in 1950 over

Table 3.2   Religious Groups in Israel

Year	Jewish	Muslim	Christian	Druze	Total	Jewish Population as a Percentage of Total Population
1949	1,013,900	111,500	34,000	14,500	1,173,900	86.37
1959	1,858,800	159,200	48,300	22,300	2,088,700	88.99
1969	2,506,800	314,500	73,500	34,600	2,929,500	85.57
1979	3,218,400	481,200	87,600	49,000	3,836,200	83.89
1989	3,717,100	655,200	107,000	80,300	4,559,600	81.52
1999	4,872,800	934,100	131,800	101,200	6,209,100	78.47
2008	5,569,200	1,240,000	153,100	121,900	7,374,000	75.52

Source: Central Bureau of Statistics, *Statistical Abstract of Israel, 2009* (Jerusalem, Central Bureau of Statistics, 2009), Table 2.2, "The Population, by Religion," www.cbs.gov.il/shnaton60/st02_02.pdf, accessed January 2010.

120,000 Iraqi Jews arrived. By the end of the 1970s, nearly 750,000 Jews from the Middle East and northern Africa had migrated to Israel.[26] Sources and numbers of immigrants to Israel are shown in table 2.1.

In recent years the rate of immigration to Israel has declined sharply (see table 3.3).[27] One of the reasons for this may be obvious: the number of Jews outside Israel seeking to resettle there has declined dramatically as a result of the overwhelming rate of past immigration. To take the example cited earlier, from 1949 to 1950 the Jewish population of Yemen was about forty-five thousand; most moved to Israel, and today there remain only about eight hundred Jews in the entire nation.[28] By the late 1970s, there were only thirty thousand Jews remaining in Morocco, just 10 percent of those who lived there when Israel declared statehood.[29] Similarly, the rate of immigration from Europe immediately following Israeli independence could not continue since the number of Jews remaining in Europe has decreased just as dramatically.

The immigration from the former Soviet Union—primarily Russia—has had a significant impact on Israel.[30] While there had been a three-to-one or four-to-one ratio between immigrants from Ashkenazic roots and those with Sephardic roots through the 1980s, the effect of Russian Jews on the equation can be seen quite clearly; the ratio of Ashkenazic to Sephardic immigrants reached almost fifteen-to-one in the 1990s, with more than 90 percent of the immigrants during the first half of the decade coming from Europe and America, primarily Russia, and more than 85 percent from the same regions during the second half of the decade.[31]

A number of agencies and offices in Israel, some official and some quasi-governmental, are active in the process of immigrant resettlement. A

Table 3.3   Jewish Immigration to Israel, 1948–2008

Period of Immigration	Total Immigration	Asia-Africa (%)*	Europe-America (%)**
1975–1979	124,827	14.3	85.7
1980–1984	83,637	27.1	72.9
1985–1989	70,196	20.4	79.6
1990–1994	609,322	6.3	93.7
1995–1999	346,997	14.7	85.3
2000–2004	181,505	21.1	78.9
2005–2008	72,282	27.7	72.3

Source: Central Bureau of Statistics, *Statistical Abstract of Israel, 2009* (Jerusalem: Central Bureau of Statistics, 2009), Table 4.2, "Immigrants by Period of Immigration and Last Continent of Residence," www.cbs.gov.il/shnaton60/st04_02.pdf, accessed January 2010.
Notes:
Asher Arian has written, "There is a very high correlation between European- or American-born and Ashkenazim, and the Asian- or African-born and Sephardim, and hence we shall use the terms interchangeably." See Asher Arian, *The Second Republic, Politics in Israel* (Chatham, N.J.: Chatham House, 1998), p. 33.
* Corresponds highly with Sephardic Jews.
** Corresponds highly with Ashkenazic Jews.

cabinet-level agency, the Ministry of Absorption, is responsible for coordinating assistance. The Ministries of Housing, Labor, Education, and Health all are important in the overall absorption process. Immigrants are eligible for up to five months' temporary housing in an absorption center, financial assistance for locating permanent housing, tax benefits and customs privileges (importing items otherwise subject to duties), job placement, language training, complete health care, and other forms of governmental assistance. Nongovernmental agencies likewise participate in the process. The Jewish Agency, the Women's International Zionist Organization (WIZO), United Jewish Appeal, and many other similar organizations contribute to the multiple support services offered to new immigrants.

SOCIAL CLASS

Despite the opinions of some early Zionist thinkers, the "ingathering of the exiles" has in some ways proven to be an insufficient common experience to produce an entirely unified society.[32] Notwithstanding a Jewish majority in a Jewish state and a resurgence of Jewish culture, recent history has shown that not all Jews are sufficiently alike to attain the degree of social cohesion expected by Zionist thinkers. Not only do we find social tensions between Israeli Jews and Israeli Arabs, and between Israeli citizens and Palestinians, but we also find social tensions between various groups of Israeli Jews.[33] The Ashkenazic-Sephardic distinction introduced earlier in this chapter has given rise to merely one aspect of social tension.

One of the most remarkable characteristics of Israeli society over the last forty years has been its heterogeneity, a direct, if presumably temporary, result of the Zionist goal of the "ingathering of the exiles." Jews from Europe, Russia and the (former) Soviet Union, Asia, Africa, North America, and South America have come together, and on occasion it has become clear that the respective "Jewishness" of these many and varied groups is not enough of a common bond to guarantee social unity.[34] Some groups have been more visible than others in Israeli society in their process and problems of assimilation. For instance, a group made up primarily of Black Americans claiming Jewish descent caused quite a stir when they arrived to establish their own community.[35]

Similarly, the appearance of Ethiopian Falashas (a tribe of Ethiopian nomads claiming to be Jews) was a highly publicized injection of a new and different community into Israeli society.[36] Much was made of the fact that most of these individuals had never even seen electric appliances or lived in modern society before arriving at a designated landing strip in Ethiopia and being airlifted to Israel.[37] They have, since their arrival, settled in and become an established community, although to a large degree they have not been assimilated or become part of the mainstream of society as many had hoped would be the case.[38]

At one point in recent years, the Government decided that in order to accelerate social interaction, immigrants from different parts of the world should be settled together in large apartment buildings. German, Moroccan, American, and Russian immigrants, to take only four examples, would occupy the same multistory apartment building. This experiment in social homogenization failed when it became clear that their common Jewishness was insufficient to make them good neighbors because their individual backgrounds and customs were simply too different to change overnight. In some cultures it is socially acceptable to do one's cooking and laundry in open, communal areas. In others, this is simply not done. These small-scale experiments in creating "melting pots" were terminated when it became clear, for example, that many European Jewish immigrants did not appreciate being given apartments next to immigrants from North Africa, who did their cooking in the stairwells![39]

One of the most successful institutions contributing to social integration has been the army.[40] Because military service is the one social phenomenon common to virtually all in society, it is in the army that Ashkenazim meet Sephardim, and it is in the army that they share a common experience.[41]

EDUCATION AND CULTURE

One of the earliest legislative acts of the government of Israel was the Compulsory Education Law (1949), which provided free and compulsory education to all children between the ages of five and fourteen. Since 1978 education has been mandatory up to the age of sixteen and free until age eighteen. Separate school systems exist for the Jewish and Arab communities, with the Jewish schools being taught in Hebrew and the Arab schools, which also serve the Druze community, being taught in Arabic. The Ministry of Education oversees both school systems.[42]

According to the U.S. State Department, while Arab-Israeli children make up about one-fourth of Israel's public school population, the support provided for schools for those children is not proportional to the population. The report indicates, "Many schools in Arab communities are dilapidated and overcrowded, lack special educational services and counselors, have poor libraries, and have no sports facilities. Arab groups also note that the mandated public school curriculum stresses the country's Jewish culture and heritage."[43]

The Jewish schools are of three types: state, state-run religious, and private religious certified by the government.[44] State schools are coeducational and essentially secular,[45] while both the private and the state-run religious schools[46] include a substantial religious component in their curricula in addition to the academic content of the "regular" schools. The non Jewish schools, both for Druze as well as other Arab groups, provide academic and religious content appropriate to those communities. Religious instruction for both the Islamic and Christian populations is offered in Arab schools, while in Druze schools it is controlled by community leaders.[47]

Israel also has many fine institutions of higher education, which are available to Jewish and non-Jewish students alike, although some studies have shown that Arab-Israeli citizens are underrepresented in most university student populations.[48] Many universities in Israel operate with very large foreign student populations. The major Israeli universities are indicated in table 3.4. There was "a veritable explosion" in Israel's student population in the 1970s, and this radical growth continued through the end of the century.[49] In Israel's early days the demand for education was affected by immigration primarily from postwar Europe and Arab countries. In the 1960s society had to adapt to a larger wave of immigration from North Africa, which ended up creating an increased need for higher education, as well. As has already been noted here, through the 1990s some eight hundred thousand Jews from the former Soviet Union relocated to Israel, a pattern that also had a significant impact upon educational resources in the nation.[50]

Israel's universities are financed to a significant extent by the government and the Jewish Agency, which together contribute the bulk of

Table 3.4 Israeli Universities

Year Open	University	Students 1979–1980	Students 1989–1990	Students 1999–2000	Students 2007–2008
1924	Technion–Israel Institute of Technology (Haifa)	7,580	9,080	12,720	12,420
1925	Hebrew University of Jerusalem	13,570	16,780	21,390	21,175
1934	Weizmann Institute of Science (Rehovot—postgraduate)	490	640	790	975
1955	Bar-Ilan (Ramat Gan, Tel Aviv)	8,070	9,330	21,770	25,890
1956	Tel Aviv University	14,380	19,270	26,480	25,130
1963	Haifa University	6,140	6,780	13,550	17,460
1969	Ben-Gurion University of the Negev (Beersheba)	4,250	5,890	16,310	17,940
Total		54,480	67,770	113,010	120,990

Source: Central Bureau of Statistics, *Statistical Abstract of Israel, 2008* (Jerusalem: Central Bureau of Statistics, 2008), Table 8.49, "Students in Universities, by Degree and Institution," pp. 426–27, www1.cbs.gov.il/reader/shnaton/templ_shnaton_e.html?num_tab=st08_49&CYear=2008, accessed January 2010.

the universities' budgets. Tuition and fees have made up most of the remainder of the university budgets in recent years.[51] Of late, Israel has also added an Open University to its resource base (founded in 1974) as well as a network of regional colleges. The regional colleges are each associated with one of the major universities, and they make it possible for students to begin their university studies at a location near their homes and later move to the university to complete the educational process.

Culture is important in the Israeli social agenda, and the Ministry of Education and Culture supports a wide range of activities in this area, as do a number of private and semiprivate agencies. Classical music is supported widely; many of the rural kibbutzim have their own string quartets and musical groups! In Israel there are numerous publishing houses, which print books, magazines, and newspapers in Hebrew, Arabic, English, Russian, French, German, and many other languages as well. A number of theater and dance companies operate across the country, too. Israel is deservedly famous for many of its museums of antiquity, but it also deserves note for many of its other museums.

HEALTH CARE AND SOCIAL SERVICES

Israel has a comprehensive and socialized health care system available to all citizens.[52] As is the case for many dimensions of Israel's governmental structure, much of the infrastructure for public support of health care can trace its roots to prestate times. During Israel's first fifty years, challenges affecting the delivery of health care in society have arisen, such as having a population that is expanding far, far more quickly than natural expansion would suggest (most recently as a result of the rapid immigration of Russian Jews), having to spend a significant proportion of the budget on defense costs, having an aging population, and having such a heterogeneous population that health care needs to be delivered in many different languages.[53]

The Ministry of Health supervises health care, although many Israelis still prefer to go to private clinics, doctors, and hospitals run by other, often political, organizations. In 2008 Israel had a total of 377 hospitals; of these, approximately half are owned by the government; others are privately owned, run as nonprofit organizations, or supported by private sick funds (health care organizations) (see table 3.5).

According to the Israeli government, the Israeli health care system includes hospitals, clinics, and mother-and-child care centers.[54] The Government passed a National Health Insurance Law, in effect since 1995, which articulates the state's responsibility to provide health services for all resi-

Table 3.5   Hospitals in Israel

	1948	*2008*
Type		
General	36	46
Psychiatric	19	13
Long-term care	11	316
Rehabilitation	—	2
Ownership		
Government: national/city	7	24
Other public	13	148
Sick fund	10	25
Private	31	180
Total	66	377

Source: Central Bureau of Statistics, *Statistical Abstract of Israel, 2009* (Jerusalem: Central Bureau of Statistics, 2009), Table 6.5, "Hospitals, by Type and Ownership," p. 319, www.cbs.gov.il/shnaton60/st06_05.pdf, accessed January 2010.

dents of the country (not including tourists). Prior to 1995 most residents had been insured by one of four comprehensive health care organizations, some with roots going back to prestate times.

In health care, like other areas concerned with social goods, Israel's Arab citizen population complains that it is not given a commitment of resources proportional to its share of the population. In addition to limiting support to Arab-Israelis, the Israeli government has worked in recent years to disengage and separate its medical structures from those on the West Bank and in Gaza that serve Palestinian noncitizens of Israel.[55]

On a broader scale, Israel has a political system committed to the welfare state approach to social services. This means that the state will make sure that certain minimal standards of social goods are available to all citizens, including education and health care, which have already been discussed, and several others. Israel has a guaranteed minimum annual income; if someone is unable to earn a certain amount of money each year, the state provides the income to the individual directly. The state runs a variety of services for families, children, and the handicapped, and also provides a guaranteed retirement plan. Included among these services are a state-supported network of preschools and other support for child care, subsidized meal plans in public schools, reduced fares on public transportation for children, socialized medicine (including both visits to doctors and hospitals and prescription drugs), physical therapy, maternity leave from jobs, unemployment compensation, job-training programs, and assistance in job placement, to name only some of the programs available.

CITIES, VILLAGES, KIBBUTZIM, AND MOSHAVIM

More than 90 percent of Israel's population lives in some form of urban setting, whether in a large city or a small town.[56] The largest cities of Israel include Jerusalem, Tel Aviv–Jaffa, Haifa, Beersheba, and Eilat, each of which has its own identity and character. As can be seen in table 3.6, the size of Jerusalem's official population has grown significantly more than any other Israeli city's in the last two decades, primarily as a result of government policy to expand Jerusalem's city limits (especially into areas that used to be Palestinian and were occupied during the 1967 war) and to move substantial numbers of new immigrants into the Jerusalem region to further strengthen its claim on lands there.

Jerusalem has been the capital of Israel since the time of King David, or roughly 1000 B.C. In the post-1860 period, a substantial Jewish community developed outside the walls of its Old City.[57] Since then Jerusalem has grown steadily and today—using new definitions of the city limits—is the largest city in Israel. Between 1949 and 1967 it was divided between Israel and Jordan, but at the end of the Six Day War the city was reunited, with many Israelis vowing that it would never again be separated. In July 1980, the Knesset passed a law permanently unifying Jerusalem and annexing the "occupied" portions of the city as Israeli territory.[58] The city limits of greater Jerusalem have expanded significantly in the last several decades to allow a far larger population to live within the city. A substantial proportion of Jerusalem's population is religiously devout, and entire neighborhoods are closed to traffic on the Sabbath.

The Israeli government suggests several major reasons that Jerusalem's population has increased so much in recent years, including (1) natural increase, (2) intra-Israel migration, and (3) immigration to Israel. A very

Table 3.6 Population of Israel's Largest Cities in 1985, 2000, and 2008

City	Population, 1985	Population, 2000	Population, 2008
Beersheba	110,800	172,900	187,200
Eilat	18,900	41,100	46,600
Haifa	225,800	270,500	264,800
Jerusalem	428,700	657,500	763,600
Tel Aviv–Jaffa	327,300	354,400	392,500

Sources: The 2008 population figures come from the Central Bureau of Statistics, *Statistical Abstract of Israel, 2009* (Jerusalem: Central Bureau of Statistics, 2009), Table 2.15, "Population and Density per Sq. Km. in Localities Numbering about 5,000 Residents on 31 XII 2008," p. 129, www.cbs.gov.il/shnaton60/st02_15. pdf, accessed January 2010. The 2000 population figures come from the Central Bureau of Statistics, *Statistical Abstract of Israel, 2001* (Jerusalem: Central Bureau of Statistics, 2001), Table 2.14, "Population in Localities Numbering above 5,000 Inhabitants on 31 XII 2000," pp. 2-44–2-46. The 1985 data comes from the 1985 edition of *Facts about Israel* (Jerusalem, Ministry of Foreign Affairs, 1985), p. 104.

important characteristic of Jerusalem's population is its very high rate of natural increase.[59] Jerusalem has a unique population balance, with approximately one-third of its population made up of Ultraorthodox Jews, approximately one-third of its population made up of non-Jewish communities (primarily Muslim Arabs), and approximately one-third of its population made up of what we might call secular Jews. Both the ultraorthodox Jewish community and the non-Jewish community have significantly higher birth rates than the secular Jews and the rest of Israel.

Another key factor in Jerusalem's growth, of course, is immigration. Most immigrants who have moved to Israel in the last several decades have wanted to relocate in Jerusalem; when the Government has tried to situate them in development towns or other rural areas, they have complained that they didn't move to Israel to live in the desert, they moved to Israel to live in Jerusalem. This was certainly true through the 1980s and 1990s with the waves of Russian Jews. Jerusalem is a highly attractive goal for new immigrants, and to the extent that they find it possible to do so, they settle in the Jerusalem area.

Jerusalem is not only Israel's largest city in terms of population, but it is also Israel's largest city in terms of size, which has changed significantly over the years as the Israeli government has purposefully expanded Jerusalem's city limits to absorb Arab communities and expand territory under Israeli control. It also has a number of "peripheral neighborhoods" that are important in its growth.[60]

Tel Aviv, originally founded in 1909 as a Jewish suburb of the Arab city of Jaffa, has grown to become the industrial and commercial center of Israel. The greater Tel Aviv area includes a population of more than 1.2 million,

Photo 3.1. A view of Jerusalem from the Mount of Olives

including suburbs such as Ramat Gan, Bat Yam, Bnei Brak, and many others.[61] Tel Aviv plays the role of Israel's financial and business center and is the headquarters of most of Israel's industrial, business, and agricultural enterprises, stock exchanges, newspapers, and publishing houses. Tel Aviv is seen as a more secular city than Jerusalem, and there have been instances of clashes between religious and secular groups over such issues as whether movie theaters and restaurants should be open on the Sabbath.

Haifa is the country's largest port city and the major city of Israel's north. It has a substantial industrial base and a major university and is significant as a commercial center because of the trade moving through its harbor. Haifa is even more secular than Tel Aviv.

In the south, Beersheba is often referred to as the capital of the Negev. Once referred to as simply a development town, today it is a rapidly growing city and regional center whose focus is on industrial and residential development. Beersheba has grown significantly in recent years and is a significant urban area today with a major university (Ben-Gurion University) and developed industries.

Further to the south lies Eilat. This port city on the Gulf of Eilat (referred to by many as the Gulf of Aqaba because of the Jordanian city immediately adjacent to Eilat at the northern end of the Gulf) provides access to the Red Sea and thereby direct access to East Africa and Asia. Today, Eilat has been developed as a major tourist center, with many major hotels and direct nonstop air connections to many European cities.

In addition to more than forty-five cities and towns, Israel has a substantial number of what are referred to as development towns—areas intended to draw industry and population away from the major centers and toward the underpopulated areas of the nation. The Government has used these development towns as targets for immigrant settlement by offering a number of financial incentives, including low-interest loans and subsidized housing, to encourage both new immigrants and already established Israelis to relocate there. These development towns have been of great significance in Israeli society for two reasons. First, they have contributed to the Israeli economy by helping to settle the land and create jobs. Second, they have provided the Government with a place to send new immigrants to settle and also to further the assimilation process.[62] These towns, which were created for reasons of economic expansion, are not the same as the new settlements established after 1967 on the West Bank for reasons of military security and religious commitment.

While most of the Israeli population lives in its towns and cities, nearly 8 percent of the population still resides in rural areas. Certainly the best-known Israeli structures in this latter category are the kibbutz and the moshav, each of which merits some discussion here. A kibbutz is a collective community in which communal ownership of property is the norm.[63] Members of a kibbutz own no substantial property of their own: the kibbutz owns the cars, trac-

tors, houses, and even the television sets and sailboats (where appropriate)
that are used by members of the community. In exchange for not being paid
salaries, members of kibbutzim (plural of kibbutz) have all of their expenses
taken care of, including housing, clothing, education, medical needs, pocket
money, and even vacations. The motto of the kibbutz is "to each according
to his need, from each according to his ability." Many might recognize this
motto as coming directly from the writings of Karl Marx; it indicates the socialist philosophy of the kibbutz. The kibbutz is run democratically, with all
adult members having a vote in the decisions of the community.[64] Today, 1.7
percent of Israel's population lives on more than 270 kibbutzim.[65]

The moshav is a slightly different type of community in which individuals and families own their own property, but in which major economic
ventures are undertaken cooperatively. For instance, the moshav may (collectively) own major agricultural equipment, although the individual farms
upon which the equipment is used will be owned privately. The moshav
may serve as an economic cooperative, helping individual farmers to market their products, although individual participants will retain their own
profits when the goods have been sold. Nearly 3.4 percent of Israel's population lives on approximately 441 moshavim in Israel today.[66]

One of the most remarkable characteristics of the kibbutz and moshav
populations in Israel is how consistent they have been and how consistent they remain. They have continued to account for approximately the
same proportion of Israel's population for the last few decades and show
no indication that their collective and socialist orientation is declining in
popularity in Israeli society.

THE ECONOMY

Israel's economy since the time of its creation can be characterized as
similar to those of other centralized economies with strong social welfare
dimensions.[67] From the time of independence, and in fact even before, the
state played a major role in providing for the well-being of its citizens. This
was true in a variety of social policy areas, including medical care, housing, employment, education, the provision of food and transportation,
and many other social goods. The Israeli economy has, since its inception,
been "planned,"[68] although since the 1980s it has seen gradual movement
toward more free market behavior.[69]

Israel's economy grew rapidly between 1948 and 1973, averaging 10
percent per year.[70] This was a consequence of factors that would not have
been found in many other nations, including a rapid expansion of the labor
force as a result of immigration and an artificially high rate of investment
provided substantially by Jews living abroad who funneled their contribu-

Photo 3.2. The name for the Israeli currency, the Shekel, is a Biblical one.

tions to the economy through such organizations as United Jewish Appeal, Hadassah, the Jewish Agency, and other Zionist organizations. As a result of the 1973 Yom Kippur War and other international factors,[71] Israel's economy slowed considerably.[72] In the summer of 1985, the Government implemented a radical emergency stabilization program to combat a very serious inflationary cycle, and inflation fell from 445 percent in 1984 to 185 percent in 1985 to 21 percent in 1989.[73] At one point inflation was running at nearly a 1,000-percent annual rate.[74]

Through the 1980s, the major difficulty facing the Israeli economy was the vast and continuing budgetary increases in the areas of defense and security.[75] Another difficulty was making economic policy in the Occupied Territories and, specifically, the appropriate role of the Israeli government there.[76] According to many, the Israeli contribution to West Bank development has been much more active and constructive since 1967 than that of Jordan during the preceding two decades, when Jordan was the occupying power there.[77] As well, in recent years the wave of immigrants has put a huge burden on the economy to provide resources for the relocation and support of new immigrants.[78]

One result of the constant strains on the Israeli economy, especially since the 1973 Yom Kippur War, has been a reexamination of and, to some extent, a retrenchment in the Government's social spending. In an effort to make some progress in balancing its budgets and with military and defense expenditures largely immune from reductions, the Government has capped and, in many cases, cut its spending on a wide range of social programs.

In the final decade of the twentieth century, Israel had one of the highest Gross Domestic Product (GDP) growth rates among Western economies, averaging almost 6 percent between 1990 and 1996; in 2006 the GDP grew by 5.1 percent. With a per capita GDP in 2006 of $20,306, it ranked forty-first of nearly two hundred nations in the World Bank database.[79]

In the first decade of the twenty-first century Israel did much better than many nations of the world in weathering the global economic challenges of the times. According to a 2009 Bank of Israel *Annual Report*, Israel's strong economic performance was due to a number of factors, including the following:

- Private consumption recovered rapidly, and by the end of 2009 it surpassed its precrisis level, contrary to the development in many other advanced economies.
- The crisis had a limited effect on Israel's financial system, more moderate than its impact on the advanced economies, and the main financial institutions remained stable.
- The factors contributing to the milder effect included a conservative financial system, and in particular a conservative and closely supervised banking system, a balanced housing market, and a successful economic policy.
- Manufacturing was the main casualty of the crisis due to the precipitous decrease in global demand for goods, especially given the high share of exports in domestic manufacturing activity.
- Construction decreased by only 1 percent, in a display of stability relative to other industries. It contributed to the stability of total economic activity despite early fears of a credit crunch induced by the current crisis.
- The Israeli labor market was in a situation of full employment when the global crisis began to affect it and thus weathered the crisis, during the first half of 2009, with only a moderate increase in unemployment relative to the developed economies and without a major decline in employment. The market started to recover already in the second half of 2009 and unemployment began to decline, even while it was increasing in the advanced economies.[80]

FOREIGN ECONOMIC RELATIONS

Foreign economic relations have traditionally been one of Israel's greatest concerns. In particular, there have been three significant sources of funding from outside the country for the Israeli government over the years: the world's Jewish population and the governments of the United States and the German Republic. These sources of funds have provided both grant funds—not requiring repayment—and loan funds.

The country's major international financial concern has traditionally been its balance-of-payments problem. The balance-of-payments issue can be characterized as the relationship between the amount of goods Israel imports and the amount of goods it exports.[81] Israel has a very significant gap between its high level of imports on one hand, and its relatively low level of exports on the other, and one goal of every Israeli government in recent years has been to cut the exports-to-imports gap.

This has proven difficult, however. Spending as much as Israel must on armaments makes it difficult to maintain a trade equilibrium when the nation's major exports include oranges and flowers, and when a major source of foreign revenue is tourism (which itself has been very severely affected by violence and political terrorism in recent years). One report has suggested that "it has not been possible for Israel to attain anything even resembling 'economic independence'" since obtaining independence.[82]

Over the first 48 years of Israel's existence, this deficit grew continuously, 45-fold (in current prices): from $222 million in 1949 to $10.1 billion in 1996. However, in relative terms, the deficit steadily decreased during that period, indicating that the problem was gradually being solved: whereas in 1950 exports financed only 14 percent of imports, in 1960 this ratio was 51 percent, and in 1996 it stood at 79 percent. Since then the actual deficit began declining, down to $4.7 billion in 2001 and to a mere $0.7 billion in 2005 with exports of goods and services thus financing all imports, with some surplus funds remaining.[83]

Israel has been able to negotiate a free-trade arrangement with the United States (1985) and with the European Community (1975), so its goods can enter both marketplaces without having to face the additional burden of import duties.

In recent years, over 85 percent of all imports of goods—amounting to $47.2 billion in 2006—have been production inputs and fuel; 54 percent of these arrived from Europe, with the Americas providing 17 percent, Asia 16 percent, and the remaining 13 percent from other countries. In the same year, 33 percent of Israel's exports of goods—amounting to $36.6 billion—were directed to Europe, 40 percent to the United States, 19 percent to Asia, and the remaining 8 percent to other countries. During most of the 1990s Israel's industrial exports to the U.S. exceeded its imports from there, and since 2000 this is true even when excluding the export of diamonds.[84]

THE POLITICAL CULTURE AND THE ECONOMY

The goal of this chapter has been to introduce a number of social and economic factors to the equation of Israeli politics. If we had to sum all of the material presented here into a single word, that word would be "diversity."

The Israeli culture is not a homogeneous one, but includes significant dimensions of both a Jewish and an Arab culture. In fact, we find tension not only between Jewish and non-Jewish elements of the Israeli population, but also within the Jewish component of the population, which is divided into two major groups, the Ashkenazim and Sephardim.

This chapter briefly discussed the significance of Israel's non-Jewish population and introduced a very important problem to which we return later in this volume; the tensions between the Jewish and non-Jewish portions of the Israeli population are exacerbated, of course, by the added complication of the role of non-Jewish noncitizens, the Arab inhabitants of the Occupied Territories of the West Bank and the Gaza Strip.

The focus of our examination in this chapter has been the majority Jewish culture of Israeli society. But even the Jewish dimension of Israeli culture is not a homogeneous one, and we have noted here both the Ashkenazic and Sephardic components of Israel's population. We identified some of the tensions that exist between these groups and the variety of ways in which these tensions can manifest themselves.

This chapter further introduced a variety of other institutional variables into the discussion, variables that affect the quality of life of Israeli citizens, including education and culture, health and other social services, and the types of communities within which Israelis live. We discussed the tremendous diversity in the lifestyles and settings in which Israeli citizens live and introduced economics as a significant factor in Israeli politics. The economy has been a major source of concern in the Israeli political arena primarily because of the country's balance-of-payments deficit and the terrible problems of inflation it has faced. Although recent coalition governments have attempted to address the problems directly, the economy must be considered a major hurdle in the day-to-day operations of Israeli politics.

This, then, is the setting within which the operation of Israeli politics takes place. As we progress in our study of the Israeli political system, we see again and again that many of the social, cultural, and economic variables introduced in this chapter play significant roles in both the generation of problems for Israel's political elite and the policy responses designed to resolve them.

FOR FURTHER READING

Ben-Basat, Avi. *The Israeli Economy, 1985–1998: From Government Intervention to Market Economics.* Cambridge, Mass.: MIT Press, 2002.

Elazar, Daniel, and M. Weinfeld,. *Still Moving: Recent Jewish Migration in Comparative Perspective.* New Brunswick, N.J.: Transaction, 2000.

Ganim, As'ad. *Ethnic Politics in Israel: The Margins and the Ashkenazi Center.* New York: Routledge, 2010.

Gitelman, Zvi. *Religion or Ethnicity? Jewish Identities in Evolution.* New Brunswick, N.J.: Rutgers University Press, 2009.

Hasson, Shlomo, and Mairam Gonen. *The Cultural Tension within Jerusalem's Jewish Population.* Jerusalem: Floersheimer Institute for Policy Studies, 1997.

Iram, Yaacov, and Miryam Shemida. *The Educational System of Israel.* Westport, Conn.: Greenwood, 1998.

Shama, Avraham. *Immigration without Integration: Third World Jews in Israel.* Cambridge, Mass.: Schenkman, 1977.

Shulewitz, Malka Hillel. *The Forgotten Millions: The Modern Jewish Exodus from Arab Lands.* New York: Continuum, 2000.

Wasserstein, Bernard. *Divided Jerusalem: The Struggle for the Holy City.* New Haven, Conn.: Yale University Press, 2001.

Yiftachel, Oren. *Ethnocracy: Land and Identity Politics in Israel/Palestine.* Philadelphia: University of Pennsylvania Press, 2006.

Zalmanovitch, Yair. *Policy Making at the Margins of Government: The Case of the Israeli Health System.* Albany: State University of New York Press, 2002.

II

THE GOVERNMENTAL INSTITUTIONS

4

The Constitutional System
and Parliamentary Government

Not all constitutional settings are alike, and Israel's constitutional system is a unique blend of the many influences in the Israeli political system. This chapter examines Israel's decision to have an unwritten constitution, with a related decision to write a constitution over time. We then review the progress made in that undertaking over the years, through 1995 when the Supreme Court of Israel declared that Israel's "unwritten" constitution was, in fact, going to be treated in many respects as if it were a written constitution. It discusses the basic structures of Israel's constitution and the changing role of the courts in Israeli politics, as well as their impact on the evolution of the Israeli constitutional system. Finally, it analyzes the implications of Israel's version of a parliamentary structure and attempts to interpret the significance of the Israeli idiosyncrasies in this regard.

By this juncture the formal creation of Israel and its contemporary social, economic, and religious features should be familiar to the reader. Our focus now shifts to a description of the constitutional principles and major structural components of the Israeli political system. Merging the societal with the structural will in turn facilitate our understanding of the system's subsequent evolution since 1948.

The establishment of a written constitution is considered essential for any modern nation-state. Constitutions have been seen as "power maps,"

The Knesset, in Jerusalem

playing an important role in political systems by providing broad guide-lines for permissible and impermissible political behavior.[1] In addition, a constitution provides the yardstick for judicial review and the set of stan-dards for monitoring legislative or executive actions.

At the same time that we acknowledge the importance of written constitu-tions, however, we must recognize that written constitutions do not guarantee constitutional government. A *written constitution* is a document that contains an expression of the fundamental principles of the regime, as well as of the political structures and processes according to which the regime must oper-ate. The term *constitutional government* has a specialized meaning for students of politics; it refers to a government of limited power, a regime in which there are policy or behavioral boundaries beyond which the government simply may not go. It is therefore possible, using this distinction, to have constitu-tional governments with formal written constitutions (the United States or France), constitutional governments without formal written constitutions (Is-rael or Britain), unconstitutional governments with formal written constitu-tions (the former Soviet Union), and unconstitutional governments without formal written constitutions (Nigeria after a military coup, Saudi Arabia). The point to note here is that it is possible to overstress the importance of a piece of paper, since the actual behavior of a regime may be more important than the extent to which it has created a set of legal documents.[2]

The political culture that has developed in Israel over the past six decades has been less concerned with formal structures.[3] Israel has no explicit bill of rights nor specifically created constitution to provide clear and unam-biguous guidelines for governmental power. Yet, the Israeli polity is a stable democracy. This investigation focuses on how such a condition of stability has come about in a culture of such remarkable diversity.

THE DEBATE OVER CREATING A WRITTEN CONSTITUTION

The United Nations resolution of November 29, 1947, advocating the par-tition of Palestine into two independent states, one Arab and one Jewish, required the states to adopt written constitutions.[4] In addition to requir-ing of each state the creation of a constitution, the resolution stipulated a number of other points:

1. Establishment of a legislature elected by secret ballot and universal suffrage, and an executive responsible to the legislature
2. Settling of international disputes peacefully
3. Acceptance of an obligation to refrain from the threat or use of force
4. Guarantee of equal nondiscriminatory rights in religious, economic, and political areas to all persons, including human rights, freedom

of religion, language, speech, education, publication, assembly, and association

5. Preservation of freedom of visitation and transit for residents and citizens of the "other" state in Palestine, "subject to considerations of national security"[5]

In the Declaration of the Establishment of the State of Israel, proclaimed on May 14, 1948, the United Nations resolution was reiterated, and a commitment was undertaken to have an elected constituent assembly meet to adopt a constitution not later than October 1, 1948. Because of Israel's national war for survival following the Arab military invasion in 1948, this commitment was not kept. During this period, however, the Provisional State Council did undertake a number of discussions and appointed a committee to work on a written constitution.

In July 1948, the Provisional State Council appointed a committee of eight as a constitutional committee. The committee was given the assignment "to assemble, study, and catalogue pertinent recommendations and material, and to prepare a draft constitution which, together with minority opinions in the committee, shall be submitted to the Constituent Assembly for its consideration."[6] This committee was not asked to consider whether a constitution should be written; its recommendations were based upon the premise that the document *would* be written.

On November 18, 1948, the Provisional State Council passed the Constituent Assembly Elections Ordinance, calling for the election of a constituent assembly. Two months later the council passed the Constituent Assembly (Transition) Ordinance, transferring all of its powers to the Constituent Assembly. The Constituent Assembly was elected on January 25, 1949, and on March 8, 1949, it transformed itself into the First Knesset.

During the three weeks of its existence, the Constituent Assembly, before it became the First Knesset, enacted the Transition Law (February 16, 1949). This law was, in fact, a miniconstitution, containing chapters on the Knesset, the president, the government, and other provisions.[7] But the assembly never fully debated—much less adopted—a written constitution. The assembly did table a draft constitution authored by Dr. Leo Kohn, a political advisor to then prime minister[8] David Ben-Gurion, but did not take it up again until it met as the First Knesset.[9]

Between May and December 1949, the Knesset Committee on Constitution, Law, and Justice devoted eight special sessions to the question of a constitution.[10] Various arguments were put forward against a written constitution. Among the leading opponents was David Ben-Gurion, who, with other leaders of the Mapai Party, argued that there was no need to rush into a task that clearly needed to be handled with care and precision.[11]

Opponents of a written constitution also looked to England for a precedent, arguing that if the British, with their history of stable democratic government, did not need a written constitution, then perhaps Israel could survive without one, too. Supporters of a written constitution, on the other hand, retorted that the parallel with the unwritten British constitution was a fallacious one, as Britain was an established democracy with literally hundreds of years of stable government operation in its history that contributed to "built-in conventional safeguards." Israel, in their estimation, had "not yet developed sufficiently powerful and respected conventions to safeguard its system. Therefore, it was argued, Israel needed a written constitution."[12]

Beyond this, however, Ben-Gurion contended that Israel's population was in such a state of flux, already having doubled by 1949 and now on the verge of tripling, that writing a constitution might not be such a good idea. He suggested that "it was rather 'basic laws' without special status that were needed."[13] "At the present time, the population of Israel represents only a small segment of world Jewry. But the aim of the State of Israel is to take in as many Jews as possible from the Diaspora countries. What right has such a State to adopt a constitution which will be binding on millions of men, women, and children yet to settle within its borders."[14] Consequently, he declared that "no written constitution [should] be adopted until Israel's population stabilized and the threat of Arab invasion vanished."[15]

Another major stumbling block to a written constitution, likewise foreseen by Ben-Gurion, concerned religious groups in the polity. The question of the degree to which religious principles should be entrenched in an Israeli constitution was one that bothered many citizens,[16] both religious and nonreligious, and was clearly one for which a solution would not be readily discovered.[17] The two camps involved disagreed profoundly. Those referred to as "secularists" advocated that Israel develop a constitution similar to those of other Western, liberal states. On the other side, spokesmen for the religious faction claimed that the Torah and its tradition should make up any written constitution, for this would be superior to any man-made legislation "since it was of divine origin." Because it was felt that constitutions are items regarding which consensus should be developed, rather than items to be imposed by majorities upon minorities, it was decided that it would be better to put together, piece by piece, legislation that would eventually form Israel's constitution.[18]

On June 13, 1950, the Knesset voted by a fifty-to-thirty margin to postpone indefinitely the adoption of a formal written constitution and decided instead to allow for its gradual creation, with the individual pieces to be designated "Fundamental Laws."[19] The resolution read

The First Knesset directs the Constitution, Law and Justice Committee to prepare a draft constitution for the State. The Constitution shall be constructed article by article in such a manner that each shall in itself constitute a fundamental law.

Each article shall be brought before the Knesset as the committee completes its work, and all the articles together shall comprise the State Constitution.[20]

An additional point that still is perceived by many to be part of the June 1950 understanding was the assumption that at some point in the future the entire body of Fundamental Laws would be consolidated into a single document to be known as the Constitution of Israel.

The outcome of the 1950 resolution has been subjected to broad interpretation. Ben-Gurion and his supporters interpreted the vote as opposition to an "entrenched" constitution and as a vote for complete constitutional flexibility; there would be no laws of a "privileged position." Since the resolution said nothing about the time frame within which the Fundamental Laws had to be written—although because the resolution stipulated that this would be done by the First Knesset, it could certainly be argued that there was an implied time parameter—Ben-Gurion and his supporters were in no hurry. Indeed, the first of the Fundamental Laws was not passed until eight years later.[21]

There were, on the other hand, a number of leaders in Israel who, for a variety of reasons, supported the creation of a written constitution. One argument, of course, was that Israel had already committed itself to writing such a document. Not doing so would be a breach of faith with major international actors, primarily the United Nations and those countries that had supported the creation of the state of Israel. Further, many saw the Fundamental Laws as not being the functional equivalent of a constitution because they would be passed by simple majorities of the Knesset and, thus, could be reversed by the same majorities. They argued instead that a constitution should be a more special and inflexible document than the Fundamental Laws would be. It should also require more than simple majorities—at least two-thirds or three-fourths of the legislature, for example—to come into existence.

In addition, a number of other arguments were put forward in favor of Israel having a written constitution:

- That a constitution would provide a firm basis for the government of the state, defining rights of the citizens, limiting the powers of authorities, and regulating relations between the branches of the government;
- That because virtually every other country in the world had a constitution, Israel should have one too;
- That a constitution has both educational and patriotic significance for the country; and
- That a constitution would be a symbol of national unity, which was especially important to Israel when it was welcoming immigrants from all over the world.[22]

In the end, the forces advocating inaction prevailed, as might have been predicted. Since the resolution of June 13, 1950, the Knesset has passed a number of Fundamental Laws (sometimes referred to as "basic laws"), but it has yet to complete its work and formally consolidate all of the Fundamental Laws into a single document. Some legal scholars have accordingly questioned the legitimacy of the Fundamental Laws because, unlike the First Knesset (which did not pass any Fundamental Laws), the Second and subsequent Knessot[23] did not have the same authority to enact "superior law" that was given to the First Knesset by the Constituent Assembly. They claim that only the First Knesset was a continuation of the Constituent Assembly. When it failed to adopt a written constitution, there was no duly authorized body to carry out that task.[24] Technically, then, they say, the Fundamental Laws cannot be considered constitutional.[25] Others respond that since the powers of one democratically elected legislature are passed to the next democratically elected legislature, all Knessot have had constitution-making legitimacy.[26] After six decades of debate, it seems safe to say, no formal consensus has been reached, although practice has indicated that the Knesset would have the power to act should it choose to do so.

Until 1995, Israel was one of a minority of states in the world without a formal, written constitution. At that time, in the case of *United Mizrachi Bank plc v. Migdal Cooperative Village*, the Supreme Court declared that the eleven Fundamental Laws that had been enacted up to that point *would* be interpreted by the Court as the nation's written constitution, whether the Knesset had formally passed final synthesizing legislation or not.[27]

THE STRUCTURES OF THE ISRAELI CONSTITUTION

A well-known scholar of Israeli politics has written that it is not clear whether the classification "Fundamental Law" includes "only such legislation as has formally received that designation, or whether it may be used to define any law dealing with constitutional matters."[28] Fundamental Laws (as we have already noted, sometimes called Basic Laws), except for their unusual titles, do not always carry specific features distinguishing them from other acts of the Knesset. As another analyst has noted,

> Since the resolution of 1950 did not define the term "Basic Law," many considered it to apply to all laws of fundamental constitutional content passed by the Knesset, like, for example, the Law of the Return (1950), which provides that every Jew has the right to immigrate to Israel, or the Nationality Law (1952). . . . At one point Knesset Chairman Kadish Luz cited twenty-two "laws of a constitutional nature" in addition to the two formal Basic Laws then on the statute books, and asserted that the task laid down in the 1950 resolution had already been largely accomplished.[29]

We noted earlier that, with only a few exceptions, Fundamental Laws can be changed at any time by a simple majority of the Knesset. One example of these exceptions can be found in Fundamental Law: The Knesset, which has clauses that can only be amended by absolute Knesset majorities (61 votes out of 120), and one clause that would require a two-thirds vote to amend, regardless of the number of members present. While a section in the Judiciary Law makes its structure and powers totally immune from emergency regulations, it is the only constitutional legislation protected in this way.

In fact, however, on those occasions when the Knesset has passed laws that have conflicted with Fundamental Law: The Knesset, and the Supreme Court of Israel has struck them down as unconstitutional, the Knesset has simply passed those same laws again with an absolute majority, and the legislation has then been interpreted as actually amending the Fundamental Law, making the legislation entirely constitutional and legal.

Thus far, eleven chapters of an Israeli constitution have been written, each of which is called a Fundamental Law. These laws are acts of the Knesset that have been passed by a regular majority (a majority of those present and voting), not an absolute majority (more than 50 percent of the 120 members of the Knesset, or 61 votes). Fundamental Laws are endowed with a special position when compared to regular legislation, but since they are simple decisions of a majority of those present and voting, they can, in principle, be modified or done away with by a simple majority as well. The eleven Fundamental Laws that have been passed by the Knesset are (1) The Knesset (1958); (2) Israel Lands (1960); (3) The President of the State (1964); (4) The Government (1968); (5) The State Economy (1975); (6) The Army (1976); (7) Jerusalem: Capital of Israel (1980); (8) The Judiciary (1984); (9) The State Comptroller (1988); (10) Human Dignity and Liberty (1992); and (11) Freedom of Occupation (1992).[30] These eleven Fundamental Laws collectively make up Israel's constitution.[31]

> Until 1992 the Knesset had enacted nine Basic Laws. . . . In general, the Basic Laws codified existing practice. Their relationship to ordinary law was problematic: did the Basic Laws limit governmental actions as superior, fundamental law, or were they to be treated as other laws of the State? By 1992 the prevailing understanding was that the Knesset's sovereignty was almost unlimited. The Supreme Court would only invalidate Knesset legislation when it conflicted with a specifically entrenched clause of a Basic Law and if it was not enacted by the specified majority.[32]

As noted above, in 1995 the Supreme Court of Israel announced that the eleven Fundamental Laws would serve as the nation's written constitution and that the Court would refer to them when it was exercising an American-style power of judicial review.

In 1992 the same frustration with the political process which led to the drastic revision of the *Basic Law: The Government* also provided the momentum for the Knesset to enact two additional Basic Laws, which, for the first time, dealt with human rights. The logjam was broken because advocates of a written constitution realized that even if it was still impossible to enact a general Bill of Rights, it was possible to enact bills which dealt with the less controversial human rights. In short, Israel's step-by-step process to constitution-making was employed in the area of human rights. The Knesset enacted the *Basic Law: Freedom of Occupation* and the *Basic Law: Human Dignity and Freedom*. This time, however, the Supreme Court utilized the language of the two new Basic Laws to proclaim a constitutional revolution.[33]

In addition to Fundamental Laws, a number of other pieces of legislation have been passed by the Knesset over the years that have taken on what might be called a *quasi*-constitutional status in terms of both their legal importance and their contribution to the country's political culture. Included among them would be the Law and Administration Ordinance (1948), which established a massive body of Ottoman and British law as Israeli law; the Law of Return (1950), which laid out the fundamental principles of the rights of Jews to immigrate to Israel and the responsibilities of the state to help them in this effort; the Equal Rights for Women Law (1951), giving women equal political and legal rights in the state; the Nationality Law (1952), which regulated the naturalization of non-Jews; the Judges' Law (1953), setting up a framework for the appointment of judges; and the Courts Law (1969), which established several different systems of courts for different classes of litigation.

The first of the Fundamental Laws to be passed, Fundamental Law: The Knesset, dealt with the relations between the branches of government. The Knesset was entrusted with electing the head of state, the president, for a five-year term. The president is responsible only to the Knesset, and it alone has the power to remove the president from office for misconduct or incapacity. Special majorities are required to elect and remove the president. Although the president has a legal obligation to sign legislation from the Knesset, he has no veto power; nor can he refuse to sign a legislative act. The president also plays a role in the formation of the Government. According to Fundamental Law: The Government, it is the job of the president to "entrust to one of the Members of the Knesset the duty of forming a Government." Before this Fundamental Law was passed, there was much debate in Israel over whether the prime minister had to be a member of Knesset (MK); since 1968 the question has been moot.[34] This was amended in the Direct Election of the Prime Minister Law, which is discussed later in this volume, but the president is now again a direct participant in the process.

In fact, Fundamental Law: The Government has been changed several times in Israel's history. Originally passed in 1968, it was amended to establish the direct election of the prime minister, and it was amended again—taking effect in January 2003—to *repeal* the direct election of the prime minister. The newest revision of this Fundamental Law was passed in March 2001 by the Fifteenth Knesset. The core of the Fundamental Law remains the same: it lays down rules for the selection of a prime minister and cabinet following an election or following the failure of an earlier Government, describing the role of the president in the process and the nature of the coalition-formation process.[35]

The presidency itself was first created in the February 1949 Transition Law and was more fully developed in Fundamental Law: The President of the State (1964). The intention was to model it after the British head of state, but in a republican rather than monarchical form of government. Chaim Weizmann, the first president of Israel, advocated an American-style "strong" presidency. His conception lost out to that of David Ben-Gurion, who advocated a "weak" head of state and a "strong" prime minister. The following anecdote illustrates the result: In 1951 the visiting American secretary of labor passed on a message from President Truman to President Weizmann expressing Truman's disappointment that Weizmann "had not taken a stronger position concerning the protection of Arab refugees. 'I am only a constitutional President,' replied Dr. Weizmann, 'and it's outside my province. My handkerchief is the only thing I can stick my nose into. Into everything else—it's Ben-Gurion's nose.'"[36]

Such colorful anecdotes are no longer common because the constitutional relationship of the president and the prime minister is well-known, yet the dual roles are maintained: When Egypt's President Sadat undertook his extraordinarily courageous trip to Jerusalem in November 1977, after his arrival at Ben-Gurion Airport he traveled to Jerusalem in a limousine with the president of Israel, Yitzhak Navon, and not with the prime minister, Menachem Begin, because Navon was the president, the head of state. Sadat negotiated, however, with Begin, the prime minister and chief executive of the Government.

The role of the Israeli president today is a symbolic one in the political world. Originally the president was elected by a Knesset majority to a five-year term of office and could be reelected once beyond this. That was changed in 1998 to a single term of seven years.[37] His (thus far all Israeli presidents have been men, although there is no constitutional stipulations regarding gender) powers are clearly limited by Fundamental Law: The President of the State and other laws. These powers include the responsibility to make a number of appointments—including judicial, diplomatic, and a number of other senior positions, such as state comptroller, the governor of the Bank of Israel, the president and deputy-president of the Supreme Court, among other public offices—although these appointments are made "on the advice" of the Government. He accepts the credentials of foreign diplomats and signs all laws passed by the Knesset and treaties negotiated with foreign countries.[38] He has the power to pardon or commute the sentences of both civilians and soldiers. He also performs a large number of public-related activities, including hosting groups, making speeches, and the like.[39] Israel has had nine presidents to date, as shown in table 4.1.

When Ehud Barak became prime minister of Israel in 1999, many felt that the time had arrived for Israel to finish the constitution-building process and entrench a constitution. This was possible because Barak had—as we show later in this volume—enough support in the Knesset to pass necessary legislation without the support of any religious parties, and Barak himself was in support of finishing the process. It was recognized, however, that even pulling together already completed pieces of legislation would be a difficult and symbolically important process, so the process could not be rushed through the Knesset with the appearance of being forced upon the Israeli public.[40] Unfortunately, other political events—which we also discuss later in this book—resulted in Barak resigning as prime minister and participating in an early election for another term as prime minister, which he lost. With that loss the issue of constitutional completion was relegated to the back burner of the Israeli political agenda.

THE ROLE OF THE COURTS IN THE CREATION OF A CONSTITUTION

Due to the absence of a written constitution, until 1995 the Supreme Court of Israel has often had no concrete source of law higher than acts of the Knesset upon which to base its decisions.[41] This has meant that when the Court has handed down decisions, it has always done so with questionable legitimacy.[42] The real reason for this may have more to do with politics than with principle.

Table 4.1 Israel's Presidents

1	Chaim Weizmann	1949–1952
2	Yitzhak Ben-Zvi	1952–1963
3	Zalman Shazar	1963–1973
4	Ephraim Katzir	1973–1978
5	Yitzhak Navon	1978–1983
6	Chaim Herzog	1983–1993
7	Ezer Weizman	1993–2000
8	Moshe Katsav	2000–2007
9	Shimon Peres	2007–

Source: Israel Ministry of Foreign Affairs, "The State: The Presidency," *Facts about Israel,* April 1, 2008, www.mfa.gov.il/MFA/Facts+About+Israel/State/THE+STATE-+The+Presidency.htm, accessed January 2010.

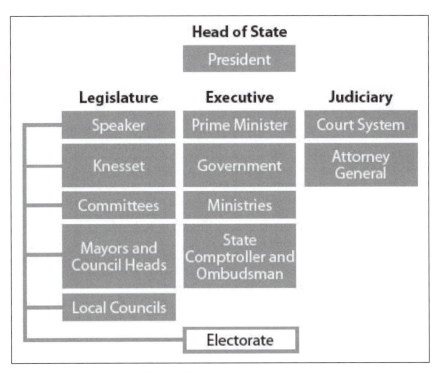

Figure 4.1. Structures of the Israeli Government
Source: Israel Ministry of Foreign Affairs, *Facts about Israel,* "The State: Political Structure," April 2008, www.mfa.gov.il/MFA/Facts+About+Israel/State/THE+STATE+Political +Structure.htm, accessed January 2010.

The Mapai Party offered one rationale in opposition to the establishment of a written constitution: a written constitution would lead to an activist Court and the development of American-style judicial review.[43] A written constitution would be a known standard against which to measure legislation and public policy and would encourage courts to be active in such measurement. If there were no such standard, courts might be more hesitant to step into the political arena. Many political leaders were hesitant to accept an arrangement that would result in taking political power away from the legislature and placing it in the hands of a nonelected judiciary. Thus, the theme of a Knesset hesitant to divest itself of any political power appears recurrently: "The idea of the sovereignty of the Knesset (on the British model) had great appeal to the strongest political party in the Knesset. Those who opposed the adoption of a written formal constitution and promised, instead, a flexible Israeli constitution were probably inspired by this political consideration."[44]

Photo 4.1.   The entrance to Israel's Supreme Court Building in Jerusalem

The importance of the principle of legislative supremacy—that the Knesset was the ultimate source of constitutional dogma by a majority vote—had several implications for the role of the Court at the time. First, the jurisdiction of the Court was limited by the Knesset; the Court was not in a position to limit the jurisdiction of the Knesset.[45] Second, when the Court chose to adjudicate, its decisions were based upon the principle of legislative sovereignty. Only very rarely did it question Knesset legislation in a specific instance, and never did it question the ability of a majority of the Knesset to do anything it wanted. Third, because of the principle of legislative supremacy, the Court could not "say what the law is," which the Court argued was the role of the

Knesset.[46] Thus, the absence of a formal, written constitution, combined with the principle of legislative supremacy, resulted until 1995 in a Court with strictly limited abilities to shape the constitution of the nation. On those occasions when the Court was willing to become more active, its rulings were limited and politically very cautious. As a group, the Court expressed the belief that its function was to uphold the law, rather than to make it.[47] A few examples of this attitude are examined here.

The earliest instance of the Court avoiding political cases was *Jabotinsky v. Weizmann* (1951). This was also the first time the term *justiciability* was used by the Court.[48] The question under review concerned the mechanics of forming a new Government. One of the president's powers as set forth in the Transition Law was to form new Governments when the need arose. After consulting with the representatives of the political parties, the president was to assign the task of actually forming the new Government to a Knesset member who was prepared to undertake the effort. In this case, after receiving a Knesset vote of no confidence, David Ben-Gurion had resigned as prime minister. The president, Chaim Weizmann, consulted with party leaders and subsequently asked Ben-Gurion to try to form a new coalition. Ben-Gurion refused. At that point, the president quit trying, and Ben-Gurion introduced a motion of dissolution calling for the election of a new Knesset.[49] Suit was brought by members of the opposition, claiming that Weizmann had failed to fulfill his duty to "entrust a member of the Knesset" with the task of forming a Government by prematurely permitting Ben-Gurion to move for its dissolution. Their argument was that Jabotinsky, the leader of the opposition, might have been able to form a coalition if he had been given the opportunity.

In rendering its verdict the Court ruled that the entire question was "political," and therefore "nonjusticiable."

> The whole subject of the duty of forming a Government . . . is nonjusticiable and beyond the scope of judicial determination. The relationships involved are in their very nature outside the field of judicial enquiry; they are relationships between the President of the State, the Government and the Knesset, that is to say the executive and parliamentary authorities. . . . The remedy must be found through parliamentary means . . . in the reaction of the Knesset to [the] Government.[50]

The principle established was very clear: henceforth the Court would avoid what it deemed to be "political" questions that dealt with issues best resolved by the legislature itself, including questions dealing with the legislature's scope of sovereignty.

The later case of *Basul v. the Minister of Interior* (1965) concerned a legislative act prohibiting pig-raising in certain areas of Israel that were to be designated on a map. At the time the bill was passed, however, the Knesset had not yet completed the design of the necessary map, so the law could not be enforced. A Muslim petitioner, resenting pig-raising in his area, appealed to the Supreme Court, claiming that the prohibition against pig-raising should still apply because it was the Knesset's fault that it did not have the map completed, rather than a problem with the law itself. Justice J. Berinson, who authored the majority opinion dismissing the case, claimed

> I doubt whether we [the Court] have the power to deny the validity of a law duly passed by the Knesset, even if it contains an error of fact or is based on faulty premises. In other words, it is doubtful whether a Court can look beyond the law and examine its correctness or compliance with the facts. . . . The Knesset is the legislative authority in the State and, as such, is sovereign.[51]

Once again the Court's reluctance to strike down legislation reflected its desire to support the Knesset and its belief that parliament should be supreme in the political system. The Court followed a doctrine of deferring action in cases that were labeled as political and disclaimed the power to amend or annul a law of the Knesset, believing that legislative supremacy was the very keystone of the Israeli constitutional system.[52]

The case of *Shalit v. the Minister of Interior* (1969) further substantiated the view that the Court's function did not include making policy. The case involved the request of a Jewish father and an agnostic mother of non-Jewish heritage that their children be registered as "of Jewish nationality but without religion."[53] The registration officer refused to register the children as Jews, claiming that according to *halachic*[54] rules "a child born to a non-Jewish mother cannot be registered as a Jew."[55] The father petitioned the Supreme Court, with the majority eventually ruling by a five-to-four margin—after two years of reflection and consideration—that the registration officer had to enroll the children in accordance with the information of the declarant "unless he had reasonable grounds to believe that the declaration was not correct."[56] The important principle in this case is that the Court refused to make law and interpret the question on religious grounds (i.e., Should the Orthodox rules about the mother's religious background be the deciding factor?), but instead simply said that the law of the Knesset indicated that the minister of interior was to register children according to parents' information.

Probably the most famous decision by the Supreme Court of Israel—often compared to the *Marbury v. Madison* decision by the Supreme Court of the United States—was the case of *Bergman v. the Minister of Interior* (1969). The plaintiff, Dr. Aaron Bergman, had brought suit before the Court seeking to prevent the minister of finance from acting under a provision of the Financing Law of 1969 that provided for governmental financing of political parties in election campaigns.[57] Dr. Bergman claimed that the Financing Law unfairly discriminated against new political parties because it provided governmental financing only for those parties that already had seats in the (outgoing) Knesset. Bergman argued that such an inequality required the Court to invalidate the Financing Law by reason of Section 4 of Fundamental Law: The Knesset, which provides, "The Knesset shall be elected by general, national, direct . . . equal elections in accordance with the Knesset elections laws. This section shall not be varied save by a majority of the members of the Knesset."

Bergman argued that the Financing Law was in conflict with Section 4 in that it produced an election that was not equal.[58] In addition, he contended that the Financing Law could not be regarded as a valid amendment to the Fundamental Law since the Financing Law was passed by less than the majority of the total membership of the Knesset, as required for a valid amendment under the terms of Section 4.

The Court's decision would clearly establish the principle of judicial review, but like the *Marbury* decision, it did so in a way that was politically acceptable at the time. Justice Landau, speaking on behalf of the Court, declared an act of the Knesset void for the first time in modern Israeli history. The Court sided with Bergman and ruled that the Financing Law was "incompatible with the equality in Section Four of the Basic Law: a Knesset elected under the Financing Law would not by terms of the Law be elected in an equal election."[59] Accordingly, the Financing Law was struck down. In fact, the Court went even further and provided the legislature with detailed advice as to how it should repair the inequality in the Financing Law, advising the Knesset that it could either reenact it with a special majority to essentially override the Fundamental Law, or it could be amended "so as to remove the lack of equality" by providing support for new political parties.[60]

The Bergman case was the foundation upon which the modern Court has based its increasingly active role in more recent years, with some of its members being unapologetically activist in nature. Of course, the view that the Court had a legitimate role in interpreting and ruling upon acts of the Knesset was not always shared by the Knesset and other observers,[61] and tensions between the Knesset and the Court have increased and decreased over time, depending upon the particular individuals involved.[62] Former chief justice Meir Shamgar once wrote that "democracy finds its expression not only in majority rule but in restraint of the majority for the sake of properly protecting the rights of the minority," and court watchers have observed that "clearly, the legislative and executive branches of government, chosen by the majority and dependent on it, can't provide that restraint; it must come from the judicial branch."[63] The problem was that some MKs didn't agree and threatened the Supreme Court with legislative retaliation—legislatively stripping the Court of some of its powers—if it became too active.[64]

As we noted earlier, a key event in the changing role of the Court was the passage in 1992 of two pieces of legislation, the Freedom of Occupation Act and the Human Dignity and Freedom Act. They limited the Knesset's authority to pass legislation violating specified rights and turned out to be significant bases for the Court to use for increasing its role in shaping social policy.[65] At that time an observer wrote, the two dominant justices on the Supreme Court have taken another step forward by hinting that in the foreseeable future they are likely to invalidate laws as well. Chief Justice Shamgar noted that in the United States, the Supreme Court assumed the power to overturn laws without an explicit constitutional mandate. In Israel, Shamgar made clear, the question of whether the court has such authority is still open. And Justice Aharon Barak wrote last year: "In principle, the possibility exists that the court will declare invalid a law that contradicts the basic principles of the system. Even if those principles are not anchored in a rigid constitution, there is nothing axiomatic about the view that a law cannot be invalidated because of its content."[66]

One of the Court's most activist members, Justice Aharon Barak,[67] has argued, "Everyone agrees that in a constitutional government that recognizes judicial review of the constitutionality of a statute, the final decision about the fundamental values is in the hands of the court."[68] Barak's view, however, has not always been met with agreement and public support.[69]

As one scholar of the Israeli Supreme Court has written, "It is routine for the Court, particularly in recent years, to appeal to the Declaration of Independence as an aid in statutory construction[70]; generally, however, its appeal is to the paragraph referring to individual rights."[71] It has also often referred to the Constitution of the United States, American constitutional law, and decisions of the U.S. Supreme Court in the justification of its opinions, such as the opinion of Justice Barak pointing out that the U.S. Constitution has permitted justices to have a "spacious view" of their role and that acts of the Knesset "should be viewed as fundamental constitutional provisions subject to . . . interpretive rules. Statutory silence is no bar to the Court's construing the law 'in light of the Declaration of Independence,' which expresses 'the vision and creed of the people.'"[72]

At the beginning of the twenty-first century, the discussion over the proper role of the Court was still actively being pursued in Israel.[73] One of the major groups of critics of the Court, as might be suspected from our discussion in earlier chapters, has been the Orthodox religious parties that have resented mightily decisions by the Court to limit their ability to determine what, precisely, "Jewishness" means in Israel and what the implications of religious orthodoxy might be. In 1999 the United Torah Judaism (*Yahdut HaTorah*) and *Shas* parties worked a resolution through the Knesset just before a weekend (when, apparently, "most coalition members had already gone home for the weekend") that "called on the Supreme Court to refrain from interfering in halachic [religious] and political issues, the legislative process, and the religious-secular status quo."[74] Shortly thereafter, the Knesset passed a resolution rescinding the critical resolution and expressing support for judicial review and the Court:

> The Knesset last night declared support for judicial review of its legislation by the Supreme Court, in a resolution that rescinded an anti-Court statement passed last

month. The resolution was passed at the end of a redebate on relations between the Knesset and the judiciary. Coalition whip Ophir Pines-Paz, who initiated the debate, said the Knesset had "saved its honor" by passing the new resolution.

It states that the Knesset must strengthen the independent status of the judiciary and "recognizes the democratic need for judicial review over its legislation," in the framework of its authority emanating from Basic Laws.[75]

In November 2000, legislation was introduced in the Knesset to create a new Constitutional Court that would formally exercise the powers of judicial review that the Supreme Court of Israel had been developing. The new Constitutional Court would have eleven members and would be made up of three justices from the Supreme Court, two religious court judges, one *kadi* (a judge ruling in accordance with Islamic religious law), four professors, and a new immigrant. The proposal, which passed a preliminary reading and vote, was seen as a legislative criticism of the increasingly political role of the Supreme Court; one of the bill's sponsors said that "the High Court of Justice is 'politicized' and as a result is not acceptable by half of the country," referring to Orthodox religious Israelis. Because the Government of the day did not support the idea, the proposal died, but it did show the degree to which some MKs were unhappy with the Court.[76]

In the spring of 2001 the discussion of the role of the Court was still on the Knesset's legislative agenda. The Knesset was holding hearings on a proposal to establish a European-style constitutional court, "thereby stripping the Supreme Court of its current role as a constitutional arbiter." Observers felt that the primary motivation behind the legislation was "the accumulated frustration with the Supreme Court's unilaterally adopted powers. Led by Barak, the Court has slowly worked to create its own constitutional powers, despite the fact that the country has no constitution."[77] This bill, too, died in Knesset committee.

The Court has had to walk a difficult line in the evolution of its role in relation to Israel's constitution, as it is not yet altogether clear what "constitutionalism" means in Israeli politics. In the United States, for example, the argument could be made that the nation was founded upon the ideals of classical liberalism, including valuing life, liberty, individual rights, and so on. At the time of Israel's creation, its founders were clearly aware of and sympathetic to the values of mid-twentieth-century liberalism, but they were also strongly committed to other ideas already presented here, including the national aspirations implied in the concept of Zionism. As one scholar has noted, "constitutional law—indeed, law in general—must somehow reconcile liberal and communitarian precepts that are not nearly so accommodating to each other as they are in the United States."[78]

The role of the Court, then, in the creation of the Israeli constitution has evolved over the years. In Israel's earliest years, the Court was very hesitant to intervene and was content to declare conflicts to be political and to leave them to the political arena, primarily to the Knesset, for resolution. The Court was consistent in ruling that the will of a simple majority of the sitting Knesset was sovereign, save in those instances in which a Fundamental Law had explicitly required special majorities for legislation designed to amend the doctrines of the Fundamental Law. This meant that the constitution continued to grow through a slow, additive process of Knesset actions on new Fundamental Laws. In more recent years, the Court has been willing to take a more visible, more political, and more proactive role—sometimes in the face of criticism for doing so—and the body of what has been called constitutional law in Israel has grown more rapidly.[79] This continues and often includes the Israeli society's most controversial and pressing concerns, issues that cannot be addressed in the legislative arena.[80]

Here, as in so many other areas, we are reminded that Israel is a young nation and that it has not reached the level of development of political practices that we find in other stable, but much older, democracies. The issue of having a written constitution is still being resolved[81] as are both the issue of the role of the Supreme Court of Israel as an activist body[82] and the issue of the very nature of what makes up constitutionalism in Israel. This theme of Israel's relative youth is one that we see repeated again and again in this volume.

ISRAEL AS A PARLIAMENTARY SYSTEM

Many scholars argue that the British model is the mother of parliamentary government and that all parliamentary systems belong in one way or another to the British family. This notion has received a good deal of attention in the Israeli context. Although there are many aspects of Israel's parliamentary system that do bear some resemblance to the British model, a good many structures are also significantly different.[83] One of the most respected studies on the subject has concluded that while Britain's "legacy" to the Knesset was "not negligible," major influences in the formation of the Knesset came primarily from the Zionist and Palestinian Jewish communities, as well as British, American, French, Yugoslav, Russian, and Turkish sources.[84]

There are a number of similarities between the Israeli parliament and the British or "Westminster model," although the changes to the Israeli electoral system in 1992—which turned out to be temporary and are discussed further in the next chapter—pulled Israel away from the Westminster model in some significant ways. The Westminster model is composed of four characteristics.[85] First, the same person who occupies the chief executive position does not act as the head of state. Second, the chief executive and his or her cabinet exercise the executive powers of Government. Third, the chief executive and the cabinet are all members of the legislature. Fourth, the chief executive and the cabinet are responsible to, and can be removed by, the legislature.

All of the above were characteristics of the Israeli polity until 1992 and are once again characteristics today. For the nine-year period from 1992 to 2001, Israel displayed the first, second, and fourth characteristics. First, there are two executives in Israel, the president and the prime minister, not one, as is found in the person of the president of the United States. Second, the prime minister and the cabinet exercise the "real" powers of the Government, while the president serves a primarily symbolic function, even though, as noted earlier, this relationship led initially to political machinations on the part of both Ben-Gurion and Weizmann before a firm relationship was established. The third characteristic was part of Israel's government until 1996 (although the law changing political structures was passed in 1992) and was reestablished as part of Israel's government in March 2001: the prime minister and most of the cabinet come from the legislature, unlike the relationship found in a presidential system in which there are specific prohibitions against membership in both branches of government.[86] In 1992 Israel decided to change to an entirely new version of Westminster-family executive elections (although it turned out to be only a temporary change); this is explained further in the next chapter. Fourth, and finally, the Knesset has the power to vote the sitting Government out of office at any time.

The Knesset is constitutionally the supreme political authority.[87] There is no executive veto of its actions and, within changing limits, the courts will not limit legislative actions by declaring them unconstitutional. Unlike in the United States, in Israel there is no longstanding tradition of widespread American-style judicial review, although that appears to be changing over the last decade.[88] The Knesset cannot be dissolved, and neither the head of state nor the chief executive can call new elections, as we would find in other parliamentary systems. Only the Knesset can cut short its electoral mandate from the voters and dissolve itself and call for new elections.

The role of the president is clearly a secondary one in the political system, as we would expect from the Westminster model. The president acts on the advice of the prime minister and, on his own, has very little discretionary power. As Sager reminds us,

> Just how limited the president's discretion can be in the determination of the premier designate was illustrated by the sequence of events that led up to the change of Government in 1983. After Prime Minister Begin declared his intention to resign, but before doing so, the *Herut* Central Committee nominated Yitzhak Shamir to succeed him, and Mr. Shamir at once met with the coalition partners of the outgoing Government and secured the necessary Knesset majority by a signed agreement. On Mr. Begin's resignation, shortly afterward, the president duly went through formal consultations with the parliamentary

groups, while his choice of Mr. Shamir to form the new Government was in fact a foregone conclusion.[89]

In short, Israel can be considered to be a parliamentary political system, but it is certainly not a clone of Britain. Israel is a good model of a constitutional, parliamentary political system, but it does have its idiosyncratic characteristics. These characteristics are the subject of our study throughout the next several chapters, in which we see that the people elect the Knesset and that a majority in the legislature chooses the leader of the executive branch, the prime minister. The prime minister stays in office only as long as he or she can command a legislative majority. In the Israeli case, this entails the construction and maintenance of coalition governments.

As with other parliamentary political systems, then, the cabinet, not the legislature, is the day-to-day focus of public attention and is the engine that drives the machinery of government. Because of the strong party discipline that exists in Israel, the role of the individual MK in the legislative process is very limited. In short, it is the political party that constitutes a key link between society and the polity. It is to this area that our discussion now must turn.

FOR FURTHER READING

Barak, Aharon. *The Judge in a Democracy.* Princeton, N.J.: Princeton University Press, 2006.

Elazar, Daniel. *Are Constitutional Limits on the High Court of Justice Democratic?* Jerusalem: Jerusalem Center for Public Affairs, 1994.

———. *The Constitution of the State of Israel.* Jerusalem: Jerusalem Center for Public Affairs, 1993.

———. *Constitutionalism: The Israeli and American Experiences.* Jerusalem: Jerusalem Center for Public Affairs, 1990.

———. *Switzerland as a Model for Constitutional Reform in Israel.* Jerusalem: Jerusalem Center for Public Affairs, 1987.

Jacobsohn, Gary. *Apple of Gold: Constitutionalism in Israel and the United States.* Princeton, N.J.: Princeton University Press, 1993.

Kretzmer, David. *The Occupation of Justice: The Supreme Court of Israel and the Occupied Territories.* Albany: State University of New York Press, 2002.

Lahav, Pnina, ed. *Law and the Transformation of Israeli Society.* Bloomington: Indiana University Press, 1998.

Sager, Samuel. *The Parliamentary System of Israel.* Syracuse, N.Y.: Syracuse University Press, 1985.

Sharfman, Daphna. *Living without a Constitution: Civil Rights in Israel.* Armonk, N.Y.: M. E. Sharpe, 1993.

Zemach, Yaacov. *Political Questions in the Courts.* Detroit, Mich.: Wayne State University Press, 1976.

5

The Prime Minister and the Knesset

If the British prime minister can be perceived as "first among equals," the Israeli prime minister can perhaps be perceived as first among unequals. Changes made in the electoral framework in 1992 significantly altered the prime minister's constitutional power base in Israel for a brief period, and although the Knesset ultimately restored the electoral system to its previous state, there were ongoing changes in the power relationship between the Knesset and the prime minister. This chapter examines the setting and organization of the Knesset, how legislation is passed, the role of individual MKs, and the nature of Israeli coalition politics. We then analyze the unusual, but highly significant, role of coalition government in Israel to understand why Israeli governments act as they do.

THE SETTING

As indicated earlier, for all but approximately nine years (1992–2001) of its existence, the Israeli government has been a fairly typical parliamentary system; that is, as with many other Westminster-model systems, the prime minister and his or her cabinet derive their authority and power from the parliament. While the chief executive can take office only after he or she has received a vote of confidence from the Knesset, the prime minister can

Prime Minister Benjamin Netanyahu addresses the Knesset while President (and former prime minister) Shimon Peres looks on.

be turned out of office at any time by a vote of no confidence in that same Knesset. Supposedly, then, the principle of *legislative supremacy* is character-istic of the Israeli political system, with the legislature doing the hiring and firing of the members of the executive branch of government.

Furthermore, the Knesset passes all legislation, serves as the pool from which the executive branch officials are drawn, controls the life of the Government (the prime minister and cabinet) by retaining the right to vote nonconfidence, elects the president for a fixed (seven-year) term, and, generally, remains the dominant political structure in Israel—at least theo-retically. In reality, as we shall see, this is not entirely the case, and through the institution of the political party and *party discipline*—the practice of members of a political party following the instructions of party leaders—the prime minister is, in fact, in control most of the time.

As noted earlier, in 1992 the Knesset approved a major change in the Israeli electoral system that for several years greatly affected the prime min-ister, the Knesset, and the balance of powers generally in the Israeli politi-cal world. With the change in the electoral system, the prime minister was directly elected by the people, rather than chosen by the president from among members of the Knesset (MKs). The new electoral system lasted un-til March 2001 and affected three Israeli prime ministerial elections—those of May 1996, May 1999, and the special election of the prime minister in February 2001.[1] Because there was significant unhappiness with the conse-quences of the new system's operation, in March 2001 the Knesset voted to restore the electoral system that had operated from independence until 1992, in which voters would cast only a single ballot for a political party to represent them in the Knesset and in which the prime minister would be chosen by the president from among MKs.[2]

In the current system there is only one national-level election: for the Knesset. People vote for members of the Knesset; then, after it is clear what the party representation in the Knesset will be and which party will have the most seats, the president will "invite" an MK—typically the person in the Knesset that the president feels has the best chance to receive support from a majority in the Knesset—to form a Government, which, given the number of political parties in the Knesset, invariably means creating a government coalition (something discussed in greater detail later in this chapter) that involves pooling the seats of several different political parties in the Knes-set to create a majority bloc. After the prime minister–designate negotiates at great length with a number of political parties, he or she goes before the Knesset for a *vote of confidence*, a demonstration that a majority of the Knes-set will, in fact, support the Government (for the time being, at least), after which the Government can be said to be in power.[3]

In the new system created in 1992 and in effect from 1996 until 2001, Israel changed from being a purely Westminster-based electoral system into a unique system when it, according to some, "presidentialized" the way it chose its prime minister.[4] The direct election of the prime minister first took place in Israel simultaneously with the 1996 elections for the Fourteenth Knesset. (Although the Knesset changed the electoral system in 1992, it did so under the condition that the changes would not take effect until the next Knesset election that took place in 1996.) The Fundamental Law: The Government, in its revised version, separated the election of the prime minister from that of the Knesset. This amendment of the basic law was proposed originally by four Knesset members following the difficulties in forming a coalition after the elections of the Twelfth Knesset (1988). The main purpose in changing the law, according to the proposals, was to strengthen the position of the prime minister and avoid the need for political horse-trading in order to form the coalition and Government.[5]

The law stated that the prime minister must be elected by more than 50 percent of the valid votes. Should no candidate win the required majority, a second round of elections would take place with the two candidates who had received the largest number of votes. In the second round, the candidate who received a majority of the votes would become prime minister.

On May 29, 1996, the first direct elections of the prime minister took place with Shimon Peres and Benjamin Netanyahu as the candidates. Netanyahu won the elections with a 50.49 percent majority. This new method of direct elections caused a significant drop in the political power of the two largest parties, Likud and Labor, which had a total of eighty-four Knesset seats in the Thirteenth Knesset and only sixty-six seats in the Fourteenth. At the same time, the number of midsize parliamentary groups (holding 5 to 10 seats) increased.

Immediately following the 1996 elections, MKs Yossi Beilin and Uzi Landau initiated a bill to cancel the direct election of the prime minister. Their justification for this move was the overall weakening of the Knesset and, specifically, of the two largest parties. Ultimately, the changes in the electoral structure were reversed in March 2001.

THE BALANCE OF POWER

In recent years a great deal of attention in political science has been focused on comparative policy making and a general tendency toward a "decline of legislatures."[6] The contention is that the increasing growth of executive government, which itself occurs for a variety of reasons, is matched by a corresponding decline in legislative influence.[7] Power in the political system is thus seen as "zero sum": every increment of growth in the executive's power is said to be matched by an equal unit of decline in the legislature's power. This situation, as has been suggested, has given rise to the de facto existence of cabinet supremacy rather than the *de jure* principle of legislative supremacy.

The principle of *cabinet supremacy* is relatively easy to express in its basic form: strong party discipline exists in parliamentary systems. Individual members of parliament are expected to follow the instructions of their party leaders. Because the leaders of the majority party or the majority coalition are almost invariably members of the cabinet, we find a situation in which the legislature, which is technically in command in the governmental structure, actually takes its orders from the leaders of the executive branch, the cabinet, because they are leaders of the parties in the Knesset; hence, the notion of cabinet supremacy.

This principle has a great deal of relevance for Israeli political figures. It means that individual MKs are not expected to engage in activities that follow only a personal agenda. Rather, they are expected to do what they are told by their leaders. Members of opposition parties are expected to follow their party leaders, just as members of Government coalition parties are expected to follow theirs (who are usually cabinet members, as well).

Because of the many political parties active in the Israeli political system, no single party has ever had an outright majority in the Knesset. *Coalitions* have therefore been the rule. A coalition can be defined as a group of nonmajority parties that pool their strength (i.e., their parliamentary seats) in the Knesset to create a majority bloc for the purpose of supporting a Government. Understanding government coalitions is a crucial starting point for any study of the political process. Because forming coalitions has always been necessary for political parties in the Knesset, there has traditionally been less latitude in individual party and legislative behavior than might otherwise be the case. Party discipline—the practice of having MKs vote together and support party policy—becomes the norm, and coalition lines are rigidly enforced.

The term *Government* in Israel refers very specifically to the prime minister and his or her cabinet.[8] The cabinet meets weekly—usually every Sunday, at the start of the work week—to discuss those issues that have found their way onto the national political agenda. The cabinet operates under the principle of collective responsibility: once a decision is reached, all members of the cabinet are expected to support that decision. Individual cabinet members' only alternative to supporting a cabinet decision is to resign.[9]

Occasionally, the media refer to an "inner" cabinet or "security" cabinet. This is a subgroup of the full cabinet, made up of the prime minister's closest advisers and those most closely involved with key issues of national security and national defense.

The office of prime minister itself does not have the same relative weight as it does in Britain, for example, primarily because of the coalition nature of Israeli cabinets. One result of this is that the prime minister may make policy suggestions to his or her cabinet colleagues that will not have the support of a majority of members of the cabinet (with the prime minister being in the minority), leaving the prime minister with only two choices: support the views of the majority of the cabinet or resign—something that would not happen in the British case.

The prime minister today is in a stronger position than he or she was prior to the brief period of direct election, however, because when the Knesset voted in 2001 to revert to the earlier system of election, it compensated for putting the prime minister in the more vulnerable position of having to assemble coalitions before coming to power by making it slightly harder for the Knesset to fire the prime minister. Between 1949 and 1996 the prime minister could be fired by a majority of those present and voting in the Knesset. A vote of no confidence could be called—with appropriate legislative warning—at any time, and if the prime minister could not demonstrate that he or she had the support of a majority of the Knesset, he or she would have to resign. While this did not happen often, it did happen. When the Knesset revised the system, they followed the model used in Germany, which is referred to as a "positive vote of non-confidence" and requires that the Knesset select a successor in the same resolution in which it expresses a lack of confidence in an incumbent. This offers greater security, of course, because it is easier to get a number of parties to agree that they do not want someone to be prime minister than it is to get them to agree on whom they will support as successor. Under the new system, if they have not already designated a successor, they cannot vote to throw the prime minister out of office.

This chapter examines the Knesset's role in the Israeli political system, along with the power held and exercised by coalition governments since 1948.[10] Although Israel is a relatively new nation in terms of the number of years that the modern state of Israel has existed, a number of traditions and customs have already developed that are uniquely Israeli and worthy of note.

LEGISLATION IN THE KNESSET

In addition to debate and discussion, probably the most important function of legislatures is passing laws. The legislative process in the Knesset follows the standard parliamentary model fairly closely; only a brief discussion of the process is needed here.[11]

An initial distinction must be made between Government bills and private members' bills (the latter are so named because they are introduced by private members, individuals acting on their own and not as members of the Government). Government bills are introduced by members of the cabinet, members of the Government. These bills tend to be authored within the ministries in the relatively vast governmental bureaucracy. Wherever they originate, these bills are passed up the chain of command in the ministry involved, eventually reaching the director general, the ministry's

Chapter 5

highest-ranking civil servant. He or she then passes the proposal along to
the minister responsible for that department, who then takes the bill to
the cabinet and, after receiving cabinet approval, introduces the bill in the
Knesset as a Government bill.

On the other hand, private members' bills are introduced by members
who are not members of the cabinet, whether they are members of parties
belonging to the Government coalition or members of opposition parties.
Historically, private members' bills have been a very small minority of the
total number of bills processed by the Knesset annually, but in the past few
years they have increased significantly in number and as a proportion of the
total amount of legislation handled in the Knesset, as shown in figure 5.1.

The Knesset has passed legislation in a remarkably broad range of areas.[12]
Whereas in the 1970s it was common for fewer than 20 percent of the total
bills introduced in the Knesset to be from private members, in the past few
years the number of private bills introduced has skyrocketed and nearly 50
percent—more than 50 percent in the Thirteenth Knesset—are introduced
by private members. Since the time of the Tenth Knesset, Menachem Begin's
second Government, the number of private members' bills has doubled in
each term of the Knesset. Despite the fact that the number of private members' bills introduced has increased drastically in the last two decades, how-

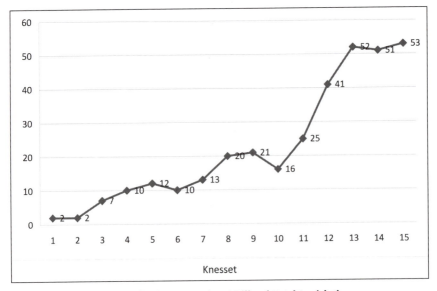

Figure 5.1.   Percentage of Private Members' Bills of Total Legislation
Source: Knesset Web page: "The Knesset at Work: Legislation," section "Data Regarding Private Members' Bills,"www.knesset.gov.il/description/eng/eng_work_mel2.htm,
accessed January 2010.

ever, it is still the case that a very, very small proportion of private members' bills are actually passed by the Knesset (see figure 5.2).

The bulk of the Knesset's output comes from Government-sponsored legislation. After approval by the cabinet, Government bills are tabled in the Knesset and entered as items for the agenda. All bills must "lie on the table" (be available for examination) for at least forty-eight hours before discussion on them begins. The Knesset committee, if it so wishes, may waive this forty-eight-hour rule, just as it can do with many other procedural rules.

The first stage in the legislative process is called the first reading.[13] The minister in charge of the bill begins with a summation of the contents of the bill and then a line-by-line reading. After the minister has finished presenting the bill, debate begins. This first reading debate is usually a general one. When the vote comes at the end of the debate, Government bills almost invariably are passed and sent to committee.[14] Private members' bills rarely meet with the same results and are usually defeated at that point in the legislative process.

The bill is then sent to whichever committee has jurisdiction.[15] If more than one committee is involved, the bill will go to the committees one after another, in whatever sequence the speaker of the Knesset selects. The committee in question may deal with a bill for three months or three hours, depending upon the importance of the bill, the committee's workload, the wishes of the Government, and the willingness of the committee to cooperate with the Government's manager of the legislation. The committee has the power to revise a bill, even to the extent of virtually rewriting it if necessary. However,

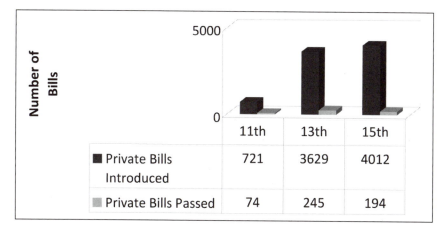

	11th	13th	15th
■ Private Bills Introduced	721	3629	4012
▨ Private Bills Passed	74	245	194

Figure 5.2. Private Members' Bills Passed by the Knesset
Source: Knesset Web page, "The Knesset at Work: Legislation," section "Data Regarding Private Members' Bills," www.knesset.gov.il/description/eng/eng_work_mel2.htm, accessed January 2010.

the Government retains the power to recall a bill to the Knesset floor in the exact form in which it was sent to committee if it believes that the committee has significantly altered the bill away from its intended direction.

At this stage the second reading takes place. This is the final major hurdle the bill must pass, because bills that pass the second reading invariably pass the third reading. Another debate takes place at this point, but in this debate only members of the committee may participate; all other members are in attendance only to vote on the bill, section by section. If no amendments to the committee report are adopted, the third reading follows immediately after the conclusion of the second. If there are amendments, the third reading is postponed for one week to allow members time to consider them. However, even if amendments have been proposed, if the Government requests an immediate third reading, it takes place immediately after the second.

Following the third reading, the bill is voted on as a whole. Since the Israeli parliamentary system is a unicameral one, bills passed by the Knesset are sent immediately to the president for signature. As noted in the last chapter, the president does not, as a custom of Israel's unwritten constitution, have a veto over legislation. Fundamental Law: The President of the State indicates, "The President of the State shall sign every Law," and the words "shall sign" have always been taken to mean that the president does not have any option but to sign an act of the Knesset.[16] One can only assume that it would cause a constitutional crisis should a president at some point in the future actually refuse to sign a piece of legislation, and such an action could be grounds for impeachment and removal from office of the president.

THE MEMBERS OF KNESSET

A general description of MKs would begin much as a description of members of parliament in most other nations. It would indicate that legislators are older on average than the general population, a higher proportion of them are male, and minorities are underrepresented.[17] Apart from their primarily Jewish religious affiliation, they differ from legislators in other nations in one very important respect. A substantial percentage of them are immigrants, although this number has decreased over the years. Twenty-two of the members of the Eighteenth Knesset (elected in February 2009) are women, 18.3 percent of the total.[18] This figure is certainly not representative of the proportion of women in the Israeli population, but it is not greatly different from that found in most European parliaments, and it is greater than the comparable figure of approximately 13.8 percent for the United States Congress (13 women in the Senate and 61 in the House of Representatives). Most MKs are also highly educated.

Most members have come to the Knesset through the ranks of their political party, with many having held some formal party office, either in the Knesset or some municipal position, prior to running for public office.[19] Many date their association with a political party from very early in their lives and were active in "youth groups" throughout their childhood. This pattern of party activity simply continued on after early childhood and led to adult political activity. Eventually, the outcome was the decision to seek a position on the party's electoral list.[20]

LEGISLATIVE BEHAVIOR OF MEMBERS OF THE KNESSET

Party discipline in the Knesset is very strict. This is especially the case in the parliamentary vote (as it is with other parliamentary regimes). On virtually all legislation in the Knesset, both in committees as well as on the floor of the main hall (called the plenum), individual members are expected to follow the party line. Failure to vote with the party can result in removal from a prestigious committee in the Knesset. Although a member cannot be expelled from the Knesset for going against his or her party, pressures brought upon MKs by the public and party colleagues have caused more than one to resign his or her legislative seat.

MKs almost never vote against their parties, and in this respect Israel is very much like other parliamentary systems. A member who feels very strongly against his or her party's position on a particular issue is more likely to go to the Knesset restaurant for a long cup of coffee in the middle of a roll call, so as to miss the roll call vote. This can sometimes be effective, although occasionally absence in itself can be a sufficient act of insubordination to warrant punishment by party leaders. From time to time, if the vote is sufficiently close, the party leader will pull in reticent members from the restaurant or elsewhere to make sure that these members vote on a given issue in the "correct" direction. The reason, of course, is that with a narrow coalition majority, a Government could "fall"—lose its ability to demonstrate control of a majority in the Knesset—as a result of only one or two "undisciplined" members.

Legislative voting is not the only dimension of activity in which the individual MK is essentially vulnerable to pressure from party leaders. Debate is another example of this relationship. Debate by itself may be the central characteristic of parliamentary bodies internationally. Regardless of the true role of legislatures in the power structures of the governments in which they are found, the one thing that they always do is debate. Debate may ensue from a formally introduced bill, a motion to add to the agenda, or a statement by the Government. Votes of confidence and no confidence would fall into the latter category.

Knesset debates can be assigned one of two labels, personal and party. Personal debate, which is the less significant, is usually employed either in nonpolitical matters that the Knesset is discussing, but that are not related to pending legislation, or in matters of legislation on which opinions are not divided along party lines. Party debate, on the other hand, makes up the bulk of Knesset debate and takes place with respect to votes of confidence, no confidence, foreign policy, the budget, and any matters that the Government regards as significant (which means virtually any bill introduced by the Government).[21] When this kind of debate takes place, the standing committee called the Knesset Committee decides how much time to allow for the total debate, then divides the total time by the total number of MKs (120), yielding a time-per-member figure.[22] This amount of time is then given to the party leaders in the Knesset to do with as they please. The leaders may choose to permit everyone in their party to speak for the allotted time per member, or they may choose to pool all of the party's time into one longer speech. In many cases the party leader himself or herself will speak, or the entire party time will be given to a senior party member who is considered the party's spokesperson on the given issue.

Here again, the individual MK is vulnerable to party leaders' actions. Should an individual MK behave (e.g., vote, speak) in a way that the party leader views as unsupportive of or disloyal to the party, that party member may find himself or herself no longer allowed to introduce legislative proposals or speak out in debates!

A significant distinction can be drawn between intralegislative and extralegislative behavior. Within the Knesset, members do not have a great deal of autonomy, nor are they expected to exercise a great deal of free will. Outside of the assembly hall and the committee rooms, however, MKs are still in a position to perform many services for the public, all of which bolster the esteem in which they are held. They respond to correspondence, provide information and policy positions to their constituents, make speeches and attend rallies, and represent the full gamut of their constituencies.

The Knesset is not currently held in terribly high standing with today's public, however. In a study commissioned by the Knesset in 2001, it received an overall score of four on a ten-point scale; "a full 88 percent are unhappy with their legislature, while 50 percent are downright ashamed of it." Individual MKs did not fare much better, also scoring a four, with respondents describing individual MKs as "lazy, selfish, and indifferent to the public. Seventy-six percent of the public believe that MKs see the Knesset as a way to make a living and get respect, and not as a mission."[23]

The term *constituency* in Israel does not have the same meaning as it does in the United States or Britain, for example. In countries with district-based voting, such as the United States, a representative's constituency is geographically delimited: lines are drawn on a map, and anyone living in the area concerned is a part of the representative's constituency. It is possible for an individual voter to know, without any doubt at all, who his or her representative is.

In Israel, on the other hand, with the electoral list system and a single national electoral district for the purposes of elections, the term *constituency* takes on what is called a "functional" meaning.[24] When individuals are placed on a party's electoral list, they are often put there as representatives of a group, and it is clear to the candidate, and to the group involved, who is on the list to represent which group.[25] A typical electoral list might have clearly designated (that is, understood, although not in writing on the list) representatives for women, teachers, blue-collar workers, farmers, kibbutz inhabitants, Yemeni immigrants, residents of Eilat, and Arabs, to name just some of the functional constituencies that might be represented. Although American citizens might react by wondering how they would know who, for example, their Labor Party representative was, an Israeli citizen would not have the same reaction. In the case of smaller party lists in the Knesset, he or she would go to any MK representing his or her party, and in the case of the larger party lists, he or she would go to one of the more "specialist" representatives.

MKs also perform much ombudsman work, in which they speak or act on behalf of members of the public to help resolve their problems. This is often the aspect of his or her job that the average MK spends the most time on and for which the MK receives the most glory (or scorn). Citizens write, telephone, or visit the MK and complain that they need help. Members contact the appropriate ministers, who are in the Knesset daily, who in turn contact the directors general of the ministries involved, and frequently, sooner or later, the problem is resolved. Actually, the MKs' success ratio in this type of activity is quite high, possibly because the political-bureaucratic system in Israel is gauged to this personalistic approach to problems.

In any case, once one distinguishes between intralegislative and extralegislative behavior, a remarkable difference in effectiveness in individual legislative behavior can be observed.[26] In aspects of intralegislative behavior, the individual MK is highly constrained and is consequently highly frustrated and cynical. It is no surprise that of the members interviewed for a study many years ago, more than 83 percent indicated that they considered themselves accountable to their party or party leaders for what they did as an MK, and 74 percent indicated that individual members had "little," "very little," or "no influence" in the formation of government policy.[27]

In extralegislative behavior, however, MKs do not feel as cynical or helpless. They indicate that they receive a great deal of mail and spend a great deal of time (many say most of their time) responding to this mail. They feel that members play a very important role in the Israeli political system and enjoy helping their constituents with problems they are having.

KNESSET ORGANIZATION

The Knesset is the central organ of the Israeli political system. The power of the Government comes from the Knesset, and Government policies are all either enacted in the Knesset's name or approved by its members. The Knesset sits for two terms a year, one in the summer and one in the winter. Under Fundamental Law: The Knesset, the two terms must total at least eight months.

Although the job of the MK is taken seriously, Israeli legislators, like most other legislators in the world, do not have the office space, secretarial help, or legislative staff budgets of their American counterparts.[28]

MKs are all afforded substantial degrees of parliamentary immunity to guarantee the freedom to perform their legislative duties without fear of possible governmental persecution. This immunity is discussed in the Immunity, Rights, and Duties of Members of the Knesset Law passed in 1951, which was based on an ordinance dating back to 1949. The protection afforded is extremely broad. The law states that a "member of the Knesset shall not be held civilly or criminally responsible, and shall be immune from legal action, with regard to any vote cast, any oral or written expression of opinion, or any other act performed in or out of the Knesset, provided that such vote, opinion, or act pertains to, or has as its purpose, the fulfillment of his mandate as a Member of the Knesset."[29]

In May 1998 the criminal immunity of Arye Deri of the *Shas* party was lifted by the Knesset upon the request of the attorney general of Israel so that Deri could be prosecuted for "alleged misuse of funds related to his personal finances."[30] More recently, in November 2001 an Arab MK, Azmi Bishara, lost his immunity for actions related to Palestinian violence against Israel:

> The Knesset voted yesterday to remove Balad leader Azmi Bishara's parliamentary immunity, so that he can stand trial for making speeches praising Hizbullah and for arranging illegal trips to Syria for Israeli Arabs.
>
> The unprecedented decisions passed with majorities of 61–30 and 65–24, making Bishara the first MK to have his immunity removed for words, not deeds. Soon after the vote, Attorney-General Elyakim Rubinstein confirmed he intends to press charges.[31]

In order to protect individual legislators, the act protects the MKs beyond their legislative behavior. Neither MKs themselves, nor their property, may be searched, except by customs officials. While they hold office, MKs are absolutely immune from arrest, unless they are caught committing a crime or an act of treason. If a member is arrested, the authorities must notify the speaker immediately, and the member may not be detained for more than ten days, unless the Knesset has revoked his or her immunity. As with other national legislatures, the Knesset building itself has immunity. Under the Knesset Buildings Law of 1952, the building and grounds are under the control of the speaker and sergeant at arms. This, too, is designed to free members from extralegislative pressures and distractions, such as demonstrations and other interruptions.

In the Knesset, chairmanships are apportioned with the major parties sharing control.[32] Seats on committees are given to parties, not to individuals, and the parties then assign their own members to the committee seats. For example, the Finance Committee might have nineteen members, representing only three large parties—Likud, Kadima, and Labor—and these parties in turn would assign their own members to the Finance Committee.

Committees provide MKs with an opportunity to specialize in their areas of interest and to keep in touch with Government ministers and high-ranking civil servants in a variety of subject areas. The committees also play a role in the legislative process, although, as already indicated, this fluctuates with the willingness of the Government to accept proposed legislative changes.

There are four types of Knesset committees that function on a regular basis: the Permanent Knesset Committees; Special Knesset Committees, which are similar to the permanent committees but have a limited term of office; Parliamentary Inquiry Committees, which deal with particular issues viewed by the Knesset as having special national importance; and the Ethics Committee, which has jurisdiction over Knesset members who have violated rules of ethics of the Knesset or who have been involved in illegal activity outside of the Knesset.

As a general rule, there are between twelve and twenty members on each of the twelve permanent standing committees, which are in turn appointed for the full term of a Knesset. In addition to the twelve permanent standing committees, temporary committees are appointed from time to time as deemed necessary by the Knesset presidium. Committees made up of members from more than one permanent standing committee are sometimes jointly appointed when legislation arises that crosses the jurisdictions of more than one permanent standing committee. The respective jurisdictions of the committees are basically self-explanatory. The committees are shown in box 5.1.

Committee meetings are usually closed to the press and public, so that all information about their proceedings must come from the committee members themselves. The committees vary in the importance they are perceived as having in the legislative process. Committee members are divided over the true role of the committee, with many saying that a committee's role depends upon the particular legislation that is before a given committee at a given time. Most members agree, however,

> that committee action is generally "meaningless" because the Government as a general rule takes no notice of committee recommendations, and although committees may spend a good deal of time modifying Government legislation, or drafting their own legislation, when the third reading of a Government bill

Box 5.1. Committees of the Knesset

Permanent Committees
- House Committee
- Finance Committee
- Economic Affairs Committee
- Foreign Affairs and Defense Committee
- Internal Affairs and Environment Committee
- Constitution, Law, and Justice Committee
- Immigration and Absorption Committee
- Education, Culture, and Sports Committee
- Labor, Welfare, and Health Committee
- State Control Committee
- Committee for the Advancement of the Status of Women
- Science and Technology Committee

Special Committees (temporary)
- Committee on Drug Abuse
- Committee on the Rights of the Child
- Committee for Foreign Workers

Parliamentary Inquiry Committees
- Ethics Committee

Source: State of Israel, Knesset Web page, "Knesset Committees," www.knesset.gov.il/description/eng/eng_work_vaada.htm, accessed January 2010.

comes on the floor of the Knesset, the Government bill is usually voted upon as it was originally introduced in the Knesset.[33]

There are exceptions to the general rule of committee ineffectiveness worth noting. The Finance Committee and the Labor Committee have been given a great deal of authority by both the Knesset and the Government to write laws in their own spheres of expertise. These committees, especially the Finance Committee, are thus considered quite powerful and influential, and positions on these committees are highly sought. The third committee to be an exception to the general rule of committee ineffectiveness is the Foreign Affairs and Security Committee. Interestingly, this committee is considered an exception to the general rule even though it has few powers and is mostly involved in oversight and debate, devoting little time to drafting legislation. However, since foreign affairs and security are priority concerns, and since MKs on this committee are privy to more classified information than MKs on the Agriculture Committee, for example, positions are in greater demand.

As indicated previously, seats on committees are given to parties and are then reassigned by party leaders to party members. Consequently, when a member bolts from the party line in a committee or speaks out of turn too often, he or she may be limited to participation in the general assembly, having been either reassigned from one committee to another or, in more extreme cases, stripped of all committee memberships. In fact, members may have no committee memberships if their party leaders feel they do not deserve such positions.

The Knesset has an elaborate framework of other organizational and behavioral rules in addition to the more formal structures of the presidium and committees. A period of time is regularly set aside for individual legislators to ask questions of the Government—the so-called Question Time. This serves the dual functions of bringing new issues to the attention of the Government as well as reminding the Government that the public is watching its overall behavior. This question period can become quite animated, as opposition members endeavor to ask the Government embarrassing questions. After Prime Minister Begin signed the Camp David Agreement (which we discuss later), opposing members within his own party used the Question Time to express their dismay and their serious concerns about the national security implications of the agreement.

In addition to parliamentary questions, another institution that should be mentioned here concerns parliamentary motions. Since the Government controls the daily calendar and thereby, in general, controls which subjects will be debated in the Knesset and for how long, a procedure is needed by which subjects that the Government may not want to talk about can be brought to the agenda to receive public scrutiny.

The Knesset has a very elaborate and highly formalized procedure by which individuals can endeavor to force the Government to schedule debates dealing with certain subject areas that it may prefer to avoid. *Motions to add to the agenda* and *urgent motions to add to the agenda* give members a potentially significant role in the process of deciding what issues are and are not discussed in the Israeli political world.[34] For example, after recent demonstrations by Israeli Jewish settlers on the West Bank against the *intifada*, some Arab MKs sought to introduce a motion to add to the agenda so that they could have the Knesset debate the Government's policy in regard to both the settlers and the way it was handling the Arab demonstrators.

COALITION POLITICS AND COALITION GOVERNMENTS

Understanding government coalitions is central to any study of Israeli politics.[35] Because political parties have traditionally had to form coalitions, there has been less opportunity for individual party and legislative behavior. Party discipline is extremely tight, and coalition lines have been rigidly enforced.

A coalition government is, very simply, one in which two or more nonmajority parties pool their seats to form a majority alliance. There is often a formal agreement drawn up among the coalition partners, indicating, among other things, their priorities and objectives, limitations upon the freedom of speech or actions of member parties, and payoffs to coalition partners (for example, the number of cabinet seats a party will receive for joining a coalition or a promise that the Government will act on certain legislative programs within a brief period of time).[36]

Since Israel's independence, there has never been what has been referred to as a *majority situation*, that is, one in which the party organizing the Government has controlled on its own more than 50 percent of the seats in the Knesset.[37] Israel, in fact, has been an oft-cited illustration of a "minority situation, majority government," one in which a party with less than a majority of parliamentary seats joins with other minority parties to create a majority Government.[38] As a result, coalitions have been formed not only after, but also between, Knesset elections. In fact, during Israel's eighteen Knessot, there have been thirty-two Governments, as shown in table 5.1.[39]

Before we turn our attention to an examination of several major themes related to Israeli coalitions, let us briefly discuss coalition governments in the abstract. When no single party has a majority in a parliamentary political system, as indicated above, the most likely outcome is the creation of a political coalition in which two or more parties will join together to create what is referred to above as a "minority situation, majority government."[40] Let us imagine a hypothetical situation with a one-hundred-seat parliament (not the 120 seats of Israel's Knesset) and five political parties, as indicated in table 5.2.

In this instance, the head of state would most likely invite the leader of Party A to form a Government, since Leader A leads the largest parliamentary group. Leader A needs to find an additional eighteen seats in order to form a majority of fifty-one (out of one hundred seats, total) to support his Government in the legislature. In this case, Leader A could go to either the leader of Party B or the leader of Party C to find a partner. Of course, Leader A could also go to more than one other party leader to try to form an ABC coalition, for example.

Usually, Leader A will have to promise the leaders of other parties involved in the coalition some sort of *payoff* for joining the coalition. In most instances, this payoff is a cabinet position (or more likely several cabinet positions). Sometimes the payoff is a promise that a certain piece of legislation that the prospective coalition partner has drafted will be passed as part of the Government's program. It should be clear, though, that the more partners Leader A has to invite into the coalition, the more different payoffs he or she will have to make. Thus, individuals charged with forming coalitions usually strive to form what are called "minimal winning coalitions,"

Table 5.1 Prime Ministers and Coalition Partners, 1949–2010

Date of Government Creation	Govt No.	Knesset	Approximate Life of Government (Months)	Prime Minister (Party)	Coalition Partners
March 10, 1949	1	I	20	Ben-Gurion (Mapai)	Left, Center, Religious
November 1, 1950	2	I	10	Ben-Gurion (Mapai)	Left, Center, Religious
September 8, 1951	3	II	15	Ben-Gurion (Mapai)	Left, Religious
December 24, 1952	4	II	13	Ben-Gurion (Mapai)	Left, Center
January 26, 1954	5	II	17	Sharett (Mapai)	Left, Center
June 29, 1955	6	III	4	Sharett (Mapai)	Left, Center, Religious
November 3, 1955	7	III	26	Ben-Gurion (Mapai)	Left, Center
January 7, 1958	8	III	24	Ben-Gurion (Mapai)	Left, Center
December 17, 1959	9	IV	23	Ben-Gurion (Mapai)	Left, Center, Religious
November 2, 1961	10	V	19	Ben-Gurion (Mapai)	Left, Religious
June 26, 1963	11	V	18	Eshkol (Mapai)	Left, Religious
December 22, 1964	12	V	13	Eshkol (Mapai)	Left, Religious
January 12, 1966	13	VI	38	Eshkol (Mapai)	Left, Religious
March 17, 1969	14	VI	9	Meir (Mapai)	Left, Religious
December 15, 1969	15	VII	51	Meir (Mapai)	Left, Religious
March 10, 1974	16	VIII	3	Meir (Mapai)	Left, Religious
June 3, 1974	17	VIII	36	Rabin (Mapai)	Left, Religious
June 20, 1977	18	IX	49	Begin (Likud)	Right, Center, Religious
August 5, 1981	19	X	26	Begin (Likud)	Right, Center, Religious
October 10, 1983	20	X	11	Shamir (Likud)	Right, Center, Religious
September 13, 1984	21	XI	25	Peres (Labor)	Left, Right, Religious
October 20, 1986	22	XI	26	Shamir (Likud)	Right, Left, Religious
December 22, 1988	23	XII	18	Shamir (Likud)	Right, Left, Religious
June 11, 1990	24	XII	25	Shamir (Likud)	Right, Religious
July 13, 1992	25	XIII	40	Rabin (Labor)	Left, Religious
November 22, 1995	26	XIII	7	Peres (Labor)	Left

Table 5.1   Prime Ministers and Coalition Partners, 1949–2010 (continued)

Date of Government Creation	Govt No.	Knesset	Approximate Life of Government (Months)	Prime Minister (Party)	Coalition Partners
June 18, 1996	27	XIV	37	Netanyahu (Likud)	Right, Religious
July 6, 1999	28	XV	20	Barak (One Israel)	Left, Center, Religious
March 7, 2001	29	XV	24	Sharon (Likud)	Right, Left, Center, Religious
February 26, 2003	30	XVI	38	Sharon (Likud)	Right, Center, Religious
May 4, 2006	31	XVII	35	Olmert (Kadima)	Center, Left, Religious
March 31, 2009	32	XVIII	–	Netanyahu (Likud)	Right, Left, Religious

Source: Israel Ministry of Foreign Affairs Web site, "The Governments of Israel: Coalitions 1949 to the Present," www.mfa.gov.il/MFA/Government/Previous+governments/The+Governments+of+Israel.htm, accessed January 2010.

Table 5.2   A Hypothetical Party Distribution in a One-Hundred-Seat Legislature

Party A	33 seats
Party B	20 seats
Party C	18 seats
Party D	16 seats
Party E	13 seats
Total	100 seats

coalitions no bigger than necessary to wield a majority (be a winning coalition) so that unnecessary payoffs will not be required.

If Leader A can reach an agreement with one or more partners to form a coalition that will control a majority of the legislature, then Leader A will receive his or her vote of confidence, a vote by a majority that it supports his or her Government, and the Government can be said to be in power. If, however, Leader A cannot find sufficient coalition partnership within a constitutionally mandated period of time, usually twenty-eight days, then Leader A must return his or her mandate to the president and inform the president of his or her inability to form a Government. At this point the president seeks out a different party leader to try to form a majority coalition.

Coalition majority governments tend to be less stable than single-party majority governments in parliamentary systems. In a single-party majority system, the prime minister must impose party discipline to keep his or her party followers in line and maintain a majority. In a coalition system, the flow of power is more diffuse. The prime minister must exercise party discipline over his or her party followers and must count on the leaders of partner coalition parties to do the same. Coalition downfalls have usually come about because of differences between party leaders—in terms of our example above, because Leader B has a disagreement with Leader A and pulls the support of Party B out of the AB coalition—not because of a failure of party discipline within Party A.

As might be expected, the complexity of the coalition-formation process is a direct function of the number of political parties in a legislature. In the examples in table 5.3, Situation I is relatively simple, Situation II is more complex, and Situation III is even more complex. One should keep in mind that in Situation III, there are only eight parties represented; in some countries, such as Israel, there are many more. In fact there are at the time of this writing *twelve* parliamentary groups represented in the Israeli Knesset, and

Table 5.3   The Complexity of the Coalition-Formation Process in a One-Hundred-Seat Legislature

Situation I: Simplest Majority Possibilities

Party A	44 Seats	
Party B	42 Seats	AB, AC, BC, ABC
Party C	14 Seats	

Situation II: More Complex Majority Possibilities

Party A	38 Seats	
Party B	20 Seats	AB, AC, AD, ABC, ABD, ABE, ACD, ACE, ADE, BCD, etc.
Party C	17 Seats	
Party D	15 Seats	
Party E	10 Seats	

Situation III: Most Complex Majority Possibilities

Party A	30 Seats	
Party B	19 Seats	
Party C	12 Seats	
Party D	9 Seats	ABC, ABD, ABE, ABF, ABG, BCDE, CDEFGH, etc.
Party E	8 Seats	
Party F	8 Seats	
Party G	7 Seats	
Party H	7 Seats	

some of those groups are blocs of several different political parties; indeed, thirty-four parties ran for seats in the 2009 election! The more parties that exist, the more possibilities there are to form a winning coalition, and the more partners there are in a coalition, the more possibilities there are for a coalition to fall apart.

The study of what has come to be called coalition theory has greatly expanded over time. Indeed, in a recent study political scientists have suggested that coalition theory is now in its third generation: the first developed theories of how coalitions work, the second tried to apply the general theories to real-world politics to see how well the models predicted what would happen, and the current generation seeks to combine the research of both the first and the second generations to make coalition theory a truly predictive model.[41]

There are, of course, a number of problems with broad theories of coalition formation. First, the theories may be more or less valid in one political system than in another. Second, the research may not be transferable; that is, research done on coalition behavior in Japan may not tell us a great deal about how coalitions work in Israel. Finally, the distribution of cabinet positions may be explained by many different theories, including the number of seats a party can claim to control, patronage, loyalty, payment for future support, and a variety of other reasons.

Several of these themes must be kept in mind when we analyze the formation of coalitions among Israeli political parties. First, political parties play an overwhelming role not only in political life, but also in social and economic life, as we noted earlier in this book. Parties publish newspapers, run medical clinics, sponsor athletic and social events, and, in short, permeate every aspect of life.[42]

Second, one must note the number of parties currently active. As many as twenty-four presented themselves at elections for the First and Second Knessot[43]; twenty-seven parties ran candidates in the Twelfth Knesset elections in 1988, and twelve won Knesset seats. Thirty-one parties ran candidates in the Fifteenth Knesset elections in 1999, and fifteen parties won seats.[44] Twenty-nine parties ran candidates in the Sixteenth Knesset elections in 2003, and fourteen parties won seats. Thirty-four parties ran candidates in the Eighteenth Knesset election campaign in 2009, and at the time of this writing there are twelve parliamentary groups represented in the Knesset, some of those blocs of several different parties.[45]

The number of political parties active in the political system may affect our ability to theorize about coalition formation. It has been noted that whereas twelve cabinets had actually formed through 1965, in those twelve cabinets there were 7,873 possible winning coalitions, to say nothing of the number of near-winning or minority coalitions possible.[46] To provide a comparison, in Belgium over a comparable period of time (1949–1965), there were fourteen actual coalitions with 463 possible winning combinations because of the smaller number of parties operating in that setting.[47]

Third, the regional military balance and national security in general have always been of paramount importance in Israeli politics. War situations, for example in 1967, have greatly influenced the size of coalitions that were formed in Israel. On several occasions coalitions have been created that were larger than they needed to be and that included parties whose support was not really necessary in order to demonstrate to the outside world that the Government in power at the time had a strong base of support. The institution of past *national unity governments* is an example of a larger-than-necessary coalition.[48]

Finally, the history and ideological nature of the Israeli party system must be considered. The party system in Israel has been called overdeveloped by many, and several political scientists have written that the large number of political parties is not really necessary. The abundance of political parties is usually attributed to the fact that most parties—or the parents of parties that have broken away from older parties—existed before the state did.[49] This history, combined with the proportional representation electoral system that encourages new parties to form by making representation in the Knesset relatively easy, has encouraged the expansion of parties, which has complicated the coalition-formation process.

The important consequences of coalition governments for the Israeli political system are several. First, they result in an increased party discipline and thereby in less individual legislative freedom, as the Government has to be sure that it can depend upon coalition members to support government policy.[50]

Second, and perhaps more important, coalitions leave the Government vulnerable to a kind of political "blackmail." If a given coalition is a "minimal" one in which the Government would lose its majority if a single party withdrew, then a relatively small coalition partner might have considerably greater leverage with the Government than its size alone would suggest. We have already seen how Israel's religious parties have had a great deal of influence over government policy. This has rarely reflected a Government's ideological commitment to religious issues. Rather, it has often been the result of smaller religious parties issuing ultimatums such as "Pass/Support our policy, or we will withdraw from the government coalition and you will lose your majority and will no longer be prime minister." Prime ministers have tended, over the years, to respond to this kind of threat.

Finally, coalitions have led to a condition termed *immobilisme*—an inability to act on a given issue. This occurs when a problem comes up and the Government knows that if it acts in one direction or another, one of its coalition partners will get angry and quit the coalition. The only solution, then, is to do nothing. A good example was seen during the Government of Menachem Begin: the minister of education told Begin that if the cabinet did not approve a significant raise for public school teachers, he would leave the cabinet and take all of his party followers with him. As a result Mr. Begin would lose his Knesset majority. In response to this threat, however, the minister of finance indicated that if Mr. Begin gave in to the minister of education and altered the fiscally tight budget he had created, *he* would leave the cabinet and take all of *his* party followers with him, which would also result in Mr. Begin's losing his majority. It was clear that whatever Mr. Begin did, or didn't do, he would lose the support of one of his coalition partners and thereby lose majority support in the Knesset. The outcome was Begin's decision to call for new elections and subsequently create a new coalition. (After the election, when a new coalition was in place with a new budget, the teachers did receive slightly higher salaries!)

THE KNESSET, THE GOVERNMENT, AND ISRAELI POLITICS

The political structure of Israel tells us a great deal about Israeli society. As was pointed out earlier, it is a stable democratic society in a part of the world in which stable democratic societies are not very common. Stability and democracy, of course, do not necessarily mean unanimity, or political quiet, and it is this characteristic of modern Israel that has led to the existence of a multiple-party political system in which so much loud and often-heated debate takes place.

Political parties, it has been argued, are the key to the political structures of the Knesset and the Government. Parties not only are the basis for governmental organization, they are also the vehicles through which virtually all of the official functions of the Knesset are undertaken. Individual legislators are to a substantial degree at the mercy of their party organizations: not only can they not run for office without being on a party list, but once they are in the Knesset, they cannot introduce bills, serve on committees, or engage in debate without a party leader's approval.

The number of political parties has led to the development of a coalition system in Israel. This, in turn, has had two broad consequences. First, Governments have on a number of occasions taken less dramatic action than otherwise might have been the case, precisely because the prime minister needed to worry about whether a more dramatic action would alienate one of his or her coalition partners. Second, this phenomenon has resulted in some of the smaller parties—most notably, of course, the orthodox religious parties—having far more influence over government policy than their size alone would have merited. The role of the small party as the keystone of Government coalitions has contributed significantly to the continued visibility of the religious question in Israeli politics and has continued to serve as a source of irritation to a substantial portion of the Israeli electorate.

FOR FURTHER READING

Elazar, Daniel, and Shmuel Sandler. *Israel's Odd Couple: The 1984 Knesset Elections and the National Unity Government.* Detroit, Mich.: Wayne State University Press, 1990.

Hazan, Reuven. *Cohesion and Discipline in Legislatures: Political Parties, Party Leadership, Parliamentary Committees and Governance.* London: Routledge, 2005.

———. *Reforming Parliamentary Committees: Israel in Comparative Perspective.* Columbus: Ohio State University Press, 2001.

Hefez, Nir, and Gadi Bloom, *Ariel Sharon: A Life.* New York: Random House, 2006.

Longley, Lawrence, and Reuven Hazan, *The Uneasy Relationships between Parliamentary Members and Leaders.* Portland, Ore.: Frank Cass, 2000.

Mahler, Gregory. *The Knesset: Parliament in the Israeli Political System.* Rutherford, N.J.: Fairleigh Dickinson University Press, 1981.

Sager, Samuel. *The Parliamentary System of Israel.* Syracuse, N.Y.: Syracuse University Press, 1985.

Swirski, Shlomo, and Yaron Yechezkel, *Women's Representation in the Legislature and the Executive in Israel and Worldwide.* Tel Aviv: Adva Center, 1999.

6

Political Parties and Interest Groups

The building blocks of Israeli democracy have been its political parties. Israel was described nearly fifty years ago as a *parteienstaat* ("party-state"), and the role of political parties in the day-to-day operation of the polity has not diminished. This chapter discusses the structure and behavior of political parties and related interest groups, how political parties are organized in Israel, what their key issues are, and how they differ from each other. Then the chapter's focus shifts to interest groups, another very important structure in the contemporary Israeli democratic arena.

THE SETTING

The political party is the underlying factor in contemporary Israel that explains a good deal of the turbulence in the political system. The Israeli political system has been referred to as a *parteienstaat* par excellence, and the description is appropriate.[1] Political parties played an important role in Israel's achieving statehood. One could even say that the state of Israel "was actually brought into existence by political parties, which were organized and developed entities . . . years before the coming of statehood."[2] Indeed, contemporary Israeli political parties are a direct link to the past in that virtually all have roots in some prestate political form.[3]

Contemporary Israeli politics operates within a diverse and pluralistic society.

The Israeli political party system could almost be classified as overdeveloped. Indeed, as we noted in the last chapter, thirty-one parties ran candidates in the Fifteenth Knesset elections in 1999, and fifteen of these parties won seats in the Knesset by winning at least 1.5 percent of the votes; twenty-nine parties ran candidates in the Sixteenth Knesset elections in 2003, and fourteen parties won seats; thirty-four parties ran candidates in the Eighteenth Knesset election campaign in 2009, and at the time of this writing there are twelve parliamentary groups represented in the Knesset, some of those blocs of several different parties.[4] Many of these lists represented temporary electoral coalitions of up to five separate political party organizations. Many Israelis believe that the system would be better off with only a very small number of parties and see no real need for so many organizations. They suggest that Israel could operate with greater stability with only a left, a right, and a religious party, with perhaps an Arab party as a fourth party. They argue in support of the position that there is no need for four individual religious parties, although many argue that Israel's various religious parties are sufficiently different from each other that one party alone would not meet all social needs.[5]

There are, of course, several reasons why the independent party organizations continue to function—and even thrive—in spite of the fact that they may be losing their autonomy within the legislature. Perhaps the most important is that party organizations engage in considerably wider ranges of activity than merely drafting legislation in the Knesset. They do not, in other words, confine their behavior to only the obviously "political." Israel's parties "have been more than electoral mechanisms and formulators of governmental policies."[6] Parties "occupy in Israel a place more prominent and exercise an influence more pervasive than in any other state with the sole exception of some one-party states," and they work for their members in a variety of ways to maintain public support.[7] One classic study of party activity, to a very large extent still quite accurate today, beautifully captures this party-member relationship:

> A person who subscribes to the party's daily newspaper, is given medical care in a party sponsored clinic, hospital, or convalescent home, spends his evenings in a party club, plays athletic games in the party's sports league, gets his books from the party's publishing house, lives in a village or in an urban development inhabited solely by other adherents of the party, and is accustomed to look to the party for the solution of many of his daily troubles—is naturally surrounded and enveloped by an all-pervasive partisan atmosphere.[8]

While this is less true today than it was at the time the article was written in 1955, political parties in Israel still perform a much broader range of services for their members than do parties in most other democracies; thus, they have stronger ties to their publics than is typical elsewhere. It therefore becomes clear that an understanding of political parties is absolutely essential for a clear understanding of the operation of the Israeli political system.

IDEOLOGY IN ISRAEL

"The style of Israeli politics is ideological."[9] Ideology refers to a set of values and beliefs pertaining to political behavior and public policy, the political "oughts" or "shoulds." In particular, Israel was born of socialist and Zionist ideologies, both of which have endured to this day.[10] In addition to these fundamental philosophies, however, a number of other ideological and policy issues have developed over time that have become the focus of much debate. Israel's political culture, in fact, "demonstrates a fascinating mix of ideology and pragmatism."[11] Many years ago a path-breaking study of political ideology in Israel was undertaken. At that time, five major issues were deemed crucial in determining party platforms:

1. Private enterprise (a) versus socialism (b)
2. Activist Arab policy (c) versus restraint (d)
3. Torah-oriented life (e) versus secularism (f)
4. Pro–Soviet Union (g) versus pro-West (h) foreign policy
5. Zionist (i) versus non-Zionist (j) approaches to the legitimacy of the state[12]

Based upon these five issues, thirty-two different political party platforms were mathematically created (e.g. acegi, acegj, acehi, acehj, etc.), of which nineteen were logically impossible or ideologically incompatible. (An example of an incompatible ideological mix would be a pro-Soviet, private enterprise, Torah-oriented, non-Zionist platform.) Ten of the remaining hypothesized platforms corresponded with platforms of political parties of the time, and three were logically possible, but had yet to be offered as political alternatives.

With the exception of the Soviet question (issue number 4 from the list above), which is not a matter of contention in Israel today (even if we substitute "pro-Russian" for "pro-Soviet," the conflict with the West is moot today), the other four issues remain active and continue to be the cause of further party fragmentation.[13] In research done in the Knesset, members were asked to position the various political parties of the time along the remaining four scales, which they were able to do without trouble. It is clear from the responses that these members felt it was possible to position parties along a number of different ideological scales in a way that adequately represented their different issue positions and, thereby, gave them their distinctive identities. It is also clear from the legislators' responses that although many of the center, left, and religious parties had similar views, they did diverge enough for the legislators to feel comfortable rating them separately.

While the total number of issue positions on four bipositional issues ("hawk" / "dove," "pro–private enterprise" / "pro-socialism") is only sixteen, some of which may be logically contradictory or incompatible, the various degrees of opinion and intensity of belief for each of the four issues leave open the possibility for more competing party organizations to form.[14] At the same time, conversely, some political parties have become firmly identified with specific ideological positions. This concept is represented in table 6.1.

It is clear how extraordinarily tenuous some of the coalition governments in Israel have been, how difficult it is for partners to be partners: they disagree, sometimes fundamentally, on many issues, including economic policy, how flexible Israel should be in negotiations with Arab powers, what Israel's policy should be with regard to settlements on the West Bank, what influence the Orthodox religious groups should have in politics, and so on.

Party ideology has been most important in times of elections. "Israeli voters tend to report that ideological considerations are important" in motivating their votes.[15] To some extent, of course, this depends upon how one defines "ideology," because in one sense all of Israeli politics is ideological. If we define "ideology" in a more specific sense to include policy positions on a wide variety of individual issues, then it is possible to conclude that electoral campaigns have become less ideological over the years. Many argue that ideological differences between the parties have decreased to such an extent that general party image and the popularity of individual party leaders have taken the place of ideology as the reason why people vote as they do.[16]

Over the years, the predominant coalition of political ideologies in Israel has been deemed to have shifted to the right toward a more conservative and hawkish position.[17] This was one of the reasons for Likud's victory and the Labor Alignment's loss in the 1977 election; the left's ideology had become stale and had fallen out of step with public opinion.[18] To some extent,

Table 6.1   Four Bipositional Issue Spectra and Possible Political Party Positions

Dimension	Policy Extremes
1	private enterprise (A) versus socialism (B)
2	"activist" Arab policy (C) versus restraint (D)
3	Torah-oriented life (E) versus secularism (F)
4	Zionist (G) versus non-Zionist (H)

Possible combinations for political parties to represent:
ACEG ACEH ACFG ACFH ADEG ADEH ADFG ADFH
BCEG BCEH BCFG BCFH BDEG BDEH BDFG BDFH

the creation of preelectoral blocs between several different political parties has tended to force some of the parties to relax their ideological rhetoric. Parties seeking to hold political office must operate in the real world, which has sometimes necessitated their making political deals with parties that take opposing ideological positions, requiring some compromise and modification of pure ideological standards.[19]

THE FUNCTIONS OF PARTIES

Quite apart from the fact that we may credit the various organizational ancestors of contemporary political parties for assisting in the formation of the state of Israel, contemporary political parties perform a significantly greater number of important functions in the political system. Although I do not mean to suggest that all Israeli parties perform all of these functions (or that they all perform them equally well), it can be suggested that *most* parties perform *most* of these functions *most* of the time.

First, parties act as personnel agencies, or mechanisms to assist in the recruitment of political leaders.[20] It is very clear that in Israel one does not become active in politics at the national level without operating within a party framework. Independents are not elected to the Knesset, and, as should have become clear in chapter 5, the Knesset does not encourage the participation of independent, nonparty members. Individuals seeking political office in Israel must operate using the vehicle of a political party. This assertion is further substantiated by the fact that when individuals break away from established political parties, they do not compete in the political arena as independents. Rather, they establish their own political parties and continue to operate in the party-dominated environment. An overarching explanation for this is the country's electoral system. The Israeli formula of proportional representation makes it impossible—legally impossible—to run for office without a party label. The nature of the electoral system likewise gives party leaders a great deal of leverage over individual members even after elections.

The second function of political parties is to help organize groups and articulate political demands.[21] Parties seek the support of various constituencies when elections for the Knesset are at hand, and they work full-time between elections to continue generating public support for their organizations. Translated into action, this means that parties publish newspapers, operate medical clinics, subsidize housing, run job-placement services, and provide a wide range of additional specialized services to their members.[22] Beyond this, when parties see new issues looming on the public agenda, they seek to stake out an advantageous position in relation to their own platforms and those of their rivals. Parties will act to mobilize groups around their issues and will speak out in an effort to attract even more popular and electoral support. This is especially true in relation to issues of social-class structure.[23] The importance of Russian immigrants is very clear in this way, with the creation of *Yisrael Ba'Aliya*, a political party focused overwhelmingly on the problems of Russian immigrants.[24] In this respect, political parties in Israel can be seen to act as movements, in addition to being simply political parties in the conventional sense of the word. It is difficult for citizens of other democracies, in which political parties serve primarily elective functions, to appreciate the extent to which parties in Israel touch a wide range of aspects in an Israeli citizen's life.

A third function involves providing an ideological or perceptual frame of reference for voters. The world is a complicated place, and very often citizens (and voters) are not sure how to perceive events happening around them. Parties perform a useful function here by staking out positions on a wide range of issues, offering general and detailed explanations for why those opinions are the "correct" opinions to hold, and thereby making the political world a more understandable place for individuals who might not otherwise grasp many of the finer points of contemporary political discourse. In this sense parties perform a crucial role in political social-ization, the process by which individuals develop beliefs, attitudes, and values related to the political world. Along with the family, schools, ethnic groups and group leaders, occupational colleagues, peers, the media, and community leaders, the political party plays a significant role as a point of orientation as the individual develops his or her views about how and why the political world operates as it does.[25]

Finally, parties serve as so-called linkage mechanisms, helping to tie the individual to the political system within which he or she resides. Although there are formal mechanisms in the Israeli political system that link mem-bers of the public to governmental structures, namely specifically elected representatives, there is a great deal of ambiguity about the role that the rep-resentative should play. Since Israelis vote for political parties, not individual candidates, and since there are no geographic districts in Israel, as we noted earlier, individual Israelis are left without their own official—governmentally designated—representatives. It is, instead, through the political party that Is-raelis relate to the political system as a whole. Israeli parties are *mass parties*— they are based upon mass membership and are truly run by the rank-and-file of the party—and it is the party that provides the opportunity for individuals to feel that they have a real say in the political process.

PARTIES AND ISSUES

Israeli political history has seen many political parties come and go over the years. Table 6.2 indicates the major parties that have been active in the

Box 6.1. Mergers and Splits among Parliamentary Groups in the Sixteenth and Seventeenth Knessot

Sixteenth Knesset

March 10, 2003—*Yisrael Be'aliyah* merged into the Likud.

June 15, 2004—*Meretz*-Democratic Choice-*Shahar* changed its name to Yahad and the Democratic Choice.

January 12, 2005—United Torah Judaism split into *Agudat Yisrael* and *Degel Hatorah*.

March 21, 2005—*Hitchabrut* split off from the National Religious Party.

May 16, 2005—*Hitchabrut* changed its name to Renewed National Religious Zionism.

May 18, 2005—One MK split off from *Shinui*–the Secular Movement and established Zionism Liberalism Equality.

May 18, 2005—*Shinui*–the Secular Movement changed its name to *Shinui*–Party for the Secular and the Middle Class.

May 23, 2005—Labor-*Meimad* and *Am Ehad* merged into one parliamentary group and Labor-*Meimad-Am Ehad*.

May 23, 2005—One MK split off from *Am Ehad* and established *Noy*.

July 27, 2005—*Yahad* and the Democratic Choice changed its name to *Meretz-Yahad* and the Democratic Choice.

November 23, 2005—Fourteen MKs from the Likud split off and formed *Achrayut Leumit*.

November 23, 2005—*Noy* merged with *Achrayut Leumit*.

January 17, 2006—*Achrayut Leumit* changed its name to *Kadima*.

January 26, 2006—*Shinui*–Party for the Secular and the Middle Class split into *Shinui*, with three members and the Secular Faction, which had eleven members.

February 1, 2006—One MK left *Ichud Leumi* and remained a Single MK.

February 1, 2006—One MK split off from *Shinui*, and formed *Ha-olim*, which then merged with *Ichud Leumi-Yisrael Beitenu-Moledet-Tekuma*.

February 1, 2006—*Ichud Leumi-Yisrael Beitenu-Moledet-Tekuma* split into *Ichud Leumi-Moledet-Tekuma* with four members and *Yisrael Beitenu* with three members.

February 5, 2006—Two MKs left the Secular Faction and established *Habayit Haleumi*.

February 7, 2006—*Hadash-Ta'al* split into Arab Movement for Renewal (*Ta-al*) and *Hadash*.

Seventeenth Knesset

June 2, 2008—Three MKs from the Gil Pensioners Party split and formed the Justice for the Elderly parliamentary group.

October 27, 2008—Two MKs from Justice for the Elderly remerged with Gil Pensioners Party. The third MK split and formed a single-member parliamentary group called the Right Way.

December 3, 2008—*Ichud Leumi*–Mafdal changed its name to Jewish Home–Mafdal and *Ichud Leumi*.

December 18, 2008—The Labor-*Meimad* parliamentary group split into two separate groups: *Meimad* and Labor Under Ehud Barak (18 MKs).

December 18, 2008—United Torah Judaism split into *Agudat Yisrael* and *Degel Hatorah*.

December 23, 2008—Jewish Home–Mafdal and *Ichud Leumi* split into Jewish Home–Mafdal, Achi, and Moledet–*Ichud Leumi*.

Source: State of Israel, Knesset Web page, "Mergers and Splits among Parliamentary Groups," www.knesset.gov.il/faction/eng/FactionHistoryAll_eng.asp#key, accessed January 2010.

last five Israeli elections, between 1992 and 2010. There are a lot of them, and their relationships are quite complex, because many have merged, broken apart, and recombined over the years. Indeed, the Thirteenth Knesset started its term in 1977 with thirteen parties, and ended its term in 1981 with twenty parties!

This process of party factionalization, recombination, and creation is a fascinating way for political organizations to stay viable and relevant to the voters—or otherwise to disappear from the political scene altogether—and shows how a political system that is very responsive to the electorate might operate. Box 6.1 shows mergers and splits among parliamentary organizations in the Sixteenth and Seventeenth Knessot—elected in 2003 and 2006, respectively—and illustrates the principle that the Knesset is organizationally very fluid.

Political parties that have participated in Israeli coalition governments can be conventionally grouped into four categories: left, center, right, and religious. (Arab parties exist, too, but have not been formal members of Government coalitions nor formally in positions of power in the Knesset.[26]) This quadripartite classification has occasionally been upset by the existence of parties that do not fit into the system, such as the Democratic Movement for Change (DMC) in the late 1970s. Here we briefly review the political parties that ran for office in the elections for the Eighteenth Knesset and won seats in that election, seeking to describe not only the basic tenets of the parties today but also the evolution of the parties and the political groups from which they have developed, if appropriate.[27]

Left Parties[28]

The **Labor Party** started in Israeli history as Mapai, an acronym for *Mifleget Poalei Israel* ("Israel Workers' Party"), in 1930. Labor is a classical social-democratic political party, with a commitment to government activism to provide social and economic benefits for the public. The Labor Party's roots

Table 6.2   Major Political Parties in Israeli Elections, 1992–2009

Symbol	Name of Party List
A	Israel Labor Party (MAPAI)
AMT	Alignment—Israel Labor Party and United Workers' Party (7th through 12th Knesset)
	Labor headed by Yitzhak Rabin (13th Knesset)
	Labor (in the 14th Knesset)
	One Israel headed by Ehud Barak—Labor, *Gesher, Meimad* (15th and 16th Knesset)
AT	Alignment—Israel Labor Party and Unity of Labor (6th Knesset)
B	National Religious Front, *Mizrahi*, and *Mizrahi* Workers
G	United Torah Judaism—*Agudat Yisrael, Degel HaTorah*, Rabbi Yizhaq Peretz *Agudat Israel* Workers (was AI/PAI)
D	*Agudat Israel* Workers (until the 9th Knesset)
D	National Democratic Alliance (BALAD)
HD	The Third Way for National Consensus
HN	Centre—*Shinui* List
W	Democratic Front for Peace and Equality, Israel Communist Party (RAKAH), Black Panthers, and Jewish and Arab Circles
ZH	Gil Pensioners Party
H	*Herut*, Freedom Party
HL	*Herut*-Liberal Front (GAHAL)
HLTAM	Likud
T	Free Center (7th Knesset)
T	*Moledet*
T	*Yahad*—Movement for National Unity (11th Knesset)
T	*Ichud Leumi, Erez Israel Shelanu, Moledet*
TB	*Ichud Leumi–Mafdal*
YT	National Union—*Moledet, Herut, Tequma*
YM	United Arab List (9th Knesset)
JS	*Ometz*—Recovery of the Economy (10th and 11th Knesset)
JS	Democratic Movement for Change (DASH) (9th Knesset)
JS	*Shinui*—Secular Movement headed by Lapid and Poraz
KA	Israel Workers' List (RAFI)
KACH	KACH—Movement founded by Rabi Meir Kahana
KN	*Shlomzion*—Realization of Zionism Movement
KN	*Yisrael Ba'Aliya* headed by Natan Sharansky
KN	*Kadima*
L	Liberal Party
L	*Yisrael Beiteinu* headed by Avigdor Liberman
LA	Independent Liberals
M-MAPAM	United Workers' Party and Nonaligned

Table 6.2   Major Political Parties in Israeli Elections, 1992–2009

Symbol	Name of Party List
MHL	*Halikud (Mahal)*—Likud, *Gesher, Zomet*
MEREZ	*Merez*—Democratic Israel, RZ, Mapam, *Shinui*
M	*Am Ahad* headed by Amir Perez—Faction of Workers and Pensioners
NJ	Israel Tradition Movement (TAMI)
ADP	Arab Democratic Party
AD	*Morasha, Mazad, Agudat Israel* Workers
AM	State List
AM	United Arab List (15th Knesset)
EZ	*Degel HaTorah*
P	Progressive List for Peace
PH	Center Party headed by Yizhaq Mordechai
PS	Flatto-Sharon—Development and Peace
TZ	*Zomet*—Movement for Zionist Renewal
K	Israel Communist Party
KN	*Moked* (*Tekhelet-Adom* Movement)
RZ	Citizens' Rights Movement and Peace
S	*HaOlam Haze*
S	*Shelli*
SHAS	Universal Association of Sephardi Observers of the Torah
Th	Resurrection, *Hatchia*
TW	Unity of Labor, *Achdut HaAvoda*
TLM	Movement for State Renewal (KEN)
–	Minorities' lists connected with the Alignment
–	Other lists

Source: Central Bureau of Statistics, *Statistical Abstract of Israel, 2009*, Table 10.01, "Elections and the Knesset: Legend to Tables 10.1–10.3," www1.cbs.gov.il/reader/shnaton/templ_shnaton_e.html?num_tab=st10_001&CYear=2009, accessed January 2010.

are based in labor and Zionist ideology, and it was founded by the same two groups that founded the *Histadrut*, the national labor federation; these groups were the *Ahdut HaAvodah* ("Unity of Labor") and *HaPoel HaTzair* ("Young Labor").

   Ahdut HaAvodah itself had a long history, tracing its roots back to 1919 when it was created from the *Poalei Tziyon* ("Workers of Zion"); *HaPoel HaTzair* was active in Palestine from 1905 to 1930 and was a leading force in building Jewish settlements in the area. Mapai was the dominant partner in the Labor Party after its creation in 1968 from the merger of Mapai, *Ahdut HaAvodah*, and Rafi. Rafi, an acronym for the *Reshuma Poaeli Israel* ("Israel Labor List"), had been created in 1965 when David Ben-Gurion and some of his supporters left Mapai after a disagreement over a policy issue. In 1968 most of those who left (but not, it should be noted, Ben-Gurion) returned to Mapai and along with *Ahdut HaAvodah* created the Labor Party.

From 1968 to 1974 the Labor Party's formal party positions were distributed on the basis of 57.3 percent for Mapai and 21.3 percent each to *Ahdut HaAvodah* and Rafi; after 1974 (when Yitzhak Rabin, Shimon Peres, and Yigal Allon were leaders of the three factions and agreed to truly merge them), Labor absorbed the three formative groups entirely. Between 1969 and 1984 Labor and Mapam, an acronym for *Mifleget Poaeli Meuchedet* ("United Workers' Party"), joined together to form the *Maarach*, or "Alignment." Mapam had been created in 1948 from the merger of two kibbutz-related political parties, *HaShomer HaTzair* ("The Young Watchman," founded in 1913) and *Ahdut HaAvodah* (some of which left in 1954 to become independent again). After 1984, in protest of the Alignment's joining the Likud in a national unity government, Mapam left the Alignment and continued as an independent party.

Labor has lost much of its strength in the years since it was assumed to be the only option for the government of Israel. Since 1977 it has continued to decline, winning only thirteen seats in the elections for the Eighteenth Knesset and likely not surviving the current Knesset in its present form; various suggestions are being made by its Knesset leaders for party division.

Meretz was founded in 1992 by a union of the Citizens' Rights Movement (CRM), Mapam, and *Shinui*. Shulamit Aloni, an MK from the Labor Party, created the CRM in 1973. The CRM put great emphasis on civil rights and was willing to make more compromises on Palestinian-related issues than was the Labor Party at the time. The focus of *Meretz*'s ideology is on human rights, and thereby *Meretz* has been associated with the peace process because it has championed Arab rights as well as Jewish rights. In the elections for the Eighteenth Knesset, *Meretz* won three seats.

The Center and Right Blocs[29]

The *Kadima* party is relatively new on the national scene. Toward the end of the Sixteenth Knesset, a new parliamentary group, *Achrayut Leumit* (which means "National Responsibility"), split off from the Likud party. Approximately two months later, *Achrayut Leumit* changed its name to *Kadima*, the name of its parallel political party outside of the Knesset. *Kadima* entered the Seventeenth Knesset with the largest number of seats (twenty-nine), and won twenty-eight seats in the election for the Eighteenth Knesset.

The *Likud* ("Union") was created at the time of the 1973 election when the Free Center Party and the Gahal bloc merged. The Free Center had been a bloc of the *Herut* ("Freedom") Party that had broken away in 1967, only to rejoin in a new form with its former partners in 1973. (The Free Center later left the Likud in 1977 and joined the reform party the DMC.) Gahal actually was another acronym, deriving from *Gush Herut Liberalim*, or *Herut*-Liberal Bloc, that was created in 1965 by *Herut* and the Liberal Party to compete more effectively in the Mapai-dominated party system. The Liberal Party was formed in 1961 from a merger of the Progressive Party and the General Zionist Party, both of which dated from before the creation of the state. *Herut* was a right-wing party founded by those who had been active in the *Irgun* in the prestate years, with an ideology based upon revisionist Zionism. *Herut* became the dominant component in the Likud, and since 1977 the *Herut*-Likud bloc on the right has been the basis of most Israeli governments, committed to a diminution of government regulation in the economy, fewer concessions to the Palestinians, and strong security concerns. It is significantly reliant on a Sephardic constituency to stay in power.

The **National Union Party** (*Halchud HaLeumi*) was created in 1999 and is itself a right-wing coalition that includes former members of *Herut*, and other right-wing parties. The platform of the party emphasizes that the land of Israel is the homeland of the Jewish people. In the elections for the Seventeenth Knesset, *Ichud Leumi* ran together with the National Religious Party (Mafdal), but that alignment did not continue into the elections for the Eighteenth Knesset when the two parties split and ran independently. The National Unity Party won four seats in the elections for the Eighteenth Knesset.

Israel Our Home (*Yisrael Beiteinu*) is a new party created before the 1999 elections with the specific goal of drawing support from new Russian-speaking immigrants. The founder of the party, Avigdor Liberman, was director general for former prime minister Benjamin Netanyahu and was a supporter of the Likud Party. He believed that forming a new party would draw more support from the new Russian immigrants than would simply waiting for them to come to the Likud. In the course of the Fifteenth Knesset, *Yisrael Beiteinu* merged with the *Ichud Hale'umi*, forming the *Ichud-Hale'umi–Yisrael Beiteinu* parliamentary group. In the elections for the Sixteenth Knesset, *Yisrael Beiteinu* was part of the *Ichud Haleumi* list. In the elections for the Seventeenth Knesset, *Yisrael Beiteinu* ran as an independent list and won eleven Knesset seats. It won fifteen seats in the elections for the Eighteenth Knesset.

The Religious Parties[30]

The **National Religious Party** (NRP), also known as Mafdal, an acronym for *Mifleget Ha Datit Leumit* ("National Religious Party"), was created in 1956 by the merger of *HaPoel HaMizrahi* ("Eastern Workers," established in 1922 as an Orthodox religious workers' party) and *Mizrahi* ("Eastern," established in 1902 as an Orthodox religious Zionist party). In 1949 *Mizrahi* joined with other religious parties to form the United Religious Front. Between

1948 and 1977, the NRP allied with Labor in coalition governments, in return for which it continually controlled the Ministry of Religious Affairs. Until 1981 the NRP fairly regularly drew about 10 percent of the vote and received about twelve seats in the Knesset; after that time there were other religious parties, and the NRP contingent in the Knesset was significantly smaller. In the elections for the Eighteenth Knesset, the National Religious Party ran under a new name, *Habayit Hayehudi* ("The Jewish Home"): the New Mafdal. It won three Knesset seats.

Shas, or Sephardic Torah Guardians, was created as a religious and theocratic party in 1984 by some former members of the *Agudat Israel* ("Society of Israel") organization as a protest against the peripheral representation of Sephardic Jews within the *Agudat Israel* party list. *Shas* is really a Sephardic copy of the Orthodox *Agudat Israel*, which was founded in Poland in 1912 and reestablished in Palestine in the 1920s. In 1949 *Agudat Israel* joined with *Mizrahi* to be part of the United Religious Front, and between 1955 and 1959 it operated with *Poalei Agudat Israei* ("Workers' Society of Israel") as the Torah Religious Front. The Torah Religious Front broke up prior to the 1961 election. *Agudat Israel* was a non-Zionist party directed by an Orthodox religious Council of Torah Sages whose primary function was religious, not political. *Shas* became a major party only in recent years when the primarily Ashkenazic-dominated *Agudat* bloc refocused its attention on Orthodox Sephardic Jews, whose support for *Shas* has turned it into the third largest party in Israel today. One of its major goals is to repair the alleged continued economic and social discrimination against the Sephardic population of Israel. *Shas* today is considered a party for the ultraorthodox Sephardim; most Ashkenazic ultraorthodox have chosen to support the United Torah Judaism (*Yahdut HaTorah*) Party. *Shas* won eleven seats in the elections for the Eighteenth Knesset.

United Torah Judaism (UTJ) is a coalition of two ultraorthodox religious parties, *Agudat Israel* (see the discussion of *Shas* above) and *Degel HaTorah* ("Flag of the Torah"). *Degel HaTorah* was formed in 1988 and is an Ashkenazic spin-off of *Shas*. UTJ won five seats in the election for the Eighteenth Knesset.

Far Left, Communist, and Arab Parties[31]

Hadash is the name adopted by the New Communist List (*Rakach*) toward the end of the Eighth Knesset, after the party outside the Knesset was joined by other left-wing noncommunist groups. From its inception *Hadash* advocated a complete Israeli withdrawal from the territories occupied in 1967, recognition of the Palestinian Liberation Organization (PLO), and the establishment of a Palestinian state alongside Israel, in addition to full equality for Israel's Arab citizens. In 1949 the Communist Party of Israel, or Maki, the acronym for *Mifleget Kommunistit Yisraeli* ("Israel Communist Party"), was created, and in 1965 it broke into two factions, Maki and Rakah. Maki continued to be primarily Jewish, while Rakah, an acronym for *Reshuma Kommunistit Hadash* ("New Communist List") was mostly made up of Arab Communist supporters. *Hadash*, which is a Jewish and Arab party, ran for the Ninth, Tenth, Thirteenth, and Fifteenth Knessets under this name. In elections for the Eleventh, Twelfth, Fourteenth, and Sixteenth Knessets, *Hadash* ran under joint names together with other parties. In the elections for the Eighteenth Knesset *Hadash* won four Knesset seats.

The **United Arab List** (UAL) is a coalition of the Arab Democratic Party and other small Islamic organizations in Israel. The Arab Democratic Party was created in 1988 and has focused on equality for Arab-Israelis and Israeli withdrawal from the West Bank. The primary focus of the UAL is the creation of a Palestinian state and the removal of all Israeli settlements in the West Bank and Gaza areas. In the elections for the Seventeenth Knesset, the United Arab List and the Arab Movement for Renewal ran together as a united list and won four Knesset seats. It won four seats again in the elections for the Eighteenth Knesset.

Table 6.3 Parties Winning Seats in the Elections for the Eighteenth Knesset, 2009

Party List Name	Percentage of Vote	Number of Seats Won	Percentage of Seats Won
Kadima	22.4	28	23.3
Likud	21.6	27	22.5
Yisrael Beytenu	11.7	15	12.5
Labor	9.9	13	10.8
Shas	8.5	11	9.2
United Torah Judaism	4.4	5	4.2
United Arab List	3.4	4	3.3
National Union	3.3	4	3.3
Hadash	3.3	4	3.3
Meretz and The New Movement	3.0	3	2.5
Habayit HaYehudi–New National Religious Party (NRP)	2.9	3	2.5
Balad	2.5	3	2.5
Total	96.9	120	99.9

Note:
Voter Turnout: 65.2%
Number of Votes Cast: 3,416,587
Number of Valid Votes: 3,373,490

Source: Israel Ministry of Foreign Affairs Web page, "Elections in Israel–February 2009," www.mfa.gov.il/MFA/History/Modern+History/Historic+Events/Elections_in_Israel_February_2009.htm, accessed January 2010.

Balad, the National Democratic Alliance, is one of Israel's major Arab parties. It is called "Balad" because of the acronym of its name in Hebrew. It advocates Israel's turning into "a state of all its citizens," the return of Arab refugees from 1948 and 1967, Israel's withdrawal to 1967 borders, and the creation of a Palestinian state. Balad was made up of a variety of factions, including the Arab Movement for Change, created in 1996. It ran for the Fourteenth Knesset in a joint list with the Democratic Front for Peace and Equality (*Hadash*). Toward the end of the Fourteenth Knesset, its two members broke away from *Hadash*-Balad and formed an independent parliamentary group. Balad received two seats in the Fifteenth Knesset, and three seats in the Sixteenth Knesset. It won three seats in the Eighteenth Knesset.

What we see in this brief examination of the Israeli party system is an almost bewildering array of political opinions and options, represented by many parties in the Eighteenth Knesset, as shown in table 6.3. The nature of the electoral system tends to permit—even encourage—a proliferation of what we can call maverick parties. It is relatively easy for a well-known political leader with a solid base of support to break away from his former party and to form a party of his own, with little that is ideologically new, just with himself or herself as the party head. This is precisely why it is difficult to pinpoint the differences in substance between many of the parties, as often there are very few substantive differences involved. What we find is a series of personal followings that form individual parties that then establish coalition blocs on the basis of ideology and programmatic preference.

INTEREST GROUPS

Interest groups are commonly defined as collections of like-minded individuals. There are many different kinds of interest groups, some highly organized, others less so. Some are large, such as organizations for Russian Jewish immigrants; others are smaller, such as groups for pensioners' rights. Regardless of their size or level of organization, interest groups are important because of the manner in which they can influence the behavior of a Government.[32] Not only do interest groups communicate the views of the public, they also help to communicate the views of the Government back to different segments of the public. Thereby, interest groups serve as linkage mechanisms in the democratic machinery of government.[33] It should be noted, however, that interest groups in Israel do not have the level of activity or importance that they do in many other democratic polities because many of the most important functions performed by interest groups elsewhere are performed by the political party organizations in Israel. In a sense, then, political parties have essentially usurped many of the roles traditionally played by interest groups.

Not all of the specialized parties have been as successful as others, however. To take only one example, the party focused on pensioners was not successful in the election of 1999 because not enough of its target membership was willing to forsake other interests to cast their votes for the pensioners' party; they apparently preferred to vote based upon their other interests. A study of that election showed that if only 10 percent of those who ostensibly would have had an interest in the issues of that party—those aged sixty-five or older—had voted for the party, the party would have elected two MKs in the election of 1999. Instead, it received less than 1.5 percent of the total vote and received no representation in the Knesset.[34]

The largest single interest group in Israel is labor, the largest organization of which is the *Histadrut*, or General Federation of Workers, which was established in 1920.[35] The *Histadrut* is often referred to as a national labor union, but it is much more than that. It owns, builds, rents, and sells property, runs housing projects, administers medical clinics, owns newspapers and publishing houses, supervises schools, and in general is responsible for a wide range of social services. Through the 1977 Knesset election—that is, as long as the Labor Party dominated Government coalitions—the *Histadrut* had very strong and close ties with the Government. Primarily this was achieved through an explicit overlap (or interlocking directorate) of personnel in leadership positions of each. In the process, *Histadrut* actually inspired many important pieces of legislation dealing with labor and employment, such as the Hours of Work and Rest Law, the Youth Employment Law, and the Labor Exchange Law.[36]

Another interest group that must be considered when examining Israeli politics is the military. The study of civil-military relations has demonstrated that the military does influence public policy in Israel.[37] Since an overwhelming percentage of Israel's adult population is either on active service or in the reserves, opinions of the military have a way of finding their way into politics. This is particularly noticeable when one examines the political recruitment process. There has been no shortage of examples—Dayan, Rabin, Weizman, Barak, Sharon—of individuals who have achieved fame through their military exploits, then have exchanged that fame for a position on a party's electoral list or have simply gone out and formed their own political party. On the whole, studies of Israeli army officers "have indicated that their political attitudes and orientations are as diverse as those of the population at large. They do not constitute a distinct or separate ideological bloc."[38]

International Jewry constitutes yet a third group that exercises an influence in Israeli politics. Diaspora Jewry has on many occasions expressed its policy preferences through a variety of mechanisms, including formal organizations such as the Jewish Agency, the World Zionist Organization, and the American Jewish Committee, as well as through direct communication between Jews in the Diaspora and Israeli politicians. It is clear that international Jewry was very important in terms of its response to the 1988 election in which its American component (at least) exerted great pressure on Yitzhak Shamir to deter him from forming a Likud-Orthodox coalition in a fashion that would force a ruling on the "Who is a Jew?" question. The eruption of this long-simmering controversy—with the Orthodox parties wanting Mr. Shamir to introduce legislation recognizing only Orthodox Jewish conversions and marriages, among other rituals—generated a tremendous amount of concern in Jewish communities outside of Israel and is an excellent case study of how overseas Jewish communities can influence domestic Israeli politics.

The fact of the matter is that the Israeli government receives a great deal of money through these international interest groups and thus is very sensitive about avoiding actions that might cause an erosion of this international support. For example, "Because of the prestige and wealth of its members, the American Jewish Committee has been especially cultivated by Israel's leaders. It is the only private organization with which the Israeli government has reached a quasi-official agreement defining a 'proper' relationship with diaspora Jewry."[39]

Finally, but not least, specific ethnic groups have begun to influence government policy in a direct way.[40] For many years, as we have already noted, the Ashkenazic group of the Israeli population dominated the political arena. Sephardic Jews were a substantial minority in Israel (even approaching majority status) but were systematically excluded from positions of leadership in the party organizations, governmental bureaucracy, and elected positions. In recent years the Sephardic groups in the Israeli population have begun to speak out, to organize, and to lobby in their own interest. Their common interests and platforms seek equal opportunity, based on the claim that they have not had the educational and career opportunities of other segments of society, nor all of the concomitant benefits that such opportunities provide. We have already seen how new political parties such as *Shas* have been created specifically to represent the interests of the Sephardim.

Shas, it must be noted, is a special kind of organization that is both an interest group and a political party. *Shas* is clearly a Sephardic religious political party, but it has been far more successful than others of its type by seeking to be integrative rather than separatist in its approach to the political world. It has tried to establish itself as a vehicle for drawing the disenfranchised into the political world and has been quite successful in doing this.[41]

A result of this activism by Sephardic groups is that the larger parties, especially Labor and Likud, have been compelled to increase their overtures to the Sephardim. Likud recognized prior to the 1977 election that the Sephardim were an untouched electoral resource, and it became identified as the party of Sephardic interests. Labor, in recent years, has tried to make inroads in this Likud constituency and some progress has been made. In brief, the Sephardim have been recognized as a significant interest group and are now receiving the kind of electoral attention that they felt in the past they deserved.

Arab political organizations are another category of interest group that has increased in visibility and significance in Israeli politics in recent years. For many years Arab interest groups were fundamentally invisible in Israeli politics. In more recent times, for reasons that are both obvious and unfortunate, Arab visibility in Israeli society has become much more significant and contentious; until the recent breakdown in civil relations between Israeli Jews and many groups of Israeli Arabs, there were some indications that Arab interest groups were becoming more effective in pressing their causes. Increased violence has changed this, and some Israelis argue that peace is not possible until Arabs are fully integrated into Israeli society and politics, while others argue that Arabs will never be welcomed into Israeli society and politics and that peace will not be possible until Arabs are fully separated from Israeli society. These arguments, sadly, are very much the same types of arguments that history has seen in different places at different times related to long-term violence and political instability, such as India with Hindus and Muslims, South Africa with black and white South Africans, Ireland with Catholics and Protestants, and the like. Arab interest groups have become increasingly organized and vocal in recent years and will likely continue to be more visible and more included in the political process.[42]

The Knesset has been a high-priority target for much lobbying in Israeli politics, and some have been concerned about the ethics and legality of much interest group behavior.[43] This has been increasingly discussed in the Israeli political arena, and the Government has paid particular attention to challenges caused by these concerns.[44]

FOR FURTHER READING

Ben-Meir, Yehuda. *Civil-Military Relations in Israel.* New York: Columbia University Press, 1995.

Cohen, Ra'anan. *Strangers in Their Homeland: A Critical Study of Israel's Arab Citizens.* Portland, Ore.: Sussex Academic Press, 2009.

Hazan, Reuven, and M. Benjamin Mollov, eds. *Israel at the Polls, 1999.* Portland, Ore.: Frank Cass, 2001.

Hazan, Reuven, and Gideon Rahat. *Democracy within Parties: Candidate Selection Methods and Their Political Consequences.* New York: Oxford University Press, 2010.

———. *Israeli Party Politics: New Approaches, New Perspectives.* London: Sage Publications, 2008.

Sharkansky, Ira. *The Politics of Religion and the Religion of Politics: Looking at Israel.* Lanham, Md.: Lexington Books, 2000.

Sprinzak, Ehud, and Larry Diamond, eds. *Israeli Democracy under Stress.* Boulder, Colo.: Lynne Rienner, 1993.

Sternhell, Zeev. *The Founding Myths of Israel: Nationalism, Socialism, and the Making of the Jewish State*. Princeton, N.J.: Princeton University Press, 1998.

Tepe, Sultan. *Beyond Sacred and Secular: Politics of Religion in Israel and Turkey*. Stanford, Calif.: Stanford University Press, 2008.

Troen, Ilan, and Noah Lucas, eds. *Israel: The First Decade of Independence*. Albany: State University of New York Press, 1995.

Van Creveld, Martin. *The Sword and the Olive: A Critical History of the Israeli Defense Force*. Oxford, U.K.: Perseus, 1999.

7

The Electoral Process
and Voting Behavior

While parties and interest groups are of great importance to an understanding of how Israeli politics operates, they cannot be understood without knowledge of the rules of the game, how they are expected (and permitted) to behave in the polity. Israel's proportional representation electoral system for Knesset elections and, in 1992, the temporary addition of a direct election for the prime minister, followed less than a decade later by a return to the original model of elections, have made elections in Israel consistently problematic. This chapter discusses key factors influencing election outcomes and examines trends in recent elections to understand the significance of the electoral framework for Israeli voting behavior and Israeli politics more generally construed.

A voter casting a ballot in the February 2009 election

THE ELECTORAL SYSTEM AND ISRAELI VOTING BEHAVIOR

The electoral system of any country is very important in terms of both its role in the selection of political leaders and its influence on the nature and style of political discussion and activity. This is clearly the case in Israel, where the electoral system itself promotes such diverse and even contradictory phenomena as a splintering of established political parties, strict party discipline, and close overall control of individual legislators within the separate party organizations. Indeed, as we noted in the last chapter, the very nature of the Israeli electoral system is often credited with being the prime reason there are so many political parties. There are few institutional incentives for factionalized parties to remain together and many for groups with a moderate amount of popular support to break away from parent political organizations and run for office under their own banners.

Conversely, individuals who do not wish to break away are left in a very vulnerable position in relation to their party leaders, for party leaders can use the electoral system as a lever—or a threat—to remind the rank and file that they would do better to act in a manner consistent with party guidelines or face the consequences. Not surprisingly, then, there have been numerous calls for reform of the Israeli electoral system over the years and, as we have already noted, a major reform of the electoral system (involving the direct election of the prime minister) was enacted by the Knesset in 1992 and came into effect in 1996, only to be repealed in 2001!

PROPORTIONAL REPRESENTATION AND ELECTIONS

Maurice Duverger, a French political scientist, once wrote that there is a direct relationship between the electoral system of a nation and the number and nature of political parties that exist in it. More specifically, Duverger wrote that proportional representation elections lead to multiple political parties.[1] That is certainly the case in Israel.

Israeli elections must be held *at least* every four years. In other words, although the maximum term of any single elected Knesset is four years, the Knesset may vote to dissolve itself prior to the normal expiration of its term and call for new elections. Unlike the situation in other parliamentary systems, however, only the Knesset, not the head of state—such as the queen in England—has the power to dissolve the Knesset prior to the expiration of its legislated term of office. On a number of occasions in Israeli history, the term of a Knesset has been less than four years, including most recently the term following the 1996 election, when new elections were held in 1999; on two occasions (1949–1951 and 1959–1961) it was less than three years.

The Fundamental Law: The Knesset says that "the Knesset shall be elected in general, national, direct, equal, secret, and proportional elections."[2] This means, in practice, that all citizens eighteen years of age or older can vote. The actual electoral system employs a single-ballot, national constituency, proportional representation electoral framework.[3] That is, the whole country is considered a single electoral district, and each voter casts his or her vote for the party whose platform and candidates he or she most prefers. The percentage of votes received by each party in the national election determines the percentage of seats it will accordingly receive in the Knesset.

Parties receiving at least 2 percent of the vote are entitled to representation. Parties receiving fewer votes than this threshold receive no Knesset representation.[4] The total number of votes in the election (minus the votes going to parties that receive less than the 2-percent threshold) is divided by 120, the total number of seats in the Knesset, thereby establishing a "key." When the Knesset seats are distributed in this way, there are typically as many as ten or fifteen seats remaining as a consequence of rounding and remainders from the division process. Seats remaining in the Knesset after the initial assignment are then distributed, in a process that appears quite complex but in actuality is not that hard to understand, among parties with high numbers of "surplus votes." The process, which has been used in Israel since 1973, is called the d'Hondt system, named after the Belgian who devised it; in Israel the d'Hondt system is referred to as the "Bader-Ofer System," named after the two members of Parliament who introduced the distribution system to Israel.[5]

For many years seats were awarded purely on the basis of the size of the remainders. This, in fact, sometimes permitted parties that had not even won a single seat to win a surplus seat because they had higher remainders (in this case, a remainder after zero seats and before one seat) than the more established parties (perhaps with more votes than needed for thirty-two seats, but not quite enough votes for thirty-three seats). The Bader-Ofer formula does not allow this and is said to favor the larger parties slightly.

This system does not necessarily give surplus Knesset seats to the largest parties or to the parties with the largest remainders, but instead puts a premium on the base of party support. The idea here is that "a party supported by a million voters must be treated differently from a party supported by 20,000 voters."[6]

The operation of the Bader-Ofer formula is reflected in table 7.1. The remaining seats are distributed by setting up a table very much like that demonstrated in table 7.1, in which each party's remaining votes are divided in turn by larger and larger divisors. In table 7.1, three hypothetical parties (A, B, and C) have remaining votes of ten thousand, eight thousand, and three thousand, respectively. After the division has taken place, the remaining seats are given, in order, to the largest dividends in the table, so that if there were fifteen remaining seats to be distributed, Party A would win seven of the seats (seats 1, 3, 5, 8, 10, 11, and 14), Party B would win six of the seats (seats 2, 4, 7, 9, 12, and 15), and Party C would win two of the seats (seats 6 and 13), as shown in table 7.2.

During the preelection period, the amount and degree of partisan campaigning reaches intense proportions. Election periods vary in length; when the Knesset passes the act dissolving itself and calling for new elections, it sets the period of the campaign. There is no standard legally mandated period, although campaigns generally tend to last for about eight to ten weeks. The election expenses of Israel's political parties through the 1960s had been among the world's highest.[7] Reform in 1969 led to limitations on overall campaign expenses and increased government oversight of party spending during the election period. Since 1973 Israeli parties have been forbidden

Table 7.1 Surplus Vote Distribution (Bader-Ofer Formula): The Computation Method

	Party A	*Party B*	*Party C*
"Surplus Votes"	10,000	8,000	3,000
Divide by			
1	10,000	8,000	3,000
2	5,000	4,000	1,500
3	3,333	2,666	1,000
4	2,500	2,000	750
5	2,000	1,600	600
6	1,666	1,333	500
7	1,428	1,142	428
8	1,250	1,000	375

Table 7.2 Surplus Vote Distribution (Bader-Ofer Formula): The Awarding of Extra Seats

	Party A	*Party B*	*Party C*
"Surplus Votes"	10,000	8,000	3,000
Divide by			
1	(1) 10,000	(2) 8,000	(6) 3,000
2	(3) 5,000	(4) 4,000	(13) 1,500
3	(5) 3,333	(7) 2,666	1,000
4	(8) 2,500	(9) 2,000	750
5	(10) 2,000	(12) 1,600	600
6	(11) 1,666	(15) 1,333	500
7	(14) 1,428	1,142	428
8	1,250	1,000	375
Total "Extra" Seats Won	7	6	2

from receiving corporate contributions.[8] Parties are given free time on television and radio for campaigning, and those that already control seats in the Knesset are given substantial allowances for the electoral campaign based upon the number of seats they control in the Knesset at the time.[9]

The role of the media has changed over time. The media are now being recognized in the scholarly literature as playing a significant role in Israeli campaigns, and the role of the Central Elections Committee is reflected in box 7.1.[10] During the last month of the campaign each party list is allocated ten free minutes of television prime time each evening, six nights a week, and parties already represented in the Knesset receive an additional four free minutes per seat they controlled in the previous Knesset.

Opinion about the quality and level of argument presented in these advertisements varies, however, to such an extent that one wonders if the editorial writers were in the same country watching the same television![11] Yeshayahu Ben-Porat wrote in an editorial in one major newspaper, "Most, if not all of the party telecasts constitute an insult to the intelligence. They are based on the assumption that the average voter is an infantile imbecile, whose vote will be determined by some jingle or electronic or graphic stunt taken from the world of video pacman games" (*Yediot Aharonot*, October 9, 1988). Avraham Schweitzer wrote in another editorial,

A few words should be said in praise of the telecast war. Labor, the Likud, Tehiya, the CRM—and even the representatives on earth of God Almighty, the religious parties—are all addressing the issues. Observers of the American presidential election are complaining about the absence or extreme paucity of substantive issues in the campaigns of Bush and Dukakis. That is not the case in Israel (*Ha'aretz*, October 7, 1988).

There is no doubt that the television campaign adds an extra dimension to the campaign. The question is, Is the extra dimension a positive one or a negative one?[12]

During the campaign, walls are covered with party advertisements, while rallies and speeches abound. All registered voters are mailed an official government publication, prepared by the Central Elections Committee, which contains information provided by all political parties that have lists of candidates on file with the Election Bureau. This Central Elections Committee is made up of MKs' parties in proportion to their strength.

Lists of candidates for Knesset elections may be submitted either by a party that is already represented or by a group of 2,500 qualified voters.[13] In 1948 the requirement was for a group of 250 qualified voters. This was raised to 750 in 1951, and it has steadily increased ever since.[14] Individuals whose names are on party lists must write to the Central Elections Committee and accept their nominations. In order to submit lists of candidates to the voters, new parties must deposit a sum of money with the Central

Box 7.1.   Announcements of the Central Elections Committee in the Special Prime Ministerial Election, 2001

The broadcasting schedule of the campaign for the special elections for prime minister, as decided on by the Central Elections Committee Plenum:

At their first meeting on Sunday, December 31st, 2000, the Central Elections Committee for the 16th Knesset and for prime minister, chaired by Supreme Court Judge Mishael Heshin, determined the broadcasting schedule for the election campaign on television and radio, to begin on Tuesday, January 16, 2001.

Representatives of the political parties and the Israel Broadcasting Authority reached agreement on the broadcasting schedule of the campaign on television (Channel 1) and radio.

However, the representatives of the political parties, of Channel 2 and of the broadcasting licensees did not reach an agreement as to the schedule for campaign broadcasts on Channel 2.

The representatives of Channel 2 and the broadcasting licensees requested that the broadcasting of the election campaign on Channel 2 be between 19:00–19:15 or 19:35–19:55. They claimed that otherwise the broadcasting schedule would be severely damaged.

The representatives of the parties, MK Ophir Pines (One Israel) and MK Michael Eitan (Likud) demanded that the election broadcasts on Channel 2 be between 20:35–20:55.

No agreement was reached between the sides, despite the intervention of the chairman of the Central Elections Committee. Judge Mishael Heshin therefore decided that the campaign broadcasts on Channel 2 take place Sunday through Thursday between 19:35–19:55.

. . .

Judge Mishael Heshin wrote in his decision: "I have based my decision on my colleagues' considerations as well as my own. I will say further that time is short and for this reason also—particularly for this reason—I will not elaborate as did my colleagues in their decisions."

The campaign broadcasts will begin on Tuesday, January 16, 2001 and will end on Monday, February 5th, 2001 at 19:00.

Each candidate for prime minister will be allowed 120 minutes for radio broadcast, 120 minutes for television broadcast on Channel 1, and 120 minutes on Channel 2.

It was further decided that each television broadcast in Hebrew will be not shorter than two minutes and will not exceed five minutes, and in Arabic will be not shorter than one minute and will not exceed five minutes.

Each radio broadcast in Hebrew, Arabic and Russian will be not less than two minutes and will not exceed five minutes.

Source: State of Israel, Knesset Web page, "Elections for the Prime Minister 2001: Central Elections Committee Announcements," www.knesset.gov.il/elections01/eannouncements.htm, accessed May 2010.

Elections Committee.[15] If the party wins at least one seat, its deposit is returned; if not, it forfeits a portion. This is designed to discourage truly unrealistic parties from campaigning. But it is clear from the number of parties that compete in Knesset elections that this desire does not stop new parties from forming.

Many of the serious parties submit lists with 120 names on them, one for each possible seat in the Knesset, even though the parties know that no single party will win 100 percent of the vote. Smaller parties and the unrealistic parties often submit smaller lists with fewer names, realizing that there is no point in their putting forward 120 names (see figure 7.1). Sometimes even the smaller parties surprise themselves, though. In the Eighth Knesset election of 1973, for example, the Citizen's Rights Movement, started by a former Mapai parliamentarian, submitted a list with only five names to the electorate, not really expecting that the party would win enough votes for even the first name on the list to be given a seat. To the surprise of many, the party won enough votes for the first three names on the party list to be given seats in the Knesset.

Some parties today use primary elections to determine the composition of their electoral lists, while others use national conventions. In the period leading up to the national elections for the Eighteenth Knesset in Febru-

Photo 7.1.   A list of all of the party ballots in the February 2009 election. Voters select a ballot with the symbol of the party that they prefer, and they place that ballot in the ballot box.

רשימות המועמדים לכנסת השמונה עשרה

לפי חוק הבחירות לכנסת [נוסח משולב], התשכ"ט-1969

בהתאם לסעיף 65 לחוק הבחירות לכנסת [נוסח משולב], התשכ"ט-1969', מתפרסמות בזה רשימות המועמדים לכנסת השמונה עשרה כפי שאושרו:

אות הרשימה : אמת

כינוי הרשימה : העבודה בראשות אהוד ברק

שם פרטי	שם משפחה	מס'	שם פרטי	שם משפחה	מס'	שם פרטי	שם משפחה	מס'
אופיר	פינס-פז	3	יצחק	הרצוג	2	אהוד	ברק	1
מתן	וילנאי	6	שלי רחל	יחימוביץ	5	אבישי	ברורמן	4
יולי	תמיר	9	בנימין פואד	בן אליעזר	8	איתן	כבל	7
שלום	שמחון	12	דניאל	בן סימון	11	ארמונד עמיר	פרץ	10
גאלב	מגדלה	15	עינת	וילף	14	אורית עירית	נוקד	13
לאון	ליטינצקי	18	יורם	מרציאנו	17	שכיב	שנאן	16
יוסף	סולימני	21	משה	סמיה	20	קולט	אביטל	19
מנחם	ליבוביץ	24	אבי	חזקיהו	23	אריק	חדר	22
עזי	גנר	27	יואב	חי	26	עפר	קורנפלד	25
נאדיה	חילו	30	אבי	שקד	29	בנימין	לוין	28
רות	דיין מדר	33	יריב	אופנהיימר	32	שמעון	שטרית	31
אמנון	זילברמן	36	דנה	אורן	35	אסתר	ביתן	34
מיקי	גולד	39	יעקב	רומי	38	ואפד	קבלאן	37
מעין	אמודאי	42	ולדימיר	סברדלוב	41	מאיר	וייס	40
זאב-ולולה	שור	45	ניקולא	מסעד	44	פייצל	אלהזייל	43
פהים	גאנם	48	אמנון	זך	47	אהרון	קראוס	46
הדסה חנה	רוסו	51	חנה	מרשק	50	מוטי	ששון	49
סימון	אלפסי	54	דב	צור	53	אלי	אורן	52
שלומי	וייזר	57	שייע יצחק	ישועה	56	יוסף	וונונו	55
לאה יונה	גבע	60	יוסף	ארבל	59	מישל שלום	חלימי	58
דקל דוד	עוזר	63	יובל	אדמון	62	ארז שלמה	אבו	61
אהרון חי	כהן	66	משה	פרנקל	65	יהונתן	מאייר עזור	64
אליהו	סדן	69	יהודית	הרן	68	אדית	אבוד	67
אברהם	הצמרי	72	אבינועם	טובים	71	רבקה	בית הלחמי	70
שרה	גנסטיל	75	שמעון	קמרי	74	רמי	אזרן	73
נורית	לוי	78	יהודית	אוליאל	77	מוטי	דותן	76
רני	אידן	81	דניאל	עטר	80	יהודה	שביט	79
צפורה	רון	84	אלון נתן	שוסטר	83	מאיר	ויזל	82
עין	שפרמן	87	מעין	סרבר	86	אהרון	ענאקי	85
צבי	איזנברג	90	אומיד	סולימני	89	אור	ורטמן	88
יואב	לוי	93	יהונתן	סבן	92	יפתח	דבוש	91
יחזקאל	אנגלר	96	חנה	בית הלחמי	95	למואל	מלמד	94
חיה	כהן	99	חנה	בן דוד	98	עמרם	לוק	97
יהודה	סעדי	102	מנחם	פרימן	101	יצחק	ירון	100
יוסף	גליצקי	105	שרה	אורי	104	משה	אדמתי	103
שמואל	קלם	108	שאול	רייכמן	107	פדינה	לוין	106
משה	ורטמן	111	שמואל	קשלס	110	שמואל	בצלאלי	109
שלמה	בן עמי	114	עמרם	מצנע	113	גדעון	בן ישראל	112
אברהם בייגה	שוחט	117	אהרון	ידלין	116	שבח	וייס	115
יצחק	נבון	120	אריה לובה	אליאב	119	משה	שחל	118

Figure 7.1. Official Electoral List for the 18th Knesset Elections for the Israel Labor Party. There are 120 names on the list. In the election thirteen members of the Labor Party were elected to the Knesset, starting with party leader Ehud Barak (number 1 in the list). As of July, 2010, two more individuals on the list—number 14, Einat Wilf, and number 15, Raleb Majadele—had entered the Knesset as replacements for two Labor Members of Knesset who had resigned (Ophir Pines-Paz and Yuli Tamir).

ary 2009, the Labor Party primary election took place in December 2008. Nearly sixty thousand registered Labor Party members were eligible to vote in the primary election. Voters had the opportunity to vote for up to eight candidates from the national list, from nineteen who were running; the ten candidates who earned the most votes would occupy slots two to eleven on the slate. In addition, voters would have the opportunity to select one of the relevant regional or sectoral candidates, which would have accounted for most of the following sixteen slots. Some positions on the party list were still "reserved" for specific groups. For example, the twelfth position on the party list "belonged" to the Moshav movement, the thirteenth position on the party list "belonged" to the Kibbutz movement, and the sixteenth position on the list was reserved for a leading Arab member of the party.[16]

The official assignment of seats in the Knesset is determined purely by position on a party list. If a party wins 25 percent of the national vote and is allotted thirty seats in the Knesset (0.25 x 120 seats = 30 seats), the seats are awarded to the first thirty names on the party list. If an MK dies during the term of the Knesset or if a member resigns for some reason, the seat is simply passed along to the next name on the list. The importance of rank order for an individual candidate on the party electoral list immediately becomes clear, then. Since most parties will put a great number of names on their lists that have no realistic chance of being elected, it is crucial to a serious candidate that he or she be placed in as high a position on the party list as possible.[17]

This positioning on electoral lists has a great deal of significance in the Israeli political recruitment process.[18] It also has an equal importance in terms of intraparty and interfactional argument over which individual is placed in which position on the electoral list. In a preelectoral coalition, in which one electoral list is submitted for a number of parties, such as some of the preelectoral alliances discussed in the preceding chapter, one's position on the list is as decisive for the component parties as for the individuals concerned. The positions are determined in a conference of party leaders, the most important party in the alignment receiving the best positions, and so on.

As a general rule, there is no overall formula for the placement of party factions in order on the list. Each position is argued over individually among the parties involved until an agreement is reached. This type of argument can sometimes lead to near crisis for the preelection party alignments. Fundamental Law: The Knesset allows for this kind of party preelectoral agreement, and parties are used to operating in the electoral environment with these arrangements.[19]

Some parties reach a compromise on list positions by determining that there shall be a rotation of office; this is especially frequent in the smaller parties, which can elect only a few members. Occasionally, in the middle of a parliamentary term a member of one small party bloc will resign because of a preelection compact within his party that required him to do so in order that a member of another party faction, who was next on the party list, could assume a seat in the Knesset.[20]

Because their position on the party list is so critical for those who want to advance their political careers, individual Knesset members in parties that do not have primary elections are extremely vulnerable to the party leaders and list makers. The member who is elected from a safe position who is too much of a maverick during the Knesset term, who votes against the party, or who speaks against the party may find his or her position on the next electoral list lowered, perhaps by only one or two positions as a warning, or perhaps more. This ability to lower a member's position on the list puts a real lever in the hands of those who demand party discipline in the Knesset.[21]

Since the assignment of a safe position on the party list, or even the assignment of a marginal position, may be entirely up to the discretion of the party leaders in a given party, a safe position is usually awarded as a prize or a reward for a history of good work and loyalty.[22] The work may involve living on a party kibbutz, working at the party's headquarters in one of the many possible full-time positions, or merely being active in campaign activities. Even being placed in an unrealistic or symbolic position can be seen as an honor for a political neophyte, for it implies that with continued good work and loyalty, a higher list rank and possibly a Knesset seat might eventually be forthcoming. The party list thus becomes a prime tool in the hands of the party leaders for recruiting new members. If leaders see an individual whom they would like to nurture and encourage to become active in the party, they can place him or her in the marginal zone, or slightly below that, with the implicit understanding that better things are to come.

In addition to recruiting individuals with the Knesset list, the party can also use the list strategically to attract groups.[23] The group may serve as the focal point in this process, where the party may offer groups safe or marginal positions on the party list in exchange for party endorsements and support.

The tendency of the large parties to work with primary elections and national conventions has changed the recruitment process in Israel from the way it operated in Israel's early years. Gone are the smoke-filled rooms and intentional symbolic structuring of the party's electoral list—when party leaders would try to include representation of formal groups in visible and symbolic positions—and instead the democratic influence of the primary electoral process has been felt.[24]

To take a recent example, the primary election for the *Kadima* party list took place in September 2008, in anticipation of the February 2009 Knesset election. Tzipi Livni ended up defeating her primary challenger for the party leadership by just more than 1 percent of the vote, leading to threats of lawsuits and involvement of the courts.[25]

All types of groups are represented on the party list, irrespective of how the group candidates are chosen. Local party organizations vie for safe places, as do union organizations, professional associations, ethnic groups, and the like. In recent years the major parties have significantly opened their nomination procedures with primary elections affecting candidates and candidates' positions on the party list, but the basis of group representation has not changed.[26]

PAST PROPOSALS FOR ELECTORAL CHANGE

Over the years many efforts have been undertaken to change the electoral system in Israel, some moderate and some much more extensive, because political leaders have realized that the electoral system as it presently exists has a significant effect upon the election outcome. If Israel had a single-member district electoral arrangement similar to that of the United States, it is doubtful that more than a dozen different political parties would be represented in the Knesset. Accordingly, many Israelis—especially those in the smaller political parties—have steadfastly fought against any proposed change in the structure of the electoral system.

One of the earliest proponents of electoral change was former prime minister David Ben-Gurion. He favored the single-member district as practiced in Britain and the United States, claiming that the Israeli proportional representation system encouraged small factions to break away from larger parties and form new, small parties, which in turn made it more difficult to form stable Government coalitions. In fact, in 1952 Ben-Gurion and the Mapai Party proposed raising the 1 percent threshold necessary to gain representation in the Knesset to 10 percent, a change that would have significantly cut Knesset representation at the time (from fifteen parties to four).[27] In 1958 Ben-Gurion and Mapai spoke out favoring an amendment providing for 120 single-member districts in Israel, but the bill was never passed.[28]

Although there were a number of subsequent and unsuccessful efforts, the next major attempt at reform came in April 1974, when a bill aimed at modifying the party list system was introduced in the Knesset. The bill would have made the Knesset members "more responsive to the wishes of the constituents and would prevent a minority from having the power to distort the wishes of the majority."[29] This proposal, sometimes referred to as the Ya'acobi Proposal (named after its primary advocate, Gad Ya'acobi), is an imaginative proposal worth brief examination here.[30]

Ya'acobi proposed that MKs be elected in two ways: most—90 of the 120—from a modified proportional representation system using eighteen small constituencies, with the rest chosen from a single national district.

One effect of this proposal would have been to raise the vote threshold from 1 percent to 20 percent. Parties receiving less than that would not win seats. This would also very likely have encouraged more preelection alliances between political parties (especially small parties) that knew they could not win sufficient votes alone but felt that in combination with other parties they might stand a chance. An additional favorable result of this system would be that members of the public would now have a stronger sense of who their representatives were.

In the second vote, there would be a single national constituency as there is today, in which the remaining thirty members would be elected at large, and a party winning, say, 10 percent of the at-large vote would receive three seats. This would enable the smaller parties to contest some of the Knesset seats; essentially, there would be a 3.3-percent threshold for these seats since 3.3 percent of the vote would net one at-large seat.

When Ya'acobi's bill was introduced in the Knesset, it barely passed with sixty-one votes. Any bills proposing changes in the electoral system are in fact proposals for amendments to the Fundamental Law: The Knesset (which describes the method of election to the Knesset), and as amendments to a Fundamental Law, in order to pass they require an absolute majority (i.e., at least 61 votes out of 120 possible votes). Since Ya'acobi's bill was a private member's bill, that is, a bill not introduced by a member of the Government (cabinet), when it received its sixty-one votes, it was sent to committee for consideration, and it never reappeared.

A more recent attempt at electoral reform took place in 1977 after the elections for the Ninth Knesset.[31] The Democratic Movement for Change (DMC) had demanded electoral reform as one of its primary campaign platforms, and when Menachem Begin invited them to join his Likud coalition, electoral reform was one of their two requirements for joining the government coalition (they also wanted Begin to appoint the DMC leader as the foreign minister). Since the 1977 election was the first in nearly thirty years in which Mr. Begin's party had emerged victorious, observers predicted that he was hardly likely to agree to change the electoral system that had put him there, which proved to be the case.

In the coalition agreement that the DMC signed with Mr. Begin, the Government agreed to set up a committee of the four coalition partners (Likud, the DMC, the National Religious Party, and *Agudat Israel*) to discuss the topic of electoral reform, although it was widely perceived that this concession was purely symbolic as the price Mr. Begin was willing to pay to broaden the coalition. With two small religious parties on the committee with the Likud, the DMC held no illusions about the likelihood that it could effect changes. The committee commenced to discuss the number of regions into which the country might be divided for district-based representation, but that was as far as the reform move went.

To no one's surprise, the DMC's proposals for electoral reform, which it characterized as central to any reform of Israeli politics, were not put into effect by the Likud Government. The leaders of the DMC knew when they signed the coalition agreement that setting up a committee to study their reform proposal was comparable to putting a cat in the cage to protect the bird; *Agudat Israel* had openly condemned the proposal before the elections, and both Likud and the NRP were skeptical at best.

The theme of electoral reform has continued to receive interest over the years, leading to one significant move in 1988 and another—that ultimately proved temporarily successful—in 1992.[32] In June 1988 the Knesset began to address a bill dealing with electoral reform. The bill proposed two possible ways for changing the Israeli electoral system. The first would divide the country into twenty electoral districts, each electing four MKs, with another forty representatives to be elected by a national proportional representation list system. A second proposal would divide the country into sixty electoral districts, each electing one representative, with the remaining sixty to be elected by a national proportional representation list system as presently exists. Both proposals were strongly opposed by the religious parties, which claimed that "the system would deprive large sections of the electorate of any share of the vote." In the final analysis, the bills were not voted on before the Knesset adjourned for the fall elections.[33]

After the 1988 election the topic of electoral reform received even more attention as a result of the initially unsuccessful efforts of Mr. Shamir and the Likud Party to form a coalition Government. In that event, since the Likud received a plurality of Knesset seats—that is, more than other parties, but less than an absolute majority—the president gave the Likud's leader, Mr. Shamir, three weeks in which to form a coalition. After a great deal of public wrangling, most of which had to do with demands by the small religious parties for an expansion of the role of Orthodox religion in the state in exchange for their support, the three-week period expired without the Likud being able to establish a coalition; Mr. Shamir was simply unwilling to give in to what he felt—and what substantial communities in Israel as well as Jewish communities overseas felt—were unreasonable demands by the Orthodox religious parties.[34]

Mr. Shamir returned to the president and asked for another three-week mandate, arguing that he was sure that he could succeed in a second period. The president gave him a second mandate, but advised him to form another national unity government with the Labor Party, something that both the Likud and the Labor parties had promised their audiences during the campaign that they would not do. The president also advised Mr. Shamir to consider making changes to the electoral system after a coalition was established that would have the effect of limiting in the future the number of small parties represented in the Knesset, something the president felt exacerbated difficulties in the coalition-formation process.

Eventually, fifty-one days after the November 1 Knesset election, Mr. Shamir succeeded in forming a broad Likud–Labor–religious unity government. The entire coalition-formation process brought honor neither upon Mr. Shamir nor upon the system of forming coalitions in Israel. One editorial writer observed,

> The Likud made exorbitant promises to [the religious parties] in order to win their support—and then systematically broke most of them. Had it not made those promises, in the field of religious legislation, settlements, and in ministries, honors and money, they would not have recommended to the President that he name Shamir to form a government, and the President would not have chosen him. Nor could Shamir have expected Labor to agree to join his government without a rotation in the premiership. The unity government could not have arisen on the conditions that it did. The government that did arise was the result of two factors: the Likud's acquiescing in most of the demands of the religious parties, and its breaking of those promises.[35]

THE 1996–2001 ELECTORAL SYSTEM FOR PRIME MINISTER

In 1992 the Knesset did, in fact, change the electoral system to include a dual ballot, with citizens voting for the Knesset by proportional representation on one ballot and directly for the prime minister on another; the Fundamental Law: The Government, in its revised version, separated the election of the prime minister from that of the Knesset.[36] The direct election of the prime minister first took place in Israel simultaneously with the 1996 elections for the Fourteenth Knesset. This amendment of the basic law was proposed originally by four Knesset members following the difficulties in forming a coalition after the elections of the Twelfth Knesset in 1988. The main purpose in changing the law, according to the proposals, was to strengthen the position of the prime minister and avoid the need for political horse-trading in order to form the coalition and Government.

The new law stated that the prime minister must be elected by more than 50 percent of the valid votes cast. If more than one candidate ran for the office of prime minister and none of the candidates won the required majority, a second round of elections would take place with the two candidates who received the largest number of votes. In the second round, the candidate who received a majority of the votes would become prime minister.

The newly elected (directly elected) prime minister would have forty-five days in which to create a majority coalition in the Knesset to support his or her Government, assuming that no single party received a majority in the Knesset. In addition, sixty-one Knesset members could bring the prime minister down in a vote of no confidence, thereby bringing about his or her resignation and early elections for the Knesset and prime minister. The same situation could also result from the following conditions: a decision of the prime minister to dissolve the Knesset, a resolution by the Knesset to dissolve itself, or failure to pass the annual budget law by the end of March of the new fiscal year.

As described in the previous chapter, because of dissatisfaction with the unintended consequences of the new electoral system—specifically the increase in support for small parties in the Knesset and the decrease in support for the previously dominant parties—many MKs supported changing the new electoral system back to its previous form. Indeed, immediately following the 1996 elections—the first election using the new system— MKs Yossi Beilin and Uzi Landau (two of the authors of the new system) initiated a bill to cancel the direct election of the prime minister and return to the system of elections used previously. Their justification for this move was the overall weakening of the Knesset and specifically of the two largest parties. Their proposal didn't pass, but in 2001 the Knesset did decide to go back to the previous electoral system; the national election of 2003 took place under the old system, with a single election held for the Knesset and the prime minister selected from among the newly elected MKs.[37]

VOTING BEHAVIOR AND ELECTORAL RESULTS

This is not the place for a comprehensive analysis of voting behavior in all of the eighteen Knesset elections. That has been done more than adequately elsewhere.[38] Our task here is to highlight some of the major themes that have been brought to light in the substantial scholarship in this area.

To begin with, overall voter turnout in Israel is high. It has ranged from a high of 86.8 percent in 1949 for the first Knesset election, to a low of 63.5 percent in 2009, with an average of about 80 percent. Turnout in 1999 was 78.7 percent, in 2003 turnout was 67.8 percent, in 2006 it was 63.5, and in 2009 it was 64.7 percent.[39] Patterns of voting turnout are shown in figure 7.2.

Even the voting turnout over time of the Bedouin voters in Israel is slightly more than 64 percent, lower than most other groups in Israel but certainly much higher than the usual American figure. One interesting difference between Jewish Israeli voting patterns and non-Jewish Israeli voting patterns has appeared in recent research: they differ significantly in their motivations for *non*participation. That is, citizens who could vote but choose *not* to vote do so for different reasons. Few Jewish Israelis fail to vote for ideological or political reasons, and their responses to interview questions indicated that when they failed to vote, it tended to be because of rea-

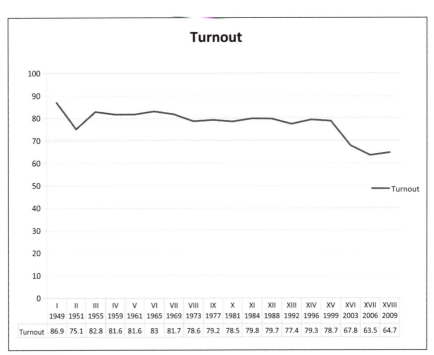

Figure 7.2.   Trends in Israeli Voting Participation, 1949–2009
Source: Central Bureau of Statistics, *Statistical Abstract of Israel*, 2009, Table 10.1 "Elections to the Knesset, by Eligible Voters and Voters, 1949–2008," www1.cbs.gov.il/reader/shnaton/templ_shnaton_e.html?num_tab=st10_01&CYear=2009, accessed February 2010.

sons such as illness, having failed to register to vote, or not having adequate identification when they intended to vote. Non-Jewish Israeli citizens, on the other hand, expressed a conscious motive in their nonparticipation: "54.6 percent of the non-Jews gave purposeful abstention as the reason for not voting, compared to 12.8 percent of the sample of Jewish voters."[40]

VOTING AND IDEOLOGY

The reasons that Israelis vote as they do have been the subject of much study over the years. Certainly one explanation has to do with ideology—what Israeli voters believe and what policy alternatives the political parties offer the voters. According to Asher Arian, "Israeli voters tend to report that ideological considerations are important in motivating the vote. The Israeli political system is, and is perceived to be, ideological in nature; one is tempted to say that this is the ideology of the system."[41] Survey research data tend to support this view: recent survey research has shown the following responses to the question: Which is the most important factor in influencing a person to vote for a particular party?

- 32 percent responded that their party identification was the most important factor
- 10 percent responded that the party's candidate was most important
- 53 percent said that the party's platform or ideology was most important
- 4 percent indicated that the party's being in Government or opposition was most important
- 2 percent offered other responses[42]

One of the real problems with political ideology in Israel, and one dimension in which we can see its direct impact upon the electoral system and electoral behavior, has to do with the number of cross pressures that individuals face. Cross pressures can be defined as conflicting claims on a voter's loyalties, with one issue pushing the voter in one direction and another pulling him or her the opposite way.

In the United States, with its loose party discipline in the legislature, this would not be such a great problem. Although various Republicans in Congress may have different opinions on some crucial issues, they can all survive as Republicans because the national party platform is (deliberately) general and vague, and because they have a great deal of legislative autonomy (including actual voting) in Congress. In the Knesset, however, with highly disciplined political parties that try to deliver on the policy promises they make, members of legislative parties cannot disagree on important policy issues. Instead, new political parties tend to be formed that represent new specific policy combinations.

In fact, some in Israel say that more parties are needed, not fewer, because of the great number of possible issue positions that can be taken. As we noted earlier, the various degrees of opinion and intensity of belief for each issue leave the possibility open for more competing party organizations to form. Given that most of the major issues in the Israeli political arena are *not* bipositional—there is a left, a right, and a center, as well as a number of intermediate positions—there is room for a wide range of parties to functionally represent the spectrum of views in Israeli politics.

ETHNICITY

Although scholarship on Israeli voting behavior has found a number of meaningful associations in recent years, one of the most important has been that pertaining to ethnicity. In brief, Likud was brought to and has stayed in power since 1977 (with only a couple of brief periods of Labor government since 1977) with the support of the Sephardim—Jews of Asian, African, or Middle Eastern background. Correspondingly, the Labor bloc has been most strongly supported by European Jews (including American Jews), the Ashkenazim.[43]

Interpretations of this phenomenon vary. Many suggest that for almost thirty years, while the Labor Alignment was in control in Israeli politics, the Sephardic Jews were systematically shut out of top political positions in the Government, the bureaucracy, and the Knesset. This was reflected directly in the electoral lists for the Knesset, although, in the early years, the Alignment "regularly won support from most groups in society."[44] Significant change in electoral behavior occurred during the 1970s. Research has shown that "in the late 1960s both parties were predominantly Ashkenazi; by 1981 the Alignment had stayed that way, and the Likud had become predominantly Sephardi. The turnabout seems to have occurred in 1977 when a majority of the Likud vote was Sephardi for the first time."[45]

Other reasons can be advanced for the increased Sephardic vote, as well. As the proportion of Sephardim in the population increased from a minority to a majority, and as awareness of their relatively lower income and education levels grew, the Sephardim became increasingly dissatisfied with the behavior of the "in" party, Labor. At the same time, Likud was seeking a new constituency, and the attraction of Likud to the Sephardim proved advantageous for both the Likud and the Sephardim themselves. In any event, for whatever reasons, ethnic politics has been more and more visible in Israel for the last three elections, and there is no indication that this will not continue to be the case, even though the Alignment has undertaken a concerted effort to break the Likud's hold on the loyalties of the Sephardim.

VOTING TRENDS

Although there have been a large number of short-term variations in the eighteen elections for the Knesset, most have been exhaustively chronicled and analyzed in specific monographs and essays.[46] Here we simply want to demonstrate a few general trends in recent elections.

First, observers of elections in Israel have seen a substantial decline in the strength of the Labor Alignment, as illustrated in figure 7.3. This has been explained as a function of both short- and long-term factors. After the 1977 election the Labor leader indicated that "corruption in his party was the major cause of the Labor defeat in the election." In fact, "during the Seventh and Eighth Knessot there were scandals in the Finance Ministry, the Bank of Israel, and personal financial illegalities committed by the Labor Prime

Minister (Rabin) and his wife. . . . These events simply led to the public perception of the Labor party as a whole becoming corrupt, and a good share of the public was looking for new leadership."[47]

In the longer term one could list ethnicity (already discussed in the preceding section), other demographic shifts, and changes in the general political setting as factors influencing voting behavior. Many analysts noted that the terrorist bombing of an innocent civilian's vehicle on the day of the 1988 Knesset election was responsible for a last-minute vote swing of several percentage points to the Likud Party. In sum, Mapai/Labor was originally the overwhelmingly dominant party on the political landscape in Israel because it was the Government party. As the role of the government has changed, the advantages for members of the public supporting Mapai, and then the Alignment, have changed, and voters have proven to be much more willing to switch to other parties when given the choice in national elections.

One high-ranking Likud Party official explained the decline of Mapai, the rise of Likud, and the subsequent equalization of parties in the Knesset as a function of governmental involvement in the economy.[48] During Israel's formative years, political party organizations were extremely important in providing services to the public as extensive as employment, housing, education, medical care, and so on. For many Israelis the party infrastructure

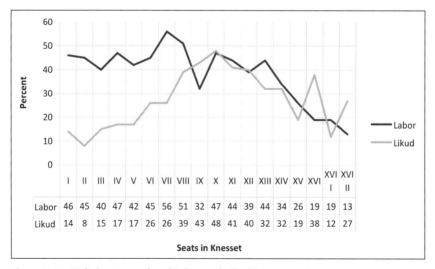

	I	II	III	IV	V	VI	VII	VIII	IX	X	XI	XII	XIII	XIV	XV	XVI	XVII	XVIII
Labor	46	45	40	47	42	45	56	51	32	47	44	39	44	34	26	19	19	13
Likud	14	8	15	17	17	26	26	39	43	48	41	40	32	32	19	38	12	27

Seats in Knesset

Figure 7.3. Relative Strengths of Labor and Likud in Knesset Seats
Source: Government of Israel, Central Bureau of Statistics, *Statistical Abstract of Israel, 2009*, Table 10.3, "Knesset Members by Main List, 1949–2009," www.cbs.gov.il/reader/shnaton/templ_shnaton_e.html?num_tab=st10_03&CYear=2009, accessed February 2010.

was even more important than the government in the provision of these services. However, as the government itself increasingly assumed responsibility and equalized the public's access to these services, there was less need for citizens to belong to a major political party like Mapai/Labor, for example, to receive these benefits.

The gradual decline in the electoral strength of Mapai, the largest party in Israel until 1977 and the party organizing the government in every coalition until that time, can be explained by this phenomenon. Since Mapai was the largest party, it had the most social goods to give to its supporters. Once these benefits—medical care, education, employment services, and the like—were being distributed equally by the government ministries, Mapai/Labor lost the advantages that it used to hold over the other, smaller parties, and consequently voters felt freer to shift their support, knowing that the governmental services would be theirs in any case.

In more recent years, foreign policy issues, the question of settlements on the West Bank, and the general issue of national security have also come to be seen as distinguishing characteristics of the two major political party blocs. Likud was the party of the strong response to the Arab challenge, while Mapai—now Labor—was perceived as the party supporting negotiation and moderation. This has been an image that Labor has tried hard to shed, but to a large extent it has not been successful, and today's political landscape continues to see the Likud positioned as the party of "national security" and a "tough response" to the Palestinian question. This led to a gradual decline in the strength of Mapai, later the Alignment and then Labor, and an increase in the strength of Likud. When this general pattern is combined with the change in degrees of ethnic support, and short-term issues such as corruption or the emergence of a new political party led by a charismatic leader are added to the equation, some drastic changes in electoral outcomes can result.

One thing is quite clear: although the Likud may have been seen in Israel's early years as a totally unrealistic alternative basis for a Government—thus leading some voters to support Mapai, or Labor, despite being ideologically predisposed not to do so—that is clearly no longer the case today.

Beyond this, as seen in figure 7.4, we can observe that both of the major parties have lost strength in recent years in terms of the overall proportion of Knesset seats that they control. Figure 7.4 shows that the proportion of seats that Labor and Likud control in the Knesset has declined significantly over time. As we noted above, much of the blame for this pattern was placed on the (temporary) new electoral system for direct election of the prime minister, which permitted individuals to vote for their preference for prime minister between the major candidates and then to vote for a smaller party for the Knesset. The pattern was not significantly reversed, however, when the system reverted to the old method of electing the Knesset.

SIGNIFICANCE OF THE ELECTORAL PROCESS FOR ISRAEL

The current Israeli electoral system has been criticized for a number of reasons, including the argument that the electoral list system makes the MK too dependent upon party leaders, which means that the MK has no reason to want to stay in contact with the voters; that power is too highly concentrated in the hands of a few party leaders; and that the current system leads to unstable government and weak coalitions because it encourages too many political parties to compete.[49] The Israeli electoral system, according to one scholar, "has been criticized on three main grounds: that in encouraging multipartism and coalition rule it impedes truly responsible government; that it facilitates undemocratic choice of candidates; and that it separates between electors and representatives."[50] A number of these points deserve additional comment here.

It is apparent that the electoral system as it is presently constituted encourages many different political parties to operate in the Israeli political world. We have seen how some proposed electoral changes would drastically alter the way that both the electoral system and the party system would operate. The point to remember, however, is that the electoral system did not originally create the many political parties that exist currently in Israel. They themselves created an electoral system that has perpetuated their exis-

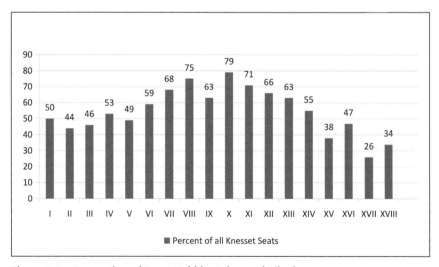

Figure 7.4. Proportion of Seats Held by Labor and Likud
Source: Data computed from Government of Israel, Central Bureau of Statistics, *Statistical Abstract of Israel, 2009*, Table 10.3, "Knesset Members by Main List, 1949–2009," www .cbs.gov.il/reader/shnaton/templ_shnaton_e.html?num_tab=st10_03&CYear=2009, accessed February 2010.

tence. As one author puts it, "Israel's choice of an electoral system . . . rested on solid precedents from the prestate period."[51] Nor should we forget that there is also a positive side to multipartism: it more accurately reflects the characteristics of the population.

We would no doubt see a quieter and calmer electoral system if Israel were divided into equal representative districts. In that case, most likely two or three larger parties would capture virtually all of the Knesset seats, leading to majority government. However, one of the very special—perhaps unpleasant, but special—characteristics of Israeli elections over the years has been the degree to which identifiable electoral minorities are able to succeed in attaining Knesset representation. There can be no question that this has forced coalition governments and given many smaller—usually religious—parties undue leverage in government policy. Still, for many this is the saving grace of the Israeli electoral framework.

This situation does, of course, have implications for responsible government and the ability of elected representatives to deliver on their promises. As we have noted earlier, no party has ever received an absolute electoral majority, thus necessitating the formation (and instability) of coalitions. As well, small electoral groups have a disproportionate influence on government policy. Where a small group becomes necessary for the creation of a coalition, that party has an undeserved influence, which has been offered as an explanation for the continuation—and indeed expansion—of legislation supporting Orthodox Jewish public policy.

This issue is not likely to go away in future years in political debates in Israel. The proportional representation system, with electoral lists composed by national party organizations, clearly limits the ability of interested individuals to enter the political arena with any likelihood of winning at all unless they operate within the framework of an established political party. Some of the political parties have opened up their list construction procedures and now stipulate that national conventions must approve positions on the party list.[52] But in many cases the closed-door or smoke-filled-room scenario is still apt.[53]

Although the process may not be entirely open, however, it is not entirely closed. The major parties make a concerted effort to recruit candidates from a variety of social, economic, ethnic, geographic, and occupational backgrounds.[54] In doing so they force themselves to be relatively open. This process may have additional benefits, in that it may do a better job of representing some of these groups than an open market approach would. One study has found that women fare better being recruited to positions on the party list than they would in a district-based electoral system.[55]

The Israeli representation system is not one in which open primary elections would be appropriate. Although it is possible for single individuals to offer themselves as one-man lists, this is not an established practice in

Israeli politics. An actor who wants to have a realistic chance of election to the Knesset must operate from a high position on an established political party's electoral list. This does, in fact, make the system less democratic in terms of a choice of candidates, especially because individual voters must vote for lists, not individuals, and a voter who strongly wants candidate number fifty-three on the Labor list must wait for the first fifty-two Laborites to be elected before his or her vote counts for the preferred candidate. This is precisely the reason for the Ya'acobi proposal for a number of smaller electoral districts. Thus, there is no doubt that the electoral system does have a significant impact upon politics in the Israeli political system.

FOR FURTHER READING

Arian, Alan, and Michal Shamir. *The Elections in Israel, 2006.* New Brunswick, N.J.: Transaction, 2008.

Diamond, Larry, and Marc Plattner, eds. *Electoral Systems and Democracy.* Baltimore: Johns Hopkins University Press, 2006.

Elazar, Daniel, and M. Benjamin Mollov. *Israel at the Polls: 1999.* Portland, Ore.: Frank Cass, 2001.

Elazar, Daniel, and Shmuel Sandler. *Israel at the Polls, 1992.* Lanham, Md.: Rowman & Littlefield, 1995.

Frenkel, Erwin. *The Press and Politics in Israel: Jerusalem Post from 1932 to the Present.* Westport, Conn.: Greenwood, 1994.

Hazan, Reuven, and Gideon Rahat. *Democracy within Parties: Candidate Selection Methods and Their Political Consequences.* New York: Oxford University Press, 2010.

———. *Israeli Party Politics: New Approaches, New Perspectives.* London: Sage, 2008.

Latner, Michael, and Anthony J. McGann. *Geographical Representation under Proportional Representation: The Cases of Israel and the Netherlands.* Irvine, Calif.: Center for the Study of Democracy, 2004.

Schofield, Norman, and Itai Sened. *Multiparty Democracy: Elections and Legislative Politics.* New York: Cambridge University Press, 2006.

Yaacobi, Gad. *The Government of Israel.* New York: Praeger, 1981.

8

The Machinery of Government

The bureaucracy and local government are significant in the day-to-day operation of Israeli politics, and it is at this point in this volume that we will—albeit briefly—turn our attention to these governmental structures to appreciate their contribution to the Israeli political world. We want to further examine Israeli judicial institutions, too; they are unique as a result of the religion-and-politics debates that were discussed earlier, and this is the point at which further discussion of the role of religion in Israeli politics should take place. Some courts deal with religious issues, while others do not. Religious courts influence the daily lives of many Israelis, however, and we examine their roles in this chapter. Another structure related to the Israeli legal system is the important—and changing—role of the attorney general, and we will see some discussion of that office here, too. Finally, we analyze the role of the much-discussed Israeli Defense Forces (IDF). The military's role in politics has changed considerably over the last fifty years, and many of the legends of the military's role are simply that, legends. The military is still highly significant in the political arena—quite apart from its role in the strategic arena—and an understanding of its structure and its organization will be of importance for a complete mastery of the material presented in this book.

Thus far, our discussion of Israeli institutions and political behavior has focused on the more traditional political structures: the constitution, political parties, elections and voting, the legislature, and the executive.

The Ministry of Finance plays a crucial role in the Israeli political system.

We cannot forget, however, that the political process includes more than these traditional components. There are other institutions and patterns of behavior that likewise satisfy the definition of "structure" and that need to be considered in our study of Israeli politics.[1] Some are inherent in modern government, such as bureaucracy; others are required in order to help control issues in daily life, such as local government. Some are formal and constitutional, such as the judiciary and the legal system; others mirror the specific requirements of the Israeli political environment, like the military.

Bureaucracy, as we shall see, is a phenomenon that many have argued is inevitable in modern governmental structures. As the scope of governmental responsibilities has grown larger and larger, infrastructures have become necessary to assist in the development and execution of public policy. Legislatures and executives are obvious structures; bureaucratic support structures may be less so. Local government is likewise often overlooked as a significant political actor, especially in centralized unitary governments. This fact notwithstanding, however, it is true that local governments in Israel are real and very important actors in the political system and need to be covered here. In this chapter we examine the scope and nature of the Israeli bureaucracy and local government to determine the role each plays in the contemporary political process.

In the United States the judiciary is considered to be a natural part of the traditional constitutional order. The principle of judicial review was established very early in American history, and the courts—especially the Supreme Court—have been significant political structures in American politics ever since. This is not the case in the majority of political systems in the world, however. In most parliamentary political systems, the courts play virtually no political role. The dominant political principle of the regimes is that of legislative supremacy, and it is virtually impossible to have a system with both legislative supremacy and absolute judicial review. The Israeli system, as we shall observe, represents something of a hybrid. Clearly, the Knesset is the supreme political body. On the other hand, there has been a political role carved out by the Supreme Court of Israel, one that has proven significant on several occasions. In addition, the role of the attorney general in the political landscape has grown significantly in recent years, and we should note that, too.

Virtually all political systems have military organizations. In most stable democracies, these organizations do not play a significant role in the political process. This is true for modern Israel, as well. Soldiers, like all Israeli citizens, are allowed and encouraged to vote, but members of the military are not allowed to run for or to hold office in the Knesset or the government while they are in the military. They do, however, become politically active *after* their period of service in the military. Nevertheless, the military is regarded as a political actor. The principle of civilian control is important, yet the military exerts a clear influence on civilian government at all levels.

In short, our examination of political institutions and political behavior in Israel will not be complete without some discussion of these four sets of actors: the bureaucracy, local governments, the judiciary and legal system, and the military. It is to an examination of each that we now turn our attention.

THE BUREAUCRACY AND THE CIVIL SERVICE

Israel, like many other modern political systems, has a civil service that has grown tremendously over the years. It has become, as one author puts it, "thoroughly bureaucratized."[2] In 1949 only four ministries—Foreign Affairs, Defense, Social Welfare, and Education and Culture—had an established civil service. Each of these, it should be noted, also evolved from a prestate organization.[3] Today, as table 8.1 indicates, their number and size have expanded considerably. The fact that the figures for 2008 show a reduction compared to 1980 is tied directly to the country's budget cutbacks and inflationary problems, to say nothing of the Likud's ideological preferences for reduced state welfarism and a less-intrusive political system. In the years since 1988, there has been a concerted effort to hold the line on the size of the public sector.[4] It should be noted, however, that the total size of the civil service in 2008 was still smaller than it was in 1980.

Israel's Civil Service Law provides job stability and security for those who work in the government. Job security for individual civil servants, however, can cause ministers great frustration when they try to staff their offices with individuals whose support and information they seek.[5] (This is, of course, the case for cabinet-level political leaders in *all* political systems that have protected civil service rosters of employees.) Indeed, ministers do not have a great deal of freedom in determining the top officers of their ministries because of the security and stability that the Civil Service Law provides to government employees. It is a rare occasion in which a minister can appoint a new high-ranking civil servant to a position.[6] Ministers may appoint some staff, such as their own personal secretaries and drivers, and they may recommend directors general for their individual ministries. Beyond that, ministers must, generally speaking, live with the ministry employees who are civil servants.

Before the formal creation of the state, the division between party and state bureaucracy was often blurred. After independence this overlap continued, as the Mapai Party controlled the government and made sure that its supporters had all the important government jobs.[7] Shortly thereafter, however, a movement was started to establish a neutral civil service.[8] Eventually, a formal Civil Service Commission was established in 1950, independent of other governmental agencies.[9] At the outset, the prime minister directed the civil service. Subsequently, it was moved to the control of the Ministry of Finance. This proved to be an ineffective home for the civil

Table 8.1   State Employees in Selected Ministries

Ministry	1980	1995	2008
Prime minister (1)	866	939	2,361
Finance (1)	7,655	7,248	6,290
Environment (2)	–	301	484
Energy/infrastructure (3)	326	230	300
Israel Lands Authority	586	721	769
Defense	2,752	2,049	2,237
Construction/housing	2,979	2,122	1,043
Health	17,561	24,816	28,186
Religious affairs (4)	372	672	–
Foreign affairs	913	947	939
Education/culture (5)	3,406	2,806	2,600
Agriculture	3,083	2,473	1,780
Economy and planning (6)	–	61	–
Science and development (5)	–	53	136
Public security	–	–	155
Justice	1,966	3,360	7,329
Labor and social welfare (7)	4,398	3,644	2,771
Interior	908	1,117	1,722
Absorption of immigration	498	594	521
Transport	1,098	986	1,017
Tourism	–	233	214
Industry and trade	1,113	620	1,446
Communications (8)	14,190	133	176
Total of listed ministries	64,670	56,125	62,657

Sources: The 1980 data comes from the Government of Israel, Central Bureau of Statistics, *Statistical Abstract of Israel* (Jerusalem: Central Bureau of Statistics, 1988), p. 565.

The 1995 data comes from the Government of Israel, Central Bureau of Statistics, *Statistical Abstract of Israel*, Table 20.9, "Government Employees, by Ministries and the Israel Police," www.cbs.gov.il/archive/shnaton47/st20-09.gif, accessed February 2010.

The 2008 data come from the Government of Israel, Central Bureau of Statistics, *Statistical Abstract of Israel*, Table 10.12, "Government Employees, Israel Police and Prison Service," www.cbs.gov.il/shnaton60/st10_12.pdf, accessed February 2010.

Notes:

(1) In 1996 the Civil Service Commission was transferred from the Ministry of Finance to the Prime Minister's Office.

(2) In 2006, the name of the Ministry of Environment was changed to the Ministry of Environmental Protection.

(3) In 1996 the name of the Ministry of Energy and Infrastructure was changed to the Ministry of National Infrastructure.

(4) In 2004, the Ministry of Religious Affairs was dissolved. Some of its powers were transferred to the national Authority of Religious Services at the Prime Minister's Office, and the Rabbinical Courts moved to the Ministry of Justice.

(5) In 1999, Culture and Sport were transferred from the Ministry of Education to the Ministry of Science.

(6) This ministry was eliminated in 1996, and its staff was transferred to the Ministry of Finance and to the Prime Minister's Office.

(7) As of 1999, the ministry does not include the workers of the Israel Institute of Productivity.

(8) Much of the Ministry of Communications was privatized in 1984.

service, and the Civil Service Department was moved back to the prime minister's office. In the mid-1950s it was once again moved back to the Finance Ministry, where it has stayed. In 1959 the Knesset passed the Civil Service (Appointments) Law, which "required civil service appointments to be made on merit and qualifications for existing positions as they become vacant and for new positions."[10]

The Civil Service Commission has a number of specific responsibilities in Israel today, as indicated in box 8.1.

Since independence, three significant changes have taken place in the civil service. First, the civil service has become progressively less politicized.[11] To a large degree this has resulted from passage of the Civil Service Law and the institutionalization of the civil service itself. An illustration of the decline of politics in the appointment process to the civil service can be found in the fact that "as a rule, new ministers do not even replace the director generals of their ministries, certainly not immediately."[12] Second, the level of education of members of the civil service has significantly increased. Today, "one can barely find a civil servant . . . who was appointed in the last ten years and who does not have an academic degree."[13] Third, although the civil service has gained personnel from other Israeli bureaucracies,[14] it has also lost many to the private sector, both as a consequence of financial factors (most notably higher salaries) and because of greater independence and opportunity to exercise their own initiative outside of government.[15]

In fact, despite a clearly delineated civil service hierarchy, it is not uncommon to hear charges of "politicization of the civil service" being directed by

Box 8.1. The Civil Service Commission's Tasks

- implement government policy regarding civil-service administration and personnel
- approve government ministry personnel quotas
- approve the structure and division of powers among government agencies and ministries
- decide on promotion tracks in various Civil Service functions
- administer tests and competitions for Civil Service vacancies
- oversee appointments, handle dismissals, and set severance pay
- supervise retirement and set pension rates
- offer in-service and general training
- devise administrative codes
- determine terms of service
- improve service to the public
- organize and streamline working methods
- tighten discipline

Source: Israeli Ministry of Foreign Affairs, MFA Library, "Civil Service Commission," www.mfa.gov.il/MFA/MFAArchive/1990_1999/1998/6/Civil+Service+Commission.htm, accessed February 2010.

one political faction at another. The philosophical question of the value of
a purely neutral civil service is one that is frequently discussed in Israel today. On one hand, most politicians agree that they do not want a blatantly
political spoils system.[16] Merit should be a central part of the appointment
and promotion process. On the other hand, government ministers must be
able to work with the directors general of their ministries, and thus they
feel that they should have some freedom in terms of their higher-level appointments.[17] One scholar notes,

> merit considerations are often spoken of, especially at the lower ranks of hi-
> erarchies. But as we move up the ladder of power and prestige, the prevalence
> of extraprofessional considerations grows. Israel is a small country, and among
> the few candidates for a senior position, the front runners are likely to be
> known. Past performance and the groups to which a candidate is affiliated can-
> not easily be separated in the minds of an appointment committee.[18]

Israel has been characterized as a nation without the semblance of a
coherent administrative culture. Indeed, its administrative system reflects
many elements of the country's heterogeneous political culture.[19] Blatant
political corruption may not be obvious and common, but *protektzia*—the
use of personal "pull"—is often the currency by which the system operates.
As Asher Arian tartly puts it,

> There is a plethora of rules, bureaucrats, and committees; but the political ele-
> ment is never far from the surface, especially if the issue is considered an impor-
> tant one. Lip service is paid to professionalism and nonpartisanship, but these
> values are likely to weaken the higher up the civil service ladder one climbs.
> There is a pretense of modern rational structure, and increasingly computerized
> techniques have been introduced; still, a solid core remains of a more personal
> and traditional form of dealing with the citizenry by the administration.[20]

Israel's "administrative culture" has been described as composed of four
identifiable strands.[21] One is an "indigenous Middle Eastern style," in
which "business is transacted at a regal pace, in a charmingly courteous,
if exasperating, fashion." This style is one in which deference to authority, status, and rank are combined to produce a bargaining situation. The
next is a remnant from the British Mandatory Period. This style involves a
"no-nonsense, orderly, condescending, bureaucratic approach, with little
room for bargaining, local initiative, or disruption." A third is composed
of "traditions brought by Jewish immigrants from their countries of origin,
as varied as the contents of a spicery." This has been described as a style
in which "paranoiac ghetto attitudes mingle with dynamic, cosmopolitan,
liberal entrepreneurship." Finally, there is the tradition of the Israeli old-
timers (*vatikim*), which combines pragmatism and personal connections.

This leads to resolving problems by taking shortcuts, operating without appropriate authorization, and similar actions.[22]

The "net result of these cultural strands," it has been argued, "is inconsistency, incoherence, and not a small measure of inefficiency."[23] Israelis seem to have a limitless supply of anecdotes of irrationality, incompetence, and agony caused by the national bureaucracy.[24] In their book *Bureaucratic Culture*, David Nachmias and David Rosenbloom report, based on a survey of the Israeli population, that Israeli citizens do not think very highly of the bureaucracy. (This, of course, is not unusual and probably duplicates public opinion in most democratic nations.) The public feels that the bureaucracy has a significant impact on individuals' lives and that it is important in terms of national and social development and democracy, but Nachmias and Rosenbloom report that the public feels "overwhelmingly negative in their characterization of the bureaucracy's impact." The report indicates that "at least 60 percent of the public gave [the bureaucracy's] activities a negative rating," and the public perceives civil servants to be "relatively dishonest, unpleasant, inefficient, passive, slow, and unstable." As a conclusion, Nachmias and Rosenbloom indicate that "Israelis find their national bureaucracy and its employees to be undesirable features of the political community, which have a considerable, yet largely unfavorable, influence upon their society."[25] While modern efforts to reform and improve the image of the civil service have continued over the years, the general reputation of the bureaucracy has not changed significantly.[26]

Civil servants often participate in the political process through their testimony in the Knesset before standing Knesset committees. It is worth noting that before a civil servant from a specific ministry may appear at a Knesset committee meeting, he or she must receive the permission of the appropriate minister. The minister must also approve the content of the civil servant's testimony before the committee or the testimony cannot take place.[27] Senior civil servants may be invited to cabinet meetings if their expertise is needed for a policy debate.[28]

LOCAL GOVERNMENT

Although they do not always receive a great deal of attention, there is a full network of subnational governments in the Israeli political system.[29] In total, after four decades of independence there were 1,409 local authorities functioning in Israel, approximately one for every 2,823 inhabitants.[30] Local governments today are especially significant in four areas: (1) the provision of governmental services, (2) the recruitment of political leaders,[31] (3) the development and maintenance of political communications networks between the public and political leaders, and (4) the "maintenance of

Box 8.2.   Functions of Local Governments in Israel

- education
- culture (including orchestras, choirs, theaters)
- health
- social welfare
- road maintenance
- firefighting
- public parks
- water and sanitation
- environmental protection
- libraries

Source: Israel Ministry of Foreign Affairs, "Israeli Democracy: How Does It Work?" www.mfa.gov
.il/MFA/Government/Branches+of+Government/Executive/Israeli+Democracy+-+How+does+it+work
.htm#local, accessed February 2010.

necessary or desired diversity within a small country where there are heavy pressures toward homogeneity."[32] Services provided by local governments include many of the most common areas in which government affects citizens, including those listed in box 8.2.

There are different levels of local authorities in Israel, indicated in table 8.2, one for urbanized areas with populations greater than twenty thousand, one for towns between two thousand and twenty thousand citizens, and one level of government that coordinates regional councils that include several villages in one region.[33] Local governments tend to be organized in similar ways, with either a mayor or a chairperson and a council, the size of which is determined by the Ministry of the Interior based upon the population of the local area. A national Union of Local Authorities helps to coordinate communications between and among various local governments, "represents them before the government, monitors relevant legislation in the Knesset, and provides guidance on issues such as work agreements and legal affairs."[34] The local council plays an important role in town planning, and local planning authorities have considerable independence under the 1965 Planning and Building Law.[35] Arab local governments have distinctive identities and play important roles in the continuity of civil service in their respective areas, as well.[36]

From one-half to two-thirds of the local governments' budgets are provided by the central government, with the remainder typically raised through property taxes.[37] "From the early 1970s to the mid-1980s, locally generated income was low and government participation was high; from then on the proportions were reversed."[38] The Ministry of the Interior has jurisdiction over local concerns and works with the various local governments to coordinate governmental policies.

Table 8.2 Types of Local Governments in Israel

Type	Total Number
Cities	66
Local councils	144
Regional councils	53
Local committees	825
Confederations of cities	32
Religious councils	204

Sources: Information on Israeli local government can be found at the Israel Ministry of Foreign Affairs Web page: "Local Government," www.mfa.gov.il/MFA/Government/Branches+of+Government/Executive/Israeli+Democracy+-+How+does+it+work.htm#local, accessed February 2010; and at the Knesset's Web page: "Local Government in Israel," www.knesset.gov.il/lexicon/eng/LocalAuthorities_eng.htm, accessed February 2010.

Local elections are based upon direct, universal, and secret ballot and take place every five years. Local legislative councils have from nine to thirty-one members, depending upon the population of the locality.[39] Until November 1978, elections for these positions were based upon proportional representation, as were elections to the Knesset, and the position of mayor was filled in the same manner as the position of prime minister, through coalitions in the local councils. Turnout for local elections has traditionally been high: "When elections for the Knesset and the local authorities have been held at the same time, voter turnout in the local elections was between 73 and 83 percent, while in the case of separate election dates, turnout has averaged around 60 percent. Voter turnout for local elections in the Arab sector has traditionally been much higher than that in the Jewish sector."[40]

After 1978, municipal elections combined the direct election of mayors with proportional election of city councils; party lists receive a number of seats on city councils that corresponds to the proportion of the votes they receive. The idea behind this was to minimize the political infighting that had been taking place in municipalities after local elections. Invariably, coalitions would be formed as in the Knesset, based upon party representation in the municipality's legislative council. The attendant interparty negotiation and factionalism often worked to weaken the mayor's position. Now the mayor is elected by direct vote, with candidates needing at least 40 percent of the total votes cast to win. If no candidate receives this, a runoff between the two candidates receiving the largest number of votes is held two weeks after the initial election, with the winner determined at that time.[41]

For administrative purposes, Israel is divided into six districts: Jerusalem, administered in Jerusalem; Northern, administered from Nazareth; Haifa, administered in Haifa; Central, administered from Ramla; Tel Aviv, administered in Tel Aviv; and Southern, administered from Beersheba. Over the years more and more regional differentiation has developed in Israel, with the various towns, cities, and regions becoming more and more distinct from each other. This has developed because of geographic patterns of settlement, regional issues, and economic circumstances.[42] Different regions have different concerns that more or less predominate, with the southern region very concerned about the availability of water and commercial links with the larger marketplaces of the north, while the Tel Aviv region is concerned about metropolitan growth, to take just two examples.[43] Some regions feel that they are slighted or underrepresented in the political arena, with Eilat and the Negev region always very sensitive about the political attention they receive.[44] Finally, the distinction between Arab regions and Jewish regions, and the different levels of government support directed to those regions—with Arab regions receiving significantly fewer resources than Jewish regions—has had major implications for the ability of Arab local governments to provide similar service levels to those provided by Jewish local governments.[45]

THE JUDICIARY AND THE LEGAL SYSTEM IN ISRAELI POLITICS

Although traces of many different legal systems can be found in Israeli law,[46] the legal system has been characterized as consisting of five basic components: Ottoman law that existed in Palestine until the end of World War I; British Mandatory regulations; British common law; the legislation of the Knesset; and religious law, coming from several different religious sources.[47] Each of these different cornerstones of the legal system merits brief discussion here.

One of the major influences on the Israeli legal system came from the Ottoman Empire. Turkish jurisprudence was the major legal system in Palestine until the British Mandate began, and there are many indications of Ottoman law to be found in Israel today. The Turkish *Majelle* ("civil code") was passed in 1869 and continued to exist in the Israeli legal system until its total repeal in 1984, although actual repeal of its sixteen volumes of over eighteen hundred sections commenced with the Knesset's enactment of the Agency Law of 1965.[48]

Another source of Israeli legal tradition was British legislation. From 1922—the date when the Mandate officially began—until 1948, this was the ultimate source of Palestinian law.[49] In a similar manner, during this period the ultimate court of appeals for Palestine was not the local Supreme Court, but instead the Judicial Committee of the Privy Council at Westminster (London). Thus, much of British common law also eventually found its way into Israel's legal system during this twenty-five-year interval.

Israeli legislation is a fourth base of the legal system.[50] The Declaration of the Establishment of the State of Israel stipulated that the People's Council, which would become the Provisional State Council, would make legislation for the new state. Among its most important acts was the Law and Administration Ordinance (1948), which reiterated that the laws in effect in Israel at that time—including British, Ottoman, and others—would remain in force unless they were specifically changed by future legislation. Subsequently, the Provisional State Council became the Knesset, and the Knesset became the font from which Israeli law flowed.[51]

Finally, religious law has played, and continues to play, a significant role in the construction and interpretation of Israeli law. During the Mandatory Period, the British gave each of the major religious groups some degree of autonomy over matters of personal status, including marriage, divorce, wills, and so on. The exercise of influence in these areas by religious courts continues today. Each of the four main religious denominations (Judaism, Islam, Christianity, and Druze) has its own system of courts. Religious courts were integrated in the political realm by the passage of the Palestine Order in Council (1922) during the Mandatory period. It provided that "jurisdiction in matters of personal status shall be exercised . . . by the courts of the religious communities" and "recognized eleven religious communities: Jewish, Muslim, and nine Christian denominations. The Israeli government later added the Presbyterian Evangelical Church and the Baha'i to this list. The Knesset also enacted a law vesting jurisdiction in the Druze religious courts."[52]

From a historical perspective, it is clear that when it passed the Marriage and Divorce Law, the Knesset abdicated its right to legislate on matters of that nature.[53] All citizens of Israel are now subject to the religious laws of their individual religious communities (individuals' identity cards indicate the religious group of which they are a member), which have their own special networks of religious courts to handle adjudication.

The legal implications of Israel's occupation of the West Bank and the Gaza Strip and legal questions raised by the Israeli-Arab conflict more generally have proven in recent years an especially problematic dimension of the Israeli legal system.[54]

While it is true that there is a separation of powers in the Israeli political system, the nature and degree of this separation is uniquely Israeli. In the American political system, there is a clear separation between and among the legislative, executive, and judicial branches.[55] In Britain, the legislative and executive functions merge in the House of Commons, and the legislative and judicial functions merge in the House of Lords. In Israel, there "exists a certain separation among the authorities. However, the functions of policy formulation, legislation, and jurisdiction are implemented in a coordinated form."[56] The Knesset passes laws, the Government enforces them, and the courts play a role in determining whether the actions of the Government are consistent with the intentions of the Knesset.[57] The courts do not have the power, generally speaking, to strike down acts of the Knesset, although as we noted earlier in this volume, this has changed significantly in recent years,[58] especially where human rights are concerned.[59]

In 1957 the Knesset passed the Courts Law, which reorganized the system
of courts that had slowly evolved until that time and guaranteed the independence of the judiciary. Israel's unitary system of government is reflected
in its courts, which are organized in a single system of general law courts as
described in the Fundamental Law: The Judiciary.[60]

Since 1957, the Supreme Court of Israel has been the highest court of
the judicial system. Below the high court, in terms of judicial organization,
are municipal courts, magistrates' courts, and district courts. There are also
special traffic, labor, juvenile, military, and municipal courts with clearly
defined jurisdictions, as well as religious and administrative courts.[61] The
magistrates' court typically has one judge and hears cases involving civil
and minor criminal offenses; it has jurisdiction in both civil and criminal
cases. The district court—typically with one or three judges—has appellate jurisdiction over magistrates' courts, with some original jurisdiction in
more important civil and criminal cases. The Supreme Court—sitting with
one, three, five, or sometimes even more judges—is the highest court in the
land and has broad appellate authority. Sitting as the High Court of Justice,
it can hear petitions against any government body or agent.[62]

Municipal courts exist in each major city and have jurisdiction over relatively minor offenses committed within the city limits. Magistrates' courts
have jurisdiction over the administrative districts (and in some cases, sub-
districts) of Israel, hearing both minor monetary claims and less serious
criminal charges, and may impose penalties of up to three years in prison.
In addition to having jurisdiction over civil cases in which the sum claimed
is no higher than one million shekels, they also "act as traffic courts, municipal courts, family courts, and small claims courts." Appeals from these
courts, as well as some initial proceedings, are heard in district courts.[63]

District courts have both original and appellate jurisdictions. There are five
district courts in Israel: in Tel Aviv, Jerusalem, Haifa, Beersheba, and Nazareth. They have original jurisdiction over issues that do not come before magistrates' courts, with the exception of religious questions, which are heard in
the separate system of religious courts described below. Examples of original
jurisdiction questions would be serious misdemeanors, felonies, and major
civil cases, that is, cases in which the sum claimed is over one million shekels.
In criminal matters they hear cases in which the penalty may involve more
than seven years of imprisonment. In most cases a single judge will hear cases
in the district court, although "a panel of three judges is established when the
court hears an appeal of a Magistrates' Court's judgment, when the accused is
charged with an offense punishable by imprisonment of ten or more years, or
when the President or Deputy President of the District Court so directs."[64]

The Supreme Court may hear appeals from district courts if the case originated in the district court. If the case was heard in the district court on appeal
from a lower court, it may be appealed to the Supreme Court only if (1) the

district court authorizes the appeal, (2) the president of the Supreme Court (or another Supreme Court justice named by the president to make the decision) authorizes the appeal, or (3) the full Supreme Court authorizes the appeal.[65]

Photo 8.1. The Supreme Court has increased in importance for Israeli government in recent years.

The Supreme Court acts both as an appellate court for lower courts as well
as a High Court of Justice to hear complaints against the Government. It also
has special jurisdiction to "hear appeals in matters of Knesset elections, rulings of the Civil Service Commission, disciplinary rulings of the Israel Bar
Association, administrative detentions, and prisoners' petitions appealed
from the District Court."[66] Judges are appointed by the president "upon
recommendation of a nominations committee comprised of Supreme Court
judges, members of the bar and public figures. Appointments are permanent,
with mandatory retirement at age 70."[67] Typically, panels of three justices, less
than the full complement of ten, hear a case. If requested by the president of
the state, cases originally heard by three justices may be given a second hearing by panels of five or more justices. The court may nullify

a. local ordinances enacted by municipal councils on the grounds that a
   city is legislating in an area which is the exclusive jurisdiction of the
   national Parliament;
b. national administrative regulations promulgated in implementation
   of Knesset legislation . . . on the grounds that they violate the property
   or other fundamental rights of the people; and
c. decisions or other actions by public administrative officials on the
   grounds that their behavior is arbitrary or illegal.[68]

In addition to these courts, other special courts exist in Israel. As noted
above, an independent framework of religious courts operates within the
framework of the Ministry of Religious Affairs. These courts have jurisdiction in matters affecting personal status: marriage, divorce, and religious
characteristics. Separate Jewish, Muslim, Christian, and Druze courts
operate for members of those communities. In cases in which a question
arises as to whether an issue falls within the jurisdiction of a religious
court, two justices from the Supreme Court and the president of the religious court concerned sit as a panel to decide the matter.[69] The Supreme
Court of Israel has heard cases in which constitutional questions related
to religion are raised.[70]

Seven rabbinical courts exist for the Jewish community in Israel,[71] appeals from which may be taken to the Grand Rabbinical Court of Appeals
in Jerusalem.[72] Appeals may not be made from a religious court to a secular
court. The jurisdiction of Jewish religious courts in some areas such as marriages and divorces extends to all Jews in Israel,[73] whether they are Israeli
citizens or not and whether they like it or not.[74] Religious courts may also
share jurisdiction with civil courts in a number of areas if all parties concerned agree with the religious courts' participation in the decision.

There are four Muslim religious courts in Israel, appeals from which
may be taken to the Muslim Appeals Court, which sits in Jerusalem. A

number of other religious courts exist for the Catholic, Protestant, Greek Orthodox, Melkite, Maronite, and Druze communities, each of which has its own religious courts with jurisdiction over its members in matters of personal status.[75]

The appointment of judges in Israel illustrates the degree of judicial independence found there. A nine-member Appointment Committee recommends individuals to the president for consideration. This committee is made up of the president of the Supreme Court and two other Supreme Court justices, the minister of justice and one other cabinet member chosen by the cabinet, two MKs elected by secret ballot, and two lawyers chosen by the Israeli Bar Association. Judges in Israel serve "during good behavior," either until they decide to retire (there is a mandatory retirement age of seventy) or until they are accused and found guilty by a special court of behavior unbefitting a judge. At that point the minister of justice can recommend their dismissal by the president.

In recent years the role of the attorney general has become increasingly significant in Israeli politics. The attorney general "serves as legal counsel for the Government and public authorities, directs the state prosecution and supervises the legal department that prepares and reviews proposed legislation," thus serving a number of very important roles, roles that have had the potential to become politicized in recent years. It is worth noting that several of Israel's recent attorneys general have gone on to become members of the Supreme Court there, too. Custom has suggested that politically active individuals and "individuals with a strong political identity" should not be appointed to this post.[76]

In recent years the attorney general has played a key role in making decisions about whether to bring indictments against (former) political leaders, such as recent inquiries about whether former prime minister Ehud Olmert violated the law while serving as prime minister.[77] He has also played a key role in discussions about whether the Government should take a legal position on a very sensitive area of conflict, and about whether it is appropriate for the Knesset to undertake legislation in areas of controversy.

The role of the courts in Israel illustrates the commitment of the political system to the rule of law and also the singular interaction of the religious and secular realms in the polity. The courts have the power, as has been explained above, to annul any administrative action that is not consistent with legislation; to annul any legislation that is not consistent with action by the Knesset, the source of the supreme law of the land; or to annul legislation by the Knesset that is not consistent with the Fundamental Laws passed by the Knesset. They have also established a clear division between religious jurisdiction and secular jurisdiction, a division that has been threatened by recent efforts of the Orthodox to expand their jurisdiction in the social realm.

THE MILITARY AND THE GOVERNMENT

Although there have been several general historical studies of the subject, some have suggested that there has been a veil of secrecy over academic research on civil-military relations in Israel.[78] Academics have avoided the study of the military because of both personal and political pressures. Since Israel has been at war for the more than sixty years since it achieved independence, with five major wars since 1948 and no period of real peace, a tendency has existed not to study the military so as to avoid inadvertently giving away something of military significance.[79]

When David Ben-Gurion took over the defense portfolio in the provisional government of Israel in 1948, he later stated,

> I made it clear to the Provisional Government when it delegated the defence portfolio to me that I would accept the ministry only under the following conditions: (1) the army that will be formed and all its branches be subordinated to the government of the people and only to that government. (2) All persons acting on behalf of the army . . . will act only according to a clearly defined function established by the government of the people.[80]

The defense ministry created by Ben-Gurion was influenced by his socialist bent.[81] It was committed to the principles of a depoliticized army, the supremacy of civilian authority and direction, and a highly centralized decision-making structure.[82] The "antimilitaristic dimension of Israeli socialism" even affected the name of the organization: it would not be called an army but a defense force.[83] The IDF was "actually the first bureaucratic structure to be successfully transformed from an autonomous pre-independence organization into a truly national institution subordinate to the government. This was achieved by taking the army out of politics."[84]

As indicated at the outset of this chapter, the principle of civilian control of the military is widely accepted in Israel. "Despite efforts of army officers to influence foreign or security policies . . . civilian control of the military has remained firm. Although army officers have ascended to top political positions including the Prime Ministry, civilian political influence has always outweighed that of the military in formation and implementation of national policies."[85]

In recent years there have been periods when the visibility of military actors becoming political has attracted the attention of the public, and while the general consensus is that the military should not become involved in politics, there is also recognition that military leaders are significant actors in the political realm. There is also recognition that, as one observer noted, because so many political leaders are ex-generals, there will be sympathy between many of the political leaders and the military.

One recent incident can be used as an example of this type of tension. In October 2001 sources in the Israeli Foreign Ministry, under Foreign

Minister Shimon Peres, were openly critical of the IDF leadership for "purposefully demolishing the ceasefire Peres brokered" in negotiations with Yasser Arafat. The Foreign Ministry felt that the IDF was "taking provocative actions against the Palestinians that have left 18 dead, mostly teenagers, since the ceasefire began." Peres was also reportedly very unhappy with statements leaked by an "anonymous officer" on the IDF general staff who "said the IDF was against the Foreign Minister's meeting with Arafat." According to one published report, "the acrimony was so bad that Defense Minister Binyamin Ben-Eliezer had to step into the ugly fray, saying any criticism should be directed at him since he approved all the IDF actions."[86] Civil-military relations have always been tense in Israel, and in this particular case the pressures between the Foreign Ministry and the Defense Ministry, each with a different short-term goal—the former's to negotiate a peaceful outcome to the *intifada*, the latter's to provide military security—led to public confrontation.

> One of the key characteristics of the IDF over the years has been that it deploys a small standing army [made up of conscripts and career personnel] with early warning capability, and a regular air force and navy. The majority of its forces are reservists, who are called up regularly for training and service, and who, in time of war or crisis, are quickly mobilized into their units from all parts of the country.[87]

The strategic implications of the small standing army and the need for nearly three days to achieve a full call-up of forces have influenced Israeli military decisions in the past in dealing with threats from neighbors.

Two significant political characteristics of the contemporary Israeli military have begun to receive more attention in the literature in recent years. First, the dynamics of the IDF have significantly changed since 1967, when much of the IDF's activity had centered on being an army of occupation in the West Bank, Gaza, and Golan areas.[88] Second, since the mid- to late 1960s, more and more senior IDF officers have left the armed forces and entered the political arena, making the military a regular channel of recruitment for the political elite.[89] In 1973, for example, there were five retired generals in the twenty-one-member cabinet of Prime Minister Meir, the largest number of former military leaders in the Government until that time.[90] Because of the principle of mandatory universal military service,[91] for women as well as men,[92] all ideological groups are represented in the military, ranging from the far left to the far right.[93]

For obvious reasons, because of its vulnerable situation in relation to national security, the Israeli military establishment and the Defense Ministry have always played a significant role in the governmental process.[94] In the recent past, the Defense Ministry alone has accounted for almost 40 percent of the national budget and virtually 20 percent of the GNP.[95]

Apart from the very obvious concern for national defense, one important function of the armed forces has been its role as a socializing institution.[96] By requiring all citizens to serve in the IDF, Israel's founding fathers "envisaged the military forces as a socializing agent, where class distinctions would be obliterated and new immigrants integrated."[97] Over the years the IDF has been responsive to the cultural and social needs of its soldiers, providing recreational and educational activities, as well as personal support services. Recruits with incomplete educational backgrounds are given opportunities to upgrade their level of education, and career officers are encouraged to study at the IDF's expense during their service. The integration of new immigrant soldiers is facilitated through special Hebrew-language instruction and other programs. Active in nation-building enterprises since its inception, the IDF also provides remedial and supplementary education to civilian populations and contributes to the absorption of newcomers among the population at large.[98]

THE BUREAUCRACY, THE JUDICIARY, AND THE MILITARY

We have seen in this chapter that in addition to the more obvious political structures contained in virtually all constitutions—the legislative and the executive branches of government and the electoral systems and voting, among others—there are at least four other political structures that must be taken into consideration in a study of the Israeli political system: the bureaucracy, local governments, the judiciary, and the military.

Israel is not unique among the nations of the world in having a well-established bureaucracy. We have seen here that the bureaucracy has grown over the years, is especially well entrenched, has many of the same faults as bureaucracies in most political systems (to say nothing of those special problems caused by the heterogeneity of the Israeli culture), and is not perceived in a positive light by much of the Israeli public.

Local governments in Israel, like local governments in many political systems, are often taken for granted and are not the primary focus of political observers. But they clearly play a significant role in Israeli politics. Many of the ordinary and nonglamorous aspects of daily life, such as garbage collection, water and electricity supply, traffic regulation, and the like, are controlled by local governments, and therefore they merit some passing recognition by the student of Israeli politics.

As in most parliamentary systems, the judiciary in Israel is not an integral part of the policy-making process at first glance. The principle of judicial review, however, as it has gradually evolved in Israeli politics, has increasingly placed the courts in significant policy-making roles. The primary political role of the courts is to ensure that the will of the Knesset is followed, but upon occasion, and the occasions have come more frequently in recent years, the courts have felt it appropriate to remind the Knesset of what they, the courts, feel the fundamental principles of the polity require. Structurally, the country has an elaborate network of courts in the criminal and civil arenas. What differentiates the Israeli judicial system from most others is the series of religious courts that exists for each of the religious communities in the nation.

Finally, the military plays a significant role in the Israeli political world. This is true not only because of the strategic importance of defense considerations, something to which we return in the next two chapters, but also because of the relatively small size of the Israeli political elite and the way in which they both react to military issues and are recruited from among the military elite.

FOR FURTHER READING

Cohen, Stuart. *Israel and Its Army: From Cohesion to Confusion.* New York: Routledge, 2008.

Hajjar, Lisa. *Courting Conflict: The Israeli Military Court System in the West Bank and Gaza.* Berkeley: University of California Press, 2005.

Heller, Mark. *Continuity and Change in Israeli Security Policy.* New York: Oxford University Press, 2000.

Hertogh, M. L. M., and Simon Halliday. *Judicial Review and Bureaucratic Impact: International and Interdisciplinary Perspectives.* New York: Cambridge University Press, 2004.

Kretzmer, David. *The Occupation of Justice: The Supreme Court of Israel and the Occupied Territories.* Albany: State University of New York Press, 2002.

Lahav, Pnina, ed. *Law and the Transformation of Israeli Society.* Bloomington: Indiana University Press, 1998.

Lebel, Udi. *Communicating Security: Civil-Military Relations in Israel.* New York: Routledge, 2008.

Lissak, Moshe. *The Unique Approach to Military-Societal Relations in Israel and Its Impact on Foreign and Security Policy.* Jerusalem: Hebrew University of Jerusalem, 1998.

Maman, Daniel, Eyal Ben-Ari, and Zeev Rosenhek. *Military, State, and Society in Israel: Theoretical and Comparative Perspectives.* New Brunswick, N.J.: Transaction, 2001.

Nachmias, David. *Israel's Senior Civil Servants: Social Structure and Patronage.* Tel Aviv: Tel Aviv University Press, 1990.

Peri, Yoram. *Generals in the Cabinet Room: How the Military Shapes Israeli Policy.* Washington, D.C.: United States Institute of Peace Press, 2006.

Rattner, Arye, and Gideon Fishman. *Justice for All? Jews and Arabs in the Israeli Criminal Justice System.* Westport, Conn.: Praeger, 1998.

Shapira, Amos, and Keren C. DeWitt-Arar. *Introduction to the Law of Israel.* Boston: Kluwer Law International, 1995.

Sheffer, Gabriel, and Oren Barak. *Militarism and Israeli Society.* Bloomington: Indiana University Press, 2010.

Vigoda-Gadot, Eran. *Building Strong Nations: Improving Governability and Public Management.* Burlington, Vt.: Ashgate, 2009.

III

FOREIGN POLICY AND THE MIDDLE EASTERN POLITICAL SETTING

9

The Foreign Policy Setting

Foreign policy is an integral component of any country's political system. This is particularly true for Israel. There are several reasons for this, the most important being the continued state of hostility that has existed between Israel and some of its Arab neighbors, and the hostile geopolitical atmosphere in which Israel has had to operate since before its creation. The study of Israeli foreign policy thus encompasses a number of important dimensions, ranging from an examination of the geopolitical and strategic contexts within which foreign policy decisions are made, to the history of Israeli and Arab foreign policies; from a consideration of military strategy and tactics, to the evolving definition of what constitutes national security. In this chapter we briefly examine each of these issues with an eye toward more fully understanding both the context within which Israeli foreign policy is made and the strategic considerations that constantly preoccupy decision makers. This chapter examines the legacy of warfare experienced in this region and analyzes the strategic considerations that have contributed to Israeli foreign policy over the last six decades. The issue of military security has traditionally been paramount in Israeli politics, and this chapter traces the history of Israeli military operations. In a parallel manner, this chapter also examines the political, diplomatic, economic, and cultural factors that have been significant in the Israeli foreign policy setting over the last six decades.

Israel's border with Lebanon was for many years the most frequently traversed of all of Israel's borders with its neighbors.

THE SETTING: THE LEGACY OF WARFARE

The foreign policy setting within which Israel has had to operate since independence has often been characterized by hostility, suspicion, and anxiety.
The central focus of the more than six decades of Arab-Israeli conflict has
been the refusal of many of the Arab states (with the exception of Egypt
and Jordan) to accept Israel's right to exist within its borders, as indicated
in map 9.1. Since the time of its Declaration of Independence, Israel has
been threatened on a number of occasions by its neighbors. The purpose
of these threats and the goal of those wars that have occurred have been
clearly articulated as the destruction of the Israeli state. Indeed, some have
referred to the principal setting within which Israel has functioned since
independence as "one long war."[1]

As we noted in chapter 1, the Arab nations surrounding Palestine in the
late 1940s rejected all British suggestions for partition into separate Jewish and Arab states. When the United Nations Special Committee recommended its own version of a partition plan for Palestine in November 1947,
it was greeted with the same response. Between then and May 14, 1948,
the projected date of Israel's formal independence, there was continued
preparation on the part of the Arab nations for an attack once the British
completed their withdrawal from Palestine.

Not surprisingly, on May 15, 1948, the combined armies of Egypt, Jordan,
Iraq, Syria, and Lebanon, assisted by forces from Saudi Arabia, launched
their invasion of the new state of Israel. Over the next fourteen months
many significant battles were fought, many sacrifices were made, and many
temporary cease-fire agreements came and went.[2] By July 1949, armistices
(not peace treaties) would be agreed to with Egypt, Lebanon, Syria, and
Jordan. Their stated purpose at the time was "to facilitate a transition to permanent peace." It was a goal not destined to be achieved in the short term
with some of the nations; it has not yet been achieved with others.

A little more than seven years later, in October 1956, the state of war
was renewed following numerous Arab violations of the 1949 armistice
agreements.[3] One of the major sources of tension contributing to this second round of warfare was Egypt's blockade of Israeli shipping through the
Straits of Tiran in 1955, which was illegal under international law because
the straits were an international waterway.[4] This had a significant impact
upon Israel since it virtually closed the port of Eilat and made it necessary
for Israeli ships bound for East Africa and the Far East to travel through the
Mediterranean and around the Horn of Africa to reach their destinations.
Israel protested the Egyptian action but was not able to resolve this crisis
either diplomatically or through unilateral action.

President Nasser of Egypt subsequently nationalized the Suez Canal on July
26, 1956. This action was upsetting to the British because at the time nearly

Map 9.1. Israel in the Middle East

a quarter of British imports passed through the canal, and nearly a third of the ships using the canal were British. Equally important to the British was their prestige in the Middle East, to say nothing of the fact that the British government owned a controlling interest in the canal.[5] The French were also upset with Egypt because Egypt was supporting the Algerian National Liberation Front in its battle for independence against France. The British and the French, accordingly, began to plan ways to retake the canal from Egypt. Their displeasure with Nasser now coincided with Israel's displeasure.

In August 1956 French interior minister Bourgès-Maunoury sent for Shimon Peres, then an assistant to Prime Minister Ben-Gurion, and asked, "If we make war on Egypt, would Israel be prepared to fight alongside us?"[6] The message was conveyed to the Israeli cabinet, which discussed the matter. Ben-Gurion was worried about the reactions of other nations, particularly the United States, the Soviet Union, and influential nonaligned countries like India.[7]

On October 24, 1956, when Egypt, Jordan, and Syria announced the creation of a joint military command, Israel's decision was made much easier.[8] In fact, historical scholarship has found that Israel's involvement in the 1956 war was heavily influenced by the French agenda and was the result of very specific issues and alliances in the short run. Overall, the question of whether Israel would have gone to war against Egypt without French and British encouragement really cannot be known.[9]

In any event, on October 29 a combined Israeli, British, and French military force seized control of the Suez Canal, along with the Gaza Strip and the entire Sinai Peninsula. The United Nations, the United States, and the Soviet Union all criticized the action, with the UN General Assembly passing an immediate cease-fire resolution demanding an Israeli withdrawal to the 1949 armistice line. On November 6, Britain and France announced that they would comply with the UN resolution, and on November 8, a UN Emergency Force was created to help maintain peace in the area. In March 1957, following promises from Egypt that it would cease all maritime blockades and guarantees from American president Dwight Eisenhower that the United States would help see that Egypt kept its word, Israel returned to Egypt all of the captured territory.[10] Egypt's promises, as it turned out, were not kept. Neither were the promises of the United States to be the guarantor of the Egyptian commitments.

By June 1967, Israel again found itself in a precarious position.[11] Both Egypt and Syria had begun a massive program of military mobilization, and it became increasingly clear to Israeli intelligence analysts that the Egyptians were preparing for another attack. Egypt ordered the UN Peacekeeping Forces out of the Sinai, where they had been maintaining a demilitarized zone,[12] moved its own forces toward the Israeli border, and again closed the Straits of Tiran to all Israeli shipping. When Israel sought American support based upon President Eisenhower's 1957 promises, President Lyndon Johnson—at this time involved in an unpopular and increasingly unsuccessful war in Vietnam—responded that the United States was "not the policeman of the world" and that Israel would have to take care of its own problems.

And so Israel did. On June 5, 1967, the Israeli Air Force launched a preemptive strike that destroyed virtually the entire Egyptian Air Force while it was on the ground.[13] At the outset, the Jordanians stayed out of the fighting. Israel assured Amman that it had no expansionist motives in the war and indicated that if Jordan stayed out of the fighting, Israel would take no action along its eastern border.[14] However, after the overwhelming Israeli successes against Egypt and Syria on the first day of the war, President Nasser of Egypt began to exert a great deal of pressure on King Hussein of Jordan, arguing that if Israel were forced to fight a three-front war—northern with Syria, southern with Egypt, and eastern with Jordan—the Arab governments would ultimately prevail. Indeed, Nasser is reported to have (untruthfully) told Hussein that three-quarters of Israel's air force had been wiped out by the Egyptian forces at the outset of the fighting and "that Egyptian armored units were fighting deep inside Israeli territory." Hussein himself later admitted that "we were misinformed about what had happened."[15] By then, of course, it was too late. Jordan did enter the war, and Israel did respond with a significant move to the east, through Jerusalem, to the Jordan River. Confounding the expectations of Nasser, at the end of six days Israel had captured the entire Sinai Desert to the south, the Golan Heights to the north, and the West Bank of the Jordan River to the east, as shown in map 9.2.[16]

After the war, Israel made a number of offers to return the captured territories in exchange for real peace treaties, not continued armistices. But at the Arab summit held in Khartoum, Sudan (about one thousand miles south of Cairo), from August 29 to September 1, 1967, the Arab governments announced their "three no" doctrine: "No recognition. No negotiation. No peace."[17] Between the spring of 1969 and the summer of 1970, Israel had to endure the so-called War of Attrition, during which Egypt regularly fired across Suez Canal cease-fire lines.[18] In August 1970, another cease-fire was negotiated between Egypt and Israel, and a temporary peace again came to the region, although it was not to last.

Although the period between 1970 and 1973 did not see outright war in the Middle East arena, neither was it a period of peace.[19] Israel was expending much effort rearming itself, improving its defenses, and maintaining its post-1967 frontiers. Egypt and Syria continued to import arms from the Soviet Union, deny Israel's right to exist, and issue various threats related to Israeli security. Tensions waxed and waned, but were never far below the surface.

In October 1973, the country was to face its most severe challenge to date.[20] Israeli intelligence notified the political leadership that it possessed clear evidence of an impending joint Egyptian-Syrian invasion. Meanwhile, President

Map 9.2.   Israeli Borders before and after the 1967 War

Anwar Sadat (who had replaced President Nasser after Nasser's death in 1970) was taking the public position that Egypt could no longer tolerate a continued Israeli presence in the Sinai. In response, some in the Israeli leadership were advocating another preemptive strike, arguing that if they were to wait for Egypt and Syria to strike first, the material and human costs to Israel would be prohibitively high, among other reasons because of the structure of the Israeli

Defense Force and the fact that a small proportion of the IDF was on active duty. Golda Meir, Israel's prime minister at the time, contacted American president Richard Nixon regarding the impending crisis. Nixon, like Johnson in 1967, urged restraint and cautioned against another preemptive strike. Even if Israel was correct that an invasion was imminent, he argued, Israel simply could not afford to be labeled again by the Arab powers as the aggressor, as had been the case in 1967. Nixon promised that if Israel would wait, it could count on American assistance, should an attack occur.

Coming from the country's principal ally and supplier, Nixon's advice carried great weight. The Israeli government's position was also influenced by the fact that Yom Kippur, the holiest day of the Jewish year, was fast approaching. The Government was loath to split up virtually every Israeli family by mobilizing the armed forces unless absolutely necessary. After extended debate the cabinet decided, finally, not to mobilize the IDF, and it adjourned from its meeting on October 5.

Early on the morning of Yom Kippur, October 6, 1973, the armed forces of Egypt and Syria launched their attack on Israel.[21] The IDF suffered extraordinarily heavy losses but managed to hold and then repel the invading armies on both fronts.[22] When Prime Minister Meir telephoned President Nixon to inform him of the invasion and request the promised American assistance, Nixon indicated that he would begin making the necessary arrangements; however, it was literally days before any American supplies reached Israel, despite repeated telephone calls from Meir to Nixon— sometimes several calls a day. Nixon's response was that it was necessary to follow required procedures, to inform Congress, and to wait for Congress to act, and that Israel should be patient and help would come.[23] Eventually, the promised American aid did begin to arrive, being airlifted in, but the delay in the process once again reminded Israel of its vulnerability.[24] A new cease-fire agreement was subsequently arranged, sponsored by the United States, after more than two weeks of fighting.

Following the 1973 war, a period of profound reassessment emerged in Israeli politics. The exuberant self-confidence that had followed the 1967 Six Day War was now severely shaken. In the first three days of the two-week 1973 war, there had been some real doubt, not hysterical, but sincere, objective, self-confidence-shattering doubt, about the conflict's likely outcome, and there were times when some actually felt that the war could be lost.[25] One consequence of this was that there were a number of significant political casualties. Long-time political leaders, including Prime Minister Meir and Defense Minister Moshe Dayan, resigned over strategic decisions made in relation to the nonmobilization. Israel, then, was increasingly sensitive to its vulnerability and the need to remain well armed.

The late 1970s and 1980s saw military action outside of Israeli territory involving Israeli troops in a highly controversial military action in Lebanon.

One of the key events during this chapter of Israeli military action occurred in June 1982 and was called by the Israeli government Operation Peace for Galilee. The IDF entered the southern part of Lebanon to seek out and destroy Palestine Liberation Organization (PLO) terrorist bases, which had long used the area to launch artillery and rocket attacks against settlements in northern Israel. This was the first military action in Israel's history in which significant portions of the Israeli population expressed vocal criticism of the Government's military policy. Indeed, many in Israel referred to this action as Israel's Vietnam. When the army finally withdrew from Lebanon in 1988, many in Israel breathed a sigh of relief, although there was substantial debate about the wisdom of leaving Lebanon, with many arguing that an Israeli withdrawal would send the wrong lesson to forces of violence in the Arab world.[26]

One of the most pointed statements after the forced Israeli withdrawal from Lebanon was a concern that this would encourage militant Palestinians. Right-wing Israelis who were opposed to the withdrawal from Lebanon worried that Palestinians would want to follow the example of Hezbollah. Hamas, the Palestinian Islamic resistance movement, made a public statement expressing just that sentiment.[27]

A "second Lebanon War" erupted in June 2006, really fought between Israel and Hezbollah, not Israel and Lebanon. Hezbollah, it will be recalled, is a Shi'a Islamist political and paramilitary organization that is based in Lebanon and that among its primary tenets is a claim that Israel lacks legitimacy and a commitment to Israel's destruction. Hezbollah first emerged as a significant military force in response to Israel's 1982 invasion of Lebanon, and it was a strong supporter of Iran's Ayatollah Khomeini, seeking to establish an Islamic regime in Lebanon. The conflict started when Hezbollah fired rockets at Israeli border towns from within Lebanon; Israel responded with significant airstrikes and ultimately a full-scale invasion of southern Lebanon. Hezbollah responded with more rocket attacks, reaching as far south as Haifa. A significant number of Lebanese civilians were killed, and a large number of Israelis were temporarily displaced from their homes around Haifa. After the cease-fire was negotiated by the United Nations in August 2006, some parts of southern Lebanon remained uninhabitable because of the number of unexploded Israeli cluster bombs that had been dropped during the fighting.[28]

A chronology of Israel's involvement in Lebanon is found in box 9.1.

Israel has also struggled with the *intifada*, an uprising on the West Bank that was originated not by the PLO but by the residents of the Occupied Territories. This uprising has continued since 1987, as shown in box 9.2, and has placed a constant pressure on Israeli authorities for several reasons. First, in many important respects the authorities were unprepared for the massive demonstrations that have occurred. Soldiers and police were

Box 9.1.   Israeli Involvement in Lebanon, 1949–2010

March 1949—War of Independence armistice is signed between Israel and Lebanon.

December 1968—Israel Defense Force (IDF) commandos raid Beirut Airport responding to terrorist attacks.

January 1969—Katyusha rocket hits Kiryat Shmona, killing two Israelis.

March 1972—IDF destroys eleven terrorist bases, killing two hundred terrorists.

March 1978—Operation Litani is launched in retaliation for that month's Coastal Road massacre. Nearly three hundred terrorists and thirty-five IDF soldiers are killed.

March 17, 1978—UN Security Council Resolution 425 calls for Israel's withdrawal from Lebanon.

July 24, 1981—Cease-fire agreement is signed with Lebanon after U.S. mediation.

June 1982—Operation Peace for Galilee begins major invasion of Lebanon in response to both the attempted assassination of Israel's ambassador to the United Kingdom and the Katyusha attacks on the north of Israel.

August 1982—IDF reaches Beirut.

November 1983—A suicide terrorist bomber kills sixty in Tyre.

June 1985—The majority of the 1982 IDF invasion force withdraws.

February 1992—A missile from an IAF helicopter gunship kills Hezbollah leader Sheikh Abbas Musawi.

July 1993—Operation Accountability is launched against terror groups, resulting in about sixty terrorists killed. During the operation the terrorists fire 142 Katyushas across the northern border.

April 1996—Operation Grapes of Wrath is launched in response to the Katyusha attacks by Hezbollah. During the campaign against the Hezbollah infrastructure, the terrorists fire 777 Katyushas at northern settlements.

September 1997—Eleven naval commandos and an army doctor are killed in an abortive raid on an Amal base.

April 1998—The Israeli cabinet decides to implement UN Security Council Resolution 425.

June 1999—Civilians are killed in a Katyusha barrage. The IDF responds by bombing Lebanese infrastructure.

May 2000—Hezbollah Katyusha attacks increase tension on the northern border, especially in Kiryat Shmona. The IAF responds with bombing raids on Lebanese infrastructure.

May 24, 2000—The last IDF soldier leaves Lebanon.

May 25, 2000—This day is declared an annual public holiday, called "Resistance and Liberation Day."

October 2000—Rafik Hariri takes office as prime minister of Lebanon for a second time.

March 2001—Lebanon begins pumping water from a tributary of the River Jordan to supply a southern border village, despite opposition from Israel.

January 2002—Elie Hobeika, a key figure in the massacres of Palestinian refugees in 1982, dies in a blast shortly after disclosing that he held videotapes and documents challenging Israel's account of the massacres.

September 2002—Row with Israel over Lebanon's plan to divert water from a border river. Israel says it cannot tolerate the diversion of the Wazzani, which provides 10 percent of its drinking water, and threatens the use of military force.

August 2003—Car bomb in Beirut kills a member of Hezbollah. Hezbollah and a government minister blame Israel for the blast.

September 2003—Israeli warplanes hit southern Lebanon in response to Hezbollah's firing antiaircraft missiles at Israeli planes in the area.

October 2003—Israel and Lebanon exchange gunfire in the disputed area known as Shebaa Farms.

September 2004—UN Security Council resolution aimed at Syria demands that foreign troops leave Lebanon. Syria dismisses the move. Parliament extends President Lahoud's term by three years. Weeks of political deadlock end with the unexpected departure of Rafik Hariri—who had at first opposed the extension—as prime minister.

February 14, 2005—Former Lebanese prime minister Rafik Hariri is assassinated. Pressure builds on Syria to withdraw its remaining troops from Lebanon, which it does in April.

June 2005—Prominent journalist Samir Qasir, a critic of Syrian influence, is killed by a car bomb. Anti-Syrian alliance led by Saad Hariri wins control of parliament following elections. New parliament chooses Hariri ally, Fouad Siniora, as prime minister.

July 2005—Lebanese prime minister Siniora meets Syria's president Assad; both sides agree to rebuild relations.

September 2005—Four pro-Syrian generals are charged over the assassination of Rafik Hariri.

December 2005—Prominent anti-Syrian MP and journalist Gibran Tueni is killed by a car bomb.

July 2006—Hezbollah militants cross into Israel, kill three Israeli soldiers, and kidnap two others in a bid to negotiate a prisoner exchange, a demand rebuffed by Israel. Another five Israeli soldiers are killed after the ambush. Israel responds with a naval blockade and by bombing hundreds of targets in Lebanon, including Beirut's airport and Hezbollah's headquarters in southern Beirut. Hezbollah responds with rocket attacks targeting northern Israeli cities. Civilian casualties are high and the damage to civilian infrastructure wide-ranging. Thousands of people are displaced.

August 2006—Truce between Israel and Hezbollah comes into effect on August 14 after thirty-four days of fighting and the deaths of around one thousand Lebanese—mostly civilians—and 159 Israelis, mainly soldiers. A UN peacekeeping force, expected to consist of fifteen thousand foreign troops, begins to deploy along the southern border.

September 2006—Lebanese government forces deploy along the Israeli border for the first time in decades.

July 2008—President Suleiman meets Syrian president Bashar al-Assad in Paris. They agree to work toward establishing full diplomatic relations between their countries. Israel frees five Lebanese prisoners in exchange for the remains of two Israeli soldiers captured by Hezbollah in July 2006. Hezbollah hails the swap as a "victory for the resistance."

October 2008—Lebanon establishes diplomatic relations with Syria for first time since both countries gained independence in the 1940s.

February 2010—Mr. Hariri expresses concern about Israeli "threats" to go to war with Lebanon. Israeli prime minister Benjamin Netanyahu had earlier said Israel sought peace with its neighbors and distanced himself from comments by a cabinet member who suggested Israel was heading for a new war with Lebanon.

Source: "Chronology of Involvement in Lebanon," *Jerusalem Post* (May 25, 2000): 5. See also CNN, "Timeline: Decades of Conflict in Lebanon, Israel," July 14, 2006, www.cnn.com/2006/WORLD/meast/07/14/israel.lebanon.timeline/, and BBC, "Timeline: Lebanon," April 28, 2010, http://news.bbc .co.uk/2/hi/middle_east/819200.stm, accessed May 2010.

untrained in how to respond to crowds throwing rocks; an army trained to fight a modern war has had to respond to challenges of urban warfare. Today the IDF has several battalions trained for low-intensity conflict, some specializing in urban warfare.[29]

In addition, the uprising caught the attention of the world in a far more sympathetic fashion than any of the past actions of the PLO. Scenes of women and children throwing rocks at armed Israeli troops were terribly effective in convincing many around the world—and many in Israel—that the occupation of the West Bank simply could not continue indefinitely. The significance of the Palestinian casualty rate has been an effective propaganda weapon for the Palestinians in supporting their argument that they are being oppressed in the Occupied Territories. The lead paragraph of an article in the *Jerusalem Post* read, "More than 600 Palestinians have died in the yearlong wave of violence known as al-Aqsa Intifada. Of these, 148 were under 18. In addition, 14,405 Palestinians have been seriously wounded or disabled."[30] The theme of the inequity of the casualty rate is one that the Palestinians have raised on many occasions, as they have emphasized the relative youth of many of the casualties.[31]

More recently, the *intifada* has evolved into a new phase with a much more aggressive and violent series of actions known as suicide bombings— referred to by the Israeli government as homicide bombings—which are a strategy to bring violence into Israel proper and to the Israeli civilian population. Major explosions killing large numbers of Israeli civilians in Israel's population centers—Tel Aviv and Jerusalem—as well as frequent incidents in less-populated areas, including bus stops in rural areas, have brought a degree of terror and a sense of vulnerability to the Israeli population that

Box 9.2.   Stages in Israeli-Palestinian Conflict, 1917–2009

November 2, 1917—The Balfour Declaration is drafted, in which the government of the United Kingdom expresses support for a homeland for the Jewish people in Palestine.

July 24, 1922—The Mandate for Palestine is approved by the League of Nations, giving Britain jurisdiction over Palestine.

November 29, 1947—UN General Assembly Resolution 181 (Partition Plan) is approved by the United Nations, dividing Palestine into Jewish and Arab states, with Jerusalem internationally administered. The Palestinians reject the plan.

May 14, 1948—The Declaration of the Establishment of the State of Israel: during the war Israel annexes territory set aside for the Arab Palestinian state, leaving only East Jerusalem, the West Bank, and the Gaza Strip in Arab hands.

April 24, 1950—Jordan annexes the West Bank and East Jerusalem, blocking efforts to form a Palestinian state there.

October 29, 1956—Israeli troops invade the Sinai Peninsula as part of an Israeli, British, and French initiative after Egypt nationalizes the Suez Canal. They withdraw under pressure from the United States and the Soviet Union.

May 28–29, 1964—The Palestine Liberation Organization (PLO) is established "to mobilize the Palestinian people to recover their usurped homes" at a meeting of the Palestine National Congress in Jerusalem.

June 5–10, 1967—Israel launches preemptive attacks on neighbors, capturing the West Bank, East Jerusalem, and Gaza, creating thousands of Palestinian refugees in what will become known as the Occupied Territories. Israel also takes Sinai and the Golan Heights.

June 27, 1967—Protection of Holy Places Law: the minister of Religious Affairs is charged with the implementation of this law.

September 1, 1967—The Khartoum Resolutions: Eight Arab heads of state attend an Arab summit conference. The resolutions advocate continued struggle against Israel and the creation of a fund to assist the economies of involved Arab states, among other things, and adopt the position of no peace with Israel, no recognition of Israel, and no negotiations with Israel.

November 22, 1967—The UN Security Council approves Resolution 242, calling for Arab recognition of Israel in return for Israeli withdrawal from occupied territories.

July 17, 1968—The Palestinian National Charter is passed, declaring Palestine to be the homeland of the Arab Palestinian people and stating that armed struggle is the only way to liberate Palestine as an overall strategy, not merely a tactical phase. It calls for commando action as the nucleus of the Palestinian popular liberation war, says that the liberation of Palestine is a national duty and attempts to repel the Zionist and imperialist aggression against the Arab homeland, aims at the elimination of Zionism in Palestine, and declares the partition of Palestine in 1947 and the establishment of the state of Israel to be entirely illegal. The Balfour Declaration, the Mandate for Palestine, and principles based upon them are deemed null and void.

February 3, 1969—Yasser Arafat, leader of Palestinian guerrilla group Fatah, is elected chairman of the PLO Executive Committee.

September 1970—The Jordanian army drives the PLO out of Jordan because of PLO activity there, an action known as "Black September." The PLO moves its base of operations to Lebanon.

September 5, 1972—Palestinian commandos kidnap Israeli Olympic team members in Munich, Germany. Eleven Israelis are killed in the raid.

October 6–22, 1973—Egypt and Syria attack Israeli forces in Sinai and Golan in the Yom Kippur War. The UN Security Council approves Resolution 338 calling for a cease-fire and "land-for-peace" Arab-Israeli negotiations.

October 22, 1973—UN Security Council Resolution 338 calls upon parties to end military activity, implement Resolution 242 (1967), and start negotiations aimed at establishing peace in the Middle East.

May 31, 1974—Separation of Forces Agreement between Israel and Syria: Israel and Syria will observe the cease-fire on land, sea, and air and refrain from military actions against each other.

October 28, 1974—At a meeting of the Arab League in Rabat, Morocco, twenty Arab heads of state adopt a resolution recognizing the PLO as "the sole legitimate representative of the Palestinian people."

March 19, 1978—UN Security Council Resolution 425 (Israeli Withdrawal from Lebanon), following the IDF invasion of Lebanon to attack PLO terrorist bases south of the Litani River, calls on Israel to withdraw and establishes a United Nations Interim Force in Lebanon (UNIFIL).

September 17, 1978—Egyptian president Anwar Sadat and Israeli prime minister Menachem Begin sign the United States–brokered Camp David Accords. The PLO does not accept the pact. One part deals with the Sinai and peace between Israel and Egypt, to be concluded within three months. The second part is a framework agreement for a format for the negotiations for the establishment of an autonomous regime in the West Bank and Gaza.

March 26, 1979—Sadat and Begin sign peace treaty. Israel returns Sinai to Egypt but keeps control of the Gaza Strip.

July 30, 1980—Basic Law: Jerusalem, Capital of Israel states that a united Jerusalem will be the capital of Israel.

December 14, 1981—The Golan Heights Law extends Israeli law to the area of the Golan Heights.

June 1982–December 1983—Israel invades Lebanon to halt guerrilla activity there, causing evacuation of PLO headquarters to Tunisia.

December 8, 1987—Rioting in the Gaza Strip leads to the beginning of the *intifada*, a prolonged Palestinian uprising against Israeli rule in the Occupied Territories.

November 15, 1988—The Palestine National Council, the PLO's legislative body, declares a Palestinian state in occupied territories. The council votes to accept UN Resolutions 242 and 338, thus recognizing Israel's right to exist.

December 14, 1988—Arafat states that the PLO recognizes Israel's right to exist and "renounces" terrorism.

May 14, 1989—Israel's Peace Initiative is formulated by Prime Minister Shamir and Defense Minister Rabin with four basic points: strengthening peace with Egypt, promoting peaceful relations with Arab states, improving refugee conditions, and advocating elections and interim self-rule for Palestinian Arabs.

August 1990—Arafat and PLO officials split with most Arab governments, backing Iraq after it invades Kuwait.

October 30, 1991—An invitation to the Madrid Peace Conference is extended to Israel, Syria, Lebanon, Jordan, and the Palestinians. This calls for a conference having no power to impose solutions, bilateral talks with Arab states bordering Israel, and talks with Palestinians on five-year interim self-rule, to be followed by talks on permanent status and multilateral talks on key regional issues, like refugees.

October 30–November 4, 1991—United States/Soviet–sponsored talks are held in Madrid with Palestinian participation. Direct Arab-Israeli negotiations involving Jordan, Lebanon, and Syria, as well as the Palestinians, continue through mid-1993.

June 23, 1992—Israeli Labor Party leader Yitzhak Rabin, pledging a concerted effort to reach peace settlements with the Arabs, leads his party to victory over the incumbent Likud right-wing bloc in general elections.

January 19, 1993—Israel's parliament repeals the 1986 law forbidding Israelis to have contact with PLO members.

August 13, 1993—Israel accepts a PLO presence in the ongoing peace talks, announcing that it will continue to negotiate with the Palestinian delegation despite the open membership of several of those delegates in the PLO.

August 30–31, 1993—Israeli foreign minister Shimon Peres announces that a preliminary accord on Palestinian self-rule in the Occupied Territories has been reached in secret talks in Norway and Tunisia between the PLO and the Israeli government.

September 10, 1993—Arafat and Rabin exchange letters of mutual recognition. Arafat says parts of the 1964 PLO covenant denying Israel's right to exist are "no longer valid"; Rabin recognizes the PLO as the representative of Palestinians.

September 13, 1993—Peres and PLO negotiator Mahmoud Abbas sign a self-rule draft accord at a ceremony in Washington, D.C. Arafat and Rabin, meeting for the first time, seal the landmark pact with a handshake.

September 13, 1993—Israel-Palestinian Declaration of Principles on Interim Self-Government: Israel and the PLO (in the Jordanian-Palestinian delegation to the Middle East Peace Conference) agree to negotiate a peace settlement.

September 14, 1993—The Israel-Jordan Common Agenda is agreed on to negotiate toward peace, specifically addressing issues of water, refugees, borders, and other areas of bilateral cooperation.

May 4, 1994—An agreement on the Gaza Strip and the Jericho Area between Israel and the PLO includes a scheduled withdrawal of the Israeli military, transfer of authority in specific areas to the PLO, agreement on the structure of the Palestinian Authority (PA), a description of its powers, and an agreement on relations between Israel and the PA, specifically covering areas of economic relations, human rights, and the rule of law.

July 25, 1994—The Washington Declaration involving Israel and Jordan: Israel and Jordan agree on basic principles and announce that they will work toward a peace treaty.

August 29, 1994—An agreement on the Preparatory Transfer of Powers and Responsibilities in the West Bank between Israel and the PLO is signed.

October 26, 1994—A treaty of peace between Israel and Jordan is signed.

September 28, 1995—An interim agreement between Israel and the Palestinians makes progress toward peace.

April 26, 1996—The Israel-Lebanon Cease-fire Understanding establishes a monitoring group for the cease-fire consisting of the United States, France, Syria, Lebanon, and Israel.

May 9, 1996—Agreement on Temporary International Presence in Hebron: as called for in the Interim Agreement on the West Bank and the Gaza Strip (September 28, 1995), Israel and the PA establish a Temporary International Presence in the city of Hebron (TIPH) to supervise demilitarization and the transfer of authority.

January 21, 1997—Agreement on TIPH: a second phase of above agreement.

October 23, 1998—Wye River Memorandum is signed to further implement the Interim Agreement on the West Bank and Gaza Strip (September 28, 1995) so that Israelis and Palestinians can carry out their responsibilities relating to redeployments and security.

September 4, 1999—Sharm el-Sheikh Memorandum on Timeline of Commitments of Agreements Signed and the Resumption of Permanent Status Negotiations: Israel and the PLO commit to full implementation of the interim agreement and other agreements between them since 1993 and all commitments from other agreements. The sides agree to permanent status negotiations, more redeployments, release of prisoners, safe passage for Palestinians in the West Bank and Gaza, the establishment of a Gaza Sea Port, Hebron issues, and security.

October 5, 1999—Protocol concerning Safe Passage between the West Bank and the Gaza Strip is signed.

July 25, 2000—Trilateral Statement on the Middle East Peace Summit at Camp David: President Clinton, Prime Minister Barak, and Chairman Arafat meet at Camp David to reach an agreement on permanent status, but are not successful.

January 27, 2001—An Israeli-Palestinian Joint Statement following a meeting at Taba, Sinai, concludes that it is impossible to reach an agreement on all of the issues involved and suggests more negotiations following the Israeli election.

April 30, 2001—A report of the Sharm el-Sheikh Fact-Finding Committee recommends that Israel and the Palestinian Authority act decisively to halt violence in the West Bank and Israel and suggests that their objectives should be to rebuild confidence and resume negotiations.

June 14, 2001—The Tenet cease-fire proposal says that the two sides are committed to a mutual, comprehensive cease-fire, applying to all violent activities.

March 12, 2002—UN Resolution 1397 refers to Resolutions 242 and 338; expresses concern at violence since September 2000; stresses the importance of the safety of civilians and the need to respect humanitarian law; demands the immediate cessation of acts of violence, including acts of terror, provocation, incitement, and destruction; and calls upon Israelis and Palestinians to cooperate in the implementation of the Tenet plan.

March 28, 2002—Beirut Declaration on Saudi Peace Initiative signed.

April 30, 2003—A Performance-Based Roadmap to a Permanent Two-State Solution to the Israeli-Palestinian Conflict (The Road Map)

November 19, 2003—UN Security Council Resolution 1515

April 18, 2004—Disengagement Plan—General Outline

June 6, 2004—Revised Disengagement Plan—Main Principles

November 15, 2005—Agreed documents on movement and access from and to Gaza

January 30, 2006—Statement by the Middle East Quartet

August 11, 2006—UN Security Council Resolution 1701

September 20, 2006—Statement by the Middle East Quartet

February 2, 2007—Statement by the Middle East Quartet

November 20, 2007—Announcement of the Annapolis Conference

November 27, 2007—Joint Understanding on Negotiation

November 9, 2008—Quartet Statement in Sharm el-Sheikh

December 16, 2008—UN Security Council Resolution 1850

January 8, 2009—UN Security Council Resolution 1860

January 16, 2009—Memorandum of Understanding between Israel and the United States Regarding Prevention of the Supply of Arms and Related Materiel to Terrorist Groups

June 26, 2009—Middle East Quartet Statement from the meeting in Trieste

September 24, 2009—Joint Statement by the Middle East Quartet

Source: Israel Ministry of Foreign Affairs, State of Israel, "Reference Documents," www.mfa.gov.il/mfa/go.asp?MFAH00pq0, accessed October 2003.

simply did not exist when all of the violence of the *intifada* was confined to the (Arab) cities of the West Bank and Gaza. This has had serious effects not only upon the morale of the Israeli population, but also on Israeli tourism and, thus, the Israeli economy.[32]

Finally, it has been difficult for many to see how to bring the uprising to an end. The leaders of the *intifada* have taken different positions in respect to the continuation of the uprising, often vowing to continue their uprising as long as Israel refuses to negotiate with the PLO. Although Israel has expressed its willingness to negotiate with moderate Palestinian leaders, it has periodically refused to have anything to do with the PLO and Yasser Arafat. The cycle of violence has been dramatic and destructive: Suicide bombings lead to Israeli occupation of refugee camps or Palestinian cities in the West Bank and the destruction of homes and infrastructure, often with Palestinian casualties. This leads to Palestinian retribution and more suicide bombing. This goes on and on. Thus, there is no light at the end of the tunnel.[33]

This problem has been exacerbated by a lack of clarity of the Palestinian leadership's goals: it has not been clear that the PLO leadership has been genuinely motivated to stop the violence that has been so problematic in recent months and years. At some points the leadership has come out against violence; at others it has encouraged a continuation of it. An illustration of this inconsistency occurred in October 2000, when the *Jerusalem Post* reported that "despite Palestinian Authority Chairman Yasser Arafat's attendance at the Sharm el-Sheikh summit convened to end three weeks of violence, Arafat's mainstream Fatah faction yesterday called on Palestinians to continue the intifada until Israel withdraws its troops from all territories captured in the 1967 Six Day War."[34]

As acts of terrorism in the West Bank and Israel proper—especially suicide bombings—have taken place in the last several years, the Israeli government has continued to demand that the PLO leadership play an active role in stopping the violence. The PLO leadership has not done so, or at least it has not done so enthusiastically and effectively. When the Palestinian leadership has made statements deploring the acts of violence, they have seemed to the Israeli government half-hearted or forced. Israeli leaders have asked whether this failure to end the violence is because of a lack of ability or a lack of will. If the PLO leadership cooperates with Israel, it faces pressure (and possibly violence) from the Palestinian side, and if it does not cooperate with Israel, it faces pressure and demonstrated violence from the Israeli side.[35]

On the whole, then, the preceding discussion has sought to demonstrate that the legacy of warfare as it exists in the Middle East is significant for its duration, intensity, and policy implications. This is true in at least three important respects. First, the entire context for decision making in Israeli foreign policy has been shaped into judging virtually every situation from a national-security perspective. Israel has been forced to engage in a struggle for national survival for its entire existence. This has had the effect of graphically and periodically reminding all citizens of Israel of their vulnerability in the sense that their neighbors (with the contemporary exception of Egypt and Jordan) do not want them to be there and that many of their neighbors and other actors (such as factions of the PLO) have the ability to affect their lives through acts of warfare and terrorism.

A second legacy of the history of warfare has conditioned Israel's relations with its neighbors. Apart from Israel's relations with Egypt and Jordan, Israel's relations with Arab nations have for the most part been hostile and threatening. Israel is still technically at war with some of its neighbors and has been since 1948. Although the last full-scale Middle East war was in 1973, the IDF was mobilized from 1982 until 2000 in Lebanon, has continued to be on alert along Israel's borders, and has continued to be very active in the cause of national security in a struggle against terrorism in the West Bank and in Israel proper in recent years. While Israeli soldiers have willingly gone to war in defense of Israel for more than six decades, the *intifada* has generated a new degree of unhappiness among the Israeli military. Soldiers have increasingly said that they are willing to go to war and risk their lives to defend the state of Israel, but they do not see serving as an army of occupation in the West Bank as a just action. This is new for Israel.[36]

A third legacy of the history of warfare has to do with Israel's relations with the superpowers. Although Israel has reestablished official diplomatic relations with Russia, the heir of the Soviet Union, from the early 1950s through the 1980s the Soviet Union was a sponsor of the Arab camp in the Middle East conflict.[37] On several occasions in the last forty years, especially during the periods of active warfare, the two superpowers have been extremely active in the Middle East arena. At one point in the 1973 Yom Kippur War, Soviet premier Leonid Brezhnev called American president Richard Nixon on the "hot line" to warn that if the United States could not convince Israel to release an Egyptian division surrounded in the Sinai Desert, the Soviet Union would be forced to send its own troops in to help the Egyptians.[38] At that point, the warning that had been articulated for

Photo 9.1.   Many soldiers say that policing civilians is not the proper duty of the army.

years—that the Middle East held the potential to start a war between the superpowers—seemed alarmingly prescient. President Nixon was able to convince the Israelis to release the Egyptians, the Soviets did not intervene (more than providing arms for the Egyptians), and the superpowers successfully avoided direct conflict.

STRATEGIC CONSIDERATIONS

Although many years have gone by since it first appeared, many still regard Michael Brecher's book *The Foreign Policy System of Israel* to be the definitive study of the Israeli foreign policy system.[39] Brecher suggests that the foreign policy system of Israel is divided into three parts: "inputs," "process," and "outputs." The "inputs" segment is in turn made up of three components, the "operational environment," "communication," and the "psychological environment." The "process" segment deals with the formulation of strategic and tactical decisions, along with the way these decisions are implemented by various structures of government. The "outputs" segment pertains to the substance of decisions and actions by the government. Each of these parts of the overall process deserves individual comment, for each makes its separate contribution to our understanding of the entire scheme.

The "external environment" suggested by Brecher includes a general consideration of the global environment, or, as he puts it, the "total web of relationships among all actors within the international system (states, blocs, organizations)."[40] All of these relationships can affect the manner in which Israel acts in any given situation. Regional relationships, or what Brecher terms "subordinate systems," focus primarily upon the Middle East, for obviously this environment has a direct bearing on foreign policy decisions. Other bilateral relationships, especially those with the superpowers/great powers, such as the relations between Israel and the United States or Israel and Russia, must also be taken into consideration in the formulation of Israeli foreign policy.

The "internal environment" is composed of the domestic factors that can influence foreign policy. Among the many factors that would be included in this category are military capability, economic strength and resources, the current political environment, and the context within which decisions are made (i.e., public opinion, government coalitions, and other short-term domestic political considerations). The degree of interest-group involvement in the political system and how divided or agreed these various segments of the public are over foreign policy options is a very significant part of the study of public opinion, as is an understanding of the competing elites and their respective strengths.

The views, or "inputs," of these various actors in the international and domestic environments are communicated to decision-making elites through a variety of communications outlets, including the mass media, the press, books, radio, television, and the bureaucracy. These decision-making elites, then, become what Brecher refers to as the "core decision-making group" of the foreign policy system, consisting of the head of Government, the foreign minister, and a relatively narrow range of other political actors.[41]

As this "core decision-making group" tries to make foreign policy decisions, its individual members must operate within their own psychological environments. Each decision maker brings with him or her a set of attitudes about the world, other nations in the foreign policy setting, ideology, tradition, and the desirability of a variety of policy alternatives. Decision makers also bring in their psychological predispositions a set of images of the environment and their perceptions of reality in the political world. These images may be more or less realistic and flexible and can color the information that the decision makers receive from the external and internal operational environments.

After the elements making up the operational environment have been communicated to the elite and then filtered through the psychological screens of individual decision makers, the policy-making process itself helps to determine what policy is chosen and how that policy is implemented. Factored in here would be the number of individuals involved in the decision-making process, the chain of command or power relationship among these individuals, whether a given policy decision is seen as a political decision, the degree to which it must be openly debated and discussed, and a variety of other factors in the Israeli political world.[42]

Brecher further suggests that there are four identifiable issue areas in Israeli foreign policy: "military-security" concerns—such as violence, warfare, or national security; "political-diplomatic" concerns—involving relations with other international actors; "economic-developmental" concerns— which pertain to trade, aid, or foreign investment; and "cultural-status" concerns—which focus on education, scientific inquiry, and other related topics.[43] Each cluster of issues is handled differently by the overall foreign policy system, and, consequently, the different clusters must be analyzed and studied with an awareness that each is distinct from the others.

MILITARY-SECURITY CONCERNS

A crucial aspect of Israeli foreign policy involves its military, as the status, structure, and operation of the IDF is not the same as that of armed forces in other nations. This is true for two reasons: (1) the relations between civilians and the military are different in Israel from the relations one finds in other settings, and (2) the underlying doctrine of Israel's military establishment differs from other armies.[44] The fact that only a small proportion of

Israel's army is on active duty at any given time has strategic implications for Israeli foreign policy considerations.

The concept of defense, in the words of one analyst, "has been a central issue in [Jewish] society ever since the beginning of the Zionist Movement in Central and Eastern Europe at the turn of the century."[45] If for no other reason, the concepts of defense and the military are very significant in Israel because of the proportion of national resources defense issues consume.[46] As a percentage of the total national budget, defense spending at its peak (1973) consumed almost 50 percent of the total budget! In the 2002 budget the Defense Ministry accounted for NIS 41,911 million out of a total budget of NIS 265,652 million, or 15.77 percent of the total. In 2009 the Defense Ministry accounted for NIS 51,529 million out of a total budget of NIS 311,434 million, or 16.54 percent of the total budget. The next largest cabinet line item was education at NIS 51,394 million, or 16.5 percent of the total budget.[47]

The military is also very visible in Israeli society.[48] It is as close to a universal social experience as exists in Israel; while women do not participate in combat, they are subject to the draft, as are men, although their military circumstances are not exactly the same. Today about 90 percent of men are drafted, while only about 60 percent of women are drafted; men serve three years in active duty and are in the reserves until the age of fifty-one, while women serve only two years in active duty and are in the reserves only until the age of twenty-five.[49] As we noted earlier in this book, the IDF has played a key role in the socialization and assimilation of generations of Israeli immigrants; it is the one characteristic of Israeli life that most Israelis have in common. Thus, even in a society that is dedicated to civilian control of the military, the Israeli military has a significant role in policy making.[50]

One direct consequence for foreign policy is the call-up pattern of military reserves.[51] Only a small proportion of the military is on active duty at any given time. It is officially calculated that the IDF needs seventy-two hours to reach a fully mobilized status, although some estimates suggest a considerably shorter period than this. For example, one study has indicated that "currently, private estimates of the partial-mobilization time needed for Israel to deflect an attack range from four to eighteen hours. . . . Full mobilization can be undertaken within 16–48 hours, considerably less than the official figure of 72 hours."[52]

Whatever the time involved, when decision makers have had to decide whether to launch a preemptive attack (as was the case in 1967) or to wait to call up the reserves (as was the case in 1973), they have known that their decision will have real consequences. The IDF suffered especially high casualties in 1973 during the first seventy-two hours, until the IDF was at full strength, and postwar analysis was very clear in its criticism of Golda Meir and her Government. Among other factors, critics noted that many of these casualties could have been avoided if the IDF had been fully mobilized prior to Yom Kippur, even if the prime minister had not ordered a preemptive strike. We saw earlier why she did not order a full mobilization and why she did not launch a preemptive strike: the call-up process and the effects of mobilization were an ingredient in the equation.

Another military-security concern in foreign policy making involves the nuclear question.[53] Although Israel has continued to insist that it does not possess nuclear weapons, many observers feel that even if it is literally true that Israel does not possess intact nuclear weapons, it possesses the ability to assemble such weapons in relatively short order. Indeed, Prime Minister Netanyahu's decision to not attend a nuclear summit organized by U.S. president Barack Obama in 2010 was seen as an indication by Israel that it was not interested in nuclear moderation at all. If this is true, a nuclear capability would permit the IDF to offset an enemy with much greater tactical strength. Israel has stated publicly on several occasions that it will not permit its Arab neighbors to develop a nuclear capability. This policy was demonstrated in 1979 when Iraq was developing a nuclear reactor ostensibly for the production of electricity. Israeli acted, and its bombers attacked and destroyed the facility, the justification being that such a facility could too readily be converted to military uses to produce hostile nuclear products.[54]

Yet another military-security issue involves what the Israelis refer to as defensible borders. We noted in chapter 3 that one of the central goals of classical Zionism was a secure Jewish population in a secure Jewish state—in fact, a Jewish majority in a Jewish state. This has been translated in more modern times into a call for secure and defensible borders.[55] The quest for stability and national security has been a continual, and as yet unrealized, goal in Israeli foreign policy. The problem, of course, is that many of Israel's neighbors today are still technically in a state of war with Israel; the armistices signed in 1949, 1956, 1967, and 1973 are not the same as peace treaties, and while Israel has signed peace treaties with Egypt and Jordan, it has not yet signed peace treaties with Lebanon, Syria, or Iraq. One of the most common descriptions of the Israeli foreign policy setting, as we have already remarked, has been that Israel has survived "one long war."[56]

The quest for secure and defensible borders has been the *sine qua non* of Israeli foreign policy since 1948 and the subject of a great deal of debate and scholarship. Israel has contended that it has a right to secure boundaries and that the only way to maintain secure boundaries is to make them as defensible as possible.[57] This means, in the case of tensions with Syria (to say nothing of Egypt and Jordan, with which Israel has signed peace agreements), that geopolitical factors must be taken into consideration.

When Israel occupied the entire Sinai Peninsula following the 1967 war, it obtained a degree of security that it had not previously possessed. With military observation stations at the southwestern tip of the Sinai, Israel would have a twenty-minute warning period from the time of its first detection of hostile Egyptian aircraft taking off from Egyptian military bases near Cairo to the time those aircraft would reach the outskirts of Tel Aviv. When Israel returned the Sinai to Egypt in 1982 and its southernmost radar units were repositioned to the middle of the Sinai mountains, the advance warning time was significantly decreased: if Israel had to rely only on ground-based radar, the time would have been decreased from twenty minutes to two minutes.[58]

Similarly, the occupation and eventual annexation of part of the Golan Heights was undertaken for strategic reasons.[59] Given the topography of northern Israel, a hostile Syria controlling all of the territory of the Golan Heights meant that entire cohorts of children living on the kibbutzim and other settlements in northern Israel frequently had to live in underground shelters for long periods of time because of the constant fear and periodic reality of Syrian sniping from high ground and attacks. Once this territory was captured in 1973, the quest for secure and defensible borders meant that Israel would not return high ground to a nation with which it was still at war until it could be confident that peace would prevail. It is still waiting for a peace treaty with Syria, and advanced technology will clearly be a part of that solution, too, as it was in the Sinai.[60]

The search for national security motivates all nation-states in their foreign policy. It is only reasonable to expect that states that have never known real security will be even more desirous of obtaining it. Israel has learned that the only way it can have real security is through military preparedness, since so many of its neighbors are committed to its destruction. Any long-term peace in the Middle East must therefore require that Israel's neighbors acknowledge Israel's right to exist within mutually recognized and secure borders before the parties involved can begin to look beyond their own immediate security needs to an examination of what they can all do to deescalate the tensions and perceived threats that exist in this part of the world.[61]

POLITICAL-DIPLOMATIC CONCERNS

On a more global level, one of Israel's major concerns since independence, of course, has simply been to be accepted by the community of nations; continued conflict with the Palestinians and continued expansion of its settlements in the Occupied Territories have not been of any help in this goal. This has not been an easy task, and Israel still has not arrived as a universally accepted member of the United Nations. Although the function of the United Nations is to play the role of a disinterested third party capable of remaining neutral in any political crisis, the United Nations is not perceived in this light in Israel.[62] Israel has felt since 1967 that it cannot get a fair hearing in the United Nations General Assembly and that the combination of the Soviet Union's influence (later Russia's influence) among Eastern Bloc and Third World nations, as well as the Arab nations' influence in the Third World (through oil politics in general, as well as regional groupings such as the Organization of African Unity), has resulted in an automatic anti-Israel majority in the General Assembly and in most UN specialized agencies.[63]

Under the rules of the United Nations Charter, for example, peacekeeping forces can only be stationed in an area if they are requested by all parties concerned—actors on both sides of the relevant border. Such forces, as is well-known, were stationed in the Middle East between 1956 and 1967, but when in 1967 President Nasser of Egypt ordered them to leave, they had no choice but to comply.[64] This, according to Israel, is one of the weaknesses of the United Nations: it has no real power of its own. In situations in which the opportunity has presented itself, Israel has accordingly favored using other multinational peacekeeping forces, rather than UN forces, so that disengagement agreements can be guaranteed.

In Israel's view the United Nations cannot be objective in its dealings with the Israeli-Arab conflict because of the UN recognition of the PLO and its granting the PLO Observer Status; therefore, the United Nations has lost virtually all of its potential to act as a credible mediator between Israel and the Palestinians or other Arab powers. Instead, Israel has appeared to favor using other parties, primarily the United States, to help it negotiate with its Arab neighbors.

Outside the confines of the United Nations, Israel has had inconsistent relations with European nations.[65] For a time France was a strong supporter of Israel, and it was during the period of Franco-Israeli harmony that Israel is said to have acquired its nuclear capability.[66] In more recent times, as the French have taken a decidedly pro-Palestinian and pro-Arab stand, relations between Israel and France have suffered accordingly. Britain has never had a particularly close relationship with Israel, a fact most Israeli leaders attribute to the unpleasant period leading up to Israeli independence. Israel's relations with West Germany were greatly affected early on by the issue of reparations to be paid to Israel by the West German government for the Holocaust.[67] Over time, however, German-Israeli relations have stabilized.[68]

Israel's greatest foreign policy successes in the early years were with the Third World. Prior to the 1967 Six Day War, in fact, Israel had extremely good relations with most Third World nations. From Independence through the 1956 Suez War, in particular, many African and Latin American states saw Israel as a fellow small nation grappling with the same kinds of development problems they faced. Israel developed a number of very popular aid programs with states in sub-Saharan Africa,[69] Asia,[70] and Latin America and had a number of political, if not military, allies.[71] Through the mid-1970s, more than fifty-five hundred Israeli experts had been sent as scientific, educational, and agricultural advisers overseas, while more than

Photo 9.2. Flags of Israel, Palestine, and the United Nations

twenty thousand citizens of African, Asian, and Latin American nations had traveled to Israel for training there.[72]

The Six Day War in 1967 significantly changed Israel's status, most prominently with African nations. Egypt especially used the Organization of African Unity to isolate Israel from allies in Africa, claiming that Israel had been the aggressor in that conflict and that the principle of pan-African solidarity required all African states to cut ties with Israel. In fact, virtually all African states did this, except for South Africa. Israel has worked at improving relations with sub-Saharan Africa since that time, but only in very recent years has significant progress been made in reestablishing links with sub-Saharan African nations.[73]

Much of Israel's linkage with the Third World, and especially with Latin America, has involved arms transactions. This linkage often involves Israel

selling Israeli-made copies of United States–designed arms systems to Third
World nations, systems that the United States sold to Israel on the condition that copies could not be sold to other nations without the approval of
the United States.[74] As Israel is a major arms supplier to the Third World,
many Latin American nations have maintained their diplomatic ties with
Israel and continued their diplomatic support it as a direct *quid pro quo* for
Israel's continuing to sell arms to them.

Clearly, the most important political-diplomatic concerns held by
Israel involve relations with the United States and Russia. Although the
United States was the first nation to recognize Israel officially as an independent state,[75] the Soviet Union was in fact Israel's strongest supporter
in the earliest years of the state.[76] By the time of the 1956 Suez War, however, it was clear that Moscow had opted to support the Arab powers in
the Middle East, while Israel was going to establish closer relations with
the West. Israel's relations with Russia have improved enormously in the
last two decades.[77] Robert Freedman has suggested that the significant
improvement began under Mikhail Gorbachev (1988–1991) and was
continued during Boris Yeltsin's tenure. Yeltsin, seeking to improve Russia's international influence, adopted a more balanced position on the
Arab-Israeli conflict and sought to promote more links with Israel than
had been the case in the past.[78]

Israel and the United States have had a close relationship since the creation
of the state.[79] In recent years Israel's closest political and diplomatic ties have
been with the United States. The subject of United States–Israeli relations
is clearly far too large and significant in the context of Israeli foreign policy
to be adequately handled in the space available here.[80] The United States is
Israel's largest supplier of aid, both civilian and military, as well as Israel's
guarantor of energy,[81] its largest trading partner, and most consistent defender
in a variety of problematic international diplomatic arenas. However, most
observers have remarked that the bilateral relationship has chilled considerably since the election of President Barak Obama, who has pressed Israel to
do more to work toward peace with the Palestinians, primarily by stopping
its building of new settlements in the Occupied Territories.[82]

The role of the United States as a mediator in the Middle East in modern times—from Secretary of State Henry Kissinger's shuttle diplomacy,[83]
through President Jimmy Carter's Camp David experience, to George Mitchell's 2010 role as a peacemaker between Israel and the Palestinians—has
been consistent and omnipresent; President Bill Clinton's intense efforts
at the end of his presidential term to break the peace impasse illustrated
this.[84] Although events in recent years have created occasional tensions in
this bilateral relationship,[85] overall the two nations have been important to
each other and good allies.[86] Israel has been important to the United States
as a source of military intelligence in a strategically significant geopolitical

setting and equally important as a stable democracy in a part of the world where stable democracies are not very common.

ECONOMIC-DEVELOPMENTAL CONCERNS

The third of Brecher's four general issue areas in foreign policy involves economic and developmental concerns. Israel's economic development has been neither as strong nor as consistent as many had hoped it would be.[87] For this, foreign policy has played a direct as well as a frequently disruptive role.

Because Israel is forced to spend so much of its budget on military- and defense-related activities, it has continually had a severe balance-of-payments problem.[88] Since independence,

Israel has required no less than $176 billion (in current figures) to cover all its annual trade deficits. Almost two thirds of this accumulated deficit was covered by unilateral transfers, such as funds brought in by immigrants, foreign pensions, donations from Jewish fund-raising organizations abroad to institutions of health, education and social services, and grants from foreign governments, especially from the United States. The rest was financed by loans from individuals, banks and foreign governments, which Israel has been repaying since its early years.[89]

The national external debt thus increased every year until 1985, when, for the first time, less was borrowed than was paid back. However, "this positive trend reverted for a few years until the net national external debt reached a new high of $20.8 billion in 1995. During the past decade it diminished considerably, down to zero, and since 2002 it is becoming growingly positive—namely, Israel is a creditor—with 'the world' owing it more than Israel owes the world, over $31 billion in 2006."[90]

Total loans to Israel outstanding at the end of the year continued to grow over time between independence and the late years of the twentieth century, but by 2000 the total external debt was significantly lower. The total foreign debt was $356 million in 1954, $543 million in 1960, $2.223 billion in 1970, $11.344 billion in 1980, $15.122 billion in 1990, and $7.353 billion in 2000. Indeed, according to the Israeli Ministry of Foreign Affairs, foreign debt was essentially eliminated in the early years of the twenty-first century, "from being 1.6 times [160%] the GDP in 1985, still 25% of the GDP in 1995, declining to less than 3% in 2001, and down to zero by 2003—with Israel since then becoming a creditor (i.e., the world economy owes it much more than Israel owes the world)."[91]

Israel is economically tied to the Western world despite its geographic setting in the Middle East. More than half of Israel's imports come from the European Community (Common Market) and almost half of Israel's exports go there. In fact, in 1977 Israel signed an agreement with the Common Market and received a "special association," providing Israel with lower tariff barriers than most non–Common Market countries would have to face, and in May 2010 Israel was admitted to the Organization for Economic Cooperation and Development.[92]

CULTURAL-STATUS CONCERNS

Educational, scientific, and cultural concerns also appear in the formulation of Israeli foreign policy. As indicated above, Israel has been concerned since 1948 with gaining acceptance and legitimacy in the world community. In many cases this desire for acceptance by other nations of the world has extended from the political realm to the cultural realm. A number of efforts to defeat Israel in the cultural realm have been made by Arab nations that have been unable to defeat Israel on the battlefield. Israel must always be prepared, in other words, to do battle in the halls of the United Nations, where attempts are regularly made to expel Israel from one or another of the United Nations' many bodies, such as the United Nations Educational, Scientific, and Cultural Organization (UNESCO), or to condemn Israel for a variety of reasons.[93]

THE FOREIGN POLICY SETTING: A RECAPITULATION

When studying the political context within which public policy is made, it is important, indeed crucial, not only to understand those factors in the domestic, or internal, environment and how they might influence policy, but to understand as well those factors in the external environment. It is clear from even a cursory examination of the foreign policy process that there are a variety of factors that influence both the formulation and the execution of Israeli foreign policy decisions.

Overall, Brecher tells us that there are eight key components to Israel's foreign policy system:

1. Israel is a self-conscious Jewish state whose historical legacy and *raison d'être* link it indissolubly to Jewish communities everywhere.
2. Israel is dependent upon one or more super and great power(s) for military and economic assistance and diplomatic support.
3. The combined voting strength of the Arab, Soviet, and nonaligned groups at the UN has made a pro-Israel resolution in the General Assembly or the Security Council impossible since the early 1960s.
4. Israel is totally isolated within the Core of the Middle East system and is confronted with a permanent challenge to its security; that condi-

tion, and its geographic position, have imposed a persistent quest for military aid.

5. Israel is vastly outnumbered by the Arab states, thereby creating a continuous demand for immigrants to augment its military and economic manpower.
6. Coalition government is a fixed element of Israel's political system, causing restraints on foreign policy choices.
7. *Ein breirah* ["no alternative"] is the lynchpin of Israel's political thought and behaviour.
8. Historical legacy and Arab enmity have created the necessity for activism and militancy in Israeli behavior.[94]

The legacy of war and the resulting pattern of tension that exists are clearly the most important factors in Israeli foreign policy. There is no legacy of goodwill, trust, faith, or confidence existing between Israel and its neighbors. While it is true that Israel and Egypt have been at peace now since 1979, and Israel and Jordan have been at peace since 1994, the peace has run hot and cold over the years, and Israelis have not perceived it as sufficiently secure to feel that they no longer need to be concerned about their southern border. All of Israel's other neighbors are still technically in a state of war, and this merely intensifies Israel's concerns about the creation of an independent state for the Palestinian people, a topic to which we turn our attention in the next chapter.

Likewise, important strategic considerations must be kept in mind. Israel must be aware of the separate environments within which policy must operate, ranging from the domestic (internal) to the regional (Middle Eastern) and international (global) levels. Psychological perceptions of leaders; their attitudes, beliefs, and values; and how these perceptions can affect policy making must also be accounted for. These factors, to say nothing of the actual policy-making process itself, all make up the strategic environment in which foreign policy decisions are made.

Equally important is the military dimension of foreign policy. The size, organizational nature, and needs of the IDF must constantly be evaluated when political leaders make policy decisions that could have military consequences. The time needed to fully mobilize the Israeli armed forces, the effect of such a mobilization on the economy, and similar factors must all be considered in the development of foreign policy. The issues of national security and defensible borders form an important part of this agenda. Because Israel is small and because some of its larger and more populous neighbors are hostile, the concept of defensible borders becomes even more important than it might be in the case of the United States and Canada, for example, two nations with the longest open and unarmed border in the world, but with a history of peace and cooperation.

Israel has existed as an independent nation now for more than six de-cades, but has not yet known a moment's peace. One of the elements that will contribute in a very significant way to the realization of a state of peace in the near future is the role of the Palestinians and the question of the future of the West Bank, the Gaza Strip, and the status of Jerusalem. It is to an examination of these questions that we turn our attention.

FOR FURTHER READING

Bar-On, Mordechai. *Never-Ending Conflict: Israeli Military History.* Mechanicsburg, Pa.: Stackpole, 2006.

Ben-Basat, Avi, ed. *The Israeli Economy, 1985–1998: From Government Intervention to Market Economics.* Cambridge, Mass.: MIT Press, 2002.

Bialer, Uri. *Between East and West: Israel's Foreign Policy Orientation, 1948–1956.* Cambridge: Cambridge University Press, 2008.

Cohen, Stuart. *Israel and Its Army: Continuity and Change.* London: Routledge, 2007.

———. *The New Citizen Armies: Israel's Armed Forces in Comparative Perspective.* London: Routledge, 2010.

Cordesman, Anthony. *The Military Balance in the Middle East.* Westport, Conn.: Praeger, 2004.

Derori, Zeev. *The Israeli Defence Force and the Foundation of Israel.* London: Frank Cass, 2004.

Freedman, Robert, ed. *Contemporary Israel: Domestic Politics, Foreign Policy, and Security Challenges.* Boulder, Colo.: Westview, 2009.

Golani, Moti. *Israel in Search of a War: The Sinai Campaign, 1955–1956.* Portland, Ore.: Sussex Academic Press, 1998.

Inbar, Efraim. *Israel's Strategic Agenda.* New York: Routledge, 2007.

Karpin, Michael. *The Bomb in the Basement: How Israel Went Nuclear and What That Means for the World.* New York: Simon and Schuster, 2006.

Maoz, Zeev. *Defending the Holy Land: A Critical Analysis of Israel's Security and Foreign Policy.* Ann Arbor: University of Michigan Press, 2006.

Mearsheimer, John, and Stephen Walt. *The Israel Lobby and U.S. Foreign Policy.* New York: Farrar, Straus and Giroux, 2007.

Oren, Michael. *Six Days of War: June 1967 and the Making of the Modern Middle East.* Oxford: Oxford University Press, 2002.

Shalom, Zaki. *Israel's Nuclear Option: Behind the Scenes Diplomacy between Dimona and Washington.* Portland, Ore.: Sussex Academic Press, 2005.

Stein, Kenneth W. *Heroic Diplomacy: Sadat, Kissinger, Carter, Begin and the Quest for Arab-Israeli Peace.* New York: Routledge, 1999.

10

The Palestinians, the West Bank and Gaza, and Jerusalem

The conflict that has existed between Israelis and Palestinians for well over fifty years is easy to find confusing. Labels used in discussion of the Middle East conflict are not value-free, and for some observers these discussions carry significant emotional attachments. This chapter discusses both the historical and the contemporary significance of concepts in the equation, concepts such as "Occupied Territories" or even *Eretz Israel*. As we have already seen in chapter 1, the term *West Bank* is rooted in history, as are the terms *Palestinian* and *Zionist*, and before a student can fully understand the nature of current debate, he or she must understand the history and current meaning of the terms involved. In this chapter we also discuss the term *Palestinian* more substantially to understand the historical and contemporary meaning of that label. Beyond this, we examine the importance of Jerusalem to the various actors in the debate.

Who should control the lands called the Occupied Territories, the West Bank and Gaza, or Palestine, as the areas under debate are variously called by the different actors involved? This is one of the simplest and yet most complex questions to be addressed in this volume because it touches upon some of the most fundamental and enduring points of contention in the Middle East debate.

We begin by reviewing some of the historical claims of the parties involved, then direct our attention to the Palestinians as a people and to their political

---

The "separation wall" has caused havoc in Palestine.

237

behavior. Linked to this is the subject of the West Bank and Gaza Strip, the major components of the Occupied Territories. Why are they so important to the Palestinians? Why are they important to the Israelis? The same holds true for the city of Jerusalem and the role that it plays in the modern history of three world religions. I do not claim that this type of systematic examination will suggest answers to all of the problems and tensions to be found in this part of the world; my goal is to increase students' understanding of these tensions, sensitivity to the issues involved, and awareness of the feelings of the political actors on both sides of the dilemma.

HISTORY

The term *West Bank* is rooted in history. Prior to the British partition of 1922,[1] in which the boundaries of Transjordan were created, the term *Palestine* was used very broadly and "generally denoted the southern third of Ottoman Syria," according to the 1911 edition of the *Encyclopedia Britannica*.[2] Eventually, the territory on the East Bank of the Jordan River became Transjordan (today called Jordan), while the area on the West Bank became known as Palestine. Transjordan itself made up 78.2 percent of the British Mandate. It was within the *other* 21.8 percent of pre-1922 Palestine that the turbulence of subsequent decades was experienced. Transjordan, later Jordan, was considered a *fait accompli* and not a subject for further discussion or negotiation.

In 1920 the San Remo Conference gave Britain a mandate over Palestine, as we described in chapter 1, and by 1922 Palestine was effectively under British administration. Britain's first high commissioner to Palestine was Sir Herbert Samuel.

During the interwar period, as we saw in chapter 1, several royal commissions were created to deal with outbreaks of violence and questions of competing nationalisms. In 1929 violence escalated, with 133 Jews and 116 Palestinians killed in Jerusalem alone. The Peel Report, issued in 1937, concluded that the Jewish and Arab communities would not be able to live together in peace and recommended partition, recognizing that "it would be difficult to draw lines that would satisfy either party and that major population displacements might ensue."[3] Under the partition proposed by Peel, *none* of what is referred to today as the West Bank would have been in the Jewish state. There would be a separate sacred-site area to be controlled by Britain. A subsequent study by another royal commission, the Woodhead Commission, produced another partition recommendation, with the Jewish state in this plan substantially smaller than the one envisioned in the Peel Report. In chapter 1 we further noted how the British had, in fact, made contradictory promises to the two major groups involved, the Zionists and the Arabs, and how the

British themselves could not decide which position to favor in relation to the demands of the Zionists. Ultimately, of course, the British simply gave up and passed the issue on to the fledgling United Nations.

In 1947, when Britain turned the Palestine question over to the United Nations for resolution, it did so to some degree because awareness of the Holocaust had shifted world public opinion strongly in favor of the Zionists over the Arab community's position on the issue. In November of that year, the UN Special Committee on Palestine issued yet another in the chain of recommendations for partition, proposing the creation of two sovereign states, one Jewish and the other Palestinian. In essence:

> The country was to be divided into a Jewish state consisting of the coastal plain, eastern Galilee, and most of the southern Negev. Its 32 percent of Palestine's population would receive about 55 percent of the land. The Arabs would retain central Galilee, the mountain district (most of which was later to become the West Bank), the southern coast (some of which was later called the Gaza Strip), and the city of Jaffa. Jerusalem and its environs would become an international enclave under U.N. Trusteeship.[4]

As we already know, the Zionists supported this proposal and the Arabs were opposed (see map 1.4).

As a result of the War of Independence and the Israeli-Jordanian Armistice of 1949, Egypt controlled the Gaza Strip, Jordan occupied the area known today as the West Bank (see map 1.5), and Jerusalem was divided into Israeli and Jordanian parts.[5] On April 1, 1949, King Abdullah proceeded to formally annex the part of Jerusalem under Jordan's control.[6] The following April (1950) both chambers of a newly elected Jordanian parliament (including representatives from the West Bank) passed legislation sealing this status and supporting "unity between the two sides of the Jordan and their union into one state, which is the Hashemite Kingdom of Jordan, at whose head reigns King Abdullah Ibn al Husain, on a basis of constitutional representative government and equality of rights and duties of all citizens."[7] The local Palestinian population did not universally endorse this act; many were strongly opposed, in fact. In addition to the leaders of the Arab League, many Palestinians themselves felt that their social and political institutions were "far more advanced than those of the indigenous Bedouin inhabitants of the East."[8] Many also saw annexation as inconsistent with their ultimate goal of Palestinian nationalism. Little more was actually done to move toward this goal, however, for the next decade and a half.

In 1964 the Arab League endorsed the establishment of the Palestine Liberation Organization, the PLO, whose first congress was held in East Jerusalem (Jordan) that May. Thus would begin a long and arduous relationship between Jordan and the PLO. Although Jordan originally supported the creation and objectives of the PLO, the fact that the PLO's goals "threatened

Jordan's effort to make Jordanians of the Palestinians" provoked tensions between the PLO delegation in Jerusalem and Jordanian government officials.[9] For the next quarter century, this relationship would vacillate between cooperation and confrontation, for any future Palestinian state, after all, would encompass both Israeli and Jordanian territory.

In June 1967, as has been described earlier in this book, Israel launched a preemptive attack on Egypt, Syria, and Iraq. Succumbing to pressure from its Arab allies, Jordan entered the war, despite assurances from Israel that no hostilities along their shared border would be forthcoming if Amman remained neutral. Israel did not, in fact, launch an offensive attack against Jordan, but once Jordan became involved, Israeli forces launched a crushing campaign. Within a matter of six days, Israel had captured the entire West Bank to the Jordan River, along with the Sinai Desert (subsequently returned to Egypt), the Gaza Strip, and part of the Golan Heights (Syrian territory that was later formally annexed by Israel).

The important points to reemphasize in discussing the historical context at this point are (1) the territory that is today known as the West Bank was not integrated as a part of Jordan between 1948 and 1967, the 1949–1950 annexation statement from Jordan notwithstanding; (2) in all of the proposed partition plans that referred to what was called Palestine, there was the intention to create a Jewish state *and* a Palestinian state—a Palestinian state independent of an already established Transjordan; and (3) a Palestinian nationalist movement existed in this region prior to 1967 and opposed the annexation of the West Bank by King Hussein, before the same movement opposed the prospect of similar annexation by Israel. Thus, it would not be correct to see the goal of today's Palestinian nationalism simply as being a reaction to Israeli occupation: its goal has been sovereignty and independence from any external control, be it Israeli or Jordanian, since before Israeli occupation. It is also clear that the politics of peacemaking will have to deal with the concept of partition and the long-term division of territory in the region.[10]

THE PALESTINIANS

Palestine as a whole has been part of the map of the Middle East for nearly two thousand years, the name first appearing during the Roman occupation of the area and lasting until 1949, when the Israeli War of Independence left the land that was to be called the State of Palestine occupied by both Jordan and Israel. The people who lived on that land were historically referred to as Palestinians.

Perhaps the late Edward Said most eloquently expressed the Palestinians' central claim:

We were on the land called Palestine; were our dispossession and our efface-
ment, by which almost a million of us were made to leave Palestine and our
society made nonexistent, justified even to save the remnant of European Jews
that had survived Nazism? By what moral or political standard are we expected
to lay aside our claims to our national existence, our land, our human rights?[11]

The idea of a Palestinian nation and the quest for an independent state,
as we noted earlier, predated the most recent tensions of the Palestinian-
Israeli conflict, as there was a movement for Palestinian nationalism prior
to the creation of the state of Israel.[12] This claim to nationalism has survived the years and is a significant part of the basis for unrest today in the
region.[13] When Abdullah I of Jordan annexed the West Bank in 1949, the
Arab League, after a period of objection, agreed to its temporary *administration* by Jordan, but continued to express its sympathy for the desire of the
indigenous Palestinians for a nation of their own.[14] In 1957 King Hussein
moved against the leadership of the Palestinian nationalist movement in
the Jordanian parliament, arresting thousands of Palestinians, especially
those living on the West Bank.[15] Ensuing demonstrations against Hussein's
actions were suppressed by the king's army, thus establishing a "pattern of
control which was to characterize Jordanian policy toward the West Bank
up until the Israeli occupation" in 1967.[16]

Historically, the relationship between the late King Hussein (who died
in February 1999 after forty-six years as Jordan's monarch and was succeeded by his son, Abdullah II) and the Palestinians was not especially
warm.[17] From the time of his ascension to the throne, he was suspicious of
the Palestinians and feared their questioning of his monarchy's legitimacy.
Many Palestinians *did*, in fact, question his legitimacy as an "outsider"
whose family was installed upon the Jordanian throne by a colonial power
(the British). Until the Israeli occupation in 1967, West Bank inhabitants
were characterized as second-class citizens within the Jordanian kingdom
and often indicated that they were "discriminated against politically and
economically."[18] In a final wave of arrests following demonstrations against
King Hussein in 1966, virtually the entire leadership of the West Bank political opposition was again imprisoned.[19] In September 1970, three years
after the Israeli occupation, the Jordanian army massacred a large number
of Palestinians in refugee camps inside Jordan itself, the goal being to crush
those Palestinian organizations opposed to the king. This event became
known as Black September.[20]

The new king, Abdullah II, quickly indicated upon succession to the
throne in 1999 that he would "preserve the course that Hussein set."[21] Abdullah said during a meeting with a number of Israeli governmental leaders
shortly after he assumed the monarchy that "King Hussein chose a path of
peace and cooperation in Israel. I promise to adhere to this policy."[22] Ob-

servers at the time interpreted this to mean that Abdullah would continue
the moderate course of his father on Middle East peace issues and political
and economic reform at home. Because in 1993 Abdullah had married a
Palestinian who came from the West Bank city of Tulkarm, and because she
had assumed the title of Princess Rania at the time of the marriage, observers expected that her Palestinian background would make a real contribution to Abdullah's standing in Jordan, where ethnic Palestinians made up
nearly 60 percent of the population.[23] In 2010, after ten years on the throne,
King Abdullah II is seen by many Jordanians as "growing" into his role as
king. Although following the moderation of his father, King Hussein, he
is being careful to walk a fine line between progressive moderation and
respect for tradition so that he doesn't weaken his base of power.

Despite this history of enmity between Jordan and the Palestinians,
many continue to believe that Jordan will have to play a significant role in
the resolution of the Palestinian situation.[24] Many students of the region
believe that King Hussein in his later years on the throne sought to play a
positive and substantive role[25] and hope that King Abdullah will continue
to play a responsible and positive role in the peace process; he has been
both visible and active in promoting discussion and advocating moderation in the region in recent months.[26] There was real hope that King Abdullah and Prime Minister Ehud Barak would make significant progress toward
peace following the Israeli election of 1999.[27] While they were unable to
reach a total peace agreement during Barak's brief period in office, they did
make steady progress in that direction and did show that they could work
together toward a common goal.

Some analysts have suggested that Arab Palestinians in the world today can
be categorized as falling into one of three groups: (1) those inside pre-1967
Israel who did not flee during the War of Independence and who are, consequently, Israeli citizens with full civil and political rights; (2) those in the
Occupied Territories who have always lived in the villages, towns, and camps
in which they are presently found or who fled during fighting from 1948 to
1949 and became refugees in the Jordanian-controlled West Bank from 1949
until 1967; and (3) those who live outside of the former Palestine (many
now in Jordan itself).[28] Geopolitics and demographics, therefore, encourage,
if not mandate, Jordanian involvement in a solution to the problem.

Ironically, one of the best historical parallels to the contemporary Palestinian situation is that of the early Zionists when they, too, were developing
a strong sense of national identity but lacked a state of their own. As Said
has written,

> There is a Palestinian people, there is an Israeli occupation of Palestinian
> lands, there are Palestinians under Israeli military occupation, there are Pal-
> estinians—650,000 of them—who are Israeli citizens and who constitute 15

percent of the population of Israel, there is a large Palestinian population in exile: these are actualities which the United States and most of the world have directly or indirectly acknowledged, which Israel too has acknowledged, if only in the forms of denial, rejection, threats of war, and punishment. . . . Short of complete obliteration, the Palestinians will continue to exist and they will continue to have their own ideas about who represents them, where they want to settle, what they want to do with their national and political future.[29]

Along with cultivating a better sense of Palestinian identity, many refugees also demand the right to return to the property from which they fled between 1948 and 1949 or 1967, or they at least want compensation from Israel for the loss of that property.[30] Israel's reply has consistently been that since the Palestinians left voluntarily and at the behest of other Arab states in 1948, Israel has no legal or moral obligation to allow their return or to compensate them for lost property.

There are many Palestinian refugees, as table 10.1 indicates. Many of these refugees respond to Israel's claim that it has no legal or moral obligation to allow their return or to compensate them for lost property by noting that they were coerced from their land. In any case, they say, whatever the cause of their departure, a variety of UN resolutions plus the International Covenant on Civil and Political Rights (1966) guarantees them the right to return. They argue that fleeing the fighting in 1948 did not constitute a permanent rejection of their property rights and, consequently, that Article 12

Photo 10.1.   A "word cloud" of terms used in relation to the Gaza Strip today.

of the 1966 International Covenant on Civil and Political Rights, officially adopted by the United Nations in 1976, applies when it notes that "No one shall be arbitrarily deprived of the right to enter his own country."[31] Following the 1967 war, tens of thousands of Palestinians moved out of the West Bank. One estimate suggests that the Arab population decreased by more than two hundred thousand between the last Jordanian census before 1967 and an Israeli census taken after the fighting ceased.[32]

PALESTINIAN STATEHOOD AND GOVERNANCE

The issue of the precise date of an official declaration of Palestinian statehood has periodically become the subject of debate itself. While the Palestinian leadership has often threatened to declare statehood as a negotiating tactic with Israel, in fact it has regularly backed away from the actual declaration because Israel has indicated that a formal declaration of Palestinian statehood would force Israel to act to prevent such an action, if it took place prior to the successful conclusion of negotiations designed to bring about peace in the region. One recent example of this kind of event took place in September 2000; the Palestinian leadership had set September 13 as a

Table 10.1   United Nations Measures of Population and Refugees, 2007

	Population Census				
OPT* Populations			Average		
	Census 1997	Census 2007	Absolute Change	Percentage Change	Annual Change
West Bank	1,873,476	2,350,583	477,107	25.47	2.55
Gaza Strip	1,022,207	1,416,543	394,336	38.58	3.86
Totals	2,895,683	3,767,126	871,443	30.09	3.01
	Refugee Census				
OPT* Refugee Population			Average		
	Census 1997	Census 2007	Absolute Change	Percentage Change	Annual Change
West Bank	523,310	643,305	119,994	22.93	2.29
Gaza Strip	664,722	962,098	297,376	44.74	4.47
Totals	1,188,032	1,605,402	417,370	35.13	3.51

Source: UNRWA, *West Bank and Gaza Strip Population Census of 2007* (January 2010), "Table 1: Census Results for the OPT, 1997 and 2007," and "Table 2: Census Results for Refugees in the OPT, 1997 and 2007," www.unrwa.org/userfiles/2010012035949.pdf, accessed May 2010.
* Occupied Palestinian Territory

deadline by which either an agreement on statehood must be reached with Israel or it would unilaterally declare statehood.[33] After pressure and mediation from the United States the Palestinian leadership once again backed away from a unilateral declaration of statehood and agreed to continue negotiations with Israel.

One by-product of Palestinian nationalism, as previously mentioned, was the establishment of the PLO in 1964.[34] A full discussion of its organization, historical evolution, and behavior is beyond the scope of our examination here, but a brief outline is appropriate at this time.[35] In January 1964 at the Arab League summit in Cairo, the decision was made "to organize the Palestinian people and to enable them to take their role in the liberation of their homeland and self-determination." On May 28 of that year the PLO was established with its national charter and the Palestine National Congress (PNC), a legislature in exile. In February 1969 at the fifth PNC meeting Yasser Arafat was elected PLO chairman, and Fatah became the dominant faction of the PLO.

In April 1972 the PNC rejected a proposal by King Hussein of Jordan for the creation of a United Arab Kingdom. The next year the PNC adopted a ten-point program, dropping the concept of the creation of a state in all of Palestine (thus, allowing for some unofficial acknowledgment that a state of Israel might exist in part of Palestine). In protest of this decision some PLO factions formed a Rejectionist Front. In October 1974 the Arab League recognized the PLO as the "sole legitimate representative of the Palestinian people"; in November 1998 the United Nations granted the PLO Observer Status.[36]

The PLO is essentially an umbrella organization comprising many different groups, including Fatah (supporters of the late Yasser Arafat), the Democratic Front for the Liberation of Palestine (DFLP), the Popular Front for the Liberation of Palestine (PFLP), Hamas, and several others, which both compete and cooperate with each other. Hamas is one of the best known of the PLO factions. It is an acronym for the *Harakat al-Muqawama al-Islamiyya* (Islamic Resistance Movement) and was established in January 1988. Hamas, which is the Arabic word for "zeal," has been among the more active and violence-prone of the PLO factions. From its birth it has been more militant and more supportive of violence than many of the other factions; in February 1988 the Muslim Brotherhood adopted it as its military arm. It also has been more oriented to the masses: "it did not address itself to the notables and merchants who were traditional [Muslim] Brotherhood supporters, and who in many instances had ties to Jordan, but instead sought recruits among younger and better-educated individuals without ties to the Palestinian establishment."[37] Accordingly, there has frequently been something of a controlled conflict between the PLO central leadership (controlled by the Fatah faction) and Hamas over the extent to which violence is appropriate as a response to Israeli occupation and policy.

About 74 percent of Gazans (Gaza's population is something more than 1.55 million people) are refugees of the 1948 war or their descendants. The majority of refugees still live in wretchedly poor and overflowing camps. The West Bank does not fare any better. Its estimated population is 2.4 million, making both the West Bank and Gaza among the fastest growing population areas in the world. Forty percent of the people of the West Bank and 45 percent of Gazans are under age fifteen.[38]

The PLO has a governmental structure called the Palestine National Authority (PNA—also referred to as the Palestinian Authority, PA), with a legislative body called the Palestinian Legislative Council. The legislative council has amended the Palestinian constitution, called the Palestinian National Charter, on more than one occasion.[39] Overall, the evolution of a constitution for a state of Palestine has made significant progress in the last decade.[40] Through the PLO's Observer Status at the United Nations,[41] it has established formal diplomatic relations with a number of countries. Its relations with Arab nations have been in flux.[42] At times Egypt and Jordan have supported the PLO and its goals; on other occasions each has, both together and separately, criticized and cut off any communications with it.[43]

In 1996 the institutionalization of Palestinian nationalism advanced significantly with the election of a legislative body and a *Ra'is*, a chairman or president.[44] The election of January 1996 was the first free and democratic election ever held for the Palestinian people. As part of the Oslo 2 Accords (further discussed in the next chapter) a substantial number of international observers were on hand to monitor the election. In fact, according to one source there were 613 international observers present.[45]

Palestinians were enthusiastic and excited about the election. In October 1995, respondents to a public opinion survey indicated that the election of the Palestinian Legislative Council would "promote the democratic process in the Palestinian community" (68.8 percent), "bring changes for the better" (74.5 percent), "lead to an improvement in economic conditions" (61.4 percent), and "lead to personal security" (74.3 percent), while only a comparatively small group of respondents answered negatively, saying that the election would "be a false election; the results are predetermined" (33.2 percent), "provide legitimacy for an unsatisfactory agreement" (37.2 percent), "provide the Authority with justification to oppress the Opposition" (40 percent), and "be a change for the worse" (17.7 percent).[46]

In a December 1995 study, researchers found that more than half of the respondents believed that the upcoming elections would be fair (56.4 percent) and that they had a civil responsibility to take part in the elections (81.7 percent "strongly agree" and "agree somewhat").[47] Just before the January election, an overwhelming majority of Palestinians were satisfied with the fairness of the election process to that point, although by that time there was a significant difference between backers of the Fatah and Hamas movements in their responses to the question, as shown in table 10.2.

The January 1996 election installed a president or chairman of the PNA and an eighty-eight-member legislative council.[48] On balance, the conclusions articulated in most media were that the first-ever elections of the Palestinian people were a success. The leader of the European Union observers said that the elections "accurately reflect the aspirations of the Palestinian voters"; others in his delegation said that the election process was "largely fair,"[49] but within a day many Palestinian candidates had filed official complaints with the Central Election Commission over the election outcomes.[50]

Yasser Arafat, whose victory was never in question, received 88.6 percent of the vote of those participating in the election for the *Ra'is*, ranging from 85.5 to 93.3 percent of the votes in the electoral districts. Fully 22 percent of the voters submitted blank ballots for the *Ra'is* vote, perhaps because it was so widely perceived that no real contest was involved in this race.

The new legislative council was dominated by members of the Fatah Party, the party of Arafat, which won fifty-two of eighty-eight seats; another fourteen seats were won by independents affiliated with Fatah. One observation made about the election results was that the election was "no step forward for women," with 42 percent of the voters being female, 3 percent of the candidates being women, and only five of the eighty-eight members of the new legislative council—5.7 percent—being women. Much discussion took place after the elections about the future need for an electoral quota for women, with some arguing that the current electoral system "will only serve to further marginalize women" if quotas aren't introduced, and others arguing that women—like all candidates—should be elected on their merits alone.[51]

In the final analysis, the successful completion of the first-ever Palestinian elections was important for three reasons. First, it provided credibility to the leadership of the Palestinian National Authority in its negotiations with the Israeli government. Second, it was important within the Palestinian community in demonstrating that a peaceful election was possible and

Table 10.2   Perceived Fairness of the Palestinian Election Campaign, 1996

"In general, are you satisfied about the fairness of the election process?"			
	All	*Fatah*	*Hamas*
Yes	51.5%	70.4%	35.8%
Somewhat satisfied	25.2%	15.7%	23.0%
No	11.3%	3.9%	24.3%
No opinion	12.0%	10.1%	16.9%

Source: Jerusalem Media and Communications Center, "Public Opinion Poll No. 12: On Palestinian Elections," January 1996, p. 7.

in showing "the Palestinian people's firm commitment to democracy."[52] Third, even taking into consideration the irregularities in the election, it helped to take the Palestinian state one step further on the road to becoming a stable democracy in a part of the world where peaceful democratic elections are not at all common.

This election did not result in a transfer of power from one administration to another. Rather, it served to formalize the already empowered administration of Yasser Arafat and his Fatah Party. The old political order in Palestine was based on consensus and traditional authoritarian leadership; the new order recognizes heterogeneity and seeks to operate democratically. Many observers have suggested that Arafat belongs to the old generation of Middle Eastern politicians, those who value results more than process, and these observers have suggested that many of the violations of the electoral process were a direct result of Arafat's authoritarian approach to the election. If this is true, then it is especially important to begin to socialize the younger generation of Palestinians to the values of free and fair democratic elections. Whatever its rough points, this election was a step along that path.

As long as Yasser Arafat was *Ra'is* of the Palestinians and in control of his Fatah bloc, the controlled conflict was able to be *kept* controlled. In November 2004 Arafat died, and it quickly became clear that his successor, President Mahmoud Abbas, was not able to exercise the same degree of control over Palestinian factionalism as had Arafat.

This "controlled conflict" evolved into outright military conflict following the Palestinian election of 2006. The 2006 election was the first for the Palestinian legislature since 1996, because scheduled intervening elections had all been canceled due to political violence and instability in the region. In the 2006 election Hamas won by a landslide the majority of seats in the legislature, winning 74 of the 132 available seats compared to Fatah winning only 45 of the seats. Hamas candidates won 41.7 percent of the overall vote with Fatah candidates winning 36.96 percent of the vote.

The electoral system had been modified from its form in the 1996 election; the number of legislators was increased from 88 to 132, with 66 of the 132 seats distributed proportionally to electoral lists that received more than 2 percent of the total votes. All voters would have two ballots in the election, one for nationwide party lists and one for constituency representation.[53] Party lists were required to include at least one woman in the first three names, at least one woman in the next four names, and at least one woman in the next five names after that. The point of this change, following the 1996 election, was to get more women into the legislature; 17 (out of 132) women were elected, compared with 5 (out of 88) in the previous legislature.

The Fatah Prime Minister Ahmed Qurei resigned and Ismail Haniya, the leader of Hamas, became prime minister. In a relatively short period of time virtual civil war erupted in Palestine, with Hamas controlling the Gaza Strip and Fatah controlling the West Bank.[54]

PALESTINIAN GOALS

The major political desire of many Palestinians today is the establishment of a Palestinian state; most immediately, they seek Israeli withdrawal from the Occupied Territories.[55] Many claim, in fact, that they already have a well-defined sense of nationhood, but simply lack a state to complete the development of their sense of Palestinian identity.[56]

Originally the PLO called for the "total liberation of all occupied Palestine." At its Twelfth National Council in Cairo in 1974, however, it changed this goal, seeking instead to establish "a national authority in every part of Palestinian territory that is liberated."[57] The major groups in the PLO, including the Fatah, the DFLP, and the PFLP, debated this position vigorously, but ultimately the view of the pragmatists carried the day. Much like Herzl seventy years earlier, they believed realism and some territory was better than purism and no territory. Negotiations over the last two decades have continued to move toward the goal of independence and nationhood; one of the more recent steps toward progress occurred in November 1998 when PLO chairman (and PNA president) Yasser Arafat signed the Wye Agreement, something that is further discussed in the next chapter. The basic contents of the Wye Agreement of 1998 are included in box 10.1.

The PLO suffered both a loss of dignity and a loss of military influence when it was driven out of its bases in Lebanon by Israeli forces in 1982. The view that the world received of PLO troops being forced onto ships and sent out of Beirut Harbor robbed it of much of its self-proclaimed record of victory and effectiveness. Although the PLO did not honor its commitment to stay out of Lebanon, its standing in Arab eyes suffered from the event.[58]

A more recent major loss of Palestinian standing in the Arab world came in 1990 when Yasser Arafat publicly supported Iraq in the first Gulf War when Iraq invaded and attempted to annex Kuwait. In March 1991 the Gulf Cooperation Council (composed of six oil-producing Arab nations in the Persian Gulf region: Kuwait, Saudi Arabia, Qatar, Bahrain, Oman, and the United Arab Emirates) announced that "council members would undertake a policy of 'no forgiveness, no forgetting' toward Iraq's allies, as retribution for the threat posed to member nations by Iraq's August 1990 invasion of Kuwait." The Gulf States had given the PLO an estimated $1 billion during the 1980s, and for many years the Palestinian institutions felt the withdrawal of Arab support acutely.[59] While Arab aid has since resumed for the PNA, the episode caused hard feelings that have not disappeared.

Box 10.1. Core Content of the Wye Accord, October 23, 1998

On October 23, 1998, Israeli prime minister Benjamin Netanyahu and Chairman Yasser Arafat of the Palestine Liberation Organization (PLO) signed a document that became known as the Wye Accord. The agreement included the following provisions:

1. Israel would withdraw from 13.1 percent of the West Bank in three stages over several months and would transfer an additional 14 percent of the West Bank to PNA control from joint Israeli-Palestinian control.
2. The Palestine National Council (PNC), the parliament of the PLO, would reconvene to reconfirm the deletion of twenty-six clauses in the Palestinians' 1964 national charter that called for the destruction of Israel.
3. The PNA would arrest a number of Palestinian terrorism suspects requested by Israel and confiscate illegal weapons in Palestinian hands.
4. The Israelis would release 750 Palestinian prisoners held in Israeli jails.
5. A Palestinian airport and an industrial park in the Gaza Strip would be opened.
6. A transportation corridor between the West Bank and Gaza Strip would be opened.
7. A joint Israeli-Palestinian committee to discuss further Israeli troop withdrawals from occupied Palestinian territory would be convened.

Source: "Middle East: Highlights of Wye Accord," *Facts on File World News Digest,* October 23, 1998, accession number: 1998114840.

Recent history has shown that no matter how much the government of Israel may declare the leadership of the PNA to be irrelevant to the process of normalizing the Middle Eastern political system,[60] there can be no peace in the Middle East until the Palestinian question is resolved.[61]

THE WEST BANK AND GAZA

The Israeli government has, over the last several decades, negotiated with its neighbors a number of agreements—both peace treaties and other types of agreements—dealing with progress toward an eventual state of peace in the Middle East. One of the first major breakthroughs to this end involved the Camp David Accords (1979), which we discuss in some detail in the next chapter.[62] More recently, many other agreements with Israel's Arab neighbors have been reached, as well. These accords, as we shall see, have called for establishing autonomy for the local population while guaranteeing the security needs of Israel.[63]

Although recent acts of violence have forced Israel to curtail many of its more flexible initiatives with Arabs both in and outside of Israel, for many years Israel's Open Bridges policy permitted Palestinians living in Occupied

Territories a remarkable degree of continued economic and social contact with Lebanon, Jordan, and Egypt.[64] Transit points were open and individuals could cross from one side of the border to the other with their commercial goods.[65] This does not imply that crossing the border has always been effortless or without challenge, but it does mean that prior to the huge increase in violence and terrorism in the territories and Israel proper, a situation of commerce and travel was permitted to continue between Israel and Lebanon, Israel and Jordan, and Israel and Egypt.[66]

Since becoming the occupying power in 1967, Israel has been responsible for fundamental social services to the West Bank and Gaza populations.[67] The government provides twelve years of free schooling, nine of them mandatory, following the curricula set in Jordan and Egypt prior to occupation in 1967, although Palestinians will note that the amount spent per child is significantly different from that spent on Israeli citizens.[68] There are also a number of universities in the Occupied Territories; they have faced very significant problems over the years because of closures by Israeli authorities in response to acts of civil disobedience and violence.[69]

Most recently, as discussed in the previous chapter, the *intifada* has been the most prominent manifestation of the underlying tension between Israel and the Palestinians. The uprising began in 1987 and has successfully—from the point of view of its organizers—exerted pressure on Israel to remove itself from the Occupied Territories, even if it has not achieved its goal of Israeli withdrawal.[70]

In the early years, the point of the *intifada* was not armed resistance, but rather continued mass demonstrations requiring Israeli military attention. These demonstrations played effectively on television: scenes of Israeli troops firing on crowds of civilians proved instrumental in mobilizing public opinion around the world against Israel's presence in the West Bank and Gaza Strip and its policies there. This attention was not achieved without cost, however, for literally hundreds of Palestinians had been killed in the demonstrations through the end of 1988, virtually all shot by Israeli troops. "More than 600 Palestinians have died in the . . . wave of violence known as al-Aqsa Intifada. Of these, 148 were under 18. In addition, 14,405 Palestinians have been seriously wounded or disabled."[71] "Yet another result of the violence, often overshadowed by the bloodshed, is that more and more Palestinians are facing crushing poverty, crumbling social services, and a frightening retreat from progress towards the establishment of a democratic civil society."[72]

Ephraim Sneh, the former head of the civil administration of the West Bank, wrote in a *Ha'aretz* editorial that an analysis of the early years of the *intifada* demonstrated both costs and benefits for the Palestinians. The costs included hundreds killed and thousands wounded, or "about 20 times the order of magnitude of the annual casualties during the previous years of the occupation." Despite the fact that most Israeli forces involved changed from firing conventional ammunition to using rubber bullets (deemed more appropriate for crowd-control situations), the casualty rate on the West Bank was still significant. Among the additional costs was the fact that the economy of the Occupied Territories was virtually destroyed and the normal balance of society upset, with schools periodically shut down, a perception of anarchy existing, and gaps between social classes widening.

As for benefits, Sneh found that the *intifada* had succeeded in placing the Palestinian problem "on the international agenda." Also, "Israeli public opinion has been rocked"; that is, "Israelis who had become used to the fact that the cost of ruling over one-and-a-half million Palestinians was limited to an easy and far-off security burden, have now been confronted with the realization that it will be impossible to continue with the status quo in the territories for much longer."[73]

The early years of the *intifada* were responsible for two other remarkable phenomena: a significant increase in the Israeli population advocating withdrawal from the Occupied Territories, and public discussions by soldiers claiming that they were not adequately trained for, nor did they want to be involved in, the types of military activities demanded on the West Bank.[74]

In the more recent stage of the *intifada*, the cycle of violence and suffering in the region has expanded. Some *intifada* leaders have advocated bringing violence to the heart of Israel, suggesting that Palestinian pain and suffering will no longer be tolerated; they want Israeli civilians to suffer, too.[75] The cycle of violence and suffering has expanded with suicide bombers (referred to by Israeli spokespersons as homicide bombers) causing the deaths of literally hundreds of Israeli civilians both in population centers of Tel Aviv, Jerusalem, and the suburbs, and in rural areas between the population centers. The Israeli government has retaliated with selective assassinations, collective punishment, mass arrests, and destruction of the homes of individuals and families related to those believed to have participated in attacks against Israel.[76]

On several occasions in recent years something closely resembling open warfare has broken out, significantly and painfully affecting the quality of life of Palestinians, especially those in Gaza. Following the January 2006 election in which Hamas won a majority in the Palestinian legislature and was rapidly condemned by the European Union, Israel, and the United States as a terrorist organization, conflict developed between followers of Hamas who claimed their victory in that election and followers of Fatah, who argued that Hamas did not have the legitimacy it needed to govern.

This led to conflict between Hamas supporters of Prime Minister Ismail Haniya and Fatah president Mahmoud Abbas; the question of which party would govern broke into open warfare that resulted in the loss of life and much destruction of property. When, in December 2006, a cease-fire was achieved, it was negotiated by leaders of two other Palestinian political groups, the Popular Front for the Liberation of Palestine and Democratic Action.[77]

In brief, the period from 1967 to the present has been a continuing source of anguish for both Israelis and Palestinians.[78] Israel has been often criticized in the international community for many of the policies it has undertaken in the Occupied Territories.[79] These criticisms and accusations[80] have included charges that Israel has engaged in illegal acquisition of Palestinian land[81]; forced resettlement of parts of the Palestinian population; refused to permit Palestinian refugees from the 1967 war to return to their homes and property; forcibly expelled and deported Arab residents of the West Bank to Lebanon or Jordan[82]; restricted local political, educational, and medical institutions from operating openly; placed prohibitions on political activity; demolished buildings and residences; imposed unreasonable curfews; held people in administrative detention without judicial hearings[83]; held prisoners in unacceptable conditions of detention and interrogation (including charges of torture and prisoner abuse); censored publications; closed universities; and, in general, committed a wide range of other human rights violations.[84]

Israel's response to many of these charges has been to argue that domestic security concerns *require* these actions. The fact of the matter is that there *is* concern about terrorism because there *are* terrorist incidents; bombs *are* placed on buses, in apartment houses, in markets, and in other public places; arms and explosives *are* smuggled into Israel; suicide bombers *have* been responsible for the deaths of many, many Israeli civilians; and demonstrations and acts of violence *do* occur in the Occupied Territories. Israel's position has been that, until the question of the future of the Occupied Territories is determined and until the security of its own territory can be assured, it has an obligation to its own citizens to ensure a safe and secure existence.[85] Whether this necessitates continuation of the status quo, some form of association with Jordan, eventual independence, or outright Israeli annexation akin to what Abdullah did in 1949 has long been one of the most contentious and partisan debates in the Israeli political system.

JERUSALEM

The city of Jerusalem itself carries with it an importance far outweighing any strategic or conventional geopolitical significance. Its historical, emotional, and international complexities make it truly unique and suggest a set of problems to be resolved that go far beyond other issues of mutually agreed-upon boundaries.[86] As one scholar has indicated,

> No other city in the world has been subject to such intense competition for control as Jerusalem during its 4,000 years of recorded history. The religious

interests of the three world faiths for whom Jerusalem is so paramount can be fulfilled without their having to hold territorial control of the city. But territorial control is an overriding issue for the two nationalisms, Arab and Jewish, whose governments are in contention for the city. In the struggle of nationalisms sovereign space cannot be shared, although some sharing of political power is possible.[87]

Jerusalem's symbolic role in the Arab-Israeli struggle and, consequently, the dispute over to whom it "belongs" are profoundly emotional and intensely personal issues. David Ben-Gurion once stated that "the struggle for Jerusalem will determine the fate not only of the country, but of the Jewish people." Jordanian king Abdullah's view was that Jerusalem "holds a special position for every Muslim nation because of the Arab, Kurdish, Circassian, and Turkish blood which has been shed on its behalf throughout the history of Islam."[88] In short, neither side is inclined to compromise on the issue of Jerusalem.

A major point of contention, then, is often simply which religious group has the stronger claim (although for many the idea of *quantifying* such a claim, which would be necessary to make a determination about one claim being "stronger" than another, is almost impossible to imagine). It is clear that the three religious traditions—Judaism, Christianity, and Islam—each have links to Jerusalem and desire to exercise control over its future. Israel's position is that "Jerusalem has a far more powerful corporate meaning for Judaism than for Christianity and Islam."[89] The most commonly articulated sequence in this regard is that Christians have Rome, Muslims have Mecca and Medina, but Jews have only Jerusalem.[90] This argument, as might be imagined, carries little persuasive power for the Christian and Muslim communities.

As Saul Cohen has noted, during most of Jerusalem's history, it was territorially united under the rule of whichever nation dominated the politics of the region.[91] The city's division in 1949 was an unusual situation and one that convinced both sides in the dispute that it could not be permitted to happen again. Long-time mayor of Jerusalem Teddy Kollek concurred:

> The Jerusalem question cannot be decided by drawing a line. The future of Jerusalem cannot be resolved by division. This does not mean that Jerusalem is an insoluble problem. It means that Jerusalem's people of differing faiths, cultures, and aspirations must find peaceful ways to live together other than by drawing a line in the sand with a stick. It is no solution to rebuild concrete walls and barbed wire through the middle of the city.[92]

The actual process of partition occurred as a strictly military consequence. There were several stages in the eventual division of the territory of Palestine as a whole, beginning with the 1922 British White Paper delimiting

Palestine and Transjordan, followed by the Peel (1936) and the Woodhead (1939) Commissions, and culminating in the United Nations Special Committee on Palestine (UNSCOP) of 1947. Yet, none of these ever advocated the partition of Jerusalem itself. Indeed, all proposed leaving the city intact, either under mandatory or international authority.[93] It was rather the 1949 armistice between Israel and Jordan that left Jerusalem divided, with Jordan controlling all of the holy places in the city's eastern sector.

Between 1949 and 1967 Jerusalem remained very significant for an Israeli government that never abandoned hope of eventually reunifying the city and securing access to Jewish holy places. In fact, during this period Jerusalem functioned as the capital of Israel. Virtually all major national governmental institutions were moved from Tel Aviv to Jerusalem, albeit to the western part of the city, as a symbolic gesture of Israel's commitment eventually to reunite Jerusalem.

When reunification came in 1967, the Israeli government in effect announced that

> the June 5th [1967, the date of the beginning of the Six Day War] map of the region had been "destroyed irrevocably," but that Israel was prepared to negotiate new frontiers with its Arab neighbors. Jerusalem was an exception, not subject to negotiation. Within a month after the cease-fire the city was incorporated into the Israeli West Jerusalem municipality.[94]

Although Israel was willing to negotiate with its Arab neighbors over a variety of territorial questions, as far as the Israeli government was concerned, the issue of Jerusalem was settled: the city would never again be divided. This unification and annexation by Knesset legislation had some curious legal consequences, as the Government made a number of efforts to facilitate adaptation to the anomalies of this new situation. For example, once the Jordanian part of the city had been incorporated, under international law the Arab population automatically became inhabitants of the state of Israel, simultaneously retaining Jordanian citizenship, since Jordan continued to claim jurisdiction over the territory.[95]

The "Jerusalem question" has been intensified by Israel's active settlement policy there, something that will be discussed in the next section of this chapter. When Israeli spokesmen state that there are nearly two hundred thousand settlers in the West Bank/Occupied Territories, they are not counting the almost two hundred thousand Israelis who are living in what is called "Greater Jerusalem," land that was *not* part of Israeli Jerusalem prior to 1967. The city limits of Jerusalem have grown significantly in the last four decades, with much of the growth coming from formerly non-Israeli territory. Map 10.1 shows the city limits of Israeli Jerusalem in 1967 and how Jerusalem has grown since that time.

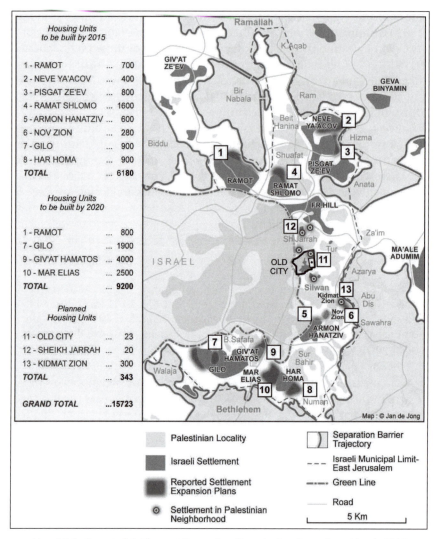

Map 10.1. Reported Settlement Expansion Plans in East Jerusalem, March 2010
Source: Foundation for Middle East Peace, "Reported Settlement Expansion Plans in
East Jerusalem, March, 2010," www.fmep.org/maps/jerusalem/is_v19_6_map_expansion
_plans.jpg/view, accessed May 2010.

Some have suggested, emotions apart, that there are geopolitical imperatives that explain why Jerusalem must remain unified, "irrespective of whatever internal geopolitical structural changes may take place."[96] Reasons offered for a united Jerusalem include

1. Historical struggles to continue ties to territories, such as those fought by the Jews through the years, create strong national values. This is especially true when the struggles have been carried out with little assistance from other national actors.
2. Jerusalem's geopolitical location in Israel makes the city and the Jerusalem corridor especially significant for Israel's development.
3. Jerusalem is a unique city, and part of its uniqueness comes from its several and varied neighborhoods. Although the whole may be greater than the sum of its parts, it is clear that the loss of some would diminish the character of the whole.
4. Jerusalem has a strategic and economic significance for Arab Palestine and, consequently, is strategically valuable to Israel, independent of any other reasons.
5. The rapid growth of the city makes it a second political core in Israel, along with Tel Aviv. Israel could not permit its second political core to be divided.

It is precisely the special status of the city and its extremely heterogeneous nature that makes the Jerusalem issue so difficult to resolve.[97] The heterogeneity of Jerusalem represents a microcosm of Israel itself, and the question of what kind of government Jerusalem should have, the administrative roles of the various ethnic groups, the relationship between religious and political questions, and other fundamental and emotional issues all serve to make the question of Jerusalem's future even more complex than it would be if it had to resolve only the question of which national actor would exercise sovereignty over it.[98]

ISRAELI ATTITUDES, INTENTIONS, AND POLICIES

Long-Term Plans

Israeli policy in the West Bank can be seen as a function of a number of different factors, including those related to ideology, history, and security, as well as a number of short-term demands of contemporary political groups. These factors, and many others, influence the attitudes and values of government leaders, and correspondingly influence the policies promulgated by the Israeli government.

The question of Israel's precise long-term intentions and plans for the Occupied Territories is one that has generated much disagreement inside the country.[99] From the outset of occupation in 1967 to the present, one of the sources of policy inconsistency has been the fact that Israeli politicians have debated repeatedly and inconclusively the status of the Occupied Territories, something that many Israelis prefer to call "the West Bank" to avoid the connotations of the term "occupied."[100] There have been those who firmly believe that the West Bank (excluding Gaza) is the same as biblical Judea and Samaria, and as such constitutes a part of what some religious Zionists believe is Greater Israel. Their solution, therefore, is annexation without further debate. Others, conversely, have argued that Israel should use the West Bank and Gaza as strategic buffer zones and bargaining chips for negotiation, being willing, in effect, to trade territory for peace. Still others have taken the position that Israel has no right to keep territories captured through warfare, whatever their status prior to capture. The territory must eventually be returned to either the Palestinians, who desire it as their state, or the Jordanians, from whom it was captured.[101]

The official position of the Labor governments in the years following the 1967 war was that the territories were occupied for security considerations and that, when it was possible, a return of the territories would be negotiated in exchange for a secure peace. In reality, there was a great deal of disagreement within the government over what its policy actually should be. Its policy positions suggested four central principles:

1. Maintenance of the status quo, with emphasis on security, under conservative local leadership supervised by Israel;
2. Economic integration of the West Bank . . . through the use of Arab labor, the marketing of Israeli products in the West Bank and of noncompetitive West Bank primary products in Israel, and the linking of West Bank infrastructure with Israel;
3. Using the West Bank as an opening wedge to the Arab world, through Moshe Dayan's "Open Bridges" policy, facilitating visits from Arab countries of "trustworthy" visitors and through export of products from Israel across the bridges to Jordan, and from Jordan to other Arab countries;
4. Establishment of Jewish settlements in selected areas as security outposts.[102]

Although it is possible to discuss the underlying principles of the Labor governments during the ten years they controlled the West Bank, they proved unable to reach an accord with Jordan or the Palestinians.[103] With the rise to power of the Likud in 1977, a significant change in direction could be perceived. Prime Minister Menachem Begin supported the Dayan policy of creating West Bank settlement "facts," and he advocated establishing so many "facts" that what was done could never be undone.[104] The number of settlements on the West Bank, and the rate of establishment of these settlements, increased dramatically.

Over the last three decades Israeli governments have taken different positions on settlements, on whether it was better to assume firm or hawkish positions in negotiations with the Palestinians, and on whether it was wise to negotiate land for peace. They have had fundamentally different attitudes about precisely how much risk is appropriate in search of peace. Prime Ministers Yitzhak Rabin (1974–1977, 1992–1995), Shimon Peres (1984–1986, 1995–1996), and Ehud Barak (1999–2001) of the Labor Party have been willing to make more concessions to the Palestinian leadership in exchange for the promise of a stable and secure peace. Prime Ministers Menachem Begin (1977–1983), Yitzhak Shamir (1983–1984, 1986–1992), Benjamin Netanyahu (1996–1999, 2009–), Ariel Sharon (2001–2006), Ehud Olmert (2006–2009), and Tsipi Livni (2009) of the Likud and, more recently, Kadima parties have put much more emphasis on negotiating from a perspective of security and not making concessions without adequate security guarantees.

There have been times over the last several decades when there appeared to be significant momentum developing toward the establishment of a stable and apparently secure peace. Time and time again, a lack of trust, an apparent unwillingness to honor previous commitments, or other factors have prevented continued progress. In July 2000 President Bill Clinton, Prime Minister Ehud Barak, and Palestinian National Authority chairman Yasser Arafat met at Camp David and came to a point at which many believed that peace really was within reach. They did not achieve it. And, in the ensuing two years, decades' worth of progress toward peace was undone. We return to this topic in the next chapter.

Settlements

Some political geographers have seen the pattern of settlements established by Israel after 1977 as a new set of walls designed to ensure a continued presence in the Occupied Territories, as well as a strategy to protect already existing Israeli settlements there. They suggest that the West Bank settlement process is an example of the "basically political nature of planning" and argue that the settlements show that "value-free planning is actually impossible."[105] Saul Cohen's geopolitical study of the Jerusalem area refers to new settlement patterns as a "third wall" around Jerusalem, despite their being some distance away from the city.[106]

It is clear, however, that the future of the Jewish communities already built in the Occupied Territories, to say nothing of future developmental plans for more communities, "largely depends on Israel's internal politics and international developments."[107] Critics of this approach have argued that the building of settlements in occupied territory is patently illegal under international law.[108] Others have suggested that the legality of the situation is basically ambiguous, but could be resolved with some action by the Israeli government.[109]

As far back as 1969 Labor Defense Minister Moshe Dayan proposed a "New Facts" doctrine, under which Israel would gradually establish new settlements and a continued presence in the Occupied Territories, arguing that Israel was in the West Bank "of right and not on sufferance."[110] Dayan proposed expanded settlement, along with increased roads, trade, commerce, and general infrastructure in the territories. Others in the Labor leadership opposed this view, for both philosophical and pragmatic reasons. For example, Finance Minister Pinhas Sapir argued that the Israeli economy would become dependent upon less-expensive Arab labor; Sapir warned that "to preserve Israel as the Jewish state . . . it would be necessary to not only maintain political separation, but to sever the economic bonds that were rapidly binding the two peoples together."[111]

Another study has indicated that two major phases may be distinguished in the establishment of settlements in the Occupied Territories, one corresponding with the Alignment (Labor) Government's term in office from 1968 to 1977, and the other corresponding with the Likud's term in office, from 1977 to 1984. Under the Alignment, the average rate of new settlers in the territories was about 770 per year; under the Likud, through 1984, the average rate was almost 5,400 per year; and in 1984, "for the first time, the growth exceeded 10,000 settlers a year." This pattern has continued since that time.[112]

In the last two decades this difference in party policies, with Labor being more moderate and more conciliatory than Likud, has been a highly visible theme in Israel's relations with its neighbors. This should come as no surprise, as foreign policy is one of the two major issue areas over which the major Israeli parties strongly disagree (the other being domestic economics). Labor's strategy has historically been more pragmatic, more supportive in principle of negotiations with Arab neighbors, and more opposed to significant expansion of Israeli settlements in the Occupied Territories, with the articulated goal of eventually exchanging land for peace. Likud, on the other hand, has been seen as far less pragmatic and far more ideologically committed to the policy of expanding settlements, supporting the Greater Israel Movement, demonstrating less flexibility with Arab neighbors, and maintaining greater suspicion of negotiations. These general party tendencies—Labor's moderate, pragmatic style versus Likud's ideological, rigid style—have been demonstrated regularly in recent Israeli foreign policy.

Table 10.3 shows the growth in the Israeli settler population in the West Bank over the last several years; the growth is even more dramatic when portrayed in a line graph as in figure 10.1. This settlement issue has been a major point of contention both within Israel and between Israel and the international community, with the international community continuing to take the position that Israeli settlements in the West Bank are illegal and are not permitted under UN resolutions.

Table 10.3 Comprehensive Settlement Population, 1972–2008

Year	West Bank	Gaza Strip	East Jerusalem	Golan Heights	Total
1972	1,182	700	8,649	77	10,608
1985	44,100	1,900	103,900	8,700	158,700
1990	78,600	3,300	135,000	10,600	227,500
1995	133,200	5,300	157,300	13,400	309,200
2000	192,976	6,678	172,250	15,955	387,859
2005	258,988	0	184,057	17,793	460,838
2007	276,462	0	189,708	18,692	484,862

Source: Based upon data provided by the Foundation for Middle East Peace, "Comprehensive Settlement Population, 1972–2008," www.fmep.org/settlement_info/settlement-info-and-tables/stats-data/comprehensive-settlement-population-1972-2006/?searchterm=None, accessed May 2010.

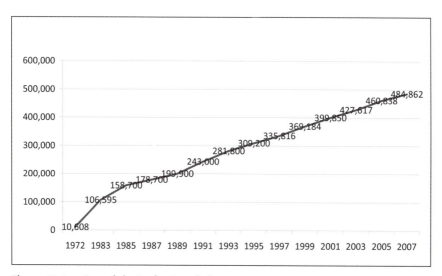

Figure 10.1. Growth in Settler Population, 1972–2007
Source: Based upon data provided by the Foundation for Middle East Peace, "Comprehensive Settlement Population, 1972–2008," www.fmep.org/settlement_info/settlement-info-and-tables/stats-data/comprehensive-settlement-population-1972-2006/?searchterm=None, accessed May 2010.

While not all sources are in agreement in terms of the absolute numbers of settlers in the West Bank and Gaza, the pattern of change is instructive. According to one source, in March 2004 there were a total of 139 settlements in the West Bank. The total population in the settlements in 2004 was approximately four hundred thousand. Nearly one hundred thousand Israelis—almost a quarter of the total settler population—reside in just eight settlements; the size of the average population of the remaining settlements is just over seven hundred people per settlement. Built-up settlement areas make up approximately 1.5 percent of the West Bank's 2,177 square miles, but settlement boundaries take much more area than this, enclosing almost 10 percent of West Bank territory.[113]

Critics of the Israeli settlements have argued that the policy of establishing settlements in the Occupied Territories is a violation of international law in a variety of respects. Among other issues involved, the UN Security Council Resolution 465 of 1980, Section 5,

> determines that all measures taken by Israel to change the physical character, demographic composition, institutional structure or status of the Palestinian and other Arab territories occupied since 1967, including Jerusalem, or any part thereof, have no legal validity and that Israel's policy and practices of settling parts of its population and new immigrants in those territories constitute a flagrant violation of the Fourth Geneva Convention relative to the Protection of Civilian Persons in Time of War and also constitute a serious obstruction to achieving a comprehensive, just and lasting peace in the Middle East.[114]

Beyond this, critics have argued that all Israeli governments since the 1967 war have engaged in the development of illegal settlements.

During the first decade of occupation after the 1967 war, Labor-led governments established the infrastructure and institutions for the creation and expansion of permanent Israeli settlement in the territories. Labor's approach was incremental, but after 1977, Begin's Likud Government embraced settlements as its raison d'être and the key to the Likud's political renaissance. Aside from the ideological imperative to settle the land, Begin viewed settlements as his opportunity to create a political constituency rooted in the settlements of the West Bank, just as Labor had done with its kibbutz and moshav settlements in prestate Israel.

In July 1977 when President Jimmy Carter asked Prime Minister Menachem Begin to freeze settlement activity, Begin refused. At the time, while there were reportedly fifty thousand Israelis living in the areas of East Jerusalem that had been annexed, only seven thousand settlers were indicated as living in forty-five civilian outposts in the West Bank and Gaza. However, this was to increase significantly in the years that followed, and Begin's minister of agriculture, Ariel Sharon, released a document titled "A Vision of Israel at Century's End," which argued for

> the settlement of 2 million Jews in the occupied territories. The Likud plan proposed settling Jews in areas of Arab habitation and for numerous settlement points as well as large urban concentrations in three principle areas: (a) a north-south axis running from the Golan through the Jordan Valley and down the east coast of Sinai; (b) a widened corridor around Jerusalem; and (c) the populated western slopes of the Samarian heartland of the West Bank.[115]

The position of successive Israeli governments has been that such settlements are entirely legal and are important to Israeli national security.[116] In 2002 the Government of Ariel Sharon released a document arguing again that, predictably, the settlements built in the territories were entirely legal. In an extended statement by the Ministry of Foreign Affairs, the Israeli government has taken the position that (1) there is historical precedent for the development of settlements in the West Bank and Gaza Strip, (2) such settlements are being developed consistently with international humanitarian law, and (3) such settlements do not violate any agreements with either the Palestinians or the Jordanians. Specifically:

- Jewish settlements in the West Bank and Gaza Strip area were recognized as legitimate in the Mandate for Palestine adopted by the League of Nations, which stated that "the Administration of Palestine . . . shall encourage . . . close settlement by Jews on the land."
- Many areas of Jewish settlement, such as the settlement in Hebron, have existed for extremely long periods.
- The only administration that has completely prohibited Jewish settlement was the Jordanian occupation administration from 1948 to 1967, which made the sale of land to Jews a capital offense.
- International humanitarian law "prohibits the forcible transfer of segments of the population of a state to the territory of another state." This is not what is taking place in the establishment of settlements in the territories; no one is being forced to move to the settlements.
- The Geneva Convention "regarding forced population transfer to occupied sovereign territory cannot be viewed as prohibiting the voluntary return of individuals to the towns and villages from which they, or their ancestors, had been ousted. Nor does it prohibit the movement of individuals to land which was not under the legitimate sovereignty of any state and which is not subject to private ownership. . . . Israeli settlements have been established only after an exhaustive investigation process, under the supervision of the Supreme Court of Israel, designed to ensure that no communities are established on private Arab land."
- The movement of individual settlers to the territory is entirely voluntary.
- The West Bank and Gaza Strip are "best regarded as territory over which there are competing claims which should be resolved in peace process negotiations. Israel has valid claims to title in this territory based not only on its historic and religious connection to the land, and its recognized security needs, but also on the fact that the territory was not under the sovereignty of any state and came under Israeli control in a war of self-defense, imposed upon Israel. At the same time, Israel recognizes that the Palestinians also entertain legitimate claims to the

area. Indeed, the very fact that the parties have agreed to conduct negotiations on settlements indicated that they envisage a compromise
on this issue."

- The agreements between the Palestinians and Israel "contain no prohibition whatsoever on the building or expansion of settlements. On
  the contrary, it is specifically provided that the issue of settlements is
  reserved for permanent status negotiations."
- The "prohibition on unilateral steps which alter the 'status' of the West
  Bank and Gaza Strip" does not apply to housing, which has no effect
  on the status of the area.[117]

Regardless of viewpoint, the pattern of settlement building has long-term
implications.[118] One of the major justifications offered by Menachem Begin
was that of "establishing facts," not unlike the proposal of Moshe Dayan
almost a decade earlier.[119] What he meant by "facts" was, in fact, the geographic pattern of settlements that would provide a security perimeter for
the bulk of the Israeli population. When enough settlers were established in
the West Bank, a critical mass would be established that would be impossible to reverse.[120]

As for the settlers themselves, scholars have suggested that there are two
general types of motives behind their behavior: ideology and self-interest.[121]
For many advocates of expanded settlement building, the justification is a
religious one: *Eretz Israel* is a concept with religious significance. The creation of more and more settlements in the Occupied Territories—or Judea
and Samaria—can be seen as fulfilling a biblical commandment.[122] The
Gush Emunim, a group representing this point of view, has been very active
in promoting more and more settlements on the West Bank,[123] although it
must be noted that "Jewish settlement in the West Bank did not start with
Gush Emunim, nor has it ended with them."[124]

Groups that settle out of self-interest tend to be less visible precisely
because they are not there for ideological reasons. Many are attracted for
purely financial reasons—the government has built villages, encouraged
industry, and offered apartments for sale (often with attractive financial
terms) at prices considerably lower than could be found in other areas.[125] It
is thus an entirely pragmatic decision on the part of many young couples.
They can now afford to purchase an apartment in a settlement on the West
Bank with guaranteed security and transportation to Jerusalem, while they
cannot afford to purchase a comparable apartment anywhere else. Their
decision to settle on the West Bank is clearly secondary to owning their
own apartment. Recently published data show quite clearly that new settlements in the West Bank are far more popular than new settlements in either
Galilee or the Negev. The study concluded that the higher demand for West
Bank apartments was at least partially caused by the government's more

generous financial incentives for settlements there, including both prices and mortgage rates. Indeed, the difference in financial incentives between high-government-priority settlements and low-government-priority settlements may be as much as 50 percent.[126]

Military Government

Among the major sources of tension to be expected in any military occupation is the fact of the occupation itself. In this regard, as described in the preceding chapter, the period from 1967 to the present has been a continuing source of anguish for both Israelis and Palestinians.[127] Israel has been criticized by many in the international community over policies it has undertaken in the Occupied Territories, including dismissal of mayors of large West Bank cities, forcible expulsion of Arab residents to Lebanon or Jordan, curfews, demolition of houses, censorship of publications, closing of universities, and a wide range of human rights violations (see chapter 9's discussion of the legacy of warfare).[128]

It is also the case, as we noted earlier, that the *intifada* has brought the military government into a much more public role than it would prefer. Its high-profile approach to dealing with the mass public demonstrations has resulted not only in the deaths of many Palestinians, but also in a great deal of domestic division within Israel over the tactics of the military government and the overall propriety of Israel's presence on the West Bank.

THE PALESTINIANS, THE WEST BANK AND GAZA, AND JERUSALEM

This chapter began by asking what appeared to be a simple question: who should control the lands called the Occupied Territories? This chapter aimed to show that an increased understanding of each party's claim to the lands might help us understand the tensions manifested through history in the region.

We began by reviewing some of the major historical themes that are relevant to the region: conflicting claims to the land, partition, lack of consensus about borders and legitimacy, and warfare. We then turned our attention to the Palestinians themselves to try to understand who they are and what their claims to the land are. We saw something of the history of their claims to a state of their own, their conflicts with Jordan as well as Israel, and the problems that having a significant refugee population have caused as far as national goals are concerned. We also examined the historical evolution of institutions of statehood, including the development of the PLO, the PNA, the legislative council, and other similar political structures.

We saw how "normal" political institutions have started to evolve, such as the election of a legislature and executive leadership in 1996, and discussed the ultimate goals of the leadership.

Some of the key issues in this chapter have involved the land and the territory itself. The West Bank and Gaza—as well as East Jerusalem and the Golan Heights—are the subject of incompatible claims by the Palestinians and the Israelis. The same goes for Jerusalem. Both sides in the past have said that they are willing to negotiate on everything and that everything is negotiable, but it has quickly become apparent that this is not true: sovereignty over Jerusalem is something upon which both sides have insisted, and they have meant unshared sovereignty over Jerusalem. The issue of sovereignty over territory, obviously, is one that must be resolved before peace can come to the region.

Finally, we briefly raised some of the issues that have to be resolved on the Israeli side before the conflict can end. We have seen earlier in this volume that national security is one of the key issues for Israel. Israeli planning has been focused on security, which has been sought through the development of settlements in the West Bank, Gaza, the Golan Heights, and occupied (and unified) Jerusalem. The idea was that "establishing facts" and putting a substantial Jewish presence on the West Bank would lead to Israeli security. Recent violence has shown that this is simply not true; to the contrary, in fact, Israeli settlements have shown themselves to be vulnerable to terrorist attack, and the existence of a significant Israeli presence in the West Bank has served as an irritant and a *casus belli* for the Palestinians.

These are all issues that simply must be resolved.

But, some progress has, in fact, been made over the years. Israel has negotiated peace treaties with both Jordan and Egypt and has been actively negotiating (albeit intermittently) with the Palestinian leadership for more than a decade now. While acts of violence (on both sides) have interrupted constructive negotiation and progress toward peace in the last several years, there still exists a foundation upon which a meaningful peace agreement could be based. It is to a discussion of the peace process in the Middle East that we now turn our attention.

FOR FURTHER READING

Abufarha, Nasser. *The Making of a Human Bomb: The Ethnography of Palestinian Resistance.* Durham, N.C.: Duke University Press, 2009.

Abu Odeh, Adnan. *Jordanians, Palestinians, and the Hashemite Kingdom in the Middle East Peace Process.* Washington, D.C.: United States Institute of Peace, 1999.

Al O'ran, Mutayyam. *Jordanian-Israeli Relations: The Peacebuilding Experience.* New York: Routledge, 2009.

Amirav, Mosheh. *Jerusalem Syndrome: The Palestinian-Israeli Battle for the Holy City.* Portland, Ore.: Sussex Academic Press, 2009.

Beinin, Joel, and Rebecca Stein. *The Struggle for Sovereignty: Palestine and Israel, 1993–2005.* Stanford, Calif.: Stanford University Press, 2006.

Bornstein, Avram. *Crossing the Green Line between the West Bank and Israel.* Philadelphia: University of Pennsylvania Press, 2002.

Cohen, Hillel. *Army of Shadows: Palestinian Collaboration with Zionism: 1917–1948.* Berkeley: University of California Press, 2008.

Frisch, Hillel. *Countdown to Statehood: Palestinian State Formation in the West Bank and Gaza.* Albany: State University of New York Press, 1998.

Gelber, Yoav. *Palestine, 1948: War, Escape, and the Emergence of the Palestinian Refugee Problem.* Portland, Ore.: Sussex Academic Press, 2001.

Grinberg, Lev Luis. *Politics and Violence in Israel/Palestine: Democracy versus Military Rule.* New York: Routledge, 2010.

Hasso, Frances. *Resistance, Repression, and Gender Politics in Occupied Palestine and Jordan.* Syracuse, N.Y.: Syracuse University Press, 2005.

Israeli, Raphael. *Jerusalem Divided: The Armistice Regime, 1947–1967.* Portland, Ore.: Frank Cass, 2002.

Kretzmer, David. *The Occupation of Justice: The Supreme Court of Israel and the Occupied Territories.* Albany: State University of New York Press, 2002.

Mahler, Gregory. *Constitutionalism and Palestinian Constitutional Development.* Jerusalem: Palestinian Academic Society for the Study of International Affairs, 1996.

Makdisi, Saree. *Palestine Inside Out: An Everyday Occupation.* New York: W. W. Norton, 2008.

Morris, Benny. *One State, Two States: Resolving the Israel/Palestine Conflict.* New Haven, Conn.: Yale University Press, 2009.

Robinson, Glenn E. *Building a Palestinian State: The Incomplete Revolution.* Bloomington: Indiana University Press, 1997.

Salinas, Moises F. *Planting Hatred, Sowing Pain: The Psychology of the Israeli-Palestinian Conflict.* Westport, Conn: Praeger, 2007.

Sayigh, Yazid. *Armed Struggle and the Search for State: The Palestinian National Movement, 1949–1993.* New York: Oxford University Press, 1997.

Shlaim, Avi. *Israel and Palestine: Reappraisals, Revisions, Refutations.* Brooklyn, N.Y.: Verso, 2009.

———. *The Politics of Partition: King Abdullah, the Zionists, and Palestine, 1921–1951.* New York: Oxford University Press, 1998.

Smith, Charles D. *Palestine and the Arab-Israeli Conflict.* Boston: Bedford/St. Martin's Press, 2007.

Tessler, Mark. *A History of the Israeli-Palestinian Conflict.* Bloomington: Indiana University Press, 1994.

Wasserstein, Bernard. *Divided Jerusalem: The Struggle for the Holy City.* New Haven, Conn.: Yale University Press, 2001.

11

The Peace Process

Israel has been in a state of war with most of its neighbors since before the time of its creation, and the challenge of peace has always been high on the nation's political agenda. The final chapter of this book discusses the elusive, frustrating, sometimes partially successful, yet ultimately (so far) unreachable goal of peace in the Middle East. This chapter also includes a brief introductory discussion of the peace process itself and of events leading up to the Camp David Peace Agreement and the peace treaty between Israel and Egypt in 1979. We also look at key events since that time, from Oslo and Madrid to Camp David (again). The chapter ends with a discussion of prospects for peace in the future.

THE QUEST FOR PEACE

We saw earlier in this volume that to a substantial extent the history of modern Israel has been the history of a nation at war. Although the often-articulated goal of Israeli foreign policy has been for the country to live in a situation of stable and secure peace with its neighbors, that situation has not yet been achieved. In chapter 1 we noted that within twenty-four hours of its Declaration of Independence on May 14, 1948, the armies of Egypt, Jordan, Syria, Lebanon, and Iraq attacked Israel. The War of Independence

---

The signing of the Camp David Accords was a major breakthrough in the Middle East peace process.

lasted fifteen months, and early in 1949 negotiations began under the aus-
pices of the United Nations between Israel and the other countries involved
in the fighting, except Iraq, which wouldn't negotiate with Israel. These
discussions resulted in armistices between Israel and its neighbors, as well
as a de facto partition of the territories, with Israel controlling more land
than had been proposed by the UN partition plan of 1947, Jordan controlling the West Bank, Egypt controlling the Gaza Strip, and Jerusalem being
divided and under the control of both Israel and Jordan.[1] (See map 1.5.)

In the more than six decades since that time, the struggle for peace has
been the central component of Israeli foreign policy.[2] Both peace-seeking
and peacemaking activities have been inconsistent over the years. At times
real, substantive progress has been made. For years following Egyptian
president Anwar Sadat's visit to Jerusalem in 1977, observers continued to
note how quickly the peace process was moving, given the historical context
within which the Middle East conflict had existed. Recent years have seen
the peace process sputter, stop, reverse directions, and apparently lie mori-
bund, to the anguish of many.

The pursuit of a secure and lasting peace has been a very complicated
challenge for both Israeli and Arab governments, not to mention nongovernmental actors such as the Palestine National Authority. The issue cannot
be resolved just on a bilateral basis by the governments involved, as there
has also been significant political conflict domestically; indeed, domestic
political issues can and do affect the peace process. Certainly, in the Israeli
case interparty and intraparty politics have affected the speed with which
Israeli governments have felt comfortable pursuing peace and negotiating
with other national and Arab groups.[3] Issues we have already covered in
this book, such as the right of return of Palestinian refugees[4] and ultimate
jurisdiction over Jerusalem,[5] not only have proven irresolvable between the
negotiating parties—specifically between Israel and the Palestine National
Authority—but also have polarized Israeli society.[6] While Israelis have
tended to agree on the need for secure borders as one of the major goals of
negotiations, others issues have been on the table, too.[7]

Significant to the peace process has been the role of the United States.[8]
As we see throughout this chapter, on several occasions over the last six
decades, only because of pressure from or guarantees by the United States
has Israel been either able or willing to make concessions necessary to move
forward—however slowly or inconsistently—in the peace process. Although
at the time of this writing the peace process has stalled, relations between
the American president and the Israeli prime minister appear to be worse
than they have ever been, and observers are far less optimistic about the
likelihood of achieving peace in the near future than they have been at other
times in the relatively recent past, the *potential* for the development of peace
remains. Once Anwar Sadat announced in 1977 that he was prepared to go

to Jerusalem to talk with the Israeli government if it would help the cause of peace, the peace treaty between Israel and Egypt came (relatively speaking) remarkably quickly: Sadat visited Jerusalem in November 1977, the Camp David Accords (discussed below) were signed in September 1978, and the peace treaty between Israel and Egypt was signed in March 1979.

In this chapter we initially take an essentially chronological approach to the quest for peace in the region, moving from the period following the establishment of the state and the War of Independence through very recent developments. At that point we step back from a purely chronological approach and discuss the several bilateral pairs of actors (Israel and Jordan, Israel and the Palestinians, Israel and Lebanon, and Israel and Syria), as we look to the future in the region and the prospects for peace in the coming months and years.

PROGRESS TOWARD PEACE, POST-1948

Although many hoped that the several armistices that were developed in 1949 would lead quickly to secure and stable peaceful relations in the region, such was not the case.[9] The "disaster" or "catastrophe" of the survival of the state of Israel in Palestine—the term in Arabic is *al-naqba*—left a situation in need of resolution.[10] Resolution, however, was not likely when the Arab states involved were committed to not speaking to Israel and not negotiating with Israel. Israel charged that not only were the Arab nations not willing to participate in negotiations for a long-lasting peace treaty, but also,

> in contradiction to the UN Security Council Resolution of 1 September 1951, Israeli and Israel-bound shipping was prevented from passing through the Suez Canal; the blockade of the Straits of Tiran was tightened; incursions into Israel of terrorist squads from neighboring Arab countries for murder and sabotage occurred with increasing frequency; and the Sinai peninsula was gradually converted into a huge Egyptian military base.[11]

As we noted earlier in this book, the political and military situation in the Middle East grew more and more difficult for Israel in 1956; after an agreement was signed by Israel's three hostile neighbors, Egypt, Syria, and Jordan, in October 1956, Israel's situation was even more bleak. This led Israel to join with Britain and France in a military action against Egypt. Following the 1956 military campaign, Israel controlled the Gaza Strip and virtually all of the Sinai Peninsula. As part of the cessation of that fighting, a United Nations Emergency Force (UNEF) contingent was stationed along the new border between Israel and Egypt, along with Egyptian assurances that there would be free navigation in the Gulf of Eilat and Israeli agreement to withdraw from the newly occupied territories.

PROGRESS TOWARD PEACE, POST-1956

The fact that Israel withdrew from territories captured in the 1956 fighting did not result in peace in the Middle East, however. Israel continued to suffer from cross-border harassment on the Jordanian and Egyptian fronts, and periodic fighting and gunfire continued along the front with Syria, affecting Israeli kibbutzim, moshavim, and development towns in the Galilee. In May 1967 Egypt ordered the United Nations peacekeeping forces out of the Sinai (and it must be recalled that under United Nations procedures, peacekeeping forces would only be deployed to situations in which both sides of the border requested their presence; if one side requested that the peacekeeping forces depart, then the forces would necessarily depart), and the general situation in the Middle East became much more hostile. Shortly thereafter, Egypt again blockaded the Straits of Tiran—in direct violation of a promise made following the 1956 war—cutting off an important shipping route for Israeli commerce.

When Israel contacted the United States about the hostile Egyptian behavior (and it must be recalled that the United States had played a key role in the termination of the 1956 fighting, promising Israel that the United States would guarantee open international waterways for Israel) and received no assistance in the resolution of the new hostilities, some kind of military action proved unavoidable. The position of the Israeli government was that "Egypt had violated the arrangements agreed upon following the 1956 Sinai Campaign" and that Israel had a right to invoke "its inherent right of self-defense, launching a preemptive strike (5 June 1967) against Egypt in the south, followed by a counterattack against Jordan in the east and the routing of Syrian forces entrenched on the Golan Heights in the north."[12]

As we noted earlier, by the end of six days of fighting, the working borders of the state of Israel were significantly greater than they had been prior to the fighting: Israel controlled all of the West Bank and Gaza Strip, the Sinai, and the Golan Heights. At that time Israel's efforts to use the results of the fighting as a diplomatic lever to bring its Arab neighbors to an arena in which peace could be negotiated were not successful. Although UN Security Council Resolution 242 called for the recognition of the sovereignty of all states in the region and their right to live in peace within secure and recognized boundaries,[13] the Arab position at the August 1967 Khartoum Summit called for what came to be known as the "three noes": "no peace with Israel, no recognition of Israel, no negotiations with it."[14] It was not until 1970 that a cease-fire was finally adopted along the Suez Canal between Egypt and Israel.

In October 1973 Egypt and Syria attacked Israel yet again. While Israel had felt that an attack would be forthcoming, it had decided, at the intense urging of the United States, not to use the strategy employed in 1967 when it launched a preemptive strike. While the fighting brought about significant and extremely traumatic costs to Israel—in terms of loss of life and even fears about the ultimate outcome of the fighting—at the end of the two-week war, Israel found itself having crossed the Suez Canal into Egypt proper and having gone beyond the Golan Heights to within twenty miles of Damascus. While Israel withdrew from most of these new territories following protracted negotiations in response to UN Security Council Resolution 338, it was clear that it would take a major diplomatic initiative to bring about a stable peace in the region.[15]

CAMP DAVID AND THE PEACE PROCESS, 1978–1982

Surely the most celebrated and controversial step toward resolution of the Middle East dilemma came in March 1979, when Israel signed its first peace treaty with an Arab state since independence in 1948. The process leading up to this watershed event was both extraordinarily rapid and excruciatingly slow. As we noted earlier, it was rapid in the sense that once Egyptian president Anwar Sadat expressed a willingness to go to Jerusalem and meet with Israeli leaders—a dramatic departure from previous Arab policy toward Israel—progress was made (in the historical context of the preceding six decades) remarkably quickly. The visit led to the Camp David negotiations and the resulting Camp David Accords, which included a framework for a comprehensive peace in the Middle East. That framework included, for the first time, a specific proposal for Palestinian self-government. On the other hand, negotiations were slow in that they were consistently frustrated and bogged down by a seemingly endless stream of issues and details. In the end it would take eighteen months of extraordinary effort to complete the treaty-making process.

That process had, of course, commenced with President Sadat's stunning announcement that he was prepared to be received in Jerusalem by Israeli leaders to discuss prospects for peace between the two nations.[16] This was the first public summit of an Israeli and an Arab head of state, and everyone involved recognized its significance. (It should be noted that secret summits had taken place between King Hussein and Israeli leaders from time to time prior to this, although they failed to produce tangible results.) Sadat made it very clear from the outset that he was not seeking a peace treaty between Israel and Egypt separate from other issues in the region. He sought an overall framework for peace in the Middle East, including progress on the question of the Palestinians and their rights. In Sadat's words, "there could be no peace without the Palestinians."[17] The major issues to be negotiated were apparent to all: peace and diplomatic recognition between Israel and Egypt in exchange for the return of the Egyptian territories occupied by Israel and progress on the Palestinian question.

After Sadat and Begin's initial negotiations in Jerusalem, they met a month later (on Christmas Day, 1977) in Ismailia, Egypt, to discuss Israel's counterproposal. Sadat rejected Begin's plan because its autonomy arrangement for the Palestinians fell significantly short of Cairo's definition of acceptable progress. At this point the United States began to play a more active role in the proceedings.[18] Washington's expanding involvement reflected the fact that after a series of meetings between Israeli and Egyptian delegations during the early part of 1978, several problems persisted.

First, the Begin Government continued to argue that it had the right to develop settlements in the Occupied Territories (something that seems strangely prescient, given today's continued stance of Israel on this issue). This view was strongly supported by significant segments of the Israeli electorate and especially by Ariel Sharon, Begin's minister of agriculture and a contender for leadership of Begin's Likud Party. The position of the Egyptians and other Arab powers, also the position of the United States, was that these settlements were not permitted under international law and thus should not be established or continued.

Second, the future of the West Bank and the Gaza Strip was the subject of much discussion, with Begin and Likud willing to consider some form of limited self-rule or autonomy and a final decision to be decided upon later, while Egypt demanded total Israeli military withdrawal.

Third, there was concern over the linkage between Israel's returning the Sinai and the establishment of direct diplomatic relations between Jerusalem and Cairo, with Egypt preferring full and immediate Israeli withdrawal and phased-in diplomatic recognition, as distinct from Israel's goal of immediate full diplomatic recognition and phased withdrawal from the Sinai.

Fourth, President Sadat continued to insist that foremost on the Israeli-Egyptian agenda had to be the Palestinian question, while Prime Minister Begin wanted the Israeli-Egyptian peace treaty to be the centerpiece.

Fifth, but by no means least important, the Jerusalem issue appeared irreconcilable, with Israel insisting on continued complete sovereignty (although it would permit Arab control of Islamic holy places) and Egypt insisting on Israeli withdrawal from East Jerusalem, thereby reestablishing the status quo ante-1967, but this time with guaranteed Israeli access to Jewish holy places.

Although American presidents Nixon and Ford had devoted great energy to the quest for peace, it was President Jimmy Carter who was able to provide the setting and the momentum for the peace process to develop. In hindsight, this was to be the highlight of Carter's presidency. (On December 10, 2002, President Carter received the Nobel Peace Prize for his role in this event.) President Carter played an active role as broker between Israel and Egypt at the Camp David Summit in September 1978 and worked hard between then and the final treaty-signing ceremony the following March to keep the movement toward peace from being halted by one group or another. Although the United States had supported a comprehensive Geneva peace conference as the preferred mechanism for the development of peace treaties in the Middle East, once the Begin-Sadat opening was made, President Carter supported that vehicle.[19]

During a thirteen-day period, from September 5 to 17, 1978, Prime Minister Begin and Presidents Sadat and Carter met at Camp David, Maryland. Carter felt that an informal setting would be more productive than negotiations conducted in the glare of international publicity. Reflecting his position as facilitator and sense of the personalities involved, Carter was convinced that progress toward peace could only come if both Begin and Sadat had the chance, once again, to meet and talk face-to-face, away from the harsh lights of the media.[20] Over those two weeks at Camp David, he held a series of one-on-one talks with both Begin and Sadat, literally shuttling back and forth between their cabins, arranging sessions with their respective advisers, then conducting direct negotiations when the prospects of gain were more favorable.

The agreement on the exchange of the Sinai for peace and diplomatic recognition between Israel and Egypt was achieved in fairly short order. The difficult issue was Sadat's predictable insistence that he would only sign a peace treaty if it were linked in some way to broader progress toward peace in the Middle East and progress on the Palestinian issue. It would take all of their skills and powers of persuasion to bridge, however imperfectly, the distance dividing them.

Eventually, two agreements were reached, as table 11.1 indicates.[21] The first, a "Framework for Peace in the Middle East," dealt with the broader question of the West Bank and Gaza. It established a five-year transitional regime for the Occupied Territories, suggested that freely elected local authorities would gradually assume power, discussed the redeployment of Israeli armed forces into less visible positions, and set the stage for final negotiations to determine the status of the West Bank, Gaza, and Israeli-Jordanian relations. It did not specifically mention the PLO.

The second document was a "Framework for the Conclusion of a Peace Treaty between Egypt and Israel." This document called for the return of the Sinai to Egypt, limitations on the number of Egyptian forces that could be stationed there, a timetable for the withdrawal of Israeli forces from the Sinai tied to the signing of an Egyptian-Israeli peace treaty, the establishment of diplomatic relations between the two countries, a date by which a total Israeli withdrawal from the Sinai was to be completed, a permanent stationing of UN troops in the Sinai, which could not be removed on the sole authority of either of the two parties alone,[22] and a guarantee of free passage for Israeli ships through the Suez Canal and the Straits of Tiran.

Table 11.1   The Camp David Accords, 1978

Framework for Peace in the Middle East	Framework for the Conclusion of a Peace Treaty between Egypt and Israel
• Five-year transitional regime for the Occupied Territories • Freely elected local authorities to receive power • Redeployment of Israeli forces into less visible positions • Final negotiations on West Bank, Gaza, and Israeli-Jordanian relations	• Return of Sinai to Egypt • Limitations on Egyptian forces in Sinai • Timetable for withdrawal of Israeli forces in Sinai • Establishment of diplomatic relations between Egypt and Israel • Schedule for Israeli withdrawal from Sinai • United Nations presence in the Sinai • Free passage through the Suez Canal and the Straits of Tiran for Israeli vessels

Source: Israel Ministry of Foreign Affairs Web site, "The Camp David Accords: September 17, 1978," www.mfa.gov.il/mfa/go.asp?MFAH00ie0, accessed May 2010.

The Arab world was not pleased with the outcome of the Camp David talks, and following the signing of the peace treaty between Israel and Egypt, many Arab states cut Egypt off in terms of trade, diplomatic relationships, or both.[23] Eventually, most of those relationships were restored, however, and "the headquarters of the Arab League, which had been transferred to Tunis, was reinstated in Cairo in the early 1980s."[24] Although Sadat had insisted on a linkage between a bilateral Israeli-Egyptian peace treaty and progress on the overall Palestinian issue, other Arab nations claimed that not *enough* progress on the broader Palestinian issue had been made, due largely to Israeli intransigence.[25] Arab criticism of Sadat increased when Israel later permitted the building of more settlements on the West Bank. In the end, the question of linkage was finessed by an agreement between Begin and Sadat on a specific timetable for negotiations on the West Bank and Gaza.

On March 26, 1979, the two treaties conceived at Camp David were finally signed in Washington, formally ending the state of war between Israel and Egypt.[26] In April 1982, under the terms of the peace treaty, Israel completed its staged withdrawal from the Sinai, returning this vast buffer zone to Egypt in exchange for a declaration of peace. In fact, to the surprise of many, the Israeli-Egyptian peace treaty was implemented remarkably smoothly. Israel pulled out of the Sinai in distinct phases as called for in the treaty, returning portions of the Sinai on May 25, July 25, September 25, November 15, and November 25, 1979, and on January 25, 1980, with the final phase occurring on April 25, 1982.[27] Egypt, correspondingly, initiated and upgraded its level of diplomatic contact with Israel, eventually establishing open borders and beginning scientific and cultural exchanges. While the peace between Israel and Egypt has run hot and cold for more than two decades, primarily as a result of Israeli policy in Lebanon and on the West Bank, the peace has held.

(The last—almost symbolic—source of tension between Israel and Egypt involved a border dispute over 250 acres of land at Taba, just south of the city of Eilat. The area was occupied by Israel after the 1967 war. The dispute was complicated by the fact that a deluxe beach resort had been built there. When Israel returned its final installment of the Sinai in April 1982, it maintained that Taba was exempt from return, using a map from 1906 that placed the land occupied by Taba inside of what is today Israel. After much negotiation within the Israeli cabinet [favored by Labor's Peres, opposed by Likud's Shamir], Israel agreed in 1986 to an Egyptian proposal to accept binding arbitration from a five-member international tribunal. In September 1988 the panel ruled that Taba belonged to Egypt.[28] From September 30, 1988, through February 1989, Israel and Egypt negotiated over the financial settlement Israel would accept for the hotel that had been built on the land. Finally, in March 1989 the Israeli flag was lowered from the front of the Sonesta Beach Hotel, and the Egyptian flag was raised, signaling the end of the final chapter of Israeli-Egyptian disputes over their precise boundary.)

While progress was being made in bilateral talks between Israel and Egypt and Israel and Jordan—to which we will return shortly—all was not well on Israel's northern borders. In June 1981 Israel attacked PLO and Syrian forces in Lebanon to try to stop the consistent cross-border acts of violence there that were so adversely affecting the quality of life in many of Israel's northern cities and villages. U.S. mediator Philip Habib was able to bring about a cease-fire between Israel and the PLO in the next month, but tensions remained high.

In October 1981 Egyptian president Anwar Sadat was assassinated. As we noted earlier, President Sadat had received a great deal of criticism from other Arab leaders for his reaching out to Israel in 1977, and while many of the other governments had ended their official sanctions against Egypt, many of the more conservative segments of Egypt's population saw Sadat as an enemy for his willingness to negotiate with Israel. The fact that Sadat was assassinated by what were called right-wing forces did not surprise observers.

Upon the assassination of Sadat, one of the first reactions of Israel was to be concerned about the state of the peace agreement with Egypt. The question was raised whether Israel, in fact, had a peace with Egypt or a peace with Sadat. President Hosni Mubarak (who had been Sadat's vice president) was quick to announce that "we are committed to all charters, treaties, and international obligations which Egypt had concluded" and stated clearly that Egypt would honor all agreements with Israel, something that relieved Israeli leaders considerably.[29]

From June through August 1982 Israel was involved militarily in southern Lebanon in what was called Operation Peace for Galilee. While Israel declared that the international boundary line with Lebanon was not being challenged,[30] the relocation of the PLO from Jordan to Lebanon in 1970 (following the Black September actions of the Jordanian government, discussed earlier) had led to increased acts of terrorism across the Israeli-Lebanese border directed at Israeli cities in the north. By the end of the military action, Yasser Arafat and his PLO forces had to leave areas of Beirut that had been under their control; they relocated their base of operation to Tunisia. Following a protracted series of negotiations mediated by the United States between Israel, Syria, and the PLO leadership, a multinational force made up of American, French, and Italian troops provided stability in Beirut during the period of PLO departure. After the PLO's departure from Lebanon, Israel maintained a security zone across the southern border of Lebanon to help prevent the cross-border acts of violence.

In September 1982 President Ronald Reagan announced a new United States initiative to settle the Arab-Israeli conflict, based upon the Camp David Accords and United Nations Resolution 242.[31] It did not prove to be successful.

There were serious problems in Lebanon associated with this period of time, including two major issues: Lebanese president Basheer Gemayel was assassinated, and a significant massacre of several hundred civilian Palestinians took place in the Sabra and Shatila refugee camps in Beirut.[32] One important dimension of that massacre by the Lebanese Christian Militia was that Ariel Sharon, Israel's defense minister at the time, was seriously implicated in the event and was forced to resign over the incident in 1983.[33] In May 1983 an American-mediated Israel-Lebanon peace and withdrawal agreement was signed, and in June 1985 Israel completed its withdrawal from most of Lebanon, retaining effective control over a narrow security zone in southern Lebanon.

In December 1987 the (first) Palestinian *intifada*, or uprising, started in the Gaza Strip, eventually spreading to the West Bank. Shortly thereafter, King Hussein of Jordan formally renounced any claims that Jordan had made to the West Bank, cutting legal and administrative ties to the territory. The following December, the Palestine National Council formally accepted the original UN partition plan (UN General Assembly Resolution 181) for Palestine, Israel's right to exist, and UN Security Council Resolutions 242 and 338. It also formally renounced terrorism, which led to the United States opening a dialogue with the PLO, the first formal contacts with the PLO in thirteen years.

ISRAEL'S PEACE INITIATIVE, 1989

In May 1989 Israel's Prime Minister Yitzhak Shamir announced a four-point Israeli peace plan that involved elections in the West Bank and Gaza "for representatives who would negotiate an agreement on interim self-rule and serve as a 'self-governing authority.'"[34] The plan proposed further talks to take place later dealing with a permanent solution to the Palestinian situation. U.S. secretary of state James Baker began an effort to mediate renewal of the peace process, but Israel rejected Baker's five-point Middle East peace plan (which had a broader role for the Palestinians and a broader interpretation of Palestinian self-government than the Israeli plan), which was originally endorsed by Egypt and accepted with some reservations by the Palestinians.[35] Domestic Israeli politics and the vulnerability of Shamir's coalition government interacted with the peace process, and Shamir's hesitancy or unwillingness to move more vigorously resulted in his Government's losing a confidence vote in the Knesset.[36]

On March 16, 1990, the Israeli Knesset voted out the Government of Prime Minister Yitzhak Shamir after he refused to accept a U.S. plan for beginning Israeli-Palestinian peace talks. It was the first time an Israeli government had fallen in a no-confidence vote.

The sixty to fifty-five vote climaxed several weeks of intense political struggle between Shamir's right-wing Likud Party and the center-left Labor Party of Shimon Peres. The two parties had shared power in an uneasy Likud-dominated coalition formed after inconclusive general elections in November 1988. A similar Labor-Likud national unity government, in which Peres and Shamir rotated the premiership, had ruled in the four years before that.[37]

In June 1990 President George H. W. Bush stopped the formal negotiations between the United States and the PLO because of American feeling that the PLO was not taking a sufficiently firm position against acts of terrorism being directed against Israel. The PLO's position vis-à-vis terrorism and refusal to strongly condemn acts of terrorism directed against Israel have remained an issue in the relations between the United States and the Palestine National Authority in recent years.

In August 1990 Iraq invaded Kuwait. The significance of this for the peace process was that Yasser Arafat declared his support for Saddam Hussein, which resulted in the Gulf States' cutting off funds to the PLO. In addition to this, tens of thousands of Palestinians were forced out of the Gulf States. After the United States and a coalition of allies (including Arab countries) attacked Iraq, Iraq responded by firing missiles at Israel. At least one of Iraq's intentions behind this strategy was to try to draw Israel into the war against Iraq so that Iraq could appeal to pan-Arab unity and break up the alliance between the United States and its Arab allies. Responding to requests from the United States, however, Israel did *not* retaliate against Iraq's missile attack. Iraq lost the war, and the Palestinians lost much political capital in the Arab world because they were among the most vocal supporters of Saddam Hussein.

In March 1991 President George H. W. Bush announced that the Gulf War victory opened a window of opportunity for the resolution of the

Arab-Israeli conflict and sent Secretary of State James Baker to the Middle East on the first of many peace missions that would ultimately lead to the Madrid Conference.[38]

THE MADRID PEACE CONFERENCE, 1991

In October 1991 President George H. W. Bush of the United States and President Mikhail Gorbachev of the Soviet Union cosponsored a conference held in Madrid, Spain.[39] At the opening of the Madrid Conference, President Bush said that the objective of the conference was

> to achieve "real peace . . . security, diplomatic relations, economic relations, trade, investment, cultural exchange, even tourism. We seek a Middle East, where vast resources are no longer devoted to armaments." Outsiders can assist, he sa[id], "but in the end, it is up to the peoples and the governments of the Middle East to shape the future of the Middle East."[40]

The conference was also attended by a delegation of Palestinians that was formally part of the Jordanian delegation. Syria and Lebanon had delegations, as well.

The framework for the Madrid Conference called for both bilateral talks (Israel-Jordan, Israel-Syria, Israel-Lebanon, and Israel-Palestine) and multilateral talks to take place in "two separate yet parallel negotiating tracks."[41] The bilateral track was constructed to "resolve the conflicts of the past," and the first direct talks between Israel and its Arab neighbors began on November 3, 1991, after the opening session of the Madrid Conference. Many rounds of bilateral talks would take place over time, as table 11.2 shows. Israeli negotiators met with the Jordanian-Palestinian delegation, the Lebanese delegation, and the Syrian delegation. At the same time, a multilateral track was designed to be future-oriented and to open negotiations focused on issues that would be important in the future. Five working groups were established, focusing on water, environment, arms control and regional security, refugees, and economic development. These talks took place in various locations around the world.

The multilateral talks were intended to permit the actors to focus on regional problems that were broader than the issues of past conflicts. As well, they were intended to serve as confidence-building measures, recognizing that after literally decades of war and mistrust, it would be unrealistic to assume that the nations involved would likely move immediately into a smoothly operating working relationship. A secure future would be achieved only with open borders, broad economic development, and regional cooperation over a period of time.[42]

In mid-December 1991 talks between Israel and the other parties resumed in Washington, D.C., and a spokesman for the U.S. Department of

Table 11.2 The Madrid Peace Conference, October 30–November 1, 1991

Track I:
Bilateral Negotiations between Israel and Other Groups

Goals	Israel–Palestinians	Israel–Jordan	Israel–Syria	Israel–Lebanon
Short-term	Interim self-government arrangements for five years			
Long-term	Permanent status	Peace treaty signed October 26, 1994	Goal of peace treaty	Goal of peace treaty

- The purpose of the bilateral negotiations was to resolve past conflicts.
- The goal of talks with Arab states was to conclude peace treaties.
- The goal of talks with the Palestinians was to achieve a two-stage settlement over five years.

Track II:
Multilateral Negotiations
Steering Committee Working Groups

Economic cooperation and development	Water	Environment	Refugees	Arms control and regional security

- The purpose of the multilateral negotiations was to reorient debate toward future issues.
- Discussion of issues should promote cooperation and build confidence in partnerships.

Source: Israel Ministry of Foreign Affairs Web page, "The Madrid Framework—Diagram," October 31, 1999, at www.mfa.gov.il/mfa/go.asp?MFAH00sj0, accessed May 2010.

State said "that the talks are continuing. . . . [This] is a very big step forward in the region that's had hostility for forty-three years."[43] The talks continued intermittently and were scheduled to take place in the United States, Moscow, Lisbon, Belgium, Japan, Canada, and London, among other sites. In the fourth round of talks, in Washington, D.C., the Palestinians proposed direct elections in the West Bank, Gaza, and Arab East Jerusalem. Israel rejected the proposal, and the talks ended inconclusively.

In the sixth round of the bilateral talks in August 1992, Israel and Syria reached a new stage of progress when Israel openly acknowledged the possibility of withdrawing from part of the Golan Heights, one of Syria's demands since the beginning of the talks. In the seventh round of talks in

October 1992, Israel continued to indicate its willingness to pull out of the Golan Heights but emphasized that it would not give up the entire region.

January 1993 began with the Israeli Knesset rescinding its 1986 ban on contacts with the PLO. The Government was committed to making the gesture to the PLO as a partner in negotiations, but a number of Israeli political leaders opposed the measure strongly. Although Prime Minister Rabin was confident that the Knesset would, in fact, pass the bill (because his Government controlled a majority in the Knesset), it was unclear how difficult it would be to have enough coalition members support the bill. At the end of the day the vote for the bill was 39 to 20 (out of 120 MKs!) in favor of the bill.[44]

In August 1993, in a major breakthrough in the peace process, the PLO announced that in secret talks in Oslo it had reached tentative agreement with Israel on partial autonomy in the Occupied Territories. Israeli foreign minister Shimon Peres announced that Israel and the PLO had reached an agreement on Palestinian autonomy in Gaza and Jericho. The agreement, which became known as the Oslo Agreement because of the location in which the secret talks took place, was seen as a true breakthrough in the peacemaking process.

THE OSLO ACCORDS, 1993[45]

As a result of the Oslo Accords, Israel and the PLO agreed to recognize each other after forty-five years of conflict, as shown in box 11.1. PLO leader Yasser Arafat signed a letter recognizing Israel and renouncing violence. As part of the agreement, Arafat's letter was hand-carried to Israel by Norwegian foreign minister Johan Joergen Holst, whose country brokered the PLO-Israel pact. At the same time, Israeli prime minister Yitzhak Rabin signed a document recognizing the PLO and agreeing to participate in a signing ceremony on August 13 in Washington, D.C.[46] American president Bill Clinton called the Oslo Agreement "a bold breakthrough." "Today marks a shining moment of hope for the people of the Middle East; indeed, of the entire world," he said.[47]

On September 13, 1993, Israeli prime minister Yitzhak Rabin and PLO chairman Yasser Arafat met and watched Israeli foreign minister Shimon Peres and PLO Executive Council member Abou Abbas sign the Oslo Agreement, witnessed by President Bill Clinton, former presidents George Bush and Jimmy Carter, and numerous dignitaries. The next day Israel and Jordan agreed to an Israel-Jordan Common Agenda in Washington, D.C., marking the end of the state of war between the two nations and paving the way for talks leading to a formal peace treaty. Rabin and Arafat met again in October to coordinate the talks and hold a minisummit.[48]

Box 11.1.   The Oslo Accords, August 1993

The accord provided for the following:

- There would be a substantial degree of Palestinian autonomy and the establishment of interim self-government. This would come first in the Gaza Strip and the West Bank town of Jericho, and later in the rest of the West Bank (excluding Jewish settlements).
- Internationally supervised elections would be held for an interim Palestinian legislature to administer limited Palestinian self-rule. Elections would be held within nine months of the formal signing of the accord.
- The legislative council would have power in the areas of taxation, health, education, welfare, culture, tourism, and the establishment of a police force.
- Israeli military would retain authority for overall security, although Israeli forces would be pulled back from Palestinian population centers, and the Israeli military would continue to supervise all border crossings.
- Negotiations on the sensitive issues of the final status of Jerusalem and the rights of Palestinian refugees and Jewish settlers would take place when talks convened on permanent arrangements for the occupied Palestinian territories, no later than two years after the signing of the self-rule accord.
- The interim legislative council would cease to exist at the end of the transitional period, which was to last no longer than five years.
- Israeli-Palestinian negotiations sought to achieve "a permanent settlement based on (U.N.) Security Council Resolutions 242 and 338."

Source: "Israel and Palestine Liberation Organization Sign Preliminary Accord; Mutual Recognition Declared," *Facts on File World News Digest,* September 13, 1993, accession number: 1993054779.

In July 1994 Israel and Jordan agreed upon a peace treaty, three years after the beginning of the 1991 Madrid Peace Conference.[49] This officially ended the forty-six-year state of war that had existed between the two nations. The next month Israel and the Palestine National Authority signed the Agreement on the Preparatory Transfer of Powers and Responsibilities at the Erez border checkpoint between Israel and the Gaza Strip.[50] The agreement covered such subjects as the expansion of Palestinian self-rule in the West Bank in such policy areas as education, taxation, social welfare, tourism, and health.

Later in the year, on October 17, 1994, the peace treaty was initialed at the border crossing between Eilat, Israel, and Aqaba, Jordan, with U.S. president Bill Clinton witnessing the ceremony. At the end of October the treaty of peace between the state of Israel and the Hashemite kingdom of Jordan was signed at the White House. Although Israel and Jordan had been de facto at war with each other for almost five decades, in fact, on many occasions during that period of time, there were secret contacts between the governments (including secret visits of Israeli prime ministers to Jordan and secret visits of Jordanian leaders to Israel). In August 1995 the Jordanian parliament rescinded its adherence to the Arab boycott of Israel.[51]

In May 1995 U.S. secretary of state Warren Christopher announced that Israel and Syria had reached a set of understandings on security arrangements.

In late September 1995 the Israeli-Palestinian Interim Agreement on the West Bank and the Gaza Strip was signed in Washington, D.C., indicating even more progress in the negotiations on some of the central issues involved in the conflict, in this case the issue of transferring power.[52] The agreement covered such subjects as redeployment of troops and security, elections, civil affairs, legal matters, economic relations, cooperation programs, and prisoner release.

On November 4, 1995, Israeli prime minister Yitzhak Rabin was assassinated by an Israeli university student, Yigal Amir, following a peace rally in Tel Aviv. Rabin was succeeded by former foreign minister Shimon Peres. Peres was strongly behind the peace initiatives that had been pursued by Rabin—indeed, he had been one of the individuals pressing Rabin to move in that direction most strongly—and he was strongly committed to doing whatever was necessary to achieve peace.

Peres found, however, that he was unable to stem the increasing tide of Palestinian violence and terrorism. Indeed, in the May 1996 elections for prime minister in Israel, Peres was defeated by Likud leader Benjamin Netanyahu, primarily on the issue of security and Netanyahu's argument that he could bring more safety against terrorism to Israelis than could Peres.

The Israeli-Palestinian peace process was faltering, however. Some said that this was unavoidable because the easier issues had already been resolved and only the harder issues remained, such as questions dealing with Israeli settlements in the Occupied Territories, the return of Palestinian refugees, control of Jerusalem, and the like. In January 1998 President Clinton met with both Prime Minister Netanyahu and Chairman Arafat in Washington to try to restart the peace process. The next month U.S. secretary of state Madeline Albright returned to the region, meeting with both Netanyahu and Arafat. In May Secretary Albright met with Prime Minister Netanyahu and Chairman Arafat in London in yet another effort to restart the peace process. She met with both leaders again in September, and both Netanyahu and Arafat met with President Clinton in Washington. In early October Secretary Albright met with both leaders again in preparation for a new meeting that would take place at the Wye River Plantation on October 23, 1998.

THE WYE RIVER MEMORANDUM, OCTOBER 23, 1998

From October 15 to 23, 1998, negotiations between the Israelis and Palestinians took place at the Wye River Conference Center in Maryland. The resulting memorandum was very significant, because it was the result of nine hard days of negotiations out of the public eye, reminiscent of the Camp David negotiations two decades earlier.[53] It demonstrated to the public that both Prime Minister Netanyahu and Chairman Arafat could negotiate with each other to a successful conclusion, something that was not certain prior to the public announcement of a productive period.

> The accord, known formally as the Wye Memorandum, would implement the second of three slated Israeli troop pullbacks from the West Bank as outlined in the second-phase agreement on interim Palestinian self-rule, signed by the two sides in September 1995.
> . . .
> Netanyahu, who had conditioned the pact on enhanced security guarantees for Israel, declared at a signing ceremony in the White House that "Israel and our entire region are more secure" as a result of the agreement. Arafat, at the signing, referred to Netanyahu as a "copartner in peace" and said, "We [Palestinians] will never leave the peace process, and we will never go back to violence and confrontation."[54]

The Wye River Memorandum was signed at the White House on October 23. A month later President Clinton hosted a Middle East Donors Conference in Washington, D.C. In addition to Clinton's promising to ask Congress to approve a contribution of $400 million to the Palestine National Authority over a five-year period, nearly forty other nations pledged over $3 billion in economic assistance to the Palestine National Authority.[55]

The point of the Wye Agreement was to get the parties involved thinking again in terms of cooperation and to urge them to continue the progress toward peace made in the past.[56] As shown in box 11.2, the agreement combined the transferring of control to the Palestinians over more territory in the West Bank and the release of a number of Palestinian prisoners in Israeli jails with an obligation on the Palestinians to arrest suspected terrorists, increase antiterrorism measures, and perform a number of actions designed to increase Israeli security. It also included agreement over a Palestinian airport and a transportation corridor to link the West Bank and Gaza Strip.

On May 17, 1999, Ehud Barak was elected prime minister of Israel, defeating Benjamin Netanyahu by a margin of 56 to 44 percent of the vote in direct voting.[57] Peace and willingness to negotiate with the Palestinians were significant issues in the campaign, and many believed that Barak would be able to guide Israel toward a lasting peace agreement with the Palestinians. This was not to be.

September 2000 marked a turning point in the peace process. On September 28 Ariel Sharon visited the Temple Mount area, including the area near the Al-Aqsa Mosque, setting off massive rioting in the West Bank. "It was not my visit that lit the fire, but Palestinian incitement," he observed in response

Box 11.2.   The Wye River Agreement, October 23, 1998

The highlights of the accord are as follows:

- Called for Israeli military withdrawal from 13.1 percent of the West Bank to be carried out in three stages over three months. In addition, the agreement included a transfer of an additional 14 percent of the West Bank to sole Palestine National Authority control from joint Israeli-Palestinian control.
- Called for a reconvening of the Palestine National Council (PNC), the Palestinian parliament, to reconfirm the deletion of twenty-six clauses in the 1964 Palestine National Charter calling for the destruction of Israel.
- Called for an increase in Palestinian Authority antiterrorism measures to enhance Israeli security.
- Called for a reduction of the Palestinian Authority police force by 25 percent.
- Called for the Palestinian Authority arrest of thirty Palestinian terrorism suspects, as well as the confiscation of illegal weapons in Palestinian hands.
- Called for the release of 750 Palestinian prisoners held in Israeli jails.
- Called for the opening of a Palestinian airport and an industrial park in the Gaza Strip.
- Called for the opening of a transportation corridor to allow Palestinians to travel between the West Bank and Gaza Strip.
- Called for the formation of a joint Israeli-Palestinian committee to discuss further Israeli troop withdrawals from occupied Palestinian territory.

Source: "Middle East: Highlights of Wye Accord," *Facts on File World News Digest*, October 23, 1998, accession number: 1998114840.

to accusations that he intentionally aggravated Palestinian tensions by making a gesture of Israeli dominance that was certain to arouse the emotions of Palestinians. Many Israelis, and many international leaders, did not agree with his interpretation of the cause of the rioting and blamed Sharon's inflammatory Temple Mount excursion for the outbreak of violence.

Sharon said his visit was intended to reaffirm Israeli sovereignty over the area, which Israel had annexed when it captured East Jerusalem in the 1967 Arab-Israeli war. Sovereignty over Jerusalem and its holy sites was one of the most contentious unresolved issues of the Palestinian-Israeli peace talks. Sharon, the leader of the opposition Likud Party, used the occasion to criticize Israeli prime minister Ehud Barak's willingness to make concessions to the Palestinians regarding Jerusalem's status.[58]

On September 28 Sharon had said of his visit, "It was no provocation whatsoever. . . . Arabs have the right to visit everywhere in the land of Israel, and Jews have the right to visit every place in the land of Israel." However, Palestinian headquarters in East Jerusalem on September 28 issued a statement saying, "The visit struck at the very heart of the peace process."[59]

Unfortunately, Barak proved to be unable to stop the acts of terrorism that took place on his watch, especially following the start of the *al-Aqsa intifada*, and his political mandate in the Knesset was not strong enough to permit him to stand up to the short-term pressures. On December 9, 2000, Barak announced his resignation as prime minister.[60] Elections were scheduled for February 2001.

In that election, Ariel Sharon was elected prime minister of Israel. During the campaign Sharon "declared that he considered the 1993 Palestinian-Israeli Oslo peace accord completely defunct. That interim agreement had provided the primary framework for all peace negotiations since 1993, and the Oslo process had been intended to culminate in Palestinian self-rule."[61] Immediately following Sharon's election, the more moderate Arab leaders—especially Egyptian president Hosni Mubarak and Jordanian prime minister Ali Abu Ragheb—appealed to other Arab leaders "not to condemn Sharon too quickly."[62]

Since the end of 2000, and especially under Prime Minister Sharon, the peace process slowed to a crawl and often stopped completely. The Ministry of Foreign Affairs assembled a Web site that listed "Palestinian Violence and Terrorism since September 2000," and included an effort to comprehensively document acts of Palestinian terrorism that have been directed toward Israel during that time.[63] Although leaders on both sides of the conflict periodically called for the cessation of violence and terrorism and the resumption of negotiations, the cycle of violence in Israel, the West Bank, and the Gaza Strip reached a level of intensity unseen in recent memory. As we noted in the last chapter, Palestinian suicide bombers started to deliver violence and casualties to Israel's heartland. Israel responded with helicopter gunship attacks on strategic targets in Palestinian cities, the destruction of homes, Palestinian casualties, and mass arrests. The Palestinians responded with more acts of terrorism. And the violence simply made negotiations for peace unimaginable.

Some government leaders considered renewed talks, but negotiations did not make great progress. In November 2000 former U.S. senator George Mitchell was asked by President Clinton to chair a fact-finding commission to look into the causes of recent violence between the Israelis and Palestinians. In April 2001 his report, known as the Sharm el-Sheikh Memorandum for the location of the announcement of the report, was released.

THE SHARM EL-SHEIKH MEMORANDUM, APRIL 30, 2001

On April 30, 2001, the Sharm el-Sheikh Fact-Finding Committee, chaired by former U.S. senator George J. Mitchell, issued its final report on what could be done to break the cycle of violence that had developed between Israel and the Palestinians and how the Israeli-Palestinian negotiations might be reenergized, leading to a solution to the conflict (see box 11.3). The report called for an immediate cease-fire, a renunciation of terrorism, and a resumption of peace talks, as well as a freeze on the construction of Jewish settlements in the West Bank and Gaza. The report indicated that "the Government of Israel and the Palestinian Authority must act swiftly and decisively to halt the violence. Their immediate objectives then should be to rebuild confidence and resume negotiations."[64] The report singled out Ariel Sharon's visit on September 28, 2000, to the Temple Mount area as significant in the start of the *al-Aqsa intifada* and suggested that Israeli

Box 11.3. The Sharm el-Sheikh Report, April 30, 2001

1. Summary of recommendations
    - End the violence
    - Rebuild confidence
    - Resume negotiations
2. Introduction
3. Discussion
4. What happened?
5. Why did it happen?
    - Divergent expectations
    - The Palestinian perspective
    - Divergent perspectives
    - The Israeli perspective
6. End the violence
    - Cessation of violence
    - Resumption of security cooperation
7. Rebuild confidence
    - Terrorism
    - Economic and social impact of violence
    - Settlements
    - Holy places
    - Reducing tension
    - International force
    - Actions and responses
    - Cross-community initiatives
    - Incitement
8. Resume negotiations
9. Recommendations
    - End the violence
    - Rebuild confidence
    - Resume negotiations

Source: See "Excerpts from the Report of the Sharm el-Sheikh Fact-Finding Committee" April 20, 2001, *Foundation for Middle East Peace*, www.fmep.org/settlement_info/settlement-freeze/excerpts-from-the -report-of-the-sharm-el-sheikh-fact-finding-committee, accessed May 2010.

settlement building, Palestinian acts of terrorism, Israeli military responses to those acts, and injudicious public statements had all contributed to the cycle of violence in the Middle East.[65]

The report concluded that leaders needed to do nothing new, nothing that had not been done before. There was no need to reinvent the wheel. All that was needed—and the report did not minimize the difficulty of doing this—was for leaders on both sides to actually *do* what they had *pledged* to do in the past.

Subsequently, other sources of ideas for a peaceful outcome were introduced. In March 2002, Crown Prince Abdullah of Saudi Arabia proposed a peaceful two-state settlement of the Arab-Israeli conflict.[66] The Saudi plan did not put much that was new on the negotiating table, as it suggested that Israel withdraw completely from all territory occupied in 1967, including the West Bank, Gaza Strip, and East Jerusalem, in return for full normalization of relations with all Arab countries. The plan's significance, however, lay in its source—the Royal Family of Saudi Arabia—which never would have been thought possible two or three decades earlier! Following the Saudi proposal's announcement, the Arab League, meeting in Beirut, adopted the Saudi proposal.

The American Role, 2002–2010

In the period between 2002 and 2010 the momentum that had started to appear in the Middle East peace process has substantially disappeared. The Israeli-Palestinian conflict was not a priority for U.S. president George W. Bush—whose foreign policy was much more concerned with international terrorism and Iraq—and he did not pursue a major American role until near the end of his eight-year term in office.[67]

As Saudi Arabia and the Arab League started to make indications that under some circumstances they might consider moving toward normalization, the United States appeared to be moving away from its position as regular mediator in the Middle East peace process. President George W. Bush did not share his predecessor's optimism that a solution to the Arab-Israeli conflict was forthcoming; moreover, his attention was focused on the escalating situation in Iraq. In the summer of 2002, Bush gave a speech evidencing a hawkish frustration with Palestinians, calling the terrorist attacks "homicide bombings" in a somewhat redundant turn of phrase meant to emphasize their indefensibility.[68]

Bush did not walk away from the situation entirely. Along with the United Nations, the European Union, and Russia, the United States proposed what became known as the "Road Map for Peace." The Road Map reiterated the call for a two-state solution, but designed the normalization process to be implemented based on the achievement of certain goals. That is, rather than imposing an external timeline on the peace process, the Road Map called on Israel and the Palestinian Authority to meet a number of identifiable benchmarks of goodwill and development, to be confirmed by the Quartet partners, at which point the next phase of the plan would begin.[69]

Chief among these benchmarks was the cessation of violence, including (and especially) suicide attacks by Palestinian insurgents. Israel was asked to issue an "unequivocal statement affirming its commitment to the two-state vision of an independent, viable, sovereign Palestinian state," as well. Israeli security and Palestinian institution-building, humanitarian assistance for Palestinians, support for civil society projects, and a commitment by the Government of Israel to dismantle settlement outposts erected after March 2001 were also included. A transition phase was to take place between June and December 2003, including an international conference, and a permanent status agreement would be tied up in 2004 or 2005. The enforcement and improvement of the Road Map were not a priority of the Bush administration, unfortunately; President Bush did not even visit the Middle East as president until 2008, the last year of his eight-year term in office. The usefulness of the Road Map has been questioned, as very few of its objectives have been met.

American attention soon turned almost exclusively to the new war in Iraq, which officially came to a head in 2003. Nonetheless, the peace process lurched along. In 2004, Prime Minister Ariel Sharon announced that as a result of not having a partner with whom to seriously negotiate—by which he meant that Israel could not trust negotiations with the Palestinians—Israel had decided to withdraw entirely from Gaza, leaving it to govern itself—but surrounded and thoroughly locked down by Israel on its borders.[70] That same year, President Yasser Arafat died. Stepping into the leadership of the Palestinian Authority, new President Mahmoud Abbas was elected in 2005, promising to advance negotiations with Israel.[71] Shortly thereafter the militant groups still embroiled in the *al-Aqsa intifada* agreed to a cease-fire with Israeli troops.

The year 2005 also saw a unilateral Israeli withdrawal from Gaza of both troops and settlers, although Israel retained control of Gazan airspace, borders, and ports. Prime Minister Ariel Sharon indicated in speeches that since Israel didn't have a dependable partner with whom to negotiate, it would have to act unilaterally. There was substantial opposition from the Israeli right-wing parties, but since Sharon knew that he could count on the support of the Israeli left-wing parties, the decision was approved by the Knesset. So, while Israel claimed that it had pulled out of Gaza, Gazans continued to claim that they were "occupied" since they could not control their own destiny.

In 2006 Palestinians went to the polls and brought to life a dilemma beloved of political scientists: what happens when the winner of a democratic election is not fully a participant in the democratic process? Specifically, Palestinians elected an overwhelming majority government of Hamas members. Long listed as a terrorist organization by the U.S. Department of State, the election of Hamas represented for many observers a move by Palestinians away from the peace process. Even the sitting government of the Palestinian Authority, long a Fatah stronghold, was surprised. The United States, the European Union, and several other European and Western countries stopped all financial assistance to the Palestinian Authority, since they viewed Hamas as a terrorist organization, and politics there ground to a halt.

Desperate to prevent the outbreak of civil war in the Palestinian Authority, Hamas and Fatah agreed to a Saudi proposal arranging a coalition government in Palestine. The two groups eyed each other warily until Hamas took over control of Gaza entirely in June 2007. At that point, Fatah declared the unity government invalid and reclaimed unilateral control of the Palestinian Authority in the West Bank, and the United States resumed its financial assistance to the area. Gaza remains under the control of Hamas— and without the benefit of international financial assistance—to this day.

In early July 2006 the first *Qassam* rocket of increased strength was fired from Gaza into Israeli territory in the city of Ashkelon. Although there were no Israeli casualties, Israel noted with great interest—and alarm—the increased range of the new generation of the *Qassam* rockets, and discussion about alternative responses ensued.

July 2006 was also the beginning of the most recent Israel-Lebanon conflict. On July 12 some Hezbollah fighters crossed the border into Israel and kidnapped two Israeli soldiers and killed three others. This, combined with Hezbollah firing rockets at northern Israeli border towns, eventually resulted in open warfare across the border, with major military action on both sides of the conflict. The fighting lasted for more than thirty days before the United Nations was able to arrange a cease-fire, and resulted in significant casualties among Lebanese civilians and significant damage in northern Israeli cities, including Haifa. Many areas of southern Lebanon are still of questionable safety because of cluster bomblets dropped by the Israeli military.

In September 2006 a virtual civil war broke out between forces of Fatah and Hamas in the Gaza Strip. The United Nations declared the Gazan situation "intolerable"[72] and many governments suggested that the Israeli blockade of Gaza could not be permitted to continue.[73]

In October 2006 a brief military campaign was launched by the Israeli Air Force against Gaza as a result of increased rocket attacks from Gaza against civilian targets in the Israeli coastal plain.

In the final year of his eight years in office as president of the United States, George W. Bush finally sought to leave his mark on the Middle East peace process. On November 20, 2007, plans for an Annapolis Peace Conference were announced and nations were invited to come to Annapolis to discuss the peace process. The conference marked the first time both sides came to negotiations agreeing upon a two-state solution, and it was also noteworthy for the number of participants who appeared and the inclusion of a number of Arab nations that had not actively participated in the peace process before.

The Annapolis Conference was held on November 27, 2007, at the United States Naval Academy in Annapolis, Maryland. The conference ended with the issuing of a joint statement from all parties saying that the Israelis and Palestinians had agreed to work toward a peace deal that would be ready before the end of 2008. The objective of the conference was to produce a substantive document on resolving the Israeli-Palestinian conflict along the lines of President George W. Bush's Road Map for Peace, with the eventual establishment of a Palestinian state. Unfortunately, the outcome was far less than that, and within a year of the conference it was clear that the end-of-2008 target would not be met and that the principal significance of the Annapolis Conference was the fact that the number of nations attending the conference (forty) was very large and included many Arab states that had not participated previously.

The pace of negotiations, to the extent that meaningful negotiations had taken place at all, was not heartening. In December 2008, after a year of on-again, off-again talks that were not producing results, President Abbas pulled out of talks after Israeli prime minister Ehud Olmert launched an offensive on Hamas-run Gaza. Operation Cast Lead was a full-scale military invasion in response to continued Hamas rocket attacks; it lasted for three weeks before a cease-fire was negotiated.

In January 2009 the newly elected American president, Barack Obama, indicated that he wanted to move purposively and vigorously toward a Middle East peace during his presidency, and he appointed George Mitchell, once the very successful mediator in the Northern Ireland talks, to be his special representative to the Middle East.

In February 2009 the elections for the Knesset took place, as we described in chapter 7 of this volume. As a result of those elections, Benjamin Netanyahu was once again prime minister, leading a coalition of right- and center-located political parties. This was not seen as a good thing by Palestinians or by Israel's Arab neighbors, and in relatively short order Netanyahu gave a signal that settlements could continue to be built in the Occupied Territories.

In June 2009 the United States and Israel engaged in some difficult communications. Both President Obama and Secretary of State Hillary Clinton pressed Prime Minister Netanyahu for an end to settlement growth, arguing that the growth was contrary to past Middle East peace agreements and unnecessarily inflammatory in the peace process. Netanyahu countered that "natural" growth of settlements—growth that came as a result of a natural population growth in the settlements, not as a result of *new* settlements—

had been allowed in the past and would continue to be supported by his Government. But, Netanyahu also accepted in principle the idea that a Palestinian state—separate from the state of Israel—should be created, as long as it could be done under conditions that would allow Israel to be secure.

Three months later, in September 2009, President Obama brought President Abbas and Prime Minister Netanyahu together at the United Nations in New York to a widely photographed handshake. Palestinians were very disappointed that President Obama appeared to be backing away from a demand that Israel stop all settlement building prior to new negotiations. Prime Minister Netanyahu announced a ten-month "partial freeze" on settlement development, arousing much criticism from the political right in Israel.

Both President Obama and Secretary of State Clinton praised Netanyahu's "partial freeze" on new West Bank settlement building, calling it "unprecedented," although critics suggested that the "partial freeze" still permitted some new building to take place. In early March 2010 the Arab League endorsed the principle of four months of "proximity talks," a structure that would allow President Abbas to resume some kind of negotiation activity with Prime Minister Netanyahu without actually meeting with Netanyahu, since Netanyahu was not agreeing to Abbas's demand that settlement building stop completely before negotiations could recommence. Hamas criticized even the notion of "proximity talks," strengthening the divisions between Fatah and Hamas.

Shortly thereafter, in the second week of March, Mr. Mitchell started meeting with Prime Minister Netanyahu and President Abbas in the indirect "proximity" format. At the same time, President Obama and Secretary of State Clinton increased their pressure on Prime Minister Netanyahu to show good faith with the Palestinians over the settlement issue. Israel responded that it would be willing to offer the Palestinians "confidence-building" steps, although precisely what those steps would be was unclear.

BILATERAL PROGRESS

Israel and Jordan

As noted above, Israel and Jordan signed the Israeli-Jordanian Common Agenda on September 14, 1993. This served as the basis for further discussions and negotiations on key bilateral issues, including water, security, refugees and displaced persons, borders, and territorial matters.[74] In July 1994 King Hussein and Prime Minister Abdel Salem al-Majali signed the Washington Declaration, which terminated the state of war between Jordan and Israel, agreed to seek a just and lasting peace based on UN Resolutions 242 and 338, and granted to Jordan a special role over Muslim holy shrines in Jerusalem. Discussion of a number of very pragmatic issues preceded the declaration as well, including telephone links, electrical grids, border crossings, tourist mobility, problems of drug smuggling, and opportunities for economic cooperation.[75]

The treaty of peace between Israel and Jordan was signed on October 26, 1994. The treaty established full diplomatic relations between the two nations and opened the door for significantly increased economic relations between the parties. Many bilateral agreements have been signed in the last eight years, covering environmental protections, commerce and trade, transportation, air transport, water, agriculture, crime and illicit drugs, communications and mail, science and culture, education, health, borders, tourism and energy, and regional development of the Eilat-Aqaba region.[76]

Israel and Lebanon

Historically, two other issues have clouded the bilateral relationship between Israel and Lebanon: Lebanon as a satellite state for Syria and Lebanon as a base of operations for Palestinian acts of terrorism. As noted above, Israel has been very clear over the years that it does not have any claims on Lebanese territory; its military actions into and against Lebanon and its security zone in southern Lebanon were motivated by the insecurity of the Lebanese-Israeli border and the acts of violence directed against the Israeli population from Lebanese territory.

In the bilateral talks that took place in Washington in 1994, Israel proposed three key principles:

1. The Lebanese army would prevent terror activities against the security zone and against Israel for six months. Three months after that period, Israel would be willing to sign a peace treaty with Lebanon.
2. Before withdrawing from Lebanon, Israel would have to be convinced that terror groups based in Lebanon had been disbanded.
3. Lebanese citizens and Southern Lebanese Army personnel who had helped Israel would not suffer after Israeli withdrawal.

In April 1996, after many months of terrorist activity coming from the Lebanese side of Israel's northern border, Israel invaded Lebanon in what was called Operation Grapes of Wrath.[77] We discussed earlier the difficulty in domestic politics caused by the Lebanese action and the resistance of Israeli soldiers to serving in Lebanon. In the campaign for the 1999 election, Ehud Barak pledged to bring Israeli troops out of Lebanon, and the guidelines of his Government indicated that "the Government will act toward bringing the IDF out of Lebanon, while guaranteeing the welfare and security of residents of the north, and aspiring to conclude a peace treaty with Lebanon."[78]

Following Barak's election, on March 5, 2000, the Government passed a resolution to redeploy the IDF forces by July of that year; on May 23, 2000, Israel completed a unilateral withdrawal of military forces from southern Lebanon. This ended an eighteen-year Israeli presence in Lebanon.[79]

In 2006, open warfare erupted between Israel and Hezbollah forces in southern Lebanon after the kidnapping of several Israeli soldiers. The war was fierce and widespread, including Hezbollah rocket attacks on Israel as far south as Haifa and Israeli aerial bombing of Lebanese territory with cluster bombs. That conflict lasted barely a month but changed the political landscape significantly, as it was generally *not* considered a success for the Israeli forces. In fact, the Hezbollah insurgents in Lebanon gleefully claimed victory, and the missing soldiers were not returned. For the first time, it was fairly widely perceived that Israel had failed at a major military objective, rocking the government internally.

Israel and Syria

In 1994 Israel and Syria engaged in several negotiation sessions, some at the ambassadorial level in Washington, D.C., and some at other levels, including one between the Israeli and Syrian chiefs of staff in December 1994 and June 1995. Later talks, in December 1995 and January 1996, focused on security and other key issues.

As we noted earlier, Israel has agreed to a key demand of Syria in negotiations: that Israel accept the general principle of withdrawal from the Golan Heights. The issue of contention in the negotiation is whether this includes total withdrawal and what trade-off Syria will offer in exchange. Specifically, in negotiations Israel has identified four key questions in need of resolution:

1. How far Israel will withdraw. Syria wants a total withdrawal; Israel has indicated that a total withdrawal is not at all automatic.
2. The schedule and duration of the withdrawal. Syria wants a rapid and brief withdrawal; Israel has indicated that it will move deliberately and carefully.
3. The linkage between the withdrawal and normalization. Syria has offered normalization after withdrawal; Israel has insisted that the two must be linked in time and that "there be a protracted phase of normalization—open borders and embassies" before withdrawal is complete.
4. Agreement about security arrangements.[80]

Prime Minister Ehud Barak was anxious to pursue negotiations with the Syrians. In the election campaign of 1999 he promised, as a response to those strongly opposed to giving territory in the Golan Heights back to Syria, that any agreement with Syria would be submitted to the Israeli public in a referendum for approval. Unfortunately, his Government was not able to reach an agreement with Syria, and negotiations with Syria stalled. While negotiations between Israel and Syria were renewed in January 2000 in Shepherdstown, West Virginia, after a pause of more than three years, no substantive outcomes appeared from the negotiations.[81]

Israel and the Palestinians

The Israeli-Palestinian bilateral negotiations have made real progress in the decade since the Oslo Accords, and on several occasions have come very, very close to reaching what many feel is a critical threshold of progress toward peace, although the status of Israeli-Palestinian relations in 2010 might make this hard to believe. While Prime Minister Barak hoped to conclude negotiations with the Palestinians for an enduring and stable peace, acts of violence against Israeli targets by terrorists reached a point during his administration at which he felt it necessary to take a time-out in the negotiations with the Palestinians.[82] The issue, again, was the association between the Palestine National Authority, on one hand, and Palestinian terrorism, on the other. The Israeli position was that while the Palestine National Authority generally, and Yasser Arafat specifically, paid lip service to the values of peace and at times criticized acts of terrorism, on other occasions the Palestinian leadership gave decidedly different messages to a different constituency.

The negotiations were adversely affected by rejectionism on both sides.[83] While the vast majority of Palestinians may prefer progress toward peace and stability, individuals, even if only a very small number, prepared to commit suicide in the process of committing acts of terrorism have the ability to derail progress toward peace by pushing the Israeli government to retaliate, which leads to more Palestinian acts of violence, and so on, and so on. The same can be said about Israeli extremists who are willing to do whatever is necessary to stop the peace process, as well as the relative minority of religiously orthodox Israelis who hold views about their claim to land in the Occupied Territory that they are not willing to compromise. Extremists on both sides have assassinated political leaders, President Anwar Sadat on the Arab side and Prime Minister Yitzhak Rabin on the Israeli side.

As we noted above, the Oslo Accords resulted from months of secret negotiations in Oslo between negotiators for Israel and the PLO. On September 9, 1993, PLO chairman Yasser Arafat sent a letter to Prime Minister Rabin recognizing Israel's right to exist, accepting UN Security Council Resolutions 242 and 338, committing the PLO to a peaceful resolution of the negotiation, renouncing terrorism and the use of violence, promising to prevent violations of agreements, and declaring that articles of the PLO covenant denying Israel's right to exist were no longer operative. In exchange, Israel recognized the PLO as the representative of the Palestinian people.[84]

The Declaration of Principles (DOP) that came from the negotiations was signed on September 13, 1993.[85] It described self-government arrangements for the Palestinians in the West Bank and the Gaza Strip.[86] The DOP had two stages. In stage one, the "Interim Self-Government Arrangements" stage, progress would be made over a multiyear period. The Gaza-Jericho Agreement was signed in May 1994 and brought about a withdrawal of Israeli forces and administration from specific areas. It also described the transfer of powers and responsibilities to the Palestine National Authority, with specific attention paid to security arrangements.

In August 1994 a second document was signed titled "Agreement on Preparatory Transfer of Powers and Responsibilities between Israel and the Palestine National Authority." This document transferred powers in specific areas other than those covered in the Gaza-Jericho Agreement, including education and culture, health, social welfare, taxation, and tourism. (An expansion of this was signed on August 27, 1995, adding labor, trade and industry, gas and gasoline, insurance, postal services, statistics, agriculture, and local government to the powers previously agreed on.)

Finally, on September 28, 1995, the Israeli-Palestinian Interim Agreement on the West Bank and the Gaza Strip was signed and dealt with the transfer of powers in the West Bank from Israel to an elected Palestinian council.[87] The Interim Agreement was the basis for a December 1995 redeployment of Israeli troops from heavily populated areas in the West Bank, the January 1996 elections to the Palestinian council, the January 1997 withdrawal of forces from Hebron, the October 1998 Wye River Memorandum, and the September 1999 Sharm el-Sheikh Memorandum.

Stage two of the DOP was supposed to focus on permanent-status arrangements, including agreement on the borders of Jerusalem, rights of refugees, policies affecting settlements, and security arrangements and borders. The negotiations started in Taba, Egypt, in May 1996. While the talks only lasted for two days (May 5–6), they ended with a joint statement that indicated a commitment to the process leading to a lasting peace. In the Wye Memorandum of October 23, 1998, both sides agreed to resume negotiations, and a meeting took place in November 1998, with no significant results. The Sharm el-Sheikh Memorandum called for the talks to resume in September 1999. As a result of these talks, Israel completed the first and second phases of the Further Redeployment (FRD) process in March 2000.

At the invitation of President Clinton, Prime Minister Barak and Chairman Arafat attended a summit at Camp David in July 2000 to resume negotiations and to try to reenergize the peace process. Unfortunately, the summit ended without any agreement being reached.

Photo 11.1. Soldier at a security checkpoint on the road from Ramallah to Jerusalem, 2010

THE COPENHAGEN TRACK

In 1995 and 1996 a group of influential Israeli and Egyptian intellectuals, politicians, and writers met in Louisiana, Denmark, at the Danish Museum of Modern Art. The idea was to inject some warmth into the cold peace between Egypt and Israel and to seek ways to advance the peace process. The Royal Danish Ministry of Foreign Affairs arranged the meetings. Participants attended the meetings in their personal capacities, and the meetings were kept secret. In the fall of 1996, it was decided to include Palestinians and Jordanians.

In January 1997 some one hundred participants, including representatives from Egypt, Israel, Jordan, and the Palestine National Authority, met in Copenhagen at a conference opened by the Danish minister for foreign affairs. The conference established "the international alliance for Arab-Israeli peace" and passed a resolution known as "The Copenhagen Declaration." Although participants of the process have held positions in their countries and several of them had close connections with their governments, the alliance was a purely nongovernmental project with the aim of promoting peace in the region. Meetings took place in each of the years between 1998 and 2003. The 2000 meeting received the European Award for Peace.

The 2003 meeting took place in May in Copenhagen. The focus of the 2003 meeting was "The Road Map" for peace, sponsored by the United

States, the European Union, Russia, and the United Nations, referred to in the agreement as "the Quartet."

The Road Map was a departure from past approaches to peace in the Middle East. "In the old model, we started walking and wanted to see how far we could go," said Danish foreign minister Per Stig Møller. The problem was that this involved "too much process and too little peace."[88]

The Road Map started with what in other peace agreements was an ending: a specific date for the creation of a Palestinian state by 2005 and security for Israel. The Road Map replaced bilateralism (Israel and Palestine, with others watching) with multilateralism: the Quartet would guarantee movement from stage to stage.

The Road Map required commitment on the part of the parties: they would agree that whatever the provocation by the other party, there would be no more conflict or terrorism sponsored by the Palestine National Authority and no more threat of invasion by Israeli tanks. The Palestinians could count on their own state.

The key ideas of the Road Map were threefold:[89]

1. The necessity of security guarantees for Israel, provided by the Quartet
2. The necessity of independence for the Palestinians and the end of occupation
3. The removal of Israeli settlements and the restoration of Palestinian infrastructure

To insulate the process from lone suicide-bomber events, the plan called for the Quartet to monitor peace, deeming international involvement essential. It specifically suggested the following:

- The Palestinians must fight violence and work for security.
- Israel must help the Palestinians, ease restrictions, withdraw from Palestinian areas, and freeze settlement activities.
- The Palestinian state must be a viable state, not a Bantu state.
- There must be a commitment to peace. Both parties must agree that they cannot permit a single extremist to derail the peace process. For example, an Egyptian soldier who started shooting at Israeli tourists many years ago did not derail the peace.
- And the final key, the ultimate territory must be the 1967 lines, plus or minus some territory. Land swaps to accommodate changes on the ground are acceptable, but the ultimate size of Palestine must correspond to 1967 lines and must include Jerusalem.

The Danish foreign minister Per Stig Møller said on more than one occasion that "Peace is not a question of who doesn't throw the first stone. Peace is a question of who doesn't throw the *second* stone."[90] The joint declaration that came from the May 2003 Copenhagen Conference ended with the phrase "Peace is too important to be left only to governments."[91]

THE QUEST FOR PEACE, AGAIN

The legitimacy of the Palestinian claim to statehood and, by extension, the legitimacy of Israeli jurisdiction over territories in the West Bank and Gaza (the other half of the agenda) has been perhaps the central issue in the quest for peace in the region since the 1967 war. As the late Edward Said has said, there *is* a Palestinian people. No party to the debate disputes that. The dispute, rather, is over what to do about the Palestinian people and their claim to land and nationhood. Related to this, of course, is the issue of Israeli security. Time and time again, when Israel has made concessions to the Palestinians without adequate security guarantees, the product of those negotiations has not long endured.

We have seen here that there are many different responses to these questions, usually intensely held and articulated, and usually not subject to change through debate and discussion. Yet, one thing remains clear: without a resolution of the Palestinian question, there can be no stability and long-term peace in the Middle East.

FOR FURTHER READING

Berger, Marshall J., and Ora Ahimeir, eds. *Jerusalem: A City and Its Future.* Syracuse, N.Y.: Syracuse University Press, 2002.

Carter, Jimmy. *Palestine: Peace Not Apartheid.* New York: Simon and Schuster, 2006.

Freedman, Robert O. *The Middle East and the Peace Process: The Impact of the Oslo Accords.* Gainesville: University Press of Florida, 1998.

Ganim, As'ad. *Palestinian Politics after Arafat: A Failed National Movement.* Bloomington: Indiana University Press, 2010.

Indyk, Martin. *Innocent Abroad: An Intimate Account of American Peace Diplomacy in the Middle East.* New York: Simon and Schuster, 2009.

Mahler, Gregory, and Alden Mahler. *The Arab-Israeli Conflict: An Introduction and Documentary Reader.* New York: Routledge, 2010.

Miller, Aaron David. *The Much Too Promised Land: America's Elusive Search for Arab-Israeli Peace.* New York: Bantam, 2008.

Muasher, Marwan. *The Arab Center: The Promise of Moderation.* New Haven, Conn.: Yale University Press, 2008.

Quandt, William B. *Peace Process: American Diplomacy and the Arab-Israeli Conflict since 1967.* Washington, D.C.: Brookings Institution Press, 2005.

Rothstein, Robert, Moshe Ma'oz, and Khalil Shiqaqi, eds. *The Israeli-Palestinian Peace Process: Oslo and the Lessons of Failure; Perspectives, Predicaments, and Prospects.* Brighton, U.K.: Sussex Academic Press, 2002.

Sher, Gilead. *The Israeli-Palestinian Peace Negotiations, 1999–2001*. New York: Routledge, 2006.

Shlaim, Avi. *War and Peace in the Middle East: A Concise History*. New York: Penguin, 1995.

Stewart, Donna. *Good Neighbourly Relations: Jordan, Israel and the 1994–2004 Peace Process.* London: Tauris, 2007.

Tessler, Mark. *A History of the Israeli-Palestinian Conflict.* Bloomington: Indiana University Press, 1994.

Notes

INTRODUCTION: THE STUDY
OF ISRAEL IN COMPARATIVE CONTEXT

1. See Ernest Barker, ed. and trans., *The Politics of Aristotle* (New York: Oxford University Press, 1970), pp. xi–xix.

2. See Gregory Mahler, *The Knesset: Parliament in the Israeli Political System* (Rutherford, N.J.: Fairleigh Dickinson University Press, 1981).

3. The specific question was, "What was the first aspect of politics that you were aware of?" See Mahler, *The Knesset*, p. 230.

4. See Joel S. Migdal, *State in Society: Studying How States and Societies Transform and Constitute One Another* (New York: Cambridge University Press, 2001).

5. David Easton, *A Framework for Political Analysis* (Englewood Cliffs, N.J.: Prentice Hall, 1965), p. 50.

6. In the January 10, 1997, issue of the *Chronicle of Higher Education*, Christopher Shea introduced a new version of a long-running debate over the value of area studies as distinct from comparative politics. See Christopher Shea, "Political Scientists Clash over Value of Area Studies," *Chronicle of Higher Education* (January 10, 1997): A13. Harvard University's Robert Bates suggests in this essay that a focus on individual regions leads to work that is "mushy and merely descriptive."

7. A very good discussion of the concept of Zionism as a nationalist movement can be found in Shlomo Avineri, *The Making of Modern Zionism* (New York: Basic Books, 1981).

8. For discussion of the Palestinian case, see Gregory Mahler, *Constitutionalism and Palestinian Constitutional Development* (Jerusalem: Palestinian Academic Society for the Study of International Affairs, 1996). See also Khalil Shikaki, "The Peace Process, National Reconstruction and the Transition to Democracy in Palestine," *Journal of Palestine Studies* 25, no. 2 (1996): 6–27.

1 HISTORY AND THE CREATION OF ISRAEL

1. *Eretz Israel*, literally "the state of Israel," will be used to generally refer to the territory roughly corresponding to what we today call Israel.

2. See Eugene Rogan and Avi Shlaim, *The War for Palestine: Rewriting the History of 1948* (New York: Cambridge University Press, 2001); Avi Shlaim, *Israel and Palestine: Reappraisals, Revisions, Refutations* (London: Verso, 2009); Benny Morris, ed., *Making Israel* (Ann Arbor: University of Michigan Press, 2007), especially the chapter by Benny Morris titled "The New Historiography: Israel Confronts Its Critics," pp. 5–48; Zeev Sternhell, *The Founding Myths of Israel: Nationalism, Socialism, and the Making of the Jewish State* (Princeton, N.J.: Princeton University Press, 1998); Efraim Karsh, *Fabricating Israeli History: The "New Historians"* (Portland, Ore.: Frank Cass, 2000); and Anita Shapira, *Israeli Historical Revisionism: From Left to Right* (Portland, Ore.: Frank Cass, 2003).

3. See Baruch Kimmerling and Joel S. Migdal, *The Palestinian People: A History* (Cambridge, Mass.: Harvard University Press, 2003).

4. See Genesis 15:13 and Exodus 12:40, respectively. Hanoch Reviv, "Until the Monarchy," in *History until 1880*, Israel Pocket History (Jerusalem: Keter Publishing, 1973), p. 7. See also H. G. M. Williamson, *Understanding the History of Ancient Israel* (New York: Oxford University Press, 2007), and Richard Gabriel, *The Military History of Ancient Israel* (Westport, Conn.: Praeger, 2003).

5. Reviv, "Until the Monarchy," p. 7; also see Genesis 15:18–21.

6. See Deuteronomy 1:7–8, 11:24, and Joshua 1:4.

7. A note should be made here regarding the date terminology used in this volume. While the traditional Christian, hence Western, format is to use the initials B.C. and A.D., both refer to historical events that occurred before or after the birth of Christ. It should be obvious to the student who thinks about it that Jewish history would not be recorded in a way that is oriented around the appearance of Christ. Indeed, a Jewish calendar does exist. Thus the year including January 2010 is the year 5770 on the Jewish calendar. For convenience, however, because many Jews have realized that they cannot expect non-Jews to be familiar with and use their calendar, they also adhere to the Christian, or Gregorian, calendar. However, rather than adopting initials that mean "before Christ" and "Anno Domini" (year of our Lord), Jewish annotation uses the initials B.C.E. and C.E. (meaning "before the common era" and "common era," respectively). In this book we shall abide by the standard American practice of using B.C. and A.D. where appropriate.

8. The uprising was called the Hasmonean Revolt, involved the Maccabees, and gave rise to the modern Jewish holiday of Hanukkah. See Menachem Stern, "Second Temple: The Hellenistic-Roman Period: 332 B.C.E.–70 C.E.," in *History until 1880*, Israel Pocket History (Jerusalem: Keter Publishing, 1973), p. 105.

9. Shmuel Safrai, "Destruction of the Second Temple to the Arab Conquest (70–634 C.E.)," in *History until 1880*, Israel Pocket History (Jerusalem: Keter Publishing, 1973), p.127.

10. Safrai, "Destruction of the Second Temple," pp. 149–50.

11. See Haim Z'ew Hirschberg, "Crusader Period, 1099–1291," in *History until 1880*, Israel Pocket History (Jerusalem: Keter Publishing, 1973), pp. 185–200.

12. See, for instance, "Mamluk Period (1291–1516)," in *History until 1880*, Israel Pocket History (Jerusalem: Keter Publishing, 1973), p. 206. See also Charles D. Smith, *Palestine and the Arab-Israeli Conflict* (Boston: St. Martin's, 2007); Kimmerling, *The Palestinian People*; or Saul Friedman, *A History of the Middle East* (Jefferson, N.C.: McFarland and Co., 2006).

13. See Avigdor Levy, ed., *Jews, Turks, Ottomans: A Shared History, Fifteenth through the Twentieth Century* (Syracuse, N.Y.: Syracuse University Press, 2002), and Haim Z'ew Hirschberg, "Ottoman Period," in *History until 1880*, Israel Pocket History (Jerusalem: Keter Publishing, 1973), pp. 212–50. See also Ilan Pappé, *A History of Modern Palestine: One Land, Two Peoples* (New York: Cambridge University Press, 2004), and A. I. Dawisha, *Arab Nationalism in the Twentieth Century: From Triumph to Despair* (Princeton: Princeton University Press, 2003).

14. See Mordechai Chertoff, ed., *Zionism: A Basic Reader* (New York: Herzl Press, 1975), and Israel Cohen, *A Short History of Zionism* (London: F. Muller, 1951), as two examples of the huge literature in this area.

15. Getzel Kressel, ed., *Zionism*, Israel Pocket History (Jerusalem: Keter, 1973), p. 1. See also S. Ilan Troen, *Imagining Zion: Dreams, Designs, and Realities in a Century of Jewish Settlement* (New Haven, Conn.: Yale University Press, 2003).

16. Hirschberg, "Ottoman Period," p. 232. "By 1880 the total population had grown considerably to 450,000, including 24,000 Jews and 45,000 Christians," p. 237.

17. Hirschberg, "Ottoman Period," p. 242.

18. Hirschberg, "Ottoman Period," p. 243. See also the Palestinian Academic Society for the Study of International Affairs, *PASSIA Diary* (Jerusalem: PASSIA, 1996), p. 239.

19. Jacob Katz, "Forerunners," in *Zionism*, Israel Pocket History, ed. Getzel Kressel (Jerusalem: Keter, 1973), p. 5.

20. Dan Horowitz and Moshe Lissak, *Origins of the Israeli Polity: Palestine under the Mandate* (Chicago: University of Chicago Press, 1978).

21. Katz, "Forerunners," p. 21.

22. Howard Sachar, *A History of Israel: From the Rise of Zionism to Our Time* (New York: Alfred A. Knopf, 1981), p. 15.

23. Asher Arian, *Politics in Israel: The Second Generation* (Chatham, N.J.: Chatham House, 1985), p. 13.

24. Yehuda Slutsky, "Under Ottoman Rule (1880–1917)," in *History from 1880*, Israel Pocket History (Jerusalem: Keter, 1973), p. 12.

25. One of the best studies of Herzl is Amos Elon's *Herzl* (New York: Holt, Rinehart, Winston, 1975). See also Irwin Wall, "Theodor Herzl (Book Review)," *Central European History* 28, no. 3 (1995): 420–22.

26. Sachar, *History*, p. 39. See also Bernard Reich, *Arab-Israeli Conflict and Conciliation: A Documentary History* (Westport, Conn.: Greenwood Press, 1995).

27. Sachar, *History*, p. 40. See Theodor Herzl, *The Jewish State* (New York: Scopus Publishing Company, 1943).

28. Sachar, *History*, p. 40.

29. Sachar, *History*, p. 38.

30. Norman Levin, *The Zionist Movement in Palestine and World Politics, 1880–1918* (Lexington, Mass.: D. C. Heath, 1974).

31. Alfred Katz, *Government and Politics in Contemporary Israel: 1948–Present* (Washington, D.C.: University Press of America, 1980), p. 5. See also Reich, *Arab-Israeli Conflict and Conciliation.*

32. Theodor Herzl, *Complete Diaries* (New York: Herzl Press, 1960).

33. Don Peretz, *The Government and Politics of Israel* (Boulder, Colo.: Westview, 1979), p. 20. See also Harvey Sicherman, "On the Centennial of the First Zionist Congress," *Orbis* 42 (1998): 153–55.

34. Sachar, *History*, pp. 60–61. A related project involved Mesopotamia; see Stuart Cohen, "Israel Zangwill's Plan for Jewish Colonization in Mesopotamia," *Middle Eastern Studies* 16, no. 3 (1980): 200–8. See also Reich, *Arab-Israeli Conflict and Conciliation.*

35. Sachar, *History*, p. 63. See Henry Regensteiner, "Theodor Herzl in Retrospect," *Midstream* 45, no. 7 (1999): 35–42, and Martin Gilbert, *Israel: A History* (New York: Morrow, 1998).

36. Peretz, *Government and Politics*, pp. 25, 26. On the subject of the Ottoman Empire and the Zionists, see Mim Kemal Oke, "The Ottoman Empire, Zionism, and the Question of Palestine, 1890–1908," *International Journal of Middle East Studies* 14, no. 3 (1982): 329–42.

37. For a thorough history, consult Moshe Burstein, *Self-Government of the Jews in Palestine Since 1900* (New Haven, Conn.: Hyperion, 1934). See also Lawrence Davidson, "Zionism, Socialism and United States Support for the Jewish Colonization of Palestine in the 1920s," *Arab Studies Quarterly* 18, no. 3 (1996): 1–17.

38. See Mark Tessler, *A History of the Israeli-Palestinian Conflict* (Bloomington: Indiana University Press, 1994), p. 174.

39. See Michael Wolffsohn, *Israel: Polity, Society and Economy, 1882–1986* (Atlantic Highlands, N.J.: Humanities Press International, 1987), p. 121.

40. This section is based upon a much longer discussion in Arian, *Politics in Israel*, pp. 13–19.

41. Ruth Kark, "Jewish Frontier Settlement in the Negev, 1880–1948," *Middle Eastern Studies* 17, no. 3 (1981): 334–56.

42. Peretz, *Government and Politics*, p. 37.

43. Israel Information Center, Government of Israel, *Facts about Israel* (Jerusalem: Israel Information Center, 1977), p. 43.

44. Arian, *Politics in Israel*, p. 16.

45. *Facts about Israel*, p. 49.

46. Sachar, *History*, p. 156.

47. *Facts about Israel*, p. 50.

48. Peretz, *Government and Politics*, p. 36. See also Wolffsohn, *Israel*, p. 121.

49. Tessler, *History*, p. 127.

50. Tessler, *History*, p. 129.

51. Tessler, *History*, p. 131.

52. See Ya'acov Ro'i, "The Zionist Attitude to the Arabs, 1908–1914," in *Palestine and Israel in the 19th and 20th Centuries*, ed. Elie Kedourie and Sylvia Haim (London: Frank Cass, 1982), p. 45. See also Gudrun Kramer, *A History of Palestine: From the Ottoman Conquest to the Founding of the State of Israel* (Princeton: Princeton University Press, 2008).

53. Sachar, *History*, p. 92. See also Isaiah Friedman, "The McMahon-Hussein Correspondence and the Question of Palestine," *Journal of Contemporary History* 5, no. 2 (1970): 83–122. For a very good historical analysis of the period leading up to parti-

tion, see Efraim Karsh and Inari Karsh, *Empires of the Sand: The Struggle for Mastery in the Middle East, 1789–1923* (Cambridge, Mass.: Harvard University Press, 1999).

54. Historians have much debated the precise role—and attitudes—of Abdullah and the extent to which he did or did not sympathize and cooperate with Zionists. See Efraim Karsh, "The Collusion That Never Was: King Abdallah, the Jewish Agency, and the Partition of Palestine," *Journal of Contemporary History* 34, no. 4 (1999): 569–88. See also Avi Shlaim, *The Politics of Partition: King Abdullah, the Zionists, and Palestine 1921–1951* (Oxford: Oxford University Press, 1998).

55. Tessler, *History*, p. 147.

56. Sachar, *History*, p. 93. See also Reich, *Arab-Israeli Conflict and Conciliation*.

57. Sachar, *History*, p. 96. See also David Pryze-Jones, *Betrayal: France, the Arabs, and the Jews* (New York: Encounter Books, 2006).

58. See Isaiah Friedman, *The Question of Palestine: British-Jewish-Arab Relations, 1914–1918* (New Brunswick, N.J.: Transaction, 1992).

59. For background on this, see Rory Miller, *Divided against Zion: Anti-Zionist Opposition in Britain to a Jewish State in Palestine, 1945–1948* (Portland, Ore.: Frank Cass, 2000).

60. Sachar, *History*, p. 109. There is a good deal of literature dealing with Lord Balfour and his views on Zionism and Palestine. See Arthur James Balfour, *Speeches on Zionism* (New York: Kraus Reprint, 1971).

61. Perhaps the definitive work on the Balfour Declaration is Leonard Stein's *The Balfour Declaration* (New York: Simon and Schuster, 1961). See also J. M. N. Jeffries, "The Balfour Declaration," in *Arab-Israeli Relations: Historical Background and Origins of the Conflict*, ed. Ian Lustick (New York: Garland, 1994).

62. See Isaiah Freedman, *The Rise of Israel: The Zionist Commission in Palestine, 1918* (New York: Garland, 1987).

63. Sachar, *History*, p. 118.

64. Sachar, *History*, p. 121.

65. Tessler, *History*, p. 154.

66. Tessler, *History*, p. 147.

67. Tessler, *History*, p. 155.

68. See D. Edward Knox, *The Making of a New Eastern Question: British Palestine Policy and the Origins of Israel, 1917–1925* (Washington, D.C.: Catholic University Press, 1981), and John McTague, "The British Military Administration in Palestine, 1917–1920," *Journal of Palestine Studies* 7, no. 3 (1978): 55–76.

69. Sachar, *History*, p. 127.

70. League of Nations, "The Mandate for Palestine," July 24, 1922, as printed in *The Arab-Israeli Conflict: An Introduction and Documentary Reader*, ed. Gregory S. Mahler and Alden R. W. Mahler (London: Routledge, 2010), pp. 58–63.

71. Michael Cohen, *Palestine, Retreat from the Mandate: The Making of British Policy, 1936–1945* (New York: Holmes and Meier, 1978).

72. Peretz, *Government and Politics*, pp. 32–33.

73. Peretz, *Government and Politics*, p. 34. See also Reich, *Arab-Israeli Conflict and Conciliation*, for a thorough history of British Palestine policy at this time.

74. Elie Kedourie, "Sir Herbert Samuel and the Government of Palestine," *Middle Eastern Studies* 5, no. 1 (1969): 44–68.

75. Tessler, *History*, pp. 241–242.

76. Aaron Klieman, *The Rise of Israel: Zionist Evidence before the Peel Commission, 1936–1937* (New York: Garland, 1987). See also Aaron Klieman, *The Rise of Israel: The Royal Commission Report, 1937* (New York: Garland, 1987), and Aaron Klieman, *The Rise of Israel: The Partition Controversy, 1937* (New York: Garland, 1987).

77. Sir John Woodhead, *Palestine Partition Commission Report* (London: Colonial Office, 1938).

78. Sachar, *History*, p. 218. See also Adam LeBor, *City of Oranges: An Intimate History of Arabs and Jews in Jaffa* (New York: Norton, 2007).

79. Sachar, *History*, p. 220.

80. Sachar, *History*, p. 222.

81. Mahler and Mahler, *The Arab-Israeli Conflict*, p. 86.

82. Sachar, *History*, p. 224.

83. Sachar, *History*, p. 224.

84. Raul Hilberg, *The Destruction of the European Jews: Revised and Definitive Edition* (New York: Holmes and Meier, 1985).

85. Peretz, *Government and Politics*, p. 45.

86. See Gideon Hausner, *Justice in Jerusalem* (New York: Holocaust Library, 1966), for a full discussion of this. Chapter 12, "The Great Powers and the Little Man" (pp. 226–64), specifically addresses the subject of the international reaction to Hitlerism.

87. James Gelvin, "Zionism and the Representation of 'Jewish Palestine' at the New York World's Fair, 1939–1940," *International History Review* 22, no. 1 (2000): 37–65.

88. See also Irving Abella and Harold Troper's *None Is Too Many: Canada and the Jews of Europe, 1933–1948* (Toronto: Lester and Orpen Dennys, 1982), which deals with Canadian policy toward Jewish refugees. There is actually quite a literature on President Harry Truman and his responses to the creation of the state of Israel. See Michael Cohen, *Truman and Israel* (Berkeley: University of California Press, 1990). See also Julius Simon, *History, Religion, and Meaning: American Reflections on the Holocaust and Israel* (Westport, Conn.: Greenwood, 2000).

89. Abba Eban, *My People: The Story of the Jews* (New York: Random House, 1968), p. 434. There is actually quite a substantial literature describing both this period and the illegal immigration actions. See, for example, Arie Eliav, *The Voyage of the Ulua* (New York: Funk and Wagnalls, 1969).

90. The term *terrorist* is clearly laden with emotional significance, especially in light of contemporary activities in the Middle East, and perspectives of the Palestinians and Israelis in relation to the problem of terrorism will be discussed later in this book. One anecdote illustrates some of the problems caused by different perspectives associated with the term: In 1975 I interviewed Menachem Begin (then leader of the Opposition Party in the Knesset) and asked, "Mr. Begin, some people would say that there is no difference between what the PLO is doing today and what you did to the British as leader of the Irgun. How would you respond to that?" Mr. Begin replied, "Of course there is a difference, Mr. Mahler. Arafat is a terrorist. I was a freedom fighter."

91. J. S. Hurewitz, *The Struggle for Palestine* (New York: Norton, 1950), p. 199. See also Leslie Stein, *The Making of Modern Israel, 1948–1967* (Cambridge: Polity, 2009).

92. One of the most interesting histories of this period is Menachem Begin's autobiography, *The Revolt* (New York: Nash, 1977). See also Michael Cohen, *The Rise of Israel: The British Return to Partition, 1943–1945* (New York: Garland, 1987).

93. For an example of this kind of incident, see Eliav, *The Voyage of the Ulua.*

94. See Eban, *My People,* p. 437, and Marie Syrkin, *Golda Meir—Israel's Leader* (New York: Putnam's Sons, 1969), p. 161.

95. For a more detailed discussion of this proposal see Katz, *Government and Politics,* pp. 14–15.

96. Katz, *Government and Politics,* p. 15.

97. Miriam Haron, "The British Decision to Give the Palestine Question to the United Nations," *Middle Eastern Studies* 17, no. 2 (1981): 241–48.

98. Oscar Kraines, *Government and Politics in Israel* (Boston: Houghton Mifflin, 1961), p. 2.

99. Kraines makes an interesting observation: "Although the [territory] allocated to the 'Jewish State' amounted to about 55 percent of the total area of Palestine, and the 'Arab State' was given nearly 45 percent, more than half of the territory assigned to the 'Jewish State' was to consist of the Negev, an arid, bare, and largely uncultivable desert area in the south bordering Transjordan and Egypt" (Kraines, *Government and Politics,* p. 4). See also Itzhak Galnoor, *The Partition of Palestine: Decision Crossroads in the Zionist Movement* (Albany: State University of New York Press, 1995).

100. Kraines, *Government and Politics,* p. 3. A very interesting analysis of the legal status of partition is to be found in N. Elarby, "Some Legal Implications of the 1947 Partition Resolution and the 1949 Armistice Agreement," *Law and Contemporary Problems* 33, no. 1 (1968): 97–109. See also Cohen, *Rise of Israel.*

101. See Phyllis Bennis, "The United Nations and Palestine: Partition and Its Aftermath," *Arab Studies Quarterly* 19, no. 3 (1997): 47–76.

102. Kraines, *Government and Politics,* p. 3.

103. On early American-Israeli relations, see John Snetsinger, *Truman, the Jewish Vote, and the Creation of Israel* (Palo Alto, Calif.: Stanford University Press, 1974).

104. See Arnold Krammer, "Soviet Motives in the Partition of Palestine, 1947–1948," *Journal of Palestine Studies* 2, no. 2 (1973): 102–19, for information on the vote. More generally, see Walter Eytan, *The First Ten Years: A Diplomatic History of Israel* (New York: Simon and Schuster, 1958).

105. Dan Kurzman, *Genesis 1948: The First Arab-Israeli War* (New York: World, 1970). See, for a broad examination of this, Joseph Heller, *The Birth of Israel, 1945–1949: Ben-Gurion and His Critics* (Gainesville: University Press of Florida, 2000). For a dramatic story of a highly controversial battle and its impact upon long-term Israeli-Palestinian relations, see Daniel McGowan and Marc Ellis, *Remembering Deir Yassin: The Future of Israel and Palestine* (New York: Olive Branch, 1998).

106. Saul Mishal, *West Bank East Bank: The Palestinians in Jordan, 1949–1967* (New Haven, Conn.: Yale University Press, 1976).

107. On the armistices, see Muassasat al-Dirasat al-Filastiniyah, *The Arab-Israeli Armistice Agreements, February–July 1949. U.N. Texts and Annexes* (Beirut: Institute for Palestine Studies, 1967). For an Israeli-authored perspective of this period, see David Ben-Gurion, *Israel: A Personal History* (New York: Funk and Wagnalls, 1971), pp. 94–330. Another excellent study is by Jon Kimche and David Kimche, *A Clash of Destinies: The Arab-Jewish War and the Founding of the State of Israel* (New York: Praeger, 1960).

108. The precise reason the hundreds of thousands of refugees fled their homes has been a point of dispute since 1949. Two very good contemporary histories by Israelis that discuss why the Arabs fled from Palestine, or were chased out by the Is-

raelis, are Tom Segev, *1949: The First Israelis* (New York: Free Press, 1986), and Benny Morris, *The Birth of the Palestine Refugee Problem, 1947–1949* (New York: Cambridge University Press, 1987). See also Ahmad Sa'di and Lila Abu-Lughod, *Nakba: Palestine, 1948, and the Claims of Memory* (New York: Columbia University Press, 2007). This is a topic to which we shall return later in this volume.

109. A good single-volume study is David Gilmour's *Dispossessed: The Ordeal of the Palestinians: 1917–1980* (London: Sidgwick and Jackson, 1980).

110. See Walter Laqueur and Barry Rubin, *The Israel-Arab Reader: A Documentary History of the Middle East Conflict*, 6th ed. (New York: Penguin, 2001).

111. Tessler, *History*, p. 69.

112. It is important to note that the phenomenon of Palestinian nationalism did not appear only as an anti-Israeli ideology. See, inter alia, Ghada Hashem Talhami, *Syria and the Palestinians: The Clash of Nationalisms* (Gainesville: University Press of Florida, 2001), and Musa Budeiri, "The Palestinians: Tensions between Nationalist and Religious Identities," in *Rethinking Nationalism in the Arab Middle East*, ed. James P. Jankowski and Israel Gershoni (New York: Columbia University Press, 1997).

113. See Elie Kedourie and Sylvia G. Haim, eds., *Zionism and Arabism in Palestine and Israel* (London: Frank Cass, 1982).

114. For a very good review, see chapter 2, "Arab History and the Origins of Nationalism in the Arab World," in Tessler, *History*, pp. 69–126. See also Ann Lesch, "The Origins of Palestine Arab Nationalism," in *Nationalism in a Non-National State: The Dissolution of the Ottoman Empire*, ed. William Haddad and William Ochsenwald (Columbus: Ohio State University Press, 1977).

115. PASSIA, *Diary, 2000*, p. 254.

116. Palestinian Academic Society for the Study of International Affairs (PASSIA), *Datebook, 1996* (Jerusalem: PASSIA, 1996), p. 190.

117. Basheer M. Nafi, *Arabism, Islamism, and the Palestine Question, 1908–1941* (Reading, U.K.: Ithaca, 1998).

118. PASSIA, *Datebook, 1996*, p. 189.

119. See Anthony Nutting, *The Tragedy of Palestine from the Balfour Declaration to Today* (London: Arab League, 1969); Sami Hadawi, *Extracts from the History of the Palestine-Israel Conflict* (Toronto, 1991); and David McDowall, *The Palestinians: The Road to Nationhood* (London: Minority Rights Publications, 1995).

120. PASSIA, *Datebook, 1996*, p. 190. See also As'ad Ganim, *The Palestinian-Arab Minority in Israel, 1948–2000: A Political Study* (Albany: State University of New York Press, 2001), and Avraham Sela and Moshe Ma'oz, *The PLO and Israel: From Armed Conflict to Political Solution, 1964–1994* (New York: St. Martin's, 1997).

121. Again, probably the best comprehensive text is Sachar's *History*.

2 ZIONISM, RELIGION, AND THE DOMESTIC POLITICAL ENVIRONMENT

1. For a discussion of the distinction between Hasidic Jews and Orthodox Jews and the nature of Hasidism generally, see Harry Rabinowicz, *Hasidism and the State of Israel* (Rutherford, N.J.: Fairleigh Dickinson University Press, 1982). See also Rebecca Torstrick, *Culture and Customs of Israel* (Westport, Conn.: Greenwood, 2004).

2. One of the most impressive and thorough histories of this period is Walter Laqueur's *A History of Zionism* (New York: Holt, Rinehart, and Winston, 1972). See also Alain Dieckhoff, *Invention of a Nation: Zionist Thought and the Making of Modern Israel* (New York: Columbia University Press, 2002); Alan Dowty, *The Jewish State: A Century Later* (Berkeley: University of California Press, 2001); and Zeev Sternhell, *The Founding Myths of Israel: Nationalism, Socialism, and the Making of the Jewish State* (Princeton, N.J.: Princeton University Press, 1999).

3. Jacob Tsur, *Zionism: The Saga of a National Liberation Movement* (New Brunswick, N.J.: Transaction, 1976), p. 9. For a very sophisticated discussion of Zionism as a national movement, comparing Zionism to nationalism found in African states, see Dan V. Segre, *A Crisis of Identity: Israel and Zionism* (Oxford: Oxford University Press, 1980), pp. 1–13. See also Ben Halpern and Jehuda Reinharz, *Zionism and the Creation of a New Society* (New York: Oxford University Press, 1998), and Sternhell, *Founding Myths*.

4. Tsur, *Zionism*, p. 10. See also Amnon Rubinstein, *From Herzl to Rabin: The Changing Image of Zionism* (New York: Holmes and Meier, 2000), and Nathan Rotenstreich, *Zionism: Past and Present* (Albany: State University of New York Press, 2007).

5. Ofira Seliktar, *New Zionism and the Foreign Policy System of Israel* (Carbondale: Southern Illinois University Press, 1986), pp. 5–6.

6. Charles S. Liebman and Eliezer Don-Yehiya, *Civil Religion in Israel: Traditional Judaism and Political Culture in the Jewish State* (Los Angeles: University of California Press, 1983). See also Arno Mayer, *Plowshares into Swords: From Zionism to Israel* (New York: Verso, 2008).

7. Government of Israel, Central Bureau of Statistics, *Statistical Abstract of Israel, 2009*, Table 2.1, "Population, by Population Group," p. 86, www.cbs.gov.il/shnaton60/st02_01.pdf, and Table 4.2, "Immigrants, by Period of Immigration and Last Continent of Residence," p. 235, www.cbs.gov.il/shnaton60/st04_02.pdf, both accessed January 2010.

8. The numbers can be a bit confusing, because according to the Central Bureau of Statistics, until 1995 the Asian republics of the former Soviet Union were included in Europe; as of 1996 the Asian republics are included in Asia. See *Statistical Abstract of Israel, 2009*, Figure 4.2, "Immigrants, by Period of Immigration and Last Continent of Residence."

9. Tsur, *Zionism*, pp. 77–79. See "Yemen's Last Jews, a World Apart," *Jerusalem Report* (August 12, 1993): CD-ROM.

10. See Natan Sharansky, "A Tale of Two 'Isms,'" *Jerusalem Report* (November 15, 1990): CD-ROM.

11. See Government of Israel, Central Bureau of Statistics, *Statistical Abstract of Israel, 2009*, Table 4.4, "Immigrants by Period of Immigration, Country of Birth, and Last Country of Residence," p. 237, www.cbs.gov.il/shnaton60/st04_04.pdf, accessed January 2010.

12. *Statistical Abstract of Israel, 2009*, Table 4.4, "Immigrants by Period of Immigration, Country of Birth, and Last Country of Resident."

13. J. J. Goldberg, "Next Year in Jerusalem, Maybe," *Jerusalem Report* (May 6, 1993): CD-ROM.

14. Goldberg, "Next Year."

15. The names Judea and Samaria are geographical names referring to land discussed in the Bible as the "traditional" land of the Jews. The Judean Mountains and

the Samarian Mountains make up the bulk of the land in what today is called the "Occupied Territory" of the West Bank.

16. Segre, *A Crisis of Identity,* p. 154. For more on the *Gush,* see David Morrison, *The Gush: Center of Modern Religious Zionism* (New York: Gefen, 2004).

17. Seliktar, *New Zionism,* p. 115. See also Mitchell Cohen, *Zion and State: Nation, Class, and the Shaping of Modern Israel* (New York: Columbia University Press, 1992).

18. "Mapai" is an acronym for *Mifleget Poelei Israel* ("Israel Labor Party"), the predecessor of the current Labor Party.

19. Seliktar, *New Zionism,* p. 80. See Eran Kaplan, *The Jewish Radical Right: Revisionist Zionism and Its Ideological Legacy* (Madison: University of Wisconsin Press, 2005).

20. Seliktar, *New Zionism,* p. 91.

21. Segre, *A Crisis of Identity,* p. 153.

22. See Sasson Sofer and Dorothea Shefer-Vanson, *Zionism and the Foundations of Israeli Diplomacy* (New York: Cambridge University Press, 1998), and Peter Demant, *Jewish Fundamentalism in Israel: Implications for the Mideast Conflict* (Jerusalem: IPCRI, 1994).

23. Liebman and Don-Yehiya, *Civil Religion,* p. 17. See also S. Almog, Jehuda Reinharz, and Anita Shapira, eds., *Zionism and Religion* (Hanover, N.H.: University Press of New England, 1998). This Jewish anti-Zionism is not a modern invention, and there was significant opposition to the creation of the state of Israel in 1948 for precisely this reason. See Rory Miller, *Divided against Zion: Anti-Zionist Opposition in Britain to a Jewish State in Palestine, 1945–1948* (Portland, Ore.: Frank Cass, 2000).

24. Seliktar, *New Zionism,* p. 97.

25. Liebman and Don-Yehiya, *Civil Religion,* p. 189.

26. Liebman and Don-Yehiya, *Civil Religion,* p. 192. See also Almog, Reinharz, and Shapira, *Zionism and Religion.*

27. See Fredelle Z. Spiegel, "A Hobby Called Judaism," *Jerusalem Report* (December 30, 1993): CD-ROM.

28. See Stuart Schoffman, "The Americanization of Israel," *Jerusalem Report* (May 18, 1995): CD-ROM. A full issue of the journal *Israel Studies* was devoted to the theme of the Americanization of Israel, with articles on the prestate period, postindependence, politics, culture, perspectives, religion, and a variety of other topics. See Glenda Abramson and S. Ilan Troen, eds., "The Americanization of Israel," *Israel Studies* 5, no. 1 (2000): 25–38.

29. See Tom Segev, *Elvis in Jerusalem: Post-Zionism and the Americanization of Israel* (New York: Metropolitan, 2002); Steven Rosenthal, *Irreconcilable Differences: The Waning of the American Jewish Love Affair with Israel* (Hanover, N.H.: University Press of New England, 2001).

30. Seliktar, *New Zionism,* p. 74.

31. A very good source for a discussion of the interaction of Jewish identity and Jewish state is the book by Boas Evron, *Jewish State or Israeli Nation?* (Bloomington: Indiana University Press, 1995).

32. Norton Mezvinsky, "The Zionist Character of the State of Israel," in *Zionism: The Dream and the Reality—A Jewish Critique,* ed. Gary Smith (New York: David and Charles, 1974), p. 244. See also Laurence J. Silberstein, *Postzionism: A Reader* (New Brunswick, N.J.: Rutgers University Press, 2008).

33. Uri Avnery, *Israel without Zionism: A Plan for Peace in the Middle East* (New York: Collier Books, 1971), pp. 251–52.

34. Sammy Smooha, *Social Research on Arabs in Israel, 1948–1977: Trends and an Annotated Bibliography* (Ramat Gan, Israel: Turtledove, 1978). See also Robert Deemer Lee, *Religion and Politics in the Middle East: Identity, Ideology, Institutions, and Attitudes* (Boulder, Colo.: Westview, 2010).

35. *Statistical Abstract of Israel, 2009*, Table 2.2, "Population by Religion," p. 88, www.cbs.gov.il/shnaton60/st02_02.pdf, accessed January 2010.

36. Ministry of Foreign Affairs, *Facts about Israel* (Jerusalem: Ministry of Foreign Affairs, 1985), pp. 86, 89.

37. See Asher Cohen and Bernard Susser, *Israel and the Politics of Jewish Identity: The Secular-Religious Impasse* (Baltimore: Johns Hopkins University Press, 2000).

38. A very good general study is Sheva Abramov, *Perpetual Dilemma: Jewish Religion in the Jewish State* (Rutherford, N.J.: Associated University Presses, 1975).

39. See Chaim Isaac Waxman, *Israel as a Religious Reality* (Northvale, N.J.: Jason Aronson, 1994).

40. *Facts about Israel*, p. 90.

41. There are significant differences within Jewish orthodoxy, too. The "Jewish Fundamentalists" have played a very significant role in recent Israeli politics, both in terms of domestic policy demands and in terms of demands having to do with foreign policy and especially the Occupied Territory of the West Bank. The latter point will be developed later in this book. For a detailed discussion of Jewish fundamentalism in Israel, see Ian Lustick's *For the Land and the Lord: Jewish Fundamentalism in Israel* (New York: Council on Foreign Relations, 1988).

42. This is a summary of a presentation of trends in modern Judaism presented in *Facts about Israel*, p. 90.

43. There is a good deal of discussion about why Reform Judaism has never caught on in Israel in the same way that it has caught on in other Western settings—such as in the United States, for example. One of the basic arguments is that "Reform's greatest success has been communal; it has provided a way for marginal Jews to remain in the community without having to do anything too demanding. . . . More than anything else, the Reform movement has found a way to provide a Jewish context for non-religious Jews." On the other hand, Israelis say, Israel already has a Jewish context and does not need what the Reform movement offers. See Ze'ev Chafets, "Reform's Opportunity," *Jerusalem Report* (December 13, 1990): CD-ROM.

44. Norman Zucker, *The Coming Crisis in Israel: Private Faith and Public Policy* (Cambridge, Mass.: MIT Press, 1973), p. 90.

45. This refers to the quorum, traditionally made up of ten adult males, required for the purposes of formal worship.

46. Chief rabbis exist in major cities and other nations around the world. See, for example, the articles on the chief rabbi of France by Nicholas Simon, "French Chief Rabbi in Fight for Second Term," *Jerusalem Report* (June 16, 1994): CD-ROM, and after the reelection contest, "French Chief Rabbi Pledges Consultation," *Jerusalem Report* (July 14, 1994): CD-ROM; or the article by Amotz-Asa-El on Rome's chief rabbi, "Rome's New Rabbi," *Jerusalem Post* (December 14, 2001): 5. For more on the Sephardic/Mizrahi distinction, see Peter Medding, *Sephardic Jewry and Mizrahi Jews* (New York: Oxford University Press, 2007).

47. For an article on Haifa's chief rabbi and his calling for clerics of all faiths to be advocates for peace, see David Rudge, "Haifa Chief Rabbi Calls on Muslim Leaders to Preach," *Jerusalem Post* (December 28, 2001): 4A.

48. At the time of this writing, the Sephardic chief rabbi of Israel is Shlomo Amar, appointed in 2006, and the Ashkenazic chief rabbi is Yona Metzger, appointed in 2003.

49. See Yossi Klein Halevi, "End of an Age," *Jerusalem Report* (December 31, 1992): CD-ROM. See Uzi Rebhun and Chaim Waxman, *Jews in Israel: Contempoary Social and Cultural Patterns* (Hanover, N.H.: University Press of New England, 2004).

50. See Asher Felix Landau, "The Woman and the Religious Council," *Jerusalem Post* (June 6, 1988): 5.

51. On the role of religious parties, see Gary Schiff, *Tradition and Politics: The Religious Parties of Israel* (Detroit, Mich.: Wayne State University Press, 1977).

52. Indeed, one of the leaders of the World Reform Judaism movement once commented that it was ironic that Reform Jews had greater freedom in Europe and America, non-Jewish states, than they had in Israel, a Jewish state. Interview with Moshe Kol, at the Knesset, Jerusalem, June 1975.

53. Charles Liebman and Eliezer Don-Yehiya, *Religion and Politics in Israel* (Bloomington: Indiana University Press, 1984), p. 19.

54. Teddy Kollek and Amos Kollek, "Put Real Issues Before Silly Slogans," *Jerusalem Post* (March 8, 1996): 11.

55. Aryei Fishman, *Judaism and Modernization on the Religious Kibbutz* (New York: Cambridge University Press, 1992).

56. For a very interesting discussion of the matter, see Eliezer Schweid's essay "What Does It Mean to Be a Jew?" in *Israel at the Crossroads*, trans. Alton Winters (Philadelphia: Jewish Publication Society of America, 1973), pp. 9–42.

57. Benjamin Akzin, "Who Is a Jew? A Hard Case," *Israel Law Review* 5, no. 2 (1970): 259–63, or Oscar Kraines, *The Impossible Dilemma: Who Is a Jew in the State of Israel?* (New York: Bloch, 1976).

58. "Israeli Court Upholds a Convert," *New York Times* (December 3, 1986): 1.

59. The question literally asks, Who should be counted as "being Jewish," and who should be counted as not being Jewish? It has its roots in issues about whether an individual can be considered Jewish only if he or she comes from a Jewish family, only if his or her mother was Jewish. More controversially, the question also arises about how—under what circumstances and under what rabbinical supervision—one converts to Judaism.

60. Editorial in *Ha'aretz*, November 24, 1988, as reprinted in "Israel Press Highlights" (New York: Institute of Human Relations, November 28, 1988), p. 1.

61. See "Conversion Paradigm," *Jerusalem Post* (January 14, 1998): 10.

62. See the editorial "Jewish Unity," *Jerusalem Post* (January 23, 1998): 8.

63. "Jewish Unity," p. 8. See also the editorial "The Conflicts over Conversion," *Jerusalem Post* (June 4, 1998): 10.

64. Shahar Ilan, ed., "Preliminary Public Opinion Research for the 'Religion and State Index' Project," p. 16, Hiddush—For Religious Freedom and Equality, www .hiddush.org/UploadFiles/file/ReligionStateIndexResearchReport2009.pdf, accessed January 2010.

65. Christians, Muslims, Druze, and followers of other religions are not under the authority of the Chief Rabbinate, but have their own religious structures.

66. Haim Shapiro, "Immigrants from 1990 on Must Prove Their Jewishness to Marry," *Jerusalem Post* (August 13, 2001): 4.

67. See Ira Sharkansky, *Rituals of Conflict: Religion, Politics, and Public Policy in Israel* (Boulder, Colo.: Lynne Rienner, 1996); Kevin Avruch and Walter Zenner, *Critical Essays on Israeli Society, Religion, and Government* (Albany: State University of New York Press, 1997).

68. Zucker, *The Coming Crisis*, p. 2. See also Eliezer Don-Yehiya, *Religion and Political Accommodation in Israel* (Jerusalem: Floersheimer Institute for Policy Studies, 1999), and Ira Sharkansky, *The Politics of Religion and the Religion of Politics: Looking at Israel* (Lanham, Md.: Lexington Books, 2000).

69. Danny Shapiro, "Israel and Religious Orthodoxy," *Jerusalem Post* (June 6, 1988): 8. See Eliezer Ben Rafael and Yohanan Peres, *Is Israel One? Religion, Nationalism, and Multiculturalism Confounded* (Boston: Brill, 2005).

70. Shapiro, "Religious Orthodoxy," p. 8. See also Eli Lederhendler, *Who Owns Judaism? Public Religion and Private Faith in America and Israel* (New York: Oxford University Press, 2001).

71. Arian, *Politics in Israel*, p. 311.

72. Ilan, "Preliminary Public Opinion Research," p. 1.

73. Although the end of the Sabbath is defined religiously as when three stars can be seen in the sky, in fact printed timetables indicate the start and end of Sabbath so that merchants and others are not at the mercy of visibility!

74. With a lowercase "g," "government" refers to the collective body of government structures of a regime. With a capitalized "g," "Government" refers to the prime minister and cabinet.

75. See the discussion of the El Al issue in Ira Sharkansky, *What Makes Israel Tick? How Domestic Policy-Makers Cope with Constraints* (Chicago: Nelson Hall, 1975), pp. 67–69.

76. Tal Muscal, "Sneh Says El Al Will Go for Full Privatization," *Jerusalem Post* (August 28, 2001): 11. See also "El Al Says It Will Not Fly on Sabbath, amid Threats of Ultra-Orthodox Boycott," *Ha'aretz*, December 22, 2006, www.haaretz.com/hasen/spages/799618.html, referenced January 2010.

77. Arian, *Politics in Israel*, p. 312.

78. What follows is a discussion based upon that offered by Liebman and Don-Yehiya, *Religion and Politics*, pp. 15–30.

79. Liebman and Don-Yehiya, *Religion and Politics*, p. 19.

80. This is based upon a much longer discussion in Asher Arian, *The Second Republic: Politics in Israel* (Chatham, N.J.: Chatham House, 1998), p. 313.

81. Ervin Birnbaum, *The Politics of Compromise: State and Religion in Israel* (Rutherford, N.J.: Fairleigh Dickinson University Press, 1970), p. 269.

82. For a full discussion of the "status quo" agreement and problems of religion and politics in Israel, see Liebman and Don-Yehiya, "The 'Status Quo' Agreement as a Solution to Problems of Religion and State in Israel," in *Religion and Politics*, pp. 31–40.

83. See Gary S. Schiff, "Israel after Begin: The View from the Religious Parties," in *The Begin Era: Issues in Contemporary Israel*, ed. Steve Heydemann (Boulder, Colo.: Westview, 1984), pp. 41–52.

84. Sharkansky, *What Makes Israel Tick?* p. 60. See also Ira Sharkansky, *Governing Israel: Chosen People, Promised Land, and Prophetic Tradition* (New Brunswick, N.J.:

Transaction, 2005). On the role of the Orthodox religious parties, see David Lehmann and Batia Siebzehner, *Remaking Israeli Judaism: The Challenge of Shas* (New York: Oxford University Press, 2006).

85. We must recall the distinction between "Israeli Arabs" and Arab residents of the Occupied Territories. Israeli Arabs are Arabs who are Israeli citizens, and who thus have full political rights in Israel. Arab residents of the Occupied Territories are not citizens and do not have such rights. See, for more on this, Rapahel Cohen-Almagor, *Israeli Democracy at the Crossroads* (New York: Routledge, 2005).

86. Israel Ministry of Foreign Affairs, "Religious Freedom," November 4, 2002, www.mfa.gov.il/mfa/go.asp?MFAH00vz0, accessed May 2010.

87. See Shimon Shetreet, "Freedom of Religion in Israel," paper presented at the World Conference against Racism, Durban, South Africa, 2001, available on the Ministry of Foreign Affairs Web page at www.mfa.gov.il/mfa/go.asp?MFAH0kdt0, accessed May 2010. Shetreet is a professor of law at Hebrew University in Jerusalem and served from 1992 to 1996 as the minister of religious affairs in the government of Prime Minister Yitzhak Rabin.

88. U.S. Department of State, *Annual Report on International Religious Freedom for 1999: Israel* (Washington, D.C.: Bureau for Democracy, Human Rights, and Labor, September 9, 1999), www.state.gov/g/drl/rls/irf/2009/127349.htm, accessed May 2010.

89. U.S. Department of State, *Background Note: Israel*, December 17, 2009, www.state.gov/r/pa/ei/bgn/3581.htm#political, accessed May 2010.

3 THE SOCIAL AND ECONOMIC CONTEXT OF POLITICS

1. Government of Israel, Central Bureau of Statistics, *Statistical Abstract of Israel, 2009*, Table 2.1, "Population, by Population Group," p. 85, www.cbs.gov.il/shnaton60/st02_01.pdf, accessed January 2010.

2. For an impressive study in this area, see Liel Leibovitz, *Aliya: Three Generations of American-Jewish Immigration to Israel* (New York: St. Martin's Griffin, 2007), or Uzi Rebhun and Chaim Waxman, *Jews in Israel: Contemporary Social and Cultural Patterns* (Lebanon, N.H.: University Press of New England, 2004).

3. See Alex Weingrod, "Recent Trends in Israeli Ethnicity," *Ethnic and Racial Studies* 2, no. 1 (1979): 55–65. See also Calvin Goldscheider's *Israel's Changing Society: Population, Ethnicity, and Development* (Boulder, Colo.: Westview, 1996) and *Population, Ethnicity, and Nation-Building* (Boulder, Colo.: Westview, 1995).

4. *Statistical Abstract of Israel, 2009*, Table 2.1, "Population, by Population Group," p. 85. For a fuller, although somewhat dated, study, see Sammy Smooha, *Social Research on Arabs in Israel, 1948–1977: Trends and an Annotated Bibliography* (Ramat Gan, Israel: Turtledove, 1978).

5. *Statistical Abstract of Israel, 2009*, Table 2.1, "Population, by Population Group," p. 85.

6. On this see Aref Abu-Rabia, *A Bedouin Century: Education and Development among the Negev Tribes in the 20th Century* (New York: Berghahn, 2001).

7. *Statistical Abstract of Israel, 2009*, Table 2.27, "Projections of Population in Israel for 2010–2030, by Population Group, Sex, and Age," p. 159, www.cbs.gov.il/shnaton60/st02_26.pdf, accessed January 2010. This shows projections of popula-

tion in Israel by different religious groups and demonstrates the "closing" of the "religion gap." See also Roni Berger, *Immigrant Women Tell Their Stories* (New York: Haworth, 2004).

8. Don Peretz, *The Government and Politics of Israel* (Boulder, Colo.: Westview, 1979), p. 4.

9. Israel Ministry of Foreign Affairs, "People: Minority Communities," April 1, 2008, *Facts about Israel*, www.mfa.gov.il/MFA/Facts+About+Israel/People/SOCIETY-+Minority+Communities.htm, accessed January 2010. See also Zeev Derori, *The Israel Defence Force and the Foundation of Israel: Utopia in Uniform* (New York: RoutledgeCurzon, 2005).

10. U.S. Department of State, *2009 Report on International Religious Freedom*, "Israel and the Occupied Territories," www.state.gov/g/drl/rls/irf/2009/127349.htm, accessed January 2010.

11. Lee Dulter, "Eastern and Western Jews: Ethnic Divisions in Israeli Society," *Middle East Journal* 31 (1977): 451–68. See Zvi Y. Gitelman, *Religion or Ethnicity? Jewish Identities in Evolution* (New Brunswick, N.J.: Rutgers University Press, 2009).

12. Harvey Goldberg, *Sephardi and Middle Eastern Jewries: History and Culture in the Modern Era* (Bloomington: Indiana University Press, 1996).

13. Asher Arian, *Politics in Israel: The Second Generation* (Chatham, N.J.: Chatham House, 1985), p. 22.

14. Asher Arian, *The Second Republic: Politics in Israel* (Chatham, N.J.: Chatham House, 1998), p. 34.

15. See Shlomo Hasson and Mairam Gonen, *The Cultural Tension within Jerusalem's Jewish Population* (Jerusalem: Floersheimer Institute for Policy Studies, 1997).

16. For a discussion of some of these characteristics, see Walter Zenner, "Sephardic Communal Organizations in Israel," *Middle East Journal* 21, no. 2 (1967): 173–86.

17. An article about this by Judy Siegel, "Religion and Politics in Israel," appeared in *Jerusalem Post Weekly Edition* (September 9, 1975): 3.

18. Arnold Lewis, *Power, Poverty, and Education* (Ramat Gan, Israel: Turtledove, 1979). See also As'ad Ganim, *Ethnic Politics in Israel: The Margins and the Ashkenazi Center* (New York: Routledge, 2010).

19. Nimrod Raphaeli, "The Senior Civil Service in Israel," *Public Administration* 48 (1970): 169–78, and "The Absorption of Orientals into Israeli Bureaucracy," *Middle Eastern Studies* 8 (1972): 85–92.

20. And, the Sephardim argued, there was clear discrimination against Sephardic Jews by the Ashkenazic Jews. See Yitchak Haberfeld and Yinon Cohen, *Earnings Gaps between Israel's Native-Born Men: Western Jews, Eastern Jews, and Arabs, 1987–1993* (Tel Aviv: Golda Meir Institute for Social and Labour Research, 1996). See, for another example of this argument, David Rabeeya, *European Jewish Racism in Israel: Fact Not Fiction* (Pennsylvania: Sepharad Press, 1999).

21. See Golda Meir's description of her early days in the Ministry of Housing in her book *My Life* (New York: Putnam, 1975).

22. David Ben-Gurion, as quoted in Peretz, *Government and Politics*, p. 52.

23. *Statistical Abstract of Israel, 2009*, Table 2.1, "Population, by Population Group," p. 85. See Gadi Ben-Ezer, *The Migration Journey: The Ethiopian Jewish Exodus* (New Brunswick, N.J.: Transaction, 2006), and Stephen Spector, *Operation Solomon: The Daring Rescue of the Ethiopian Jews* (New York: Oxford University Press, 2005).

24. See Colin Shindler, *Exit Visa: Detente, Human Rights, and the Jewish Emigration Movement in the USSR* (London: Bachman, Turner, 1978).

25. Moshe Gat, *The Jewish Exodus from Iraq, 1948–1951* (Portland, Ore.: Frank Cass, 1997).

26. Peretz, *Government and Politics*, p. 53. See also Malka Hillel Shulewitz, *The Forgotten Millions: The Modern Jewish Exodus from Arab Lands* (New York: Continuum, 2000).

27. See Daniel Elazar and M. Weinfeld, *Still Moving: Recent Jewish Migration in Comparative Perspective* (New Brunswick, N.J.: Transaction, 2000).

28. See "Yemen's Last Jews, a World Apart," *Jerusalem Report* (August 12, 1993): CD-ROM.

29. Peretz, *Government and Politics*, p. 53.

30. See Daniel Siegel, *The Great Immigration: Russian Jews in Israel* (New York: Berghahn, 1998).

31. *Statistical Abstract of Israel, 2009*, Table 4.4, "Immigrants by Period of Immigration Country of Birth and Last Country of Residence," p. 237, www.cbs.gov.il/shnaton60/st04_04.pdf, accessed January 2010.

32. See Oren Yiftachel, *Ethnocracy: Land and Identity Politics in Israel/Palestine* (Philadelphia: University of Pennsylvania Press, 2006). For a very interesting book on this topic, see Marla Brettschneider, ed., *The Narrow Bridge: Jewish Views on Multiculturalism* (New Brunswick, N.J.: Rutgers University Press, 1996).

33. Sammy Smooha, "Ethnic Stratification and Allegiance in Israel," *Il Politico* 41, no. 4 (1976): 635–51. See Judith Shuval, *Immigrants on the Threshold* (New Brunswick, N.J.: Transaction, 2006).

34. Yochanan Peres, "Ethnic Relations in Israel," *American Journal of Sociology* 76, no. 6 (1971): 1021–47.

35. Israel Gerber, *Heritage Seekers: American Blacks in Search of Jewish Identities* (New York: Jonathan David, 1977). See also Aziza Khazzoom, *The Formation of Ethnic Inequality: Jews in Israel* (Stanford, Calif.: Stanford University Press, 2007).

36. A good story in *Jerusalem Report* discussed some of the challenges faced by this group. See Tom Sawicki, "A Long Road Still to Travel," *Jerusalem Report* (May 7, 1992): CD-ROM.

37. Louis Rapoport, *The Lost Jews: Last of the Ethiopian Falashas* (New York: Stein and Day, 1980).

38. Avraham Shama, *Immigration without Integration: Third World Jews in Israel* (Cambridge, Mass.: Schenkman, 1977).

39. Georges Tamarin, "Three Decades of Ethnic Coexistence in Israel: Recent Developments and Patterns," *Plural Societies* 11, no. 1 (1980): 3–46. See also Yinon Cohen, Yitchak Haberfeld, and Tali Kristal, *Ethnicity and Mixed Ethnicity: Educational Gaps Among Israeli-Born Jews* (Tel Aviv: English Books, 2004).

40. Maurice Roumani, ed., "From Immigrant to Citizen: The Contribution of the Army in Israel to National Integration; The Case of Oriental Jews," *Plural Societies* 9, nos. 2–3 (1978): 1–145.

41. Victor Azarya and Baruch Kimmerling, "New Immigrants in the Israeli Armed Forces," *Armed Forces and Society* 6, no. 3 (1980): 455–82.

42. See Yaacov Iram and Miryam Shemida, *The Educational System of Israel* (Westport, Conn.: Greenwood, 1998).

43. U.S. Department of State, *Annual Report on International Religious Freedom for 2009: Israel and the Occupied Territories*. See also Zama Coursen-Neff, *Second Class: Discrimination against Palestinian Arab Children in Israel's Schools* (New York: Human Rights Watch, 2001).

44. Joseph S. Bentwich, *Education in Israel* (London: Routledge, 1998).

45. We say "essentially" secular because although they do not include a substantial religious component, they do recognize all official Jewish holidays sanctioned by the government.

46. Varda Schiffer, *The Haredi Education in Israel: Allocation, Regulation and Control* (Jerusalem: Floersheimer Institute for Policy Studies, 1999).

47. Israel Ministry of Foreign Affairs, "Education: Primary and Secondary," April 1, 2008, *Facts about Israel*, www.mfa.gov.il/MFA/Facts+About+Israel/Education/EDUCATION-+Primary+and+Secondary.htm, accessed January 2010.

48. U.S. Department of State, *Annual Report*.

49. Michael Wolffsohn, *Israel: Polity, Society, and Economy, 1882–1986* (Atlantic Highlands, N.J.: Humanities Press International, 1987), p. 198.

50. See Israel Ministry of Foreign Affairs, "Education: Challenges," April 1, 2008, *Facts about Israel*, www.mfa.gov.il/MFA/Facts+About+Israel/Education/Education.htm, accessed January 2010.

51. Wolffsohn, *Israel*, p. 201.

52. Alan Arian, "Health Care in Israel: Political and Administrative Aspects," *International Political Science Review* 2, no. 1 (1981): 43–56. See also Yair Zalmanovitch, *Policy Making at the Margins of Government: The Case of the Israeli Health System* (Albany: State University of New York Press, 2002).

53. Don Chernichovsky and Sara Markowitz, *Toward a Framework for Improving Health Care Financing for an Aging Population: The Case of Israel* (Cambridge, Mass.: National Bureau of Economic Research, 2001).

54. See Israel Ministry of Foreign Affairs, "Health: Health Services," April 1, 2008, *Facts about Israel*, www.mfa.gov.il/MFA/Facts+About+Israel/Health+-+Social+Services/HEALTH-+Health+Services.htm, accessed January 2010.

55. Tamara Barnea and Rafiq Husseini, *Separate and Cooperate, Cooperate and Separate: The Disengagement of the Palestine Health Care System from Israel and Its Emergence As an Independent System* (Westport, Conn.: Praeger, 2002).

56. *Facts about Israel* indicates that "About 92 percent of Israelis live in urban areas." See Israel Ministry of Foreign Affairs, "The Land: Urban Life," April 1, 2008, *Facts about Israel*, www.mfa.gov.il/MFA/Facts+About+Israel/Land/THE+LAND-+Urban+Life.htm, accessed January 2010.

57. One of the most remarkable books on Israel, Jerusalem, and Israeli political history is Saul B. Cohen's *Jerusalem: Bridging the Four Walls; A Geopolitical Perspective* (New York: Herzl, 1977).

58. See Bernard Wasserstein's wonderful study *Divided Jerusalem: The Struggle for the Holy City* (New Haven, Conn.: Yale University Press, 2001), especially chapter 5, "Two Jerusalems," and chapter 6, "Annexation." Other sources include Ira Sharkansky, *Governing Jerusalem: Again on the World's Agenda* (Detroit, Mich.: Wayne State University Press, 1996). See also the Israel Ministry of Foreign Affairs Web page: "Jerusalem: Urban Characteristics and Major Trends in the City's Development," > "Part I: Population Characteristics," > "Section A2: Factors behind Jerusalem's

Population Growth," www.mfa.gov.il/MFA/MFAArchive/1996-1997/Jerusalem-+Ur ban+Characteristics+and+Major+Trends.htm, accessed January 2010.

59. Israel Ministry of Foreign Affairs, "Section A2: Factors behind Jerusalem's Population Growth."

60. Israel Ministry of Foreign Affairs, "Section A2: Factors behind Jerusalem's Population Growth."

61. *Statistical Abstract of Israel, 2009*, Table 2.9 "Localities and Population, by District, Sub-District, and Type of Locality," p. 108, www.cbs.gov.il/shnaton60/st02_09x.pdf, accessed January 2010.

62. On the subject of development towns, see Myron Aronoff, "Political Change in Israel: The Case of a New Town," *Political Science Quarterly* 89, no. 3 (1974): 613–26.

63. See Israel Ministry of Foreign Affairs, "The Land: Rural Life," April 1, 2008, *Facts about Israel*, www.mfa.gov.il/MFA/Facts+About+Israel/Land/THE+LAND-+Rural+Life.htm, accessed January 2010. See also Eliyahu Kanovsky, *The Economy of the Israeli Kibbutz* (Cambridge, Mass.: Harvard University Press, 1966).

64. Lionel Tiger and Joseph Sheper, *Women in the Kibbutz* (New York: Harcourt, Brace, Jovanovich, 1975), and Daniel Katz and Naphtali Golomb, "Integration, Effectiveness, and Adaptation in Social Systems: A Comparative Analysis of Kibbutzim Communities," *Administration and Society* 6, no. 4 (1975): 389–422.

65. See Israel Ministry of Foreign Affairs, "The Land: Rural Life."

66. See Israel Ministry of Foreign Affairs, "The Land: Rural Life."

67. Benjamin Akzin and Y. Dror, *Israel: High Pressure Planning* (Syracuse, N.Y.: Syracuse University Press, 1966).

68. Raphaella Bilski, *Can Planning Replace Politics? The Israeli Experience* (Boston: Martinus Nijhoff, 1980). See also Carmel Chiswick, Tikva Lecker, and Nava Kahana, *Jewish Society and Culture: An Economic Perspective* (Ramat Gan: Bar-Ilan University Press, 2007).

69. Avi Ben-Basat, *The Israeli Economy, 1985–1998: From Government Intervention to Market Economics* (Cambridge, Mass.: MIT Press, 2002). See also Jonathan Nitzan, *The Global Political Economy of Israel: From War Profits to Peace Dividends* (London: Pluto, 2001).

70. David Horowitz, *The Enigma of Economic Growth: A Case Study of Israel* (New York: Praeger, 1972).

71. Edi Karni, "The Israeli Economy, 1973–1976," *Economic Development and Cultural Change* 28, no. 1 (1979): 63–76.

72. Israel Ministry of Foreign Affairs, "Economy: Challenges and Achievements," April 1, 2008, *Facts about Israel*, www.mfa.gov.il/MFA/Facts+About+Israel/Economy/ECONOMY-+Challenges+and+Achievements.htm, accessed January 2010; Wolffsohn, *Israel*, p. 223.

73. Israel Ministry of Foreign Affairs, "Economy: The Economic Picture," April 1, 2008, *Facts about Israel*, www.mfa.gov.il/MFA/Facts+About+Israel/Economy/ECONOMY-+Inflation+and+the+Public+Sector.htm, accessed January 2010.

74. For an excellent analysis of the economic problems of the first Begin government and the 1977 to 1984 economic policy of the Israeli government, see Yakir Plessner, "Israel's Economy in the Post-Begin Era," in *Israel after Begin*, ed. Gregory Mahler (Albany: State University of New York Press, 1990), pp. 291–306.

75. Eliyahu Kanovsky, *The Economic Impact of the Six Day War* (New York: Praeger, 1970), and Marion Mushkat, "The Socio-Economic Malaise of Developing Countries As a Function of Military Expenditures: The Case of Egypt and Israel," *Co-existence* 15, no. 2 (1978): 135–45.

76. Antoine Mansour, "Monetary Dualism: The Case of the West Bank under Occupation," *Journal of Palestine Studies* 11, no. 3 (1982): 103–16.

77. Arie Bregman, *The Economy of the Administered Areas, 1968–1973* (Jerusalem: Bank of Israel, 1975).

78. Israel Ministry of Foreign Affairs, "Economy: The Economic Picture."

79. Israel Ministry of Foreign Affairs, "Economy," April 1, 2008, *Facts about Israel*, www.mfa.gov.il/MFA/Facts+About+Israel/Economy/ECONOMY.htm, accessed January 2010. See also World Bank, "Data and Statistics, Quick Reference Tables, GDP 2008," http://web.worldbank.org/WBSITE/EXTERNAL/DATASTATISTICS/0,,co ntentMDK:20399244~menuPK:1192694~pagePK:64133150~piPK:64133175~theSit ePK:239419~isCURL:Y,00.html, accessed January 2010.

80. Bank of Israel, *Annual Report, 2009*, www.bankisrael.gov.il/deptdata/mehkar/doch09/eng/summ09e.htm.

81. See Haim Levy and Azriel Levy, *The Management of Foreign Exchange Reserves with Balance-of-Payments and External Debt Considerations* (Jerusalem: Maurice Falk Institute for Economic Research in Israel, 1998).

82. Wolffsohn, *Israel*, p. 255.

83. Israel Ministry of Foreign Affairs, "Economy: The National Economy," April 1, 2008, *Facts about Israel*, www.mfa.gov.il/MFA/Facts+About+Israel/Economy/ECONOMY-+Balance+of+Payments.htm, accessed January 2010.

84. Israel Ministry of Foreign Affairs, "Economy: The National Economy."

4 THE CONSTITUTIONAL SYSTEM
AND PARLIAMENTARY GOVERNMENT

1. Ivo Duchacek, *Power Maps: Comparative Politics of Constitutions* (Santa Barbara, Calif.: Clio, 1973).

2. Leonard Ratner, "Constitutions, Majoritarianism, and Judicial Review: The Function of a Bill of Rights in Israel and the United States," *American Journal of Comparative Law* 26, no. 3 (1978): 373–97.

3. Martin Edelman, "Politics and Constitution in Israel," *State Government* 53, no. 3 (1980): 171–82.

4. See paragraph 10, section B, part I of UN General Assembly Resolution 181 (II) of November 29, 1947, Official Records of the Second Session of the General Assembly, Resolutions, September 16–November 29, 1947, January 8, 1948, p. 135.

5. See paragraph 10, section B, part I of UN General Assembly Resolution 181 (II) of November 29, 1947, pp. 135–38.

6. Asher Zidon, *The Knesset: The Parliament of Israel* (New York: Herzl, 1967), p. 285.

7. A full text of the Law of Transition can be found in David Ben-Gurion, *Israel: A Personal History* (New York: Funk and Wagnalls, 1971), pp. 336–38.

8. Although the new constitution was not yet written, Ben-Gurion had the title of prime minister because the understanding was that the Israeli political system was to be generally modeled after the British Westminster system, and that system called its chief executive—also unwritten in law—the prime minister.

9. Oscar Kraines, *Government and Politics in Israel* (Boston: Houghton Mifflin, 1961), p. 28.

10. A very good discussion of the major background issues of the argument for and against a written document can be found in Yehoshua Freudenheim, *Government in Israel* (Dobbs Ferry, N.Y.: Oceana, 1967), pp. 24–37.

11. Ben-Gurion, *Israel*, pp. 331–34.

12. Ervin Birnbaum, *The Politics of Compromise: State and Religion in Israel* (Rutherford, N.J.: Fairleigh Dickinson University Press, 1970), p. 74.

13. Samuel Sager, *The Parliamentary System of Israel* (Syracuse, N.Y.: Syracuse University Press, 1985), p. 36.

14. Zidon, *The Knesset*, p. 291.

15. Kraines, *Government*, p. 29.

16. See Arnold Enker, "The Issue of Religion in the Israeli Supreme Court," *The Constitutional Bases of Political and Social Change in the United States*, ed. Shlomo Slonim (New York: Praeger, 1990), or Ehud Sprinzak, "Three Models of Religious Violence: The Case of Jewish Fundamentalism in Israel," in *Fundamentalisms and the State: Remaking Polities, Economies, and Militance*, ed. Martin E. Marty and R. Scott Appleby (Chicago: University of Chicago Press, 1993).

17. One of the best general discussions of this type of tension over the degree of religious institutionalization of the state can be found in Birnbaum, *The Politics of Compromise*.

18. Asher Arian, *Politics in Israel: The Second Generation* (Chatham, N.J.: Chatham House, 1985), p. 179.

19. Sometimes the term is translated as "basic law" rather than "fundamental law." Here we will use the translation "fundamental law."

20. Kraines, *Government*, p. 30.

21. Sager, *The Parliamentary System of Israel*, p. 39.

22. Zidon, *The Knesset*, p. 289.

23. The plural of Knesset is Knessot.

24. Melville Nimmer, "The Uses of Judicial Review in Israel's Quest for a Constitution," *Columbia Law Review* 70 (1970): 1219.

25. Nimmer, "The Uses of Judicial Review," pp. 1239–40.

26. Claude Klein, "A New Era in Israel's Constitutional Law," *Israel Law Review* 6 (1971): 382. See also Ruth Gavison, "Constitutions and Political Reconstruction? Israel's Quest for a Constitution," in *Constitutionalism and Political Reconstruction*, ed. Said Amir Arjomand (Boston: Brill, 2007).

27. Martin Edelman, "The New Israeli Constitution," *Middle Eastern Studies* 36, no. 2 (April, 2000), p. 13.

28. Zidon, *The Knesset*, p. 297.

29. Sager, *The Parliamentary System of Israel*, p. 40.

30. Sager, *The Parliamentary System of Israel*, p. 40.

31. Michael Wolffsohn, *Israel: Polity, Society, and Economy, 1882–1986* (Atlantic Highlands, N.J.: Humanities International, 1987), p. 6.

32. Edelman, "The New Israeli Constitution," p. 14.

33. Edelman, "The New Israeli Constitution," p. 15.

34. Although it is worth noting that cabinet members do not have to be members of Knesset, many members of Knesset, upon appointment to the cabinet, resign their seats to devote their full attention to their cabinet duties, allowing party colleagues to take their places in the legislature. This method of succession is explained in chapter 7.

35. See the Web page of The Knesset, "The Existing Basic Laws: Summary," www .knesset.gov.il/description/eng/eng_mimshal_yesod2.htm, accessed January 2010.

36. Kraines, *Government*, pp. 124–25.

37. See Israel Ministry of Foreign Affairs, "The State: The Presidency," April 1, 2008, *Facts about Israel*, www.mfa.gov.il/MFA/Facts+About+Israel/State/THE+STATE-+The+Presidency.htm, accessed January 2010.

38. Fundamental Law: The President of the State indicates that "the President of the State *shall* sign every Law," not that he *may* sign laws passed by the Knesset [Section 11 (a) (1)]. The interpretation of this has been that the president has no choice but to sign all legislation that reaches his desk, and thus far no president has tested this assumption.

39. See Israel Ministry of Foreign Affairs, "The Presidents of the State of Israel,"www.mfa.gov.il/MFA/Government/Branches+of+Government/Executive/The +Presidents+of+the+State+of+Israel.htm, accessed January 2010.

40. Arik Carmon, "A State Ready for a Constitution," *Jerusalem Post* (September 18, 2000): 8. See also Gil Hoffman, "Beilin: Accelerate Steps to Prepare Constitution," *Jerusalem Post* (September 13, 2000): 3.

41. Max Goldweber, "Israel's Judicial System," *Queen's Bar Bulletin* (April 1960): 204. See also Aharon Barak, *The Judge in a Democracy* (Princeton, N.J.: Princeton University Press, 2006).

42. Meir Shangman, "On the Written Constitution," *Israel Law Review* 9 (1974): 352. See also Kate Malleson, "Judicial Appointments and Promotions in Israel," in *Appointing Judges in an Age of Judicial Power: Critical Perspectives from around the World*, ed. Peter Russell and Kate Malleson (Toronto: University of Toronto Press, 2006).

43. Klein, "A New Era," p. 382.

44. Klein, "A New Era," p. 383.

45. J. Sussman, "Law and Judicial Practice in Israel," *Journal of Comparative Legislation and International Law* 32 (1950): 30.

46. Ariel Bin-Nun, "The Borders of Justiciability," *Israel Law Review* 5 (1980): 569.

47. Shimon Shetreet, "Reflection on the Protection of the Rights of Individual: Form and Substance," *Israel Law Review* 12 (1977): 42.

48. Alfred Witkon, "Justiciability," *Israel Law Review* 1 (1966): 40.

49. Yaacov Zemach, *Political Questions in the Courts* (Detroit, Mich.: Wayne State University Press, 1976), p. 44.

50. Zemach, *Political Questions*, p. 45.

51. Witkon, "Justiciability," p. 54.

52. Eliahu S. Likhovski, "The Courts and the Legislative Supremacy of the Knesset," *Israel Law Review* 3 (1968): 351.

53. Felix Landau, *Selected Judgments of the Supreme Court of Israel* (Jerusalem: Ministry of Justice, 1971), p. 35.

54. Meaning "religiously orthodox."

55. Landau, *Judgments*.

56. Zemach, *Political Questions*, pp. 130–31.

57. Nimmer, "The Uses of Judicial Review," p. 1221.

58. Zemach, *Political Questions*, p. 58.

59. Nimmer, "The Uses of Judicial Review," p. 1221.

60. Zemach, *Political Questions*, p. 60.

61. See Rivka Amado, "Checks, Balances, and Appointments in the Public Service: Israeli Experience in Comparative Perspective," *Public Administration Review* 61, no. 5 (2001): 569–84. Amado argues that the intervention of the Court in cases involving appeals in the appointment process in the 1990s was inappropriate and dangerous because it "imposes a legal solution when a political solution is called for, and it is counterproductive because frequent judicial intervention weakens both the judiciary and the political process."

62. See Yaacov Zemach, *The Judiciary of Israel* (Jerusalem: Institute of Judicial Training for Judges, 1993). Emanuele Ottolenghi's article, "Carl Schmitt and the Jewish Leviathan: The Supreme Court vs. the Sovereign Knesset," *Israel Studies* 6, no. 1 (2001), pp. 101–25, discusses the notion of sovereign power in Israel and the way the Court and the Knesset have acted in recent years.

63. Moshe Negbi, "Power to the Court," *Jerusalem Report* (January 23, 1992): CD-ROM.

64. See Daniel Elazar, "Constitution-Making: The Pre-Eminently Political Act," chapter 1 in *Constitutionalism: The Israeli and American Experiences* (Jerusalem: Jerusalem Center for Public Affairs, 1990).

65. Moshe Negbi, "Surprise! We Have a Bill of Rights," *Jerusalem Report* (February 23, 1995): CD-ROM. See also Daniel Elazar, *The Constitution of the State of Israel* (Jerusalem: Jerusalem Center for Public Affairs, 1993), and Ran Hirschel, "The Political Origins of Judicial Empowerment through Constitutionalization: Lessons from Israel's Constitutional Revolution," *Comparative Politics* 33, no. 3 (2001): 315–35.

66. Negbi, "Power to the Court."

67. Barak became chief justice of the Supreme Court of Israel in 1995. See Peter Hirschberg, "The Lawgiver," *Jerusalem Report* (August 24, 1995): CD-ROM.

68. Gary Jacobsohn, *Apple of Gold: Constitutionalism in Israel and the United States* (Princeton, N.J.: Princeton University Press, 1993), p. 156.

69. See "Israel's Other Barak," *Economist* (April 10, 1999): 43–44.

70. See Emanuel Gutmann, *The Declaration of the Establishment of the State of Israel* (Jerusalem: Israel Information Center, 1998).

71. Jacobsohn, *Apple*, p. 153. See also Daphna Sharfman, *Living without a Constitution: Civil Rights in Israel* (Armonk, N.Y.: M. E. Sharpe, 1993).

72. Jacobsohn, *Apple*, 154.

73. In 1994 Daniel Elazar—one of the foremost students of Israeli constitutionalism—wrote *Are Constitutional Limits on the High Court of Justice Democratic?* (Jerusalem: Jerusalem Center for Public Affairs, 1994), a piece that does a good job of describing the constitutional debate at that time.

74. Nina Gilbert, "Knesset Shows Support for Judicial Review," *Jerusalem Post* (December 15, 1999): 4.

75. Gilbert, "Knesset Shows Support," p. 4.

76. Nina Gilbert, "Wide Knesset Support for Constitutional Court Proposal," *Jerusalem Post* (November 23, 2000): 5.

77. "Reform Judiciously," *Jerusalem Post* (May 10, 2001): 8.

78. Jacobsohn, *Apple*, p. 149.

79. See "The Judicialization of Politics," a symposium in *International Political Science Review* 15 (April 1994): 91–197.

80. See, for example, David Kretzmer's *The Occupation of Justice: The Supreme Court of Israel and the Occupied Territories* (Albany: State University of New York Press, 2002), or Yoav Dotan's "Judicial Rhetoric, Government Lawyers, and Human Rights: The Case of the Israeli High Court of Justice during the Intifada," *Law and Society Review* 33, no. 2 (1999): 319–63.

81. A very interesting publication is Daniel Elazar, *Switzerland as a Model for Constitutional Reform in Israel* (Jerusalem: Jerusalem Center for Public Affairs, 1987).

82. A very good recent study is Pnina Lahav, ed., *Law and the Transformation of Israeli Society* (Bloomington: Indiana University Press, 1998). It includes a strong introduction by Lahav, a chapter titled "The Role of a Supreme Court in a Democracy" by Aharon Barak, and a chapter titled "The Politics of Rights in Israeli Constitutional Law" by Aeyal Gross, among others.

83. Leslie Wolf-Phillips, "The 'Westminster Model' in Israel?" *Parliamentary Affairs* 26 (1973): 415–39.

84. Samuel Sager, "Pre-State Influences on Israel's Parliamentary System," *Parliamentary Affairs* 25 (1972): 29–49.

85. Gregory Mahler, *Comparative Politics: An Institutional and Cross-National Approach* (Upper Saddle River, N.J.: Prentice Hall, 2003), p. 187.

86. Fundamental Law: The Government (1968) states that the president "shall entrust to one of the Members of the Knesset the duty of forming a Government." This made formal what prior to 1968 had been only convention—that the prime minister would have to be a member of Knesset itself. Prior to that year, when the Fundamental Law: The Government was passed, there was considerable debate as to whether the president could invite a nonmember of Knesset to be prime minister. However, as we have already noted, with the exception of the prime minister, cabinet members do not have to be members of Knesset, and many MKs resign from the Knesset after being named to the cabinet to allow party colleagues to inherit their seats in the legislature.

87. Benjamin Akzin, "Israel's Knesset," *Ariel* 15 (1966): 5–11.

88. Likhovski, "The Courts," pp. 345–67.

89. Sager, *The Parliamentary System of Israel*, pp. 196–97.

5 THE PRIME MINISTER AND THE KNESSET

1. Israel Ministry of Foreign Affairs, "Israeli Democracy: How Does It Work?" www.mfa.gov.il/MFA/Government/Branches+of+Government/Executive/Israeli+Democracy+-+How+does+it+work.htm, accessed January 2010. A good perspective can be found in Thomas Poguntke and Paul Webb, *The Presidentialization of Politics: A Comparative Study of Modern Democracies* (New York: Oxford University Press, 2005).

2. For more detailed discussion of the actual change back to the previous electoral system, see Evelyn Gordon, "Fix the Fatal Flaws," *Jerusalem Post* (March 6, 2001): 8; Nina Gilbert and Dan Izenberg, "Knesset Set to Repeal Direct Elections," *Jerusalem Post* (March 7, 2001): 4; Sarah Honig, "(Not) 'The Way Things Were,'" *Jerusalem Post* (March 8, 2001): 1; Nina Gilbert, "Direct Elections System Nixed," *Jerusalem Post* (March 8, 2001): 4; and Daniel Bloch, "Good Riddance," *Jerusalem Post* (March 11, 2001): 6. The text of the electoral system for the prime minister is found in Fundamental Law: The Government (2001), found on the Web page of the Ministry of Foreign Affairs, "Basic Law: The Government (2001)", www.mfa.gov.il/MFA/MFAArchive/2000_2009/2001/3/Basic%20Law-%20The%20Government%20-2001-, accessed January 2010.

3. See Ethan Bueno de Mesquita, "Strategic and Nonpolicy Voting: A Coalition Analysis of Israeli Electoral Reform," *Comparative Politics* 33, no. 1 (2000): 63–80.

4. See Avraham Brichta, "The New Premier-Parliamentary System in Israel," *Annals of the American Academy of Political and Social Science* 555 (January 1998): 180–92.

5. See Gregory Mahler, "Israel's New Electoral System: Effects on Policy and Politics," *Middle East Review of International Affairs* 1, no. 2 (1997), meria.idc.ac.il/journal/1997/issue2/jv1n2a2.html, accessed January 2010; Gregory Mahler, "The Formation of the Netanyahu Government: Coalition Formation in a Quasi-Parliamentary Setting," *Israel Affairs* 3, nos. 3–4 (1997): 3–27; Henri Stellman, "Electing a Prime Minister and a Parliament: The Israeli Election 1996," *Parliamentary Affairs* 49 (1996): 648–60.

6. Gerhard Loewenberg, *Modern Parliaments: Change or Decline?* (Chicago: Atherton, 1971), p. 3.

7. Joseph LaPalombara, *Politics within Nations* (Englewood Cliffs, N.J.: Prentice Hall, 1974), pp. 221–25.

8. With a lowercase "g," "government" refers to the collective body of government structures of a regime. With a capitalized "g," "Government" refers to the prime minister and cabinet.

9. See Don Peretz, *The Government and Politics of Israel* (Boulder, Colo.: Westview, 1983), p. 159, for a description of one instance in which this type of resignation caused the breaking apart of a coalition and the fall of a Government, in fact.

10. For a wonderful collection of essays on this topic, see Lawrence D. Longley and Reuven Hazan, *The Uneasy Relationships between Parliamentary Members and Leaders* (Portland, Ore.: Frank Cass, 2000). Hazan's article in this collection is titled "Yes, Institutions Matter: The Impact of Institutional Reform on Parliamentary Members and Leaders in Israel." Two good recent biographies of modern prime ministers are those by Nir Hefez and Gadi Bloom, *Ariel Sharon: A Life* (New York: Random House, 2006), and Dennis Abrams, *Ehud Olmert* (New York: Chelsea House, 2008). Zakai Shalom's volume *Ben-Gurion's Political Struggles: A Lion in Winter* (New York: Routledge, 2005) is a fascinating study of the prime minister's final years as head of government.

11. For a more detailed description of this process, see Asher Zidon, *Knesset: The Parliament of Israel* (New York: Herzl, 1967).

12. For an indication of some of the laws of special interest passed by the Knesset, see the Web page of the Israel Ministry of Foreign Affairs, "Selected Laws of the State of Israel," www.mfa.gov.il/mfa/government/law/selected%20legislation/, accessed January 2010.

13. A detailed description of Knesset procedures can be found on the Knesset Web page, "Rules of Procedure," www.knesset.gov.il/rules/eng/contents.htm, accessed January 2010.

14. An edited collection of major debates in the Knesset between 1948 and 1981 has been compiled by Netanel Lorch, former secretary of the Knesset. See Netanel Lorch, *Major Knesset Debates, 1948–1981* (Lanham, Md.: University Press of America, 1991).

15. The definitive work on parliamentary committees is Reuven Hazan's *Reforming Parliamentary Committees: Israel in Comparative Perspective* (Columbus: Ohio State University Press, 2001).

16. Fundamental Law: The President of the State, Section 11 (a) (1). See the Knesset Web page, "Basic Law: The President of the State," www.knesset.gov.il/laws/speciaL/eng/basic12_eng.htm, accessed January 2010.

17. Data on demographic characteristics of members of Knesset, as well as information on their political upbringing, can be found in Gregory Mahler, *The Knesset: Parliament in the Israeli Political System* (Rutherford, N.J.: Fairleigh Dickinson University Press, 1981), chapter 5, "The Member of Knesset," pp. 106–37.

18. See the Knesset Web page for a list of women in the current Knesset, "Women Knesset Members," www.knesset.gov.il/mk/eng/mkindex_current_eng.asp?view=3. For a historical perspective, see Avraham Brichta, "Women in the Knesset," *Parliamentary Affairs* 28 (1974): 31–50. See also Shlomo Swirski and Yaron Yechezkel, *Women's Representation in the Legislature and the Executive in Israel and Worldwide* (Tel Aviv: Adva Center, 1999).

19. Moshe Czudnowski, "Legislative Recruitment under Proportional Representation in Israel: A Model and a Case Study," *Midwest Journal of Political Science* 14 (1970): 216–48, and Moshe Czudnowski, "Sociocultural Variables and Legislative Recruitment," *Comparative Politics* 4 (1972): 561–87.

20. Mahler, *The Knesset*, pp. 138–59, includes a thorough study of the political recruitment of members of Knesset.

21. See Shlomo Swirski et al., *The Role of the Knesset in the Budget-Making Process: A Critical Analysis and Proposal for Reform* (Tel Aviv: Adva Center, 2000). See also Reuven Hazan, *Cohesion and Discipline in Legislatures: Political Parties, Party Leadership, Parliamentary Committees and Governance* (London: Routledge, 2005).

22. In order to provide the small parties (one or two members) with some debate time, Knesset rules state that no party shall have less than ten minutes' time in a four-hour debate and fifteen minutes' time in a five-hour debate.

23. Nina Gilbert, "Study: Knesset Rates 4 on Scale of 1–10," *Jerusalem Post* (April 4, 2001): 1.

24. See Reuven Hazan, "Constituency Interests without Constituencies: The Geographical Impact of Candidate Selection on Party Organization and Legislative Behavior in the 14th Israeli Knesset, 1996–1999," *Political Geography* 18, no. 7 (1999): 791–811.

25. See the article on the Labor Party convention by Myron Aronoff, "Better Late Than Never: Democratization in the Labor Party," in *Israel since Begin*, ed. Gregory Mahler (Albany: State University of New York Press, 1990).

26. For a thorough analysis of this intralegislative frustration and extralegislative effectiveness, see Mahler, *The Knesset*, chapter 8.

27. Mahler, *The Knesset,* p. 103. See also Lawrence Longley and Reuven Hazan, *The Uneasy Relationships between Parliamentary Members and Leaders* (London: Frank Cass, 2000).

28. Mahler, *The Knesset,* p. 98; Samuel Sager, *The Parliamentary System of Israel* (Syracuse, N.Y.: Syracuse University Press, 1985), pp. 68–69, 139.

29. Zidon, *Knesset,* p. 40.

30. See Liat Collins, "Deri Defends His Record during Knesset Immunity Hearings," *Jerusalem Post* (May 27, 1998): 5.

31. Articles that are representative of the press coverage of this event include the following: Miriam Shaviv, "Bishara Stripped of Immunity, May Face Prosecution," *Jerusalem Post* (November 8, 2001): 1; Jafar Farah, "Free Speech: For Jews Only?" *Jerusalem Post* (November 8, 2001): 3; Miriam Shaviv, "Immediately after Bishara Vote—Loyalty Bill Passes First Test," *Jerusalem Post* (November 8, 2001): 3; David Addleman, "Abusing Democracy," *Jerusalem Post* (November 8, 2001): 6; Miriam Shaviv, "Immunity Deficiencies," *Jerusalem Post* (November 9, 2001): 2B; and Dan Izenberg, "Bishara Charged with Supporting Hizbullah," *Jerusalem Post* (November 13, 2001): 6.

32. On the organization of the Knesset, committee assignments, and the like, see the Knesset Web page, "The Organization of the Work of the Knesset," www.knesset .gov.il/description/eng/eng_work_org.htm, accessed January 2010.

33. Mahler, *The Knesset,* p. 89. See also Reuven Hazan, *Reforming Parliamentary Committees: Israel in Comparative Perspective* (Columbus: Ohio State University Press, 2001).

34. For a thorough discussion of parliamentary questions and the various categories of motions to add to the agenda, see the Knesset's Web page, "Knesset Rules of Procedure," > "Part B: Business of the Knesset," www.knesset.gov.il/rules/eng/ contents.htm, accessed January 2010.

35. This has been an extremely popular area of research related to Israeli politics. Older studies might include the following: Gregory Mahler and Richard Trilling, "Coalition Behavior and Cabinet Formation: The Case of Israel," *Comparative Political Studies* 8 (1975): 200–33; Dan Felsenthal, "Aspects of Coalition Payoffs: The Case of Israel," *Comparative Political Studies* 12 (1979): 151–68; David Nachmias, "Coalition Politics in Israel," *Comparative Political Studies* 7 (1974): 316–33, and "A Note on Coalition Payoffs in a Dominant Party System: Israel," *Political Studies* 21, no. 3 (1973): 301–5; and K. Z. Paltiel, "The Israeli Coalition System," *Government and Opposition* 10 (1975): 396–414. A more recent study is Michael Laver and Ian Budge, *Party Policy and Government Coalitions* (New York: St. Martin's, 1992).

36. A discussion of these payoffs can be found in Mahler, *The Knesset,* pp. 74–80.

37. Valerie Herman and John Pope, "Minority Governments in Western Democracies," *British Journal of Political Science* 3 (1973): 191.

38. Herman and Pope, "Minority Governments," p. 191.

39. See Israel Ministry of Foreign Affairs, "The Governments of Israel—Coalitions 1949 to the Present," www.mfa.gov.il/mfa/government/previous%20governments/ the%20governments%20of%20israel, accessed January 2010, for a list of all Governments between that of David Ben-Gurion, formed March 10, 1949, and that of Benjamin Netanyahu, formed in March 2009.

40. See Itai Sened, "A Model of Coalition Formation: Theory and Evidence," *Journal of Politics* 58 (1996): 350–72.

41. Eric Browne and Mark Franklin, "Editors' Introduction: New Directions in Coalition Research," *Legislative Studies Quarterly* 11, no. 4 (1986): 471. The entire issue of *Legislative Studies Quarterly* in which this article appears is devoted to the study of coalition theory.

42. Benjamin Akzin, "The Role of Parties in Israeli Democracy," *Journal of Politics* 17 (1955): 507–45.

43. "Knessot" is plural for "Knesset."

44. The data can be found on the Knesset Web page; the list of parties running for office can be found at "Lists Running in the '99 Knesset Elections," www.knesset.gov.il/elections/eindex.html, accessed January 2010.

45. The data can be found in the Ministry of Foreign Affairs Web page on the Knesset and Knesset elections: "The State: Elections," www.mfa.gov.il/MFA/Facts+About+Israel/State/THE+STATE-+Elections.htm, accessed January 2010. See the Knesset Web page, "Currently Functioning Parliamentary Groups," www.knesset.gov.il/faction/eng/FactionCurrent_eng.asp, accessed January 2010.

46. Eric Browne, "Testing Theories of Coalition Formation in the European Context," *Comparative Political Studies* 3 (1971): 400.

47. Browne, "Testing Theories," p. 402.

48. Discussion of the 1984 Government can be found in Daniel Elazar and Shmuel Sandler, *Israel's Odd Couple: The 1984 Knesset Elections and the National Unity Government* (Detroit, Mich.: Wayne State University Press, 1990).

49. Scott Johnston, "Party Politics and Coalition Cabinets in the Knesset," *Middle Eastern Affairs* 13 (1962): 130.

50. See Amnon Rapoport and Eythan Weg, "Dominated, Connected, and Tight Coalitions in the Israeli Knesset," *American Journal of Political Science* 30 (August 1986): 577–96.

6 POLITICAL PARTIES AND INTEREST GROUPS

1. Emanuel Gutmann, "Israel," *Journal of Politics* 25 (1963): 703. See also Norman Schofield and Itai Sened, *Multiparty Democracy: Elections and Legislative Politics* (New York: Cambridge University Press, 2006).

2. Scott Johnston, "Politics of the Right in Israel," *Social Science* 40 (1965): 104.

3. For a description of the history of parties in Israel, see Benjamin Akzin, "The Role of Parties in Israeli Democracy," *Journal of Politics* 17 (1955): 507–45.

4. See Government of Israel, Central Bureau of Statistics, *Statistical Abstract of Israel, 2009*, Table 10.2, "Valid Votes in the Elections to the Knesset, by Main List, 1992–2008," www.cbs.gov.il/shnaton60/st10_02.pdf, accessed January 2010. More recent data can be found in the Ministry of Foreign Affairs Web page on the Knesset and Knesset elections: "The State: Elections," www.mfa.gov.il/MFA/Facts+About+Israel/State/THE+STATE-+Elections.htm, accessed January 2010.

5. See Ira Sharkansky, *The Politics of Religion and the Religion of Politics: Looking at Israel* (Lanham, Md.: Lexington Books, 2000), especially chapter 7, "Representing Judaism in Israel: Religious Political Parties." See also Sultan Tepe, *Beyond Sacred and Secular: Politics of Religion in Israel and Turkey* (Stanford, Calif.: Stanford University Press, 2008).

6. C. Paul Bradley, *Parliamentary Elections in Israel: Three Case Studies* (Grantham, N.H.: Thompson and Rutter, 1985), p. 11.

7. Akzin, "Role of Parties," p. 509.

8. Akzin, "Role of Parties," p. 520. See also Reuven Hazan and Gid'on Rahat, *Israeli Party Politics: New Approaches, New Perspectives* (London: Sage, 2008).

9. Asher Arian, *Politics in Israel: The Second Generation* (Chatham, N.J.: Chatham House, 1985), p. 8.

10. For discussion of some of these ideological bases of the Israeli system, see Daniel Elazar, "Israel's Compound Polity," in *Israel at the Polls: The Knesset Elections of 1977*, ed. Howard Penniman (Washington, D.C.: American Enterprise Institute, 1979), pp. 1–38.

11. Arian, *Politics in Israel*, p. 8.

12. Thomas Goodland, "A Mathematical Presentation of Israel's Political Parties," *British Journal of Sociology* 8 (1957): 263–66.

13. See, for example, Zeev Ben-Sira, "The Image of Political Parties and the Structure of a Political Map," *European Journal of Political Research* 6, no. 3 (1978): 259–84.

14. And it must be recalled that these four issues are not really bipositional issues. That is, few people are really on the far, far left or far, far right end of the ideological spectrum on any of these issues. They are much more likely to distribute themselves widely from the far left to the far right, through varying degrees of moderation and middle-of-the-road positions.

15. Arian, *Politics in Israel*, p. 134.

16. Arian, *Politics in Israel*, pp. 253–54.

17. Arian, "The Electorate," p. 71, in *Politics in Israel*. See also Giora Goldberg, "The Electoral Fall of the Israeli Left," in *Israel at the Polls, 1996*, ed. Daniel Elazar and Shmuel Sandler (Portland, Ore.: Frank Cass, 1998).

18. Myron J. Aronoff, "The Decline of the Labor Party: Causes and Significance," in *Israel at the Polls: The Knesset Elections of 1977*, ed. Howard Penniman (Washington, D.C.: American Enterprise Institute, 1979), pp. 120–21.

19. Asher Arian, "Conclusion," in *Israel at the Polls: The Knesset Elections of 1977*, ed. Howard Penniman (Washington, D.C.: American Enterprise Institute, 1979), pp. 287–88.

20. One of the classic studies of this phenomenon outside of the Israeli context is Austin Ranney's *Pathways to Parliament: Candidate Selection in Britain* (Madison: University of Wisconsin Press, 1965). A more recent study of the importance of political parties for the Israeli Knesset is found in the book by Reuven Hazan and Gideon Rahat, *Democracy within Parties: Candidate Selection Methods and Their Political Consequences* (New York: Oxford University Press, 2010).

21. Amitai Etzioni, "Agrarianism in Israel's Party System," *Canadian Journal of Economics and Political Science* 23, no. 3 (1957): 363–75.

22. A good illustration of this can be found in Paul Burstein, "Political Patronage and Party Choice among Israeli Voters," *Journal of Politics* 38 (1976): 1024–32.

23. See, for example, Paul Burstein, "Social Cleavages and Party Choice in Israel: A Log-Linear Analysis," *American Political Science Review* 72 (1978): 96–109, or M. Roshwald, "Political Parties and Social Classes in Israel," *Social Research* 23, no. 2 (1956): 199–218.

24. See Etta Bick, "Sectarian Party Politics in Israel: The Case of Yisrael Ba'Aliya, the Russian Immigrant Party," in *Israel at the Polls, 1996*, ed. Daniel Elazar and Shmuel Sandler (Portland, Ore.: Frank Cass, 1998); Vladimir Khanin, "Israeli 'Russian' Parties and the New Immigrant Vote," in *Israel at the Polls, 1999*, ed. Daniel Elazar and M. Benjamin Mollov (Portland, Ore.: Frank Cass, 2001). See also Zvi Gitelman and Ken Goldstein, "The 'Russian' Revolution in Israeli Politics," in *The Elections in Israel, 1999*, ed. Alan Arian and Michal Shamir (Albany: State University of New York Press, 2002).

25. For a more thorough discussion of the process of political socialization in Israel, see Gregory Mahler, *The Knesset: Parliament in the Israeli Political System* (Rutherford, N.J.: Fairleigh Dickinson University Press, 1981), pp. 113–30. A more recent study of the role of Israeli parties in these issues is by Reuven Hazan and Gideon Rahat, *Israeli Party Politics: New Approaches, New Perspectives* (London: Sage, 2008).

26. See "Israel's Arabs Discover Their Identity: Election Boycott," *Economist* 358 (February 10, 2001): 48.

27. Unless otherwise indicated, the general background material on contemporary political parties in Israel comes from the following sources: Helen Chapin Metz, *Israel: A Country Study* (Washington, D.C.: Federal Research Division, Library of Congress, 1988), especially "Appendix B: Political Parties and Organizations," and the Knesset Web page "Currently Functioning Parliamentary Groups," www.knesset .gov.il/faction/eng/FactionCurrent_eng.asp, accessed January 2010.

28. For a more detailed description of both the prestate background and the more modern history of the alignment parties, see Arian, *Politics in Israel*, pp. 73–79. See also Myron Aronoff, *Power and Ritual in the Israeli Labor Party: A Study in Political Anthropology* (Assen, Amsterdam: Van Gorcum, 1977).

29. For a good brief history of the Likud, see Ilan Greilsammer, "The Likud," in *Israel at the Polls, 1981*, ed. Howard Penniman and Daniel Elazar (Washington, D.C.: American Enterprise Institute, 1986), pp. 65–92; Arian, *Politics in Israel*, pp. 79–86; Benjamin Akzin, "The Likud," p. 93, in *Israel at the Polls: The Knesset Elections of 1977*, ed. Howard Penniman (Washington, D.C.: American Enterprise Institute, 1979); and David Nachmias, "The Right Wing Opposition in Israel," *Political Studies* 24 (1976): 268–80.

30. A good general discussion of the religious parties is to be found in Shmuel Sandler, "The Religious Parties," in *Israel at the Polls, 1981*, ed. Howard Penniman and Daniel Elazar (Washington, D.C.: American Enterprise Institute, 1986), pp. 105–27. See also Gary Schiff, *Tradition and Politics: The Religious Parties of Israel* (Detroit, Mich.: Wayne State University Press, 1977); Stephen Oren, "Continuity and Change in Israel's Religious Parties," *Middle East Journal* 27 (1973): 36–54; David Schnall, "Native Anti-Zionism: Ideologies of Radical Dissent in Israel," *Middle East Journal* 31 (1977): 157–74; Yael Yishai, "Factionalism in the National Religious Party: The Quiet Revolution," in *The Elections in Israel, 1977*, ed. A. Arian (Jerusalem: Jerusalem Academic Press, 1980), pp. 50–60; Shimshon Zelnicker and Michael Kahan, "Religion and Nascent Cleavages: The Case of Israel's National Religious Party," *Comparative Politics* 9 (1976): 21–48; Bradley, *Parliamentary Elections*, pp. 54–55; Elyakim Rubinstein, "The Lesser Parties in the Israeli Elections of 1977," in *Israel at the Polls: The Knesset Elections of 1977*, ed. Howard Penniman (Washington, D.C.: American Enterprise Institute, 1979), pp. 173–99, at 180; Eliezer Don-Yehiya,

"Origins and Developments of the Agudah and Mafdal Parties," *Jerusalem Quarterly* (Summer 1981): 49–64; and Rael Isaac, *Party and Politics in Israel: Three Visions of a Jewish State* (New York: Longman, 1981).

31. Alain Greilsammer, "Communism in Israel: 13 Years after the Split," *Survey* 23 (1977–1978): 172–92, and Martin Slann, "Ideology and Ethnicity in Israel's Two Communist Parties," *Studies in Comparative Communism* 7, no. 4 (1974): 359–74. For two very good studies, one current, the other more historical, of the Communist Party in Israel, see Moshe Czudnowski and Jacob Landau, *The Israeli Communist Party and the Elections for the Fifth Knesset, 1961* (Stanford, Calif.: Hoover Institution, 1965), and Dunia Nahas, *The Israeli Communist Party* (New York: St. Martin's, 1976). See also Ra'anan Cohen, *Strangers in Their Homeland: A Critical Study of Israel's Arab Citizens* (Portland, Ore.: Sussex Academic Press, 2009).

32. See Yael Yishai, "Three Faces of Associational Politics: Interest Groups in Israel," *Political Studies* 40 (1992): 124–36.

33. See Clive S. Thomas, *Political Parties and Interest Groups: Shaping Democratic Governance* (Boulder, Colo.: Lynne Rienner, 2001).

34. See Esther Iecovich, "Pensioners' Political Parties in Israel," *Journal of Aging and Social Policy* 12, no. 3 (2001): 87–107.

35. On the role of the labor movement in Israel, see inter alia the following: Zeev Sternhell, *The Founding Myths of Israel: Nationalism, Socialism, and the Making of the Jewish State* (Princeton, N.J.: Princeton University Press, 1998); Yitzhak Greenberg, "The Contribution of the Labor Economy to Immigrant Absorption and Population Dispersal During Israel's First Decade," in *Israel: The First Decade of Independence,* ed. Ilan Troen and Noah Lucas (Albany: State University of New York Press, 1995); Yitchak Haberfeld, "Why Do Workers Join Unions? The Case of Israel," *Industrial and Labor Relations Review* 48 (1995): 656–70; Giora Goldberg, "Trade Unions and Party Politics in Israel: A Decline of Party Identification," *Journal of Social, Political, and Economic Studies* 23, no. 1 (1998): 53–73; and Shmuel Tzabag, "Cooperation in the Shadow of a Power Struggle: Israel; The Likud Governments and the Histadrut, 1977–1984," *Middle Eastern Studies* 31 (1995): 849–88.

36. Don Peretz, *The Government and Politics of Israel* (Boulder, Colo.: Westview, 1979), p. 120.

37. Two classic works are Yoram Peri, *Between Battles and Ballots: Israeli Military in Politics* (Cambridge, U.K.: Cambridge University Press, 1983), and Amos Perlmutter, *Military and Politics in Israel* (New York, Praeger, 1969), especially chapter 5. More recent studies of the role of the military in domestic politics would include Yehuda Ben-Meir, *Civil-Military Relations in Israel* (New York: Columbia University Press, 1995); Martin Edelman, *Courts, Politics, and Culture in Israel* (Charlottesville: University Press of Virginia, 1994); Martin Van Creveld, *The Sword and the Olive: A Critical History of the Israeli Defense Force* (Oxford, U.K.: Perseus, 1999); Moshe Lissak, "The Civilian Components of Israel's Security Doctrine: The Evolution of Civil-Military Relations in the First Decade," in *Israel: The First Decade of Independence,* ed. S. Ilan Troen and Noah Lucas (Albany: State University of New York Press, 1995); Eva Etzioni-Halevy, "Civil-Military Relations and Democracy: The Case of the Military-Political Elites' Connection in Israel," *Armed Forces and Society* 22 (1996): 401–17; and Gad Barzilai, "War, Democracy, and Internal Conflict: Israel in a Comparative Perspective," *Comparative Politics* 31, no. 3 (1999): 317–36.

38. Peretz, *Government and Politics,* p. 128.

39. Peretz, *Government and Politics,* p. 131.

40. See on this topic the following: Gabriel Bar-Haim, "Revista Mea: Keeping Alive the Romanian Community in Israel," in *Ethnic Minority Media: An International Perspective,* ed. Stephen Riggins (Newbury Park, Calif.: Sage, 1992); Sammy Smooha, "Class, Ethnic, and National Cleavages and Democracy in Israel," in *Israeli Democracy under Stress,* ed. Ehud Sprinzak and Larry Diamond (Boulder, Colo.: Lynne Rienner, 1993); Hannah Herzog, "Midway between Political and Cultural Ethnicity: An Analysis of the 'Ethnic Lists' in the 1984 Elections," in *Israel's Odd Couple: The 1984 Knesset Elections and the National Unity Government,* ed. Daniel Elazar and Shmuel Sandler (Detroit, Mich.: Wayne State University Press, 1990); and As'ad Ghanem and Sarab Ozacky-Lazar, "Israel As an Ethnic State: The Arab Vote," in *The Elections in Israel, 1999,* ed. Alan Arian and Michal Shamir (Albany: State University of New York Press, 2002).

41. See Yoav Peled, "Towards a Redefinition of Jewish Nationalism in Israel? The Enigma of Shas," *Ethnic and Racial Studies* 21, no. 4 (1998): 703–27.

42. See Adham Saouli, "Arab Political Organizations within the Israeli State," *Journal of Social, Political, and Economic Studies* 26, no. 2 (2001): 443–60, or Dan Rabinowitz, "The Common Memory of Loss: Political Mobilization among Palestinian Citizens of Israel," *Journal of Anthropological Research* 50 (1994): 27–49.

43. See Yael Yishai, "Regulation of Interest Groups in Israel," *Parliamentary Affairs* 51, no. 4 (1998): 568–78.

44. See Yael Yishai, "Civil Society in Transition: Interest Politics in Israel," *Annals of the American Academy of Political and Social Science* 555 (January 1998): 147–62.

7 THE ELECTORAL PROCESS AND VOTING BEHAVIOR

1. Maurice Duverger, *Political Parties* (New York: John Wiley, 1963), p. 239. See also Norman Schofield and Itai Sened, *Multiparty Democracy: Elections and Legislative Politics* (New York: Cambridge University Press, 2006).

2. Fundamental Law: The Knesset, Section 4.

3. For a fuller explanation, see Asher Zidon, *The Knesset* (New York: Herzl, 1967), pp. 23–29. See also Michael Latner and Anthony J. McGann, *Geographical Representation under Proportional Representation: The Cases of Israel and the Netherlands* (Irvine, Calif.: Center for the Study of Democracy, 2004); Colin Shindler, *A History of Modern Israel* (New York: Cambridge University Press, 2008); and Alan Arian and Michal Shamir, eds., *The Elections in Israel, 2006* (New Brunswick, N.J.: Transaction, 2008).

4. See the Knesset Web page, "The Electoral System in Israel," section "The Electoral System," www.knesset.gov.il/description/eng/eng_mimshal_beh.htm#7, accessed February 2010.

5. For an expanded explanation of this process, see Yehoshua Freudenheim, *Government in Israel* (Dobbs Ferry, N.Y.: Oceana, 1967), p. 126. A more recent discussion can be found in the essay by Gideon Rahat and Reuven Hazan, "Israel: The Politics of an Extreme Electoral System," in *The Politics of Electoral Systems,* ed. Michael Gallagher and Paul Mitchell (New York: Oxford University Press, 2008).

6. Asher Arian, *Politics in Israel: The Second Generation* (Chatham, N.J.: Chatham House, 1985), p. 123.

7. Samuel Sager, *The Parliamentary System of Israel* (Syracuse, N.Y.: Syracuse University Press, 1985), 67. See his section on "Financing of Elections," pp. 67–72.

8. Sager, *The Parliamentary System of Israel*, p. 69. See also Jesper Strombock and Lynda Lee Kaid, eds., *The Handbook of Election News Coverage around the World* (New York: Routledge, 2008).

9. Leon Boim, "The Financing of Elections," in *Israel at the Polls, 1977*, ed. Howard Penniman (Washington, D.C.: American Enterprise Institute, 1979). See Tamir Shaefer, Gabriel Weimann, and Yariv Tsfati, "Campaigns in the Holy Land: The Content and Effects of Election News Coverage in Israel," in *Handbook of Election News Coverage around the World*, ed. Jesper Strombock and Lynda Lee Kaid (New York: Routledge, 2008).

10. See Akiba A. Cohen and Gadi Wolfsfeld, "Overcoming Adversity and Diversity: The Utility of Television Political Advertising in Israel," in *Political Advertising in Western Democracies: Parties and Candidates on Television*, ed. Lynda Lee Kaid and Christina Holtz-Bacha (Thousand Oaks, Calif.: Sage, 1995); Dafna Lemish and Chava Tidhar, "Still Marginal: Women in Israel's 1996 Television Election Campaign," *Sex Roles* 41, nos. 5–6 (1999): 389–412; Dan Caspi, "American-Style Electioneering in Israel: Americanization Versus Modernization," in *Politics, Media, and Modern Democracy: An International Study of Innovations in Electoral Campaigning and Their Consequences*, ed. David L. Swanson and Paolo Mancini (Westport, Conn.: Praeger, 1996); Sam Lehman-Wilzig, "The Media Campaign: The Negative Effects of Positive Campaigning," in *Israel at the Polls, 1996*, ed. Daniel Elazar and Shmuel Sandler (Portland, Ore.: Frank Cass, 1998); Erwin Frenkel, *The Press and Politics in Israel: Jerusalem Post from 1932 to the Present* (Westport, Conn.: Greenwood, 1994); or the article by Judith Elizur, "The Role of the Media in the 1981 Knesset Elections," in *Israel at the Polls, 1981*, ed. Howard R. Penniman and Daniel Elazar (Bloomington: Indiana University Press, 1986), pp. 186–212.

11. Editorial comments cited here come from "The Election Campaign on Television," edited by Gary Wolf, part of the series of news releases *Israeli Press Highlights* (New York: Institute of Human Relations, American Jewish Committee, October 10, 1988), pp. 1–2.

12. An article by Joel Brinkley titled "Israeli TV Political Ads Lowering the Low Road," *New York Times* (October 8, 1988): 18, developed this theme, pointing out that the ads do help to raise issues but that they also use character defamation, propaganda, misrepresentation, deceptive photography, and alteration of pictures and quotations, and, generally, "a loose version of facts." See also Gabriel Weimann, Yariv Tsfati, and Tamir Sheafer, "Media Coverage of the 2006 Campaign: The Needs and Attitudes of the Public Vis-à-vis the Functioning of the News Media," in *The Elections in Israel, 2006*, ed. Alan Arian and Michal Shamir (New Brunswick, N.J.: Transaction, 2008).

13. Israel Ministry of Foreign Affairs, "Political Structure and Elections," section on "Elections," www.mfa.gov.il/MFA/MFAArchive/2000_2009/2001/6/Political+Structure+and+Elections.htm, accessed February 2010.

14. Zidon, *The Knesset*, pp. 23–24; Sager, *The Parliamentary System of Israel*, p. 46.

15. Arian, *Politics in Israel*, p. 121; Sager, *The Parliamentary System of Israel*, p. 46.

16. See the article by Roni Singer-Heruti and Ofri Ilani, "Labour Postpones Its Primary Election until Thursday," *Ha'Aretz* (December 2, 2008) on *Haaretz.com*, www.haaretz.com/hasen/spages/1042934.html, accessed February 2010.

17. Gregory Mahler, "The Effects of Electoral Systems upon the Behavior of Members of a National Legislature: The Israeli Knesset Case Study," *Journal of Constitutional and Parliamentary Studies* 14, no. 4 (1980): 305–18. See also Guy Lardeyret, "The Problem with P.R.," in *Electoral Systems and Democracy*, ed. Larry Diamond and Marc Plattner (Baltimore: Johns Hopkins University Press, 2006).

18. Moshe Czudnowski, "Legislative Recruitment under Proportional Representation in Israel: A Model and a Case Study," *Midwest Journal of Political Science* 14 (1970): 216–48.

19. See the Knesset's Web page, "The Electoral System in Israel," the section titled "The Distribution of Seats among the Lists," www.knesset.gov.il/description/eng/eng_mimshal_beh.htm#6, accessed February 2010.

20. *Jerusalem Post*, overseas edition (November 12, 1975): 3.

21. Avraham Brichta, "Selection of Candidates to the Tenth Knesset: The Impact of Centralization," in *Israel at the Polls, 1996*, ed. Daniel Elazar and Shmuel Sandler (Portland, Ore.: Frank Cass, 1998), pp. 18–35.

22. Steven Hoffman, "Candidate Selection in Israel's Parliament: The Realities of Change," *Middle East Journal* 34 (1980): 285–301.

23. Moshe Czudnowski, "Sociocultural Variables and Legislative Recruitment," *Comparative Politics* 4 (1972): 561–87.

24. Gregory Mahler, *The Knesset: Parliament in the Israeli Political System* (Rutherford, N.J.: Fairleigh Dickinson University Press, 1981), pp. 46–47.

25. See the article "Livni Wins Kadima Primaries By Narrow Margin," *YNET News*, September 18, 2008, http://www.ynet.co.il/english/articles/0,7340,L-3598425,00.html, accessed February 2010.

26. Myron Aronoff has written a fascinating analysis of reforms in the Labor Party. See his "Better Late Than Never: Democratization in the Labor Party," in *Israel since Begin*, ed. Gregory Mahler (Albany: State University of New York Press, 1990).

27. Alfred Katz, *Government and Politics in Contemporary Israel, 1948–Present* (Washington, D.C.: University Press of America), p. 56.

28. Sager, *The Parliamentary System of Israel*, p. 63. See also Gallagher and Mitchell, *The Politics of Electoral Systems*.

29. Katz, *Government and Politics*, p. 58.

30. This is based upon more extended discussion in Arian, *Politics in Israel*, pp. 130–31. See also Gad Yaacobi, *The Government of Israel* (New York: Praeger, 1982), p. 307.

31. Avraham Brichta, "1977 Elections and the Future of Electoral Reform in Israel," in *Israel at the Polls, 1977*, ed. Howard Penniman (Washington, D.C.: American Enterprise Institute, 1979).

32. See Reuven Hazan, "The Electoral Consequences of Political Reform: In Search of the Center of the Israeli Party System," in *The Elections in Israel, 2006*, ed. Alan Arian and Michal Shamir (New Brunswick, N.J.: Transaction, 2008); Ethan Bueno de Mesquita, "Strategic and Nonpolicy Voting: A Coalitional Analysis of Israeli Electoral Reform," *Comparative Politics* 33, no. 1 (2000): 63–80; or Gideon

Doron and Michael Harris, *Public Policy and Electoral Reform* (Lanham, Md.: Lexington Books, 2000).

33. There was substantial media coverage of the bill during its brief legislative life. See *Jerusalem Post* (June 8, 1988): 2.

34. This is discussed in "The Coalition Talks Drag On," in *Israeli Press Highlights*, ed. Gary Wolf (New York: Institute of Human Relations, American Jewish Committee, October 10, 1988), pp. 1–3.

35. Dov Goldstein in *Ma'ariv* (December 22, 1988), quoted in "The New Israeli Government," in *Israeli Press Highlights*, ed. Gary Wolf (New York: Institute of Human Relations, American Jewish Committee, October 10, 1988), p. 1.

36. See Avraham Brichta, "The New Premier-Parliamentary System in Israel," *Annals of the American Academy of Political and Social Science* 555 (1998): 180–92; Henri Stellman, "Electing a Prime Minister and a Parliament: The Israeli Election, 1996," *Parliamentary Affairs* 49 (1996): 648–60. See also Reuven Hazan, "Constituency Interests without Constituencies: The Geographical Impact of Candidate Selection on Party Organization and Legislative Behavior in the 14th Israeli Knesset, 1996–1999," *Political Geography* 18, no. 7 (1999): 791–811, and Emanuele Ottolenghi, "Why Direct Election Failed in Israel," in *Electoral Systems and Democracy*, ed. Larry Diamond and Marc Plattner (Baltimore: Johns Hopkins University Press, 2006).

37. See Emanuele Ottolenghi, "Why Direct Election Failed in Israel," *Journal of Democracy* 12, no. 4 (2001): 109–22.

38. See, among many other sources, the following for references to the last few elections: Penniman and Elazar, eds., *Israel at the Polls, 1981*; Daniel Elazar and Shmuel Sandler, *Israel's Odd Couple: The 1984 Knesset Elections and the National Unity Government* (Detroit, Mich.: Wayne State University Press, 1990); Daniel Elazar and Shmuel Sandler, eds., *Who's the Boss in Israel: Israel at the Polls, 1988–89* (Detroit, Mich.: Wayne State University Press, 1992); Daniel Elazar and Shmuel Sandler, *Israel at the Polls, 1992* (Lanham, Md.: Rowman & Littlefield, 1995); Elazar and Sandler, *Israel at the Polls, 1996*; and Daniel Elazar and M. Benjamin Mollov, *Israel at the Polls: 1999* (Portland, Ore.: Frank Cass, 2001).

39. See the Government of Israel, Central Bureau of Statistics, *Statistical Abstract of Israel, 2009*, Table 10.1, "Elections to the Knesset, by Eligible Voters and Voters, 1949–2009," www1.cbs.gov.il/reader/shnaton/templ_shnaton_e.html?num_tab=st10_01&CYear=2009, accessed February 2010.

40. Arian, *Politics in Israel*, p. 133.

41. Arian, *Politics in Israel*, p. 134. See also Jonathan Mendilow, "Party Strategy in the 2006 Elections: Kadima, Likud, and Labor," in *The Elections in Israel, 2006*, ed. Alan Arian and Michal Shamir (New Brunswick, N.J.: Transaction, 2008).

42. Arian, *Politics in Israel*, p. 136.

43. Arian, *Politics in Israel*, pp. 139–44.

44. Arian, *Politics in Israel*, p. 140.

45. Arian, *Politics in Israel*, p. 142. See also Sultan Tepe and Roni Baum, "Shas' Transformation to 'Likud with Kippa?' A Comparative Assessment of the Moderation of Religious Parties," in *The Elections in Israel, 2006*, ed. Alan Arian and Michal Shamir (New Brunswick, N.J.: Transaction, 2008).

46. Among the many journal articles dealing with specific electoral outcomes in the last three decades—a number of general books on Israeli elections have already

been referred to—the following might be included: Alan Arian, "Were the 1973 Elections in Israel Critical?" *Comparative Politics* 8 (1975): 152–65; Alan Arian and Shevah Weiss, "Split Ticket Voting in Israel," *Western Political Quarterly* 22 (1969): 375–89; Yael Azmon, "The 1981 Elections and the Changing Fortunes of the Israeli Labour Party," *Government and Opposition* 16, no. 4 (1981): 432–46; Marver Bernstein, "Israel's Ninth General Election," *International Studies* 17 (1978): 27–50; Don Peretz, "The War Election and Israel's Eighth Knesset," *Middle East Journal* 28 (1974): 111–25; Don Peretz, "Israel's 1969 Election Issues—The Visible and the Invisible," *Middle East Journal* 24, no. 1 (1970): 31–71; Don Peretz and Sammy Smooha, "Israel's Tenth Knesset Elections: Ethnic Upsurgence and Decline of Ideology," *Middle East Journal* 35 (1981): 506–26.

47. Mahler, *The Knesset*, p. 214. Following the 1977 election loss to Menachem Begin, Shimon Peres indicated that the Alignment's electoral defeat was attributable to "a number of domestic and international trends," but he also cited the "failure of demoralized party activists to push hard for victory," adding that "corruption hurt us the most." See the *Jerusalem Post*, international edition (May 24, 1977): 6.

48. Yechiel Kadashai, secretary and first assistant to Likud Party leader Menachem Begin. Information was gathered in an interview held on April 3, 1975, in the Knesset in Jerusalem. See Mahler, *The Knesset*, p. 41.

49. Avraham Brichta, "1977 Elections and the Future of Electoral Reform in Israel," in *Israel at the Polls, 1977*, ed. Howard Penniman (Washington, D.C.: American Enterprise Institute, 1979), pp. 45–46. See also the three articles by Reuven Hazan, Jonathan Spyer, and Neill Lochery on Kadima, Likud, and Labour in *Israel at the Polls, 2006*, ed. Shmuel Sandler, Manfred Gerstenfeld, and Jonathan Rynhold (London: Routledge, 2008).

50. Sager, *The Parliamentary System of Israel*, p. 48.

51. C. Paul Bradley, *Parliamentary Elections in Israel* (Grantham, N.H.: Tompson and Rutter, 1985), p. 20.

52. See Steven Hoffman, "Candidate Selection," 285–301; and Aronoff, "Better Late than Never."

53. Sager, *The Parliamentary System of Israel*, p. 51.

54. Moshe Czudnowski, "Legislative Recruitment," pp. 216–48; and Moshe Czudnowski, "Sociocultural Variables," pp. 561–87.

55. Shevah Weiss, "Women in the Knesset: 1949–1969," *Parliamentary Affairs* 28, no. 1 (1969/1970): 31–50.

8 THE MACHINERY OF GOVERNMENT

1. This is the interpretation of the term offered by Gabriel Almond. See Gabriel Almond and G. Bingham Powell Jr., *Comparative Politics: A Developmental Approach* (Boston: Little, Brown, and Company, 1966), p. 21.

2. David Rosenbloom and Gregory Mahler, "The Administrative System of Israel," in *Administrative Systems Abroad*, ed. Krishna Tummala (Washington, D.C.: University Press of America, 1982), p. 24. See also Eva Etzioni-Halevy, "Administrative Power in Israel," in *Developments in Israeli Public Administration*, ed. Moshe Maor (Portland, Ore.: Frank Cass, 2002), and Eran Vigoda-Gadot, *Building Strong Nations: Improving Governability and Public Management* (Burlington, Vt.: Ashgate, 2009).

3. Foreign Affairs was a continuation of the political department of the Jewish Agency; Defense evolved from the Haganah; Social Welfare developed from the National Council of the Yishuv's Welfare Department; and Education and Culture had been the education department of the National Council. See Don Peretz, *The Government and Politics of Israel* (Boulder, Colo.: Westview, 1979), p. 171.

4. The Knesset actually passed legislation requiring a rollback in the size of the civil service. See David Harris, "Public Sector Workforce up 3.8 in 97. Increase Leads to Rise in State's Actuarial Debt," *Jerusalem Post* (August 24, 1998): 19, and "Hollander: 1 in 6 Civil Servants Are Non-Permanent," *Jerusalem Post* (February 20, 1998): 10.

5. E. Samuel, "Efficiency in the Israeli Civil Service," *Canadian Public Administration* 4, no. 2 (1961): 191–96.

6. Gad Yaacobi, *The Government of Israel* (New York: Praeger, 1982), p. 204. See also David Nachmias, *Israel's Senior Civil Servants: Social Structure and Patronage* (Tel Aviv: Tel Aviv University Press, 1990).

7. Dan Horowitz and Moshe Lissak, *Origins of the Israeli Polity* (Chicago: University of Chicago Press, 1978), p. 196.

8. E. Samuel, "Growth of the Israel Civil Service, 1948–1956," *Revue Internationale de Science Administrative* 22, no. 4 (1956): 17–40.

9. E. Samuel, "A New Civil Service for Israel," *Public Administration* (London) 34, no. 2 (1956): 135–41.

10. Oscar Kraines, *Government and Politics in Israel* (Boston: Houghton Mifflin, 1961), p. 208.

11. Donna Divine, "The Modernization of Israeli Administration," *International Journal of Middle Eastern Studies* 5 (1974): 295–313.

12. Yaacobi, *Government*, p. 208.

13. Yaacobi, *Government*, p. 208.

14. Miron Mushkat Jr., "Transferring Administrative Skills from the Military to the Civilian Sector in the Process of Development," *Il Politico* 46, no. 3 (1981): 427–42.

15. Yaacobi, *Government*, p. 208.

16. The term *spoils system* is said to have been created in the United States to describe the practice of political leaders distributing appointive offices to loyal members of their own political party. According to *The Columbia Encyclopedia*, the name derives from a speech by Senator William Learned Marcy in which he stated, "to the victor belong the spoils." The practice was said to have been developed by the early presidents, especially Thomas Jefferson. "The system soon became entrenched in state politics and was practiced more extensively on a national scale during the administration of Andrew Jackson, who declared (1829) that the federal government would be bettered by having civil servants rotate in office. He replaced incumbent officeholders with members of his own party. Nevertheless, during Jackson's eight years in office not more than one fifth of officeholders were replaced. The dispensation of offices by strict party allegiance was followed in succeeding years and critical opposition grew. The corruption and inefficiency bred by the system reached staggering proportions in the administration of Ulysses S. Grant, and reaction against this helped bring about civil service reform, which was inaugurated by creation of the Civil Service Commission in 1871." See "Spoils System," *The Columbia Encyclopedia*, 6th ed. (New York: Columbia University Press, 2002), www.bartleby.com/65, accessed November 2002.

17. See Thomas H. Hammond, *Veto Points, Policy Preferences, and Bureaucratic Autonomy in Democratic Systems* (East Lansing: Michigan State University, Institute for Public Policy and Social Research, 1997).

18. Asher Arian, *Politics in Israel: The Second Generation* (Chatham, N.J.: Chatham House, 1985), pp. 233–34.

19. Arian, *Politics in Israel,* p. 232. On the Israeli political culture, more generally, see Myron J. Aronoff, "The Origins of Israeli Political Culture," in *Israeli Democracy under Stress,* ed. Ehud Sprinzak and Larry Diamond (Boulder, Colo.: Lynne Rienner, 1993).

20. Arian, *Politics in Israel,* p. 232.

21. The four major points that follow are based upon analysis of Gerald Caiden, *Israel's Administrative Culture* (Berkeley: Institute of Government Studies, University of California, 1970), pp. 17–19.

22. See also Brenda Danet, "The Language of Persuasion in Bureaucracy: 'Modern' and 'Traditional' Appeals to the Israel Customs Authorities," *American Sociology Review* 36, no. 5 (1971): 847–49.

23. Rosenbloom and Mahler, "Administrative System," p. 29.

24. Brenda Danet and Harriet Hartman, "Coping with Bureaucracy: The Israeli Case," *Social Forces* 51, no. 1 (1972): 7–22.

25. David Nachmias and David Rosenbloom, *Bureaucratic Culture: Citizens and Administrators in Israel* (New York: St. Martin's Press, 1978), as cited in Rosenbloom and Mahler, "Administrative System," p. 30. See also A. Friedberg, "Norms of Behavior for Public Officials in the Administrative System of Israel," *International Journal of Public Administration* 16, no. 1 (1993): 57; and Alon Peled, "First-Class Technology—Third-Rate Bureaucracy: The Case of Israel," *Information Technology for Development* 9, no. 1 (2000): 45–58.

26. See David Rosenbloom and Allon Yaroni, "The Transferability of New Public Management Reforms: Caveats from Israel," in *Public Policy in Israel,* ed. David Nachmias and Gila Menachem (Portland, Ore.: Frank Cass, 2002).

27. Yaacobi, *Government,* p. 60.

28. Yaacobi, *Government,* p. 222.

29. Some of the material in this section is a condensation of information presented in *Facts about Israel* (Jerusalem: Ministry of Information, 1975), pp. 102–3.

30. Daniel Elazar, *Israel: Building a New Society* (Bloomington: Indiana University Press, 1986), p. 87.

31. Efraim Torgovnik, "Urban Political Integration in Israel: A Comparative Perspective," *Urban Affairs Quarterly* 11, no. 4 (1976): 469–88.

32. Elazar, *Israel,* p. 83. See also Morton Rubin, *The Walls of Acre: Intergroup Relations and Urban Development in Israel* (New York: Holt, Rinehart, and Winston, 1974); and Benjamin Gidron, "A Resurgent Third Sector and Its Relationship to Government in Israel," in *Government and the Third Sector: Emerging Relationships in Welfare States,* ed. Benjamin Gidron, Ralph Kramer, and Lester Salamon (San Francisco: Jossey-Bass, 1992).

33. See *The Golden Book: Encyclopedia of Israel's Towns and Settlements* (Tel Aviv: Center for Local Governments of Israel, 1991). See also David Newman and Lawrence Applebaum, "Conflicting Objectives for Rural Local Government: Service Provision to Exurban Communities in Israel," *Environment and Planning* 13, no. 3 (1995): 253–70.

34. Israel Ministry of Foreign Affairs, "The State: Local Government," *Facts about Israel*, www.mfa.gov.il/MFA/Facts+About+Israel/State/THE+STATE-+Local+Government .htm, accessed February 2010.

35. Israel Ministry of Foreign Affairs, "The State: Local Government." See also David Janner-Klausner, *Municipal Strategic Planning: The Reshaping of Israeli Local Government* (Elmsford, N.Y.: Pergamon, 1994).

36. Majid Al Haj and Henry Rosenfeld, *Arab Local Government in Israel* (Boulder, Colo.: Westview, 1990).

37. Ernest Alexander, "The Development of an Entitlement Formula for Capital Budget Allocations to Local Government in Israel," *Planning and Administration* 7, no. 2 (1980): 13–25. See also Abraham Carmeli, "A Conceptual and Practical Framework of Measuring Performance of Local Authorities in Financial Terms: Analysing the Case of Israel," *Local Government Studies* 28, no. 1 (2002): 21–37.

38. See Chaim Kalchheim and Shimon Rozevitch, "Deficits in Local Government Budgets in Israel: A Reflection of Political Cycles and an Expression of Local Autonomy," *Public Budgeting and Finance* 10, no. 1 (1990): 67–77.

39. Kraines, *Government*, pp. 218–19.

40. See the Knesset Web page, "Local Government in Israel," www.knesset.gov.il/ lexicon/eng/LocalAuthorities_eng.htm, accessed February 2010.

41. Arian, *Politics in Israel*, p. 239.

42. Elazar, *Israel*, pp. 96–97. See also Oren Yiftachel, "Israel: Metropolitan Integration or Fractured Regions? An Alternative Perspective," *Sage Public Administration Abstracts* 25, no. 3 (1998): 371–80.

43. See Efraim Ben-Zadok, *Local Communities and the Israeli Polity: Conflict of Values and Interests* (Albany: State University of New York Press, 1993).

44. See Raphael Bar-El, Michal Avraham, and Dafna Schwartz, *Urban Growth Centers in the Galilee: A Strategy for Aliyah Absorption and Galilee Regional Development* (Rehovot: Jewish Agency, 1991); and Harvey Lithwick and Irwin Lithwick, *Regional Economic Development Policy: Lessons for Israel* (Jerusalem: Brookdale Institute of Gerontology and Adult Human Development, 1993).

45. See Oren Yiftachel, *Planning a Mixed Region in Israel: The Political Geography of Arab-Jewish Relations in the Galilee* (Brookfield, Vt.: Ashgate, 1992).

46. See Amos Shapira and Keren C. DeWitt-Arar, *Introduction to the Law of Israel* (Boston: Kluwer Law International, 1995); see also Alfredo Mordechai Rabello, ed., *European Legal Traditions and Israel: Essays on Legal History, Civil Law and Codification, European Law, Israel Law* (Jerusalem: Hebrew University of Jerusalem, 1994–1996); and several articles by Daniel Friedman: "The Effect of Foreign Law on the Law of Israel," *Israel Law Review* 10, no. 2 (1975): 192–206; "Infusion of the Common Law into the Legal System of Israel," *Israel Law Review* 10, no. 3 (1975): 324–77; and "Independent Development of Israeli Law," *Israel Law Review* 10, no. 4 (1975): 515–65.

47. Kraines, *Government*, pp. 137–42. The several paragraphs that follow are a condensation of much more detailed treatment of the fundamental elements of Israeli law found in Kraines's discussion. See also Henry Baker, *The Legal System of Israel* (Jerusalem: Israel University Press, 1968); and Izhak Englard, "The Law of Torts in Israel: The Problems of Common Law Codification in a Mixed Legal System," *American Journal of Comparative Law* 22, no. 2 (1974): 302–29.

48. Samuel Sager, *The Parliamentary System of Israel* (Syracuse, N.Y.: Syracuse University Press, 1985), p. 182.

49. Yaacov Zemach, *Political Questions in the Courts* (Detroit, Mich.: Wayne State University Press, 1976), p. 21.

50. One of the very best sources in this area is the work by Pnina Lahav, ed., *Law and the Transformation of Israeli Society* (Bloomington: Indiana University Press, 1998).

51. See *Israel's Written Constitution: Verbatim English Translations of the Declaration of Independence and of Eleven Basic Laws* (Haifa: A. G. Publications, 1993).

52. See the Israel Ministry of Foreign Affairs Web page, "The Judiciary: The Court System," the section "Religious Courts" found under "Tribunals with Limited Jurisdiction," www.mfa.gov.il/MFA/Government/Branches+of+Government/Judicial/The+Judiciary-+The+Court+System, accessed February 2010. It is worth noting that the Ministry of Foreign Affairs adds that "The [Palestine Order in Council] order also grants jurisdiction to the District Courts in matters of personal status for foreigners who are non-Muslims, stating that they 'shall apply the personal law of the parties concerned.' Regarding foreigners, this was defined as 'the law of his nationality.' Case law determined that regarding non-foreigners, 'the court . . . [has] . . . to apply the religious or communal law of the parties.'"

53. Horowitz and Lissak, *Origins*, p. 199.

54. See Ian Lustick, ed., *Economic, Legal, and Demographic Dimensions of Arab-Israeli Relations* (New York: Garland, 1994); Arye Rattner and Gideon Fishman, *Justice for All? Jews and Arabs in the Israeli Criminal Justice System* (Westport, Conn.: Praeger, 1998); David Kretzmer, *The Occupation of Justice: The Supreme Court of Israel and the Occupied Territories* (Albany: State University of New York Press, 2002); Human Rights Watch, *Israel, the Occupied West Bank and Gaza Strip, and the Palestinian Authority Territories: Justice Undermined; Balancing Security and Human Rights in the Palestinian Justice System* (New York: Human Rights Watch, 2001); Amnesty International, *Israel and the Occupied Territories: The Military Justice System in the Occupied Territories* (New York: Amnesty International, 1991); and Raja Shehadeh, *The Declaration of Principles and the Legal System in the West Bank* (Jerusalem: Palestinian Academic Society for the Study of International Affairs, 1994).

55. See Zeev Segal, *The Israeli Legal System vis-à-vis the American Legal System: Constitutional and Administrative Law* (Columbus, Ohio: Capital University, 1991).

56. Yaacobi, *Government*, p. 3. See also Yaacov Zemach, *The Judiciary of Israel*, 2nd ed. (Jerusalem: Institute of Judicial Training for Judges, 1998).

57. Eliahu Likhovski, "The Courts and the Legislative Supremacy of the Knesset," *Israel Law Review* 3, no. 3 (1968): 345–67.

58. This is the general focus of the definitive work on this subject, Zemach's *Political Questions in the Courts*. See also Martin Edelman, *Courts, Politics, and Culture in Israel* (Charlottesville: University Press of Virginia, 1994); Martin Edelman, "Israel," in *The Global Expansion of Judicial Power*, ed. C. Neal Tate and Torbjorn Vallinder (New York: New York University Press, 1995); and Alfred Witkin, "Some Reflections on Judicial Law-Making," *Israel Law Review* 2, no. 4 (1967): 475–87.

59. See Pnina Lahav, "Rights and Democracy: The Court's Performance," in Sprinzak and Diamond, *Israeli Democracy under Stress*; see also Yoav Dotan, "Legalising the Unlegaliseable: Terrorism, Secret Services and Judicial Review in Israel, 1970–2001,"

in *Judicial Review and Bureaucratic Impact: International and Interdisciplinary Perspectives*, ed. M. L. M. Hertogh and Simon Halliday (New York: Cambridge University Press, 2004); and Yoav Dotan, "Judicial Accountability in Israel: The High Court of Justice and the Phenomenon of Judicial Hyperactivism," in *Developments in Israeli Public Administration*, ed. Moshe Maor (Portland, Ore.: Frank Cass, 2002).

60. This is based upon a more complex discussion on the Ministry of Foreign Affairs Web page, "The Judiciary: The Court System," the section "The General Law Courts," www.mfa.gov.il/MFA/Government/Branches+of+Government/Judicial/The+Judiciary-+The+Court+System.htm, accessed February 2010.

61. This material is a condensation of material found in Israel Ministry of Foreign Affairs, *Facts about Israel*, online edition: "Judiciary: The Court System," www.mfa.gov.il/MFA/Government/Branches+of+Government/Judicial/The+Judiciary-+The+Court+System.htm, accessed February 2010.

62. This material is also a condensation of material found in Israel Ministry of Foreign Affairs, "Judiciary: The Court System." See also Peretz, *Government and Politics*, pp. 193–96.

63. See Israel Ministry of Foreign Affairs, "Judiciary: The Court System."

64. See Israel Ministry of Foreign Affairs, "Judiciary: The Court System."

65. Kraines, *Government*, p. 144.

66. Israel Ministry of Foreign Affairs, "Judiciary: The Court System."

67. Israel Ministry of Foreign Affairs, "Judiciary: The Court System."

68. Kraines, *Government*, p. 148.

69. Peretz, *Government and Politics*, p. 186.

70. See some of the discussion of the role of the Court in shaping the constitution in chapter 4 in this volume.

71. See Ervin Birnbaum, *The Politics of Compromise: State and Religion in Israel* (Rutherford, N.J.: Fairleigh Dickinson University Press, 1970), p. 210. See also M. Chiger, "The Rabbinical Courts in the State of Israel," *Israel Law Review* 2, no. 2 (1967): 147–81, and Martin Edelman, "The Rabbinical Courts in the Evolving Political Culture of Israel," *Middle Eastern Studies* 16 (1980): 145–66.

72. Kraines, *Government*, p. 149.

73. See also Boaz Cohen, *Law and Tradition in Judaism* (New York: Jewish Theological Seminary of America, 1959); and Saul Lubetski, *Religion and State* (New York: New York University Press, 1994).

74. Arian, *Politics in Israel*, p. 181.

75. Kraines, *Government*, p. 150.

76. Information on the role and duties of the attorney general can be found at the Ministry of Foreign Affairs Web page: "The Attorney General," www.mfa.gov.il/MFA/MFAArchive/2000_2009/2000/9/The%20Attorney%20General, accessed February 2010.

77. See the article "Israel's Attorney General Mulls Indicting Olmert," *Reuters*, March 1, 2009, www.reuters.com/article/idUSTRE5202EG20090301, accessed February 2010. See also the article by Mazan Mualem in *Ha'Aretz*, "Netanyahu puts off decision on splitting Attorney General role," November 16, 2009, www.haaretz.com/hasen/spages/1128544.html, accessed February 2010.

78. Two very good general studies of the IDF are those by Edward Luttwak and Dan Horowitz, *The Israeli Army* (New York: Harper and Row, 1975); and Gunther

Rothenberg, *The Anatomy of the Israeli Army: The Israeli Defense Force, 1948–1978* (New York: Hippocrene, 1979). More recently, see Mark Heller, *Continuity and Change in Israeli Security Policy* (New York: Oxford University Press, 2000); and Stuart Cohen, *Israel and Its Army: From Cohesion to Confusion* (New York: Routledge, 2008). A good recent study is Ze'ev Schiff's "Fifty Years of Israeli Security: The Central Role of the Defense System," *Middle East Journal* 53, no. 3 (1999): 434–42.

79. Yoram Peri, *Between Battles and Ballots: Israeli Military in Politics* (London: Cambridge University Press, 1983), p. l. See also Yehuda Ben-Meir, *Civil-Military Relations in Israel* (New York: Columbia University Press, 1995); Daniel Maman, Eyal Ben-Ari, and Zeev Rosenhek, *Military, State, and Society in Israel: Theoretical and Comparative Perspectives* (New Brunswick, N.J.: Transaction, 2001); Uri Ben-Eliezer, "Rethinking the Civil-Military Relations Paradigm: The Inverse Relation between Militarism and Praetorianism through the Example of Israel," *Comparative Political Studies* 30, no. 3 (1997): 356–75.

80. Amos Perlmutter, *Military and Politics in Israel: Nation-Building and Role Expansion* (New York: Praeger, 1969), p. 54. See also A. Yaniv, *National Security and Democracy in Israel* (Boulder, Colo.: Lynne Rienner, 1993); and Moshe Lissak, *The Unique Approach to Military-Societal Relations in Israel and Its Impact on Foreign and Security Policy* (Jerusalem: Hebrew University of Jerusalem, 1998).

81. Yigal Allon, *The Making of Israel's Army* (New York: Universe Books, 1970), or *Shield of David: The Story of Israel's Armed Forces* (New York: Random House, 1970).

82. Perlmutter, *Military*, p. 55. See also Ronald Krebs, *Fighting for Rights: Military Service and the Politics of Citizenship* (Ithaca, N.Y.: Cornell University Press, 2006).

83. Elazar, *Israel*, p. 81. See also Udi Lebel, *Communicating Security: Civil-Military Relations in Israel* (New York: Routledge, 2008).

84. Perlmutter, *Military*, p. 59.

85. Peretz, *Government and Politics*, 128. See Moshe Lissak, "The Civilian Components of Israel's Security Doctrine: The Evolution of Civil-Military Relations in the First Decade," in *Israel: The First Decade of Independence*, ed. S. Ilan Troen and Noah Lucas (Albany: State University of New York Press, 1995). See also Yoram Peri, *Generals in the Cabinet Room: How the Military Shapes Israeli Policy* (Washington, D.C.: United States Institute of Peace Press, 2006).

86. Arieh O'Sullivan, "Who's Giving the Orders Here?" *Jerusalem Post* (October 5, 2001): 1B. See also Yehuda Ben-Meir, "A Crisis in Civil-Military Relations," *Jerusalem Post* (October 15, 2001): 1; and Lisa Hajjar, *Courting Conflict: The Israeli Military Court System in the West Bank and Gaza* (Berkeley: University of California Press, 2005).

87. See Israel Ministry of Foreign Affairs, "The State: Israel Defense Forces (IDF)," *Facts about Israel*, www.mfa.gov.il/MFA/Facts+About+Israel/State/THE+STATE-+Israel+Defense+Forces+-IDF-.htm, accessed February 2010.

88. See Efraim Karsh, ed., *Between War and Peace: Dilemmas of Israeli Security* (Portland, Ore.: Frank Cass, 1996); Abraham Becker, *Israel and the Palestinian Occupied Territories: Military-Political Issues in the Debate* (Santa Monica, Calif.: Rand, 1971); and Nimrod Raphaeli, "Military Governments in the Occupied Territories," *Middle East Journal* 23, no. 2 (1969): 177–208. For an example of a very critical study of the IDF in this regard, see Geoffrey Aronson, "Israel's Policy of Military Occupation," *Journal of Palestine Studies* 7, no. 4 (1978): 79–98; David Eshel, "Following the Recent Unrest in the West Bank, Gaza Strip and Israel, David Eshel As-

sesses the Security Implications for the IDF," *Jane's Defence Weekly* 34, no. 15 (2000): 36–37; "Israel Refocuses on Urban Warfare—In the Cauldron of West Bank Street Fighting, the IDF has Embraced Helicopters and Unmanned Aircraft," *Aviation Week and Space Technology* 156, no. 19 (2002): 24–25.

89. Peri, *Battles and Ballots*, p. 9. See his chapter 5, "Generals in Mufti As Politicians," pp. 101–30. See also Amos Perlmutter, "The Israeli Army in Politics," *World Politics* 20, no. 4 (1968): 606–43.

90. Peretz, *Government and Politics*, p. 127.

91. "Men under 29 and women under 26 are called up for regular service of up to 36 months for men and 24 months for women, the exact term depending on the conscript's age on recruitment. . . . Married women, mothers, and pregnant women are exempted. Exemption is also granted to women on grounds of religious conviction. . . . After their term of national service, men and childless women are in the Reserves until the ages of 55 and 34 respectively. . . . Until they are 40, men report for 31 days' training annually, and, from then until they are 55, for 14 days," *Facts about Israel*, pp. 104–5.

92. See Martin Van Creveld, "Women of Valor: Why Israel Doesn't Send Women into Combat," *Policy Review* 62 (1992): 65–67.

93. Indeed, surveys of army officers substantiate the fact that the ideological views of ex-army officers range widely. See Peretz, *Government and Politics*, p. 129.

94. Two very good general studies of the interplay of the military and politics are Amos Perlmutter's *Military and Politics in Israel: Nation-Building and Role-Expansion* and his *Politics and the Military in Israel: 1967–1977* (London: F. Cass, 1978).

95. Peretz, *Government and Politics*, p. 178.

96. Gabriel Sheffer and Oren Barak, *Militarism and Israeli Society* (Bloomington: Indiana University Press, 2010).

97. Peretz, *Government and Politics*, p. 147. See also Victor Azarya and Baruch Kimmerling, "New Immigrants in the Israeli Armed Forces," *Armed Forces and Society* 6, no. 3 (1980): 455–82, and Maurice Roumani, "From Immigrant to Citizen: The Contribution of the Army in Israel to National Integration; The Case of Oriental Jews," *Plural Societies* 9, nos. 2–3 (1978): 1–145.

98. See Israel Ministry of Foreign Affairs, "The State: Israel Defense Forces (IDF)."

9 THE FOREIGN POLICY SETTING

1. The discussion that follows is partially based upon the extended discussion in *Facts about Israel* (Jerusalem: Ministry of Foreign Affairs, 1985), pp. 39–40. See also Efraim Karsh, *Israel: The First Hundred Years* (Portland, Ore.: Frank Cass, 1999), and three very good more recent discussions of Israeli security concerns by Zeev Maoz, *Defending the Holy Land: A Critical Analysis of Israel's Security and Foreign Policy* (Ann Arbor: University of Michigan Press, 2006); Uri Bialer, *Between East and West: Israel's Foreign Policy Orientation, 1948–1956* (Cambridge: Cambridge University Press, 2008); and Mordechai Bar-On, *Never-Ending Conflict: Israeli Military History* (Mechanicsburg, Pa.: Stackpole, 2006).

2. Some good general military histories of this period include work by Efraim Inbar, *Israel's Strategic Agenda* (New York: Routledge, 2007); S. Ilan Troen and Noah Lucas,

eds., *Israel: The First Decade of Independence* (Albany: State University of New York Press, 1995); and Zeev Derori, *The Israeli Defence Force and the Foundation of Israel* (London: Frank Cass, 2004). Histories with a different perspective include Efraim Karsh, *Fabricating Israeli History: The "New Historians"* (Portland, Ore.: Frank Cass, 2000); Eugene Rogan and Avi Shlaim, eds., *The War for Palestine: Rewriting the History of 1948* (New York: Cambridge University Press, 2001); Joseph Heller, *The Birth of Israel, 1945–1949: Ben-Gurion and His Critics* (Gainesville: University Press of Florida, 2000); Laila Parsons, *The Druze between Palestine and Israel, 1947–1949* (New York: St. Martin's, 2000); and Charles D. Smith, *Palestine and the Arab-Israeli Conflict* (Boston: St. Martin's, 2001).

3. Some reference material for this event includes Moti Golani, *Israel in Search of a War: The Sinai Campaign, 1955–1956* (Portland, Ore.: Sussex Academic Press, 1998); and Robert Henriques, *A Hundred Hours to Suez: An Account of Israel's Campaign in the Sinai Peninsula* (New York: Viking, 1957). A very good, more historical examination is Benny Morris's *Israel's Border Wars, 1949–1956: Arab Infiltration, Israeli Retaliation, and the Countdown to the Suez War* (Oxford: Clarendon, 1997).

4. See, for example, B. Andrews, "Suez Canal Controversy," *Albany Law Review* 21, no. 1 (1957): 14–33, or Simcha Dinitz, "The Legal Aspects of the Egyptian Blockade of the Suez Canal," *Georgetown Law Journal* 45, no. 2 (1957): 166–99.

5. Howard Sachar, *A History of Israel: From the Rise of Zionism to Our Time* (New York: Alfred A. Knopf, 1981), p. 486.

6. Sachar, *History of Israel*, p. 489.

7. Sachar, *History of Israel*, p. 494.

8. Alfred Katz, *Government and Politics in Contemporary Israel, 1948–Present* (Washington, D.C.: University Press of America, 1980), p. 155.

9. See David Tal, "Israel's Road to the 1956 War," *International Journal of Middle East Studies* 28 (1996): 59–81. On Israel and the Sinai, see Golani, *Israel in Search*; Morris, *Israel's Border Wars*; and Mordechai Bar-On, *The Gates of Gaza: Israel's Road to Suez and Back, 1955–1957* (New York: St. Martin's, 1995).

10. Gideon Rafael, *Destination Peace: Three Decades of Israeli Foreign Policy; A Personal Memoir* (New York: Stein and Day, 1981), p. 64.

11. There is a very good, and detailed, discussion of this in Rafael, *Destination Peace*, pp. 153–90. One of the best analyses of the decision-making process involved here is to be found in Michael Brecher's *Decisions in Israel's Foreign Policy* (New Haven, Conn.: Yale University Press, 1975), pp. 318–453. See also Ami Gluska, *The Israeli Military and the Origins of the 1967 War: Government, Armed Forces, and Defence Policy, 1963–1967* (London: Routledge, 2007).

12. On this subject, see Indar Rikhye, *The Sinai Blunder: Withdrawal of the United Nations Emergency Force Leading to the Six Day War of June, 1967* (Totowa, N.J.: Frank Cass, 1980).

13. A fascinating discussion of the value of preemption is found in Robert Harkavy, *Pre-emption and Two Front Conventional Warfare* (Jerusalem: Hebrew University Press, 1977). See also Richard Bordeaux Parker, *The Six-Day War: A Retrospective* (Gainesville: University Press of Florida, 1996); and S. Ilan Troen, Zakai Shalom, and Moshe Tlamim, "Ben-Gurion's Diary for the 1967 Six-Day War: Introduction and Diary Excerpts," *Israel Studies* 4, no. 2 (1999): 195–220.

14. On this subject, see David Ben-Gurion, *Israel: A Personal History* (New York: Funk and Wagnalls, 1971), pp. 774–86.

15. Sachar, *History of Israel*, p. 643.

16. On the Six Day War in general, see David Kimche, *The Sandstorm: The Arab-Israeli War of 1967* (New York: Stein and Day, 1968); Michael Brecher, *Decisions in Crisis: Israel, 1967 and 1973* (Berkeley: University of California Press, 1980); Michael Oren, *Six Days of War: June 1967 and the Making of the Modern Middle East* (Oxford: Oxford University Press, 2002); and Randolph Churchill, *The Six Day War* (Boston: Houghton, Mifflin, 2001).

17. *Facts about Israel*, p. 39.

18. On this war see Yaacov Bar-Simon-Tov, *The Israeli-Egyptian War of Attrition, 1969–1970* (New York: Columbia University Press, 1980).

19. See George Gawrych, *The Albatross of Decisive Victory: War and Policy between Egypt and Israel in the 1967 and 1973 Arab-Israeli Wars* (Westport, Conn.: Greenwood, 2000).

20. Rafael, *Destination Peace*, pp. 281–303.

21. Michael Handel, *Perception, Deception, and Surprise: The Case of the Yom Kippur War* (Jerusalem: Hebrew University Press, 1975).

22. There is a significant literature on the 1973 war. Examples of the analyses that have been published would include the following: Avraham Adnan, *On the Banks of the Suez: An Israeli General's Personal Account of the Yom Kippur War* (San Rafael, Calif.: Presidio, 1980); Peter Allen, *The Yom Kippur War* (New York: Scribner, 1982); Riad Ashkar, "The Syrian and Egyptian Campaign," *Journal of Palestine Studies* 3, no. 2 (1974): 15–33; Michael Brecher, *Decisions in Crisis: Israel, 1967 and 1973* (Berkeley: University of California Press, 1980); E. Monroe, *The Arab-Israeli War, 1973* (London: International Institute for Strategic Studies, 1974); and Zeev Schiff, *October Earthquake: Yom Kippur, 1973* (Tel Aviv: University Publishing Projects, 1974).

23. Edmund Ghareeb, "The U.S. Arms Supply to Israel during the October War," *Journal of Palestine Studies* 3, no. 2 (1974): 114–21.

24. See Walter J. Boyne, *The Two O'Clock War: The 1973 Yom Kippur Conflict and the Airlift that Saved Israel* (New York: Thomas Dunne, 2002).

25. Alon Ben-Meir, "Israel in the War's Long Aftermath," *Current History* 80, no. 462 (1981): 23–26; Harold Hart, *Yom Kippur Plus 100 Days* (New York: Har, 1974). See also P. R. Kumaraswamy, ed., *Revisiting the Yom Kippur War* (Portland, Ore.: Frank Cass, 2000).

26. See Shmuel Gordon, *The Vulture and the Snake: Counter-Guerrilla Air Warfare; The War in Southern Lebanon* (Ramat Gan, Israel: Begin-Sadat Center for Strategic Studies, Bar-Ilan University, 1998); Jamal El-Hajj, *UNIFIL in Lebanon: The Past and the Future* (Carlisle Barracks, Pa.: Army War College, 1998). For a very dramatic example of this, see Jacobo Timmerman, *The Longest War: Israel in Lebanon* (New York: Knopf, 1982). Another interesting study is Yohanan Ramati's "Strategic Effects of Israel's Campaign in Lebanon," *Midstream* 28, no. 7 (1982): 3–4.

27. Daoud Kuttab, "The Lebanon Lesson," *Jerusalem Post* (May 25, 2000): 8; see also Arieh O'Sullivan, "The Great Gamble: Leaving Lebanon," *Jerusalem Post* (January 9, 1998): 15.

28. See Greg Jaffe, "Short '06 Lebanon War Stokes Pentagon Debate," *Washington Post* online, April 6, 2009, for an interesting discussion of how the United States military analyzed the war. The article can be found at www.washingtonpost.com/wp-dyn/content/article/2009/04/05/AR2009040502235.html, accessed May 2010.

29. See Arieh O'Sullivan, "Nahshon Ready for Urban Warfare," *Jerusalem Post* (October 27, 2000): 4A. See also Stuart Cohen, "The Israel Defense Forces (IDF): From a 'People's Army' to a 'Professional Military'—Causes and Implications," *Armed Forces and Society* 21, no. 2 (1995): 237–54; "Israel Refocuses on Urban Warfare—In the Cauldron of West Bank Street Fighting, the IDF Has Embraced Helicopters and Unmanned Aircraft," *Aviation Week and Space Technology* 156, no. 19 (2002): 24–26; Dan Izenberg, "Israel Searches for More Humane Riot Control Tools," *Jerusalem Post* (November 16, 2000): 2; and David Eshel, "Following the Recent Unrest in the West Bank, Gaza Strip and Israel, David Eshel Assesses the Security Implications for the IDF," *Jane's Defence Weekly* 34, no. 15 (2000): 36–38.

30. See Eetta Prince Gibson, "The Fiber of Our Society Is Being Destroyed," *Jerusalem Post Magazine* (September 14, 2001): 18.

31. See Reuters, "Hamas, Fatah Vow 'Eye for an Eye'," *Jerusalem Post* (August 26, 2001): 3. See the very good volume by Baruch Kimmerling and Joel Migdal, *The Palestinian People* (Cambridge, Mass.: Harvard University Press, 2003).

32. See "Keeping the Downtown Up," *Jerusalem Post* (December 28, 2001): 3.

33. See Efraim Karsh, "Israel's War," *Commentary* 113, no. 4 (2002): 23–28. See also "The Beginning of the End of the Palestinian Uprising?" *Economist* 360 (September 29, 2001): 50–51.

34. See Lamia Lahoud, "Fatah Calls for Intifada Despite Summit," *Jerusalem Post* (October 17, 2000): 4.

35. One example of this kind of issue is found in "Arafat's Choice," *Economist* 361 (December 15, 2001): 39–40. See also David Rudge, "Arafat and Palestinian Authority Stronger Than Ever—Expert," *Jerusalem Post* (May 22, 2001): 2; Arieh O'Sullivan, "Israel, PA Now in 'Armed Conflict,'" *Jerusalem Post* (January 11, 2001): 2; Chris Hedges, "The New Palestinian Revolt," *Foreign Affairs* 80, no. 1 (January/February 2001): 124–138; Alexander Bligh, "The Intifada and the New Political Role of the Israeli Arab Leadership," *Middle Eastern Studies* 35, no. 1 (1999): 134–64; Yezid Sayigh, "Arafat and the Anatomy of a Revolt," *Survival* (England) 43, no. 3 (2001): 47–60; Lahoud, "Fatah Calls for Intifada," p. 4; and Gal Luft, "Who Is Winning the Intifada?" *Commentary* 112, no. 1 (July/August 2001): 28–33.

36. See Ruth Linn, "When the Individual Soldier Says 'No' to War: A Look at Selective Refusal During the Intifada," *Journal of Peace Research* 33 (November 1996): 421–31; Asher Arian, Michal Shamir, and Raphael Ventura, "Public Opinion and Political Change: Israel and the Intifada," *Comparative Politics* 24 (April 1992): 317–34; Efraim Infar, "Israel's Small War: The Military Response to the Intifada," *Armed Forces and Society* 18 (Fall 1991): 29–50; and Tamar Liebes and Shoshana Blum-Kulka, "Managing a Moral Dilemma: Israeli Soldiers in the Intifada," *Armed Forces and Society* 21 (Fall 1994): 45–68.

37. For a discussion of why the Soviet Union turned increasingly hostile to Israel during the 1949–1953 period, see Sachar, *History of Israel*, pp. 461–63. Studies of the role of the Soviets in the 1973 war include Galia Golan, *The Soviet Union and the Arab-Israeli War of October, 1973* (Jerusalem: Hebrew University Press, 1974), and *Yom Kippur and After: The Soviet Union and the Middle East* (New York: Cambridge University Press, 1977); and Foy Kohler, *The Soviet Union and the October 1973 Middle East War* (Coral Gables, Fla.: University of Miami Press, 1974), among others.

38. See Viktor Levonovich Israelian, *Inside the Kremlin During the Yom Kippur War* (University Park: Pennsylvania State University Press, 1995), or Galia Golan, "The Soviet Union and the Yom Kippur War," in *Revisiting the Yom Kippur War*, ed. P. R. Kumaraswamy (Portland, Ore.: Frank Cass, 2000).

39. Michael Brecher, *The Foreign Policy System of Israel: Setting, Images, Process* (New Haven, Conn.: Yale University Press, 1972). Another excellent general study of Israeli foreign policy strategy is Yoav Ben-Horin and Barry Posen's *Israel's Strategic Doctrine* (Santa Monica, Calif.: Rand Corporation, 1981).

40. Brecher, *The Foreign Policy System*, p. 5.

41. Brecher, *The Foreign Policy System*, p. 11.

42. A very good analysis of the kinds of decisions that are made and how the policy-making process works, especially in military decisions, can be found in Yoram Peri, *Between Battles and Ballots: Israeli Military in Politics* (Cambridge, U.K.: Cambridge University Press, 1983), pp. 156–74.

43. Brecher, *The Foreign Policy System*, p.13.

44. See Stuart Cohen, *Studying the Israel Defense Forces: A Changing Contract with Israeli Society* (Ramat Gan, Israel: BESA Center for Strategic Studies, Bar-Ilan University, 1995). See also Ze'ev Schiff, "Fifty Years of Israeli Security: The Central Role of the Defense System," *Middle East Journal* 53, no. 3 (1999): 434–42.

45. Peri, *Between Battles and Ballots*, p. 20. See also Mordechai Bar-On, *Never-Ending Conflict: Israeli Military History* (Mechanicsburg, Pa.: Stackpole, 2006).

46. See Paul Rivlin, "The Burden of Israel's Defence," *Survival* 20, no. 4 (1978): 146–54. See also Stuart Cohen, *Israel and Its Army: Continuity and Change* (London: Routledge, 2007).

47. Peri, *Between Battles and Ballots*, p. 21. For 2002 budget data, see Government of Israel, Central Bureau of Statistics, *Statistical Abstract of Israel, 2003*, Table 10.8, "Government Expenditure," at 194.90.153.197/reader, accessed October 2003; 2008 data come from *Statistical Abstract of Israel, 2009*, Table 10.8, "General Government Expenditure by Unit and Function," www.cbs.gov.il/shnaton60/st10_08.pdf, accessed May 2010.

48. Major studies of the Israeli army include Yigal Allon, *The Making of Israel's Army* (New York: Universe, 1970); Edward Luttwak and Dan Horwitz, *The Israeli Army* (New York: Harper and Row, 1975); and Gunther Rothenberg, *The Anatomy of the Israeli Army: The Israel Defense Force, 1948–1978* (New York: Hippocrene, 1979). A comparative study was recently published by Stuart Cohen, *The New Citizen Armies: Israel's Armed Forces in Comparative Perspective* (London: Routledge, 2010).

49. See Martin Van Creveld, "Women of Valor: Why Israel Doesn't Send Women into Combat," *Policy Review* 62 (1992): 65–67.

50. Peri, *Between Battles and Ballots*, p. 22.

51. See Gabriel Ben-Dor, Ami Pedahzur, and Badi Hasisi, "Israel's National Security Doctrine under Strain: The Crisis of the Reserve Army," *Armed Forces and Society* 28, no. 2 (2002): 233–55.

52. John E. Mroz, *Beyond Security: Private Perceptions Among Arabs and Israelis* (New York: Pergamon Press, 1980), p. 47. See also Zaki Shalom, *Israel's Nuclear Option: Behind the Scenes Diplomacy between Dimona and Washington* (Portland, Ore.: Sussex Academic Press, 2005).

53. On this subject, see Efraim Inbar, "Israeli National Security, 1973–1996," *Annals of the American Academy of Political and Social Science* 555 (January 1998): 62–81; Michael Karpin, *The Bomb in the Basement: How Israel Went Nuclear and What That Means for the World* (New York: Simon and Schuster, 2006); Louis Rene Beres, "Power and Survival: Why Israel Needs Nuclear Weapons," *International Journal of Group Tensions* 26, no. 1 (1996): 21–27, "Limits of Nuclear Deterrence: The Strategic Risks and Dangers to Israel of False Hope," *Armed Forces and Society* 23, no. 4 (1997): 539–69, and "The Question of Palestine and Israel's Nuclear Strategy," *Political Quarterly* 62 (1991): 451–60; Israel Shahak, *Open Secrets: Israeli Nuclear and Foreign Policies* (Chicago: Pluto, 1997); Shai Feldman, *Israeli Nuclear Deterrence: A Strategy for the 1980s* (New York: Columbia University Press, 1982); and Efraim Karsh, *Between War and Peace: Dilemmas of Israeli Security* (Portland, Ore.: Frank Cass, 1996).

54. On Netanyahu's nonparticipation in the 2010 nuclear summit, see Ed Henry's article titled "Netanyahu to Skip Obama's Nuclear Security Summit," *CNN World Online*, April 8, 2010, www.cnn.com/2010/WORLD/meast/04/08/us.israel.netanyahu/index.html, accessed May 2010. See also Timothy L. H. McCormack, *Self-Defense in International Law: The Israeli Raid on the Iraqi Nuclear Reactor* (New York: St. Martin's, 1996).

55. For discussions of this concept, see Yigal Allon, "Israel: The Case for Defensible Borders," *Foreign Affairs* 55 (1976): 38–53; and Dan Horowitz, *Israel's Concept of Defensible Borders* (Jerusalem: Institute for International Relations, 1975).

56. Indeed, one of the classic works of military history in Israel is the volume of the same title by Netanel Lorch, *One Long War: Arab Versus Jew Since 1920* (Jerusalem: Keter, 1976). The volume traces the history of wars in Israel from the prestate period, but begins in detail with the 1948 War of Independence and continues through the 1973 Yom Kippur War. See also the volume by Anthony Cordesman, *The Military Balance in the Middle East* (Westport, Conn.: Praeger, 2004).

57. One of the classic references is the study by Yehuda Z. Blum, *Secure Boundaries and Middle East Peace* (Jerusalem: Faculty of Law, Hebrew University, 1971), especially part 2, "On Israel's Right to Secure Boundaries," pp. 61–110.

58. In September 1988, Israel launched its own spy satellite, designed to observe troop movements and military activities in the Middle East from space. This factor, Israel claimed, would help to make up for relatively small geopolitical area of the state and would help to provide some of the advanced warning security Israel had given up in its peace negotiations with Egypt.

59. On the importance of the Golan to Israel see, inter alia, the following: Muhammad Muslih, "The Golan: Israel, Syria, and Strategic Calculations," *Middle East Journal* 47 (1993): 611–32; Eyal Ziser, "June 1967: Israel's Capture of the Golan Heights," *Israel Studies* 7, no. 1 (2002): 168–94; William Caldwell, Fandall Falk, and Timothy Malone, *Peacekeeping on the Golan Heights: Assessing U.S. Participation* (Carlisle Barracks, Pa.: U.S. Army War College, 1996).

60. See Dov S. Zakheim, "Hi-Tech Eyes and Ears," *Jerusalem Post* (July 30, 1999): 8A.

61. Mroz, *Beyond Security.*

62. Michael Curtis, "The United Nations and the Middle East Conflict, 1967–1975," *Middle East Review* 3 (1975): 18–22. See also Brian Urquhart, "The United Nations in the Middle East: A 50-Year Retrospective," *Middle East Journal* 49 (1995):

572–81; and Kofi Annan, "Israel and the United Nations," *Journal of Palestine Studies* 27, no. 4 (1998): 145–50. On UN peacekeeping in the Middle East, see H. B. Walker, "The United Nations: Peacekeeping and the Middle East," *Asian Affairs* (London) 27 (1996): 13–19.

63. Israel Information Center, Government of Israel, *Facts about Israel* (Jerusalem: Israel Information Center, 1977), p. 192.

64. Alfred Katz, *Government and Politics*, p. 155.

65. See Rosemary Hollis, "Europe and the Middle East: Power by Stealth?" *International Affairs* 73 (1997): 15–29; Paul-Marie de la Gorce, "Europe and the Arab-Israel Conflict: A Survey," *Journal of Palestine Studies* 26, no. 3 (1997): 5–17; or Efrayim Ahiram, Alfred Tovias, and Paul Pasch, *Whither EU-Israeli Relations? Common and Divergent Interests* (New York: P. Lang, 1995).

66. See Benjamin Pinkus, "Atomic Power to Israel's Rescue: French-Israeli Nuclear Cooperation, 1949–1957," *Israel Studies* 7, no. 1 (2002): 104–38; see also Raymond Aron, *DeGaulle, Israel, and the Jews* (New York: Praeger, 1969), and Sylvia Crosbie, *A Tacit Alliance* (Princeton, N.J.: Princeton University Press, 1974).

67. Brecher, "Images."

68. Nicholas Balabkins, *West German Reparations to Israel* (New Brunswick, N.J.: Rutgers University Press, 1971); Inge Deutschkron, *Bonn and Jerusalem* (Philadelphia: Clinton Books, 1970); Nicholas Balabkins, "The Course of West German-Israeli Relations," *Orbis* 14, no. 3 (1970): 776–818.

69. For example, see Samuel Decalo, *Israel and Africa: Forty Years, 1956–1996* (Gainesville, Fla.: Academic Press, 1998); Ade Adefuye, "Nigeria and Israel," *International Studies* 18, no. 4 (1979): 629–40; Y. Kohn, "Israel and the New Nation-States of Asia and Africa," *Annals of the American Academy of Political and Social Science* 324 (1959): 96–102; Mordechai Kreinin, *Israel and Africa: A Study in Technical Cooperation* (New York: Praeger, 1964), or A. Rivkin, "Israel and the Afro-Asian World," *Foreign Affairs* 37, no. 3 (1959): 486–95.

70. Michael Curtis and Susan Gitelson, *Israel in the Third World* (New Brunswick, N.J.: Transaction, 1976); Jonathan Goldstein, *China and Israel, 1948–1998: A Fifty Year Retrospective* (Westport, Conn.: Praeger, 1999); or R. Kozicki, "India and Israel: A Problem in Asian Politics," *Middle Eastern Affairs* 9, no. 5 (1958): 162–71.

71. Curtis and Gitelson, *Israel in the Third World*; Edy Kaufman, *Israeli-Latin American Relations* (New Brunswick, N.J.: Transaction, 1979); Rudiger Dornbusch and Sebastian Edwards, *Reform, Recovery, and Growth: Latin America and the Middle East* (Chicago: University of Chicago Press, 1995); or Y. Shapira, "Israel's International Cooperation Program with Latin America," *Inter-American Economic Affairs* 30, no. 2 (1976): 3–32.

72. *Facts about Israel (1977)*, p. 195.

73. See H. S. Chabra, "The Competition of Israel and the Arab States for the Friendship with the African States," *India Quarterly* 31, no. 4 (1976): 362–70; Susan Gitelson, *Israel's African Setback in Perspective* (Jerusalem: Hebrew University Press, 1974); Ethan Nadelmann, "Israel and Black Africa: A Rapprochement?" *Journal of Modern African Studies* 19, no. 2 (1981): 183–220; or Frank Sankari, "The Costs and Gains of Israel's Pursuit of Influence in Africa," *Middle Eastern Studies* 15 (1979): 270–79.

74. See Abel Jacob, "Israel's Military Aid to Africa, 1960–1966," *Journal of Modern African Studies* 9, no. 2 (1971): 165–88; Duncan Clarke, "Israel's Unauthorized

Arms Transfers," *Foreign Policy* 99 (Summer 1995): 89–109; Yitzhak Shichor, "Israel's Military Transfers to China and Taiwan," *Survival* (London) 40, no. 1 (Spring 1998): 68–91, or Yaroslav Trofimov, "Friends Indeed: India and Israel Discover Common Interests," *Far Eastern Economic Review* 157 (November 3, 1994): 20. A consequence of U.S. pressure on Israel not to sell Israeli-manufactured weapons systems based upon American-designed weapons was reflected in the article by Miles A. Pomper, "Israel Won't Sell Radar to China: Cancellation of Phalcon Sale," *Congressional Quarterly Weekly* 58, no. 29 (July 2000): 1744.

75. See John Snetsinger, *Truman, the Jewish Vote, and the Creation of Israel* (Palo Alto, Calif.: Stanford University Press, 1974), and Evan Wilson, *Decision on Palestine: How the U.S. Came to Recognize Israel* (Stanford, Calif.: Hoover Institution Press, 1979).

76. Arnold Krammer, *The Forgotten Friendship: Israel and the Soviet Bloc, 1947–1953* (Urbana: University of Illinois Press, 1974); Yaacov Ro'i, *Soviet Decision-Making in Practice, the USSR and Israel, 1947–1954* (New Brunswick, N.J.: Transaction, 1980); Avigdor Dagan, *Moscow and Jerusalem: Twenty Years of Relations between Israel and the Soviet Union* (New York: Abelard-Shuman, 1970); R. Khan, "Israel and the Soviet Union: A Review of Postwar Relations," *Orbis* 9, no. 4 (1966): 999–1012.

77. Examples of research in this area would include Aryeh Levin, *Envoy to Moscow: Memoirs of an Israeli Ambassador, 1988–1992* (London: Frank Cass, 1996); Krammer, *The Forgotten Friendship*; Galia Golan, *Yom Kippur and After*; Dagan, *Moscow and Jerusalem*; E. Satanovskii, "Russia and Israel in the 21st Century," *International Affairs* (Moscow) 6 (1988): 13; or M. Confino and S. Shamir, eds., *The U.S.S.R. and the Middle East* (New York: Wiley, 1973).

78. Robert O. Freedman, "Israeli-Russian Relations since the Collapse of the Soviet Union," *Middle East Journal* 49 (Spring 1995): 233–47.

79. Among other sources, see Robert Drinan, *Honor the Promise: America's Commitment to Israel* (Garden City, N.J.: Doubleday, 1977). See John Mearsheimer and Stephen Walt, *The Israel Lobby and U.S. Foreign Policy* (New York: Farrar, Straus and Giroux, 2007).

80. A good collection is David W. Lesch, ed., *The Middle East and the United States: A Historical and Political Reassessment* (Boulder, Colo.: Westview, 1996). See also Yaacov Bar-Siman-Tov, "The United States and Israel Since 1948: A 'Special Relationship'?" *Diplomatic History* 22, no. 2 (1998): 231–63; Gabriel Sheffer, ed., *U.S.-Israeli Relations at the Crossroads* (Portland, Ore.: Frank Cass, 1997); Bernard Reich, *Securing the Covenant: United States-Israel Relations after the Cold War* (Westport, Conn.: Greenwood, 1995); and Samuel W. Lewis, "The United States and Israel: Evolution of an Unwritten Alliance," *Middle East Journal* 53, no. 3 (1999): 364–79.

81. Duncan Clarke, Daniel B. O'Connor, and Jason Ellis, *Send Guns and Money: Security Assistance and U.S. Foreign Policy* (Westport, Conn.: Praeger, 1997); Martin Feinrider, "America's Oil Pledges to Israel: Illegal but Binding Executive Agreements," *New York University Journal of International Law and Politics* 13, no. 3 (1981): 525–70; or Bishara Bahbah, "The United States and Israel's Energy Security," *Journal of Palestine Studies* 11, no. 2 (1982): 113–31.

82. See, for examples of the coverage that the bilateral Obama-Netanyahu relationship has received, the article in the *Times* (London) by Giles Whittell, "Binyamin Netanyahu humiliated after Barack Obama 'dumped him for dinner,'" (March 26, 2010), www.timesonline.co.uk/tol/news/world/us_and_americas/article7076431.ece,

accessed May 2010, or the article by Aluf Benn in *Ha'aretz* titled "How will Netanyahu respond to Obama's ultimatum?" www.haaretz.com/print-edition/opinion/how-will-netanyahu-respond-to-obama-s-ultimatum-1.284607, accessed May 2010. See also Bernard Reich, "The United States and Israel: The Nature of a Special Relationship," in Lesch, *The Middle East and the United States*; Peter J. Hahn, "Alignment by Coincidence: Israel, the United States, and the Partition of Jerusalem, 1949–1953," *Peace Research Abstracts* 39, no. 5 (2002): 611–755; or Robert Freedman, "Israel and the United States," in *Contemporary Israel: Domestic Politics, Foreign Policy, and Security Challenges*, ed. Robert Freedman (Boulder, Colo.: Westview, 2009).

83. Kenneth W. Stein, *Heroic Diplomacy: Sadat, Kissinger, Carter, Begin and the Quest for Arab-Israeli Peace* (New York: Routledge, 1999); or Gil C. Alroy, *The Kissinger Experience: American Policy in the Middle East* (New York: Horizon, 1975).

84. On George Mitchell, see the article published by Voice of America by Robert Berger, "US Envoy Launches New Mideast Peace Mission," (May 10, 2010), www1.voanews.com/english/news/usa/US-Envoy-Launches-New-Mideast-Peace-Mission-91835909.html, accessed May 2010. A good study of executive leadership in this relationship is Herbert Druks's *The Uncertain Friendship: The U.S. and Israel from Roosevelt to Kennedy* (Westport, Conn.: Greenwood, 2001). See also Michael T. Benson, *Harry S. Truman and the Founding of Israel* (Westport, Conn.: Praeger, 1997); and Abraham Ben-Zvi, *Decade of Transition: Eisenhower, Kennedy, and the Origins of the American-Israeli Alliance* (New York: Columbia University Press, 1998).

85. See Donna Cassata, "Disagreement among Friends Strains U.S.-Israeli Ties," *Congressional Quarterly Weekly Report* 56 (January 10, 1998): 85–86; see also George Gruen's essay "Israeli-United States Relations in the Post-Begin Era," in *Israel in the Post-Begin Era*, ed. Gregory Mahler (Albany: State University of New York Press, 1990). An example of a more specific study is James Ennes, *Assault on the Liberty: The True Story of the Israeli Attack on an American Intelligence Ship* (New York: Random House, 1979). Critical studies of the relation between American Jewish supporters of Israel and American political institutions include Ghassan Bishara, "Israel's Power in the U.S. Senate," *Journal of Palestine Studies* 10 (1980): 58–79.

86. Shlomo Slonim, *United States–Israel Relations, 1967–1973* (Jerusalem: Hebrew University Press, 1974). See also Moshe Arens, *Broken Covenant: American Foreign Policy and the Crisis between the U.S. and Israel* (New York: Simon & Schuster, 1995); Bernard Reich, "Israel and the United States: The Special Relationship Reexamined," in *Issues in Contemporary Israel: The Begin Era*, ed. Steven Heydemann (Boulder, Colo.: Westview, 1984), pp. 1–20.

87. A good overall analysis of Israel's first two decades can be found in Nadav Halevi and Ruth Klinow-Malul's *The Economic Development of Israel* (New York: Praeger, 1968). See also David Horowitz, *The Enigma of Economic Growth: A Case Study of Israel* (New York: Praeger, 1972).

88. Marion Mushkat, "The Socio-Economic Malaise of Developing Countries As a Function of Military Expenditures: The Case of Egypt and Israel," *Co-Existence* 15, no. 2 (1978): 135–45. See also Haim Levy and Azriel Levy, *The Management of Foreign Exchange Reserves with Balance-of-Payments and External Debt Considerations: The Case of Israel* (Jerusalem: Maurice Falk Institute for Economic Research in Israel, 1998); or Avi Ben-Basat, ed., *The Israeli Economy, 1985–1998: From Government Intervention to Market Economics* (Cambridge, Mass.: MIT Press, 2002).

89. See Israel Ministry of Foreign Affairs, "Economy: The National Economy," section "Balance of Payments," *Facts about Israel*, April 1, 2008, www.mfa.gov .il/MFA/Facts+About+Israel/Economy/ECONOMY-+Balance+of+Payments.htm, accessed May 2010. See the very good essay by Ofira Seliktar, "The Israeli Economy," in *Contemporary Israel: Domestic Politics, Foreign Policy, and Security Challenges*, ed. Robert Freedman (Boulder, Colo.: Westview, 2009).

90. Israel Ministry of Foreign Affairs, "Economy: The National Economy," section "Balance of Payments."

91. See Israel Ministry of Foreign Affairs, "Economy: Challenges and Achievements," section "Recent Achievements," *Facts about Israel*, April 1, 2008, www.mfa.gov .il/MFA/Facts+About+Israel/Economy/ECONOMY-+Challenges+and+Achievements .htm, accessed May 2010.

92. Israel Ministry of Foreign Affairs, "Economy: Challenges and Achievements," section "Recent Achievements." See also *Ha'aretz*, "Stocks Leap as OECD Admits Israel," May 12, 2010, www.haaretz.com/print-edition/business/stocks-leap-as-oecd -admits-israel-euro-bloc-unveils-rescue-1.289553, accessed May 2010.

93. See, for example, Janine Zacharia, "'No Movement' on Ridding UN Text of Anti-Israel Content," *Jerusalem Post* (August 2, 2001): 4, or Saul Singer, "Dissecting Durban," *Jerusalem Post* (September 7, 2001): 9A.

94. Brecher, *The Foreign Policy System*, p. 555.

10 THE PALESTINIANS, THE WEST BANK AND GAZA, AND JERUSALEM

1. An expanded discussion of this material can also be found in chapter 1. See Avi Shlaim, *The Politics of Partition: King Abdullah, the Zionists, and Palestine, 1921–1951* (New York: Oxford University Press, 1998). One of the best and most comprehensive reference works on this area is Mark Tessler's *A History of the Israeli-Palestinian Conflict* (Bloomington: Indiana University Press, 1994). See also the sixth edition of Charles D. Smith's classic work *Palestine and the Arab-Israeli Conflict* (Boston: Bedford/St. Martin's, 2007).

2. Don Peretz, *The West Bank: History, Politics, Society, and Economy* (Boulder, Colo.: Westview, 1986), p. 4. Much of what follows is based upon the substantially greater and more detailed analysis found in Peretz, *The West Bank*, pp. 13–42. See also Abd al-Azzia Ayyad, *Arab Nationalism and the Palestinians, 1850–1939* (Jerusalem: Palestinian Academic Society for the Study of International Affairs, 1999).

3. Peretz, *The West Bank*, p. 26. See David McDowall, *The Palestinians: The Road to Nationhood* (London: Minority Rights Publications, 1995). See also Itzhak Galnoor, *The Partition of Palestine: Decision Crossroads in the Zionist Movement* (Albany: State University of New York Press, 1995), and for a different perspective, Hillel Cohen, *Army of Shadows: Palestinian Collaboration with Zionism: 1917–1948* (Berkeley: University of California Press, 2008).

4. Peretz, *The West Bank*, p. 29. See the publication by the United Nations, Special Unit on Palestinian Rights, *The Origins and Evolution of the Palestine Problem* (New York: United Nations Press, 1967). See also Bernard Reich, *Arab-Israeli Conflict and Conciliation: A Documentary History* (Westport, Conn.: Greenwood, 1995); Phyl-

lis Bennis, "The United Nations and Palestine: Partition and Its Aftermath," *Arab Studies Quarterly* 19, no. 3 (1997): 47–77; and Sanford Silverburg, *Palestine and International Law: Essays on Politics and Economics* (Jefferson, N.C.: McFarland, 2002).

5. See Raphael Israeli, *Jerusalem Divided: The Armistice Regime, 1947–1967* (Portland, Ore.: Frank Cass, 2002); Bernard Wasserstein, *Divided Jerusalem: The Struggle for the Holy City* (New Haven, Conn.: Yale University Press, 2001); or Rashid Khalidi, "The Future of Arab Jerusalem," in *Arab Nation, Arab Nationalism*, ed. Derek Hopwood (New York: St. Martin's, 2000).

6. Jan Metzger, Martin Orth, and Christian Sterzing, *This Land Is Our Land* (London: Zed, 1983), p. 133. See also Shlaim, *The Politics of Partition*.

7. Peretz, *The West Bank*, p. 32.

8. Peretz, *The West Bank*, p. 36.

9. Peretz, *The West Bank*, p. 40.

10. See David Newman, "The Geopolitics of Peacemaking in Israel-Palestine," *Political Geography* 221, no. 5 (June 2002): 629–46; Gadi Taub, "Israel, Palestine, and Territorial Partition," *Dissent* 48, no. 3 (Summer 2001): 22–26.

11. Edward Said, *The Question of Palestine* (New York: Vintage, 1980), pp. xvi–xvii.

12. W. F. Abboushi, "The Road to Rebellion: Arab Palestine in the 1930s," *Journal of Palestine Studies* 6, no. 3 (1977): 23–46. See also Rashid Khalidi, "The Formation of Palestinian Identity: The Critical Years, 1917–1923," in *Rethinking Nationalism in the Arab Middle East*, ed. James Jankowski and I. Gershoni (New York: Columbia University Press, 1997); Benny Morris, *One State, Two States: Resolving the Israel/Palestine Conflict* (New Haven, Conn.: Yale University Press, 2009); and Helena Lindholm Schulz, *The Reconstruction of Palestinian Nationalism between Revolution and Statehood* (New York: St. Martin's, 1999).

13. See the historical analysis by William B. Quandt, "Political and Military Dimensions of Contemporary Palestinian Nationalism," in *The Politics of Palestinian Nationalism*, ed. William B. Quandt, Fuad Jabber, and Ann M. Lesch (Berkeley: University of California Press, 1973), esp. pp. 45–52, "The Eclipse of Palestinian Nationalism, 1947–1967."

14. Metzger, Orth, and Sterzing, *This Land*, p. 133. See also Adnan Abu Odeh, *Jordanians, Palestinians, and the Hashemite Kingdom in the Middle East Peace Process* (Washington, D.C.: United States Institute of Peace, 1999); and Frances Susan Hasso, *Resistance, Repression, and Gender Politics in Occupied Palestine and Jordan* (Syracuse, N.Y.: Syracuse University Press, 2005).

15. King Hussein—Hussein bin Talal al-Hashem, born in Amman on November 14, 1935—was born to Crown Prince Talal bin Abdullah and Princess Zein al-Sharaf bint Jamil. "Hussein was crowned May 2, 1953, at the age of 17, a year after his father, King Talal, had abdicated his throne because of mental illness. Talal had become king September 6, 1951, after King Abdullah had been assassinated at Al-Aqsa mosque in East Jerusalem while attending prayer services with Talal and Hussein." See "Jordan: Facts on King Hussein," *Facts on File*, accession number: 1999126160.

16. Metzger, Orth, and Sterzing, *This Land*, p. 134.

17. See "Jordan's King Hussein Dies; Abdullah Sworn In, Pledges to Continue Policies," *Facts on File*, February 7, 1999, accession number: 1999126140.

18. Saul Mishal, *West Bank East Bank: The Palestinians in Jordan, 1949–1967* (New Haven, Conn.: Yale University Press, 1976).

19. Metzger, Orth, and Sterzing, *This Land*, p. 135.

20. See Russell Stetler, ed., *Palestine: The Arab-Israeli Conflict* (San Francisco: Ramparts Press, 1972), especially part 3, "Black September," pp. 223–89. In September 1972 the Olympic Games in Munich were disrupted by terrorists kidnapping and killing eleven Israeli athletes. "Eight terrorists invaded the Olympic Village in Munich and took 11 Israeli sportsmen hostage, killing two outright. After hours of tense negotiations, a bungled German rescue effort ended with the remaining nine Israelis and five of the terrorists dead on the tarmac of the Munich airport." This, too, has become known as "Black September." See Tom Tugend, "One Day in September," *Jerusalem Post Magazine* (February 11, 2000): 26.

21. See Lamis Andoni, "King Abdallah in His Father's Footsteps?" *Journal of Palestine Studies* 29, no. 3 (2000): 77–90. See also Mutayyam Al O'ran, *Jordanian-Israeli Relations: The Peacebuilding Experience* (New York: Routledge, 2009).

22. Nina Gilbert, "Abdullah: We'll Continue the Peace," *Jerusalem Post* (February 12, 1999): 4.

23. King Abdullah II's rise to the throne was interesting. He was declared at birth in 1962 to be Hussein's successor and was given the title of crown prince. He remained the heir apparent until 1965, when King Hussein, after facing assassination attempts, oversaw a change in the Jordanian constitution that permitted him to name his brother, Hassan, as crown prince in Abdullah's place. However, in January 1999, after returning to Jordan from treatment for cancer in the United States, King Hussein "made public the severity of a rift that had developed with his younger brother" and announced a change in the constitution and declared that Abdullah would, in fact, succeed him to the crown. See "King Hussein of Jordan Names New Successor," *Facts on File*, January 19, 1999, accession number: 1999125580; and "Jordan: Facts on King Abdullah II," *Facts on File*, accession number: 1999126150.

24. Clinton Bailey, "Changing Attitudes toward Jordan in the West Bank," *Middle East Journal* 32, no. 2 (1978): 155–66. See also Al O'ran, *Jordanian-Israeli Relations*.

25. See Arthur Day, *East Bank/West Bank: Jordan and the Prospects for Peace* (New York: Council on Foreign Relations, 1986), especially chapter 6, "Jordan's Future and the Palestinian Question."

26. See, for example, "Jordan: Abdullah and Bush Discuss Trade Pact," *Facts on File*, April 10, 2001, accession number: 2001211420.

27. See Ben Lynfield, "Barak, Abdullah Expected to Work Well Together," *Jerusalem Post* (June 10, 1999): 2.

28. Said, *Question*, p. 46.

29. Said, *Question*, p. 51. See also Glenn E. Robinson, *Building a Palestinian State: The Incomplete Revolution* (Bloomington: Indiana University Press, 1997). See also Lamia Lahoud, "Palestinians: U.S. Endorsement Moving Us Closer to Statehood," *Jerusalem Post* (November 15, 2001): 2.

30. David Gilmour, *Dispossessed: The Ordeal of the Palestinians 1917–1980* (London: Sidgwick and Jackson, 1980). See also Yoav Gelber, *Palestine, 1948: War, Escape, and the Emergence of the Palestinian Refugee Problem* (Portland, Ore.: Sussex Academic Press, 2001); Alex Takkenberg, *The Status of Palestinian Refugees in International Law* (New York: Clarendon Press, 1998); and Michael Fischbach, "The United Nations and Palestinian Refugee Property Compensation," *Journal of Palestinian Studies* 31,

no. 2 (2002): 34–52. A study that generated much discussion was Avi Shlaim's *Israel and Palestine: Reappraisals, Revisions, Refutations* (Brooklyn, N.Y.: Verso, 2009).

31. Said, *Question*, pp. 47–48. See also Benjamin Schiff, *Refugees unto the Third Generation: U.N. Aid to Palestinians* (Syracuse, N.Y.: Syracuse University Press, 1995); Regina Sharif, "The United Nations and Palestinian Rights, 1974–1979," *Journal of Palestine Studies* 9, no. 1 (1979): 21–45; and W. Thomas Mallison and Sally V. Mallison, *The Palestine Problem in International Law and World Order* (London: Longman, 1986).

32. Peretz, *The West Bank*, pp. 89–90.

33. See "Middle East Peace Process: Palestinians Defer Declaration of Statehood," *Facts on File*, September 10, 2000, accession number: 2000186010: "The Palestine Liberation Organization (PLO) Central Council September 10 voted to defer making a unilateral declaration of statehood, to allow further attempts at reaching agreement in flagging Middle East peace talks. The Palestinians a year earlier had set a September 13 deadline for declaring statehood, coinciding with a September 13 deadline for reaching a final Israeli-Palestinian peace agreement. Peace negotiations had stalled, and the deadline passed without an accord." See also Lamia Lahoud, "PCC Backs Arafat on Declaration of State," *Jerusalem Post* (July 4, 2000): 1; and Michael Arnold, "Birth of a Nation," *Jerusalem Post* (September 8, 2000): 1B.

34. Rashid Hamid, "What Is the PLO?" *Journal of Palestine Studies* 4, no. 4 (1975): 90–109; and Naveed Ahmad, "The Palestine Liberation Organization," *Pakistan Horizon* 28, no. 4 (1975): 81–115. See also Joel Beinin and Rebecca Stein, *The Struggle for Sovereignty: Palestine and Israel, 1993–2005* (Stanford, Calif.: Stanford University Press, 2006).

35. See Helena Cobban, *The Palestinian Liberation Organization: People, Power, and Politics* (New York: Cambridge University Press, 1984), for a thorough study of the development of the movement, the internal relations of its many factions, and its external ties to the Arab powers, other nations, and international organizations, such as the United Nations. See also Avraham Sela and Moshe Ma'oz, eds., *The PLO and Israel: From Armed Conflict to Political Solution, 1964–1994* (New York: St. Martin's, 1997); and Charles D. Smith, *Palestine and the Arab-Israeli Conflict* (Boston: St. Martin's, 2001), especially the chapter "From Pariah to Partner: The PLO and the Quest for Peace in Global and Regional Contexts, 1984–1993."

36. Palestinian Academic Society for the Study of International Affairs, *PASSIA Diary, 2000* (Jerusalem: PASSIA, 2000), p. 281. See also Al O'ran, *Jordanian-Israeli Relations*.

37. Tessler, *History*, pp. 694–95.

38. See the C.I.A. World Factbook, "Gaza Strip," and "West Bank," https://www.cia.gov/library/publications/the-world-factbook/geos/gz.html, accessed May 2010. See also Mahmood Monshipouri, "The PLO Rivalry with Hamas: The Challenge of Peace, Democratization and Islamic Radicalism," *Middle East Policy* 4, no. 3 (March 1996): 95.

39. Cobban, *The Palestinian Liberation Organization*, pp. 267–70. A more critical examination of the covenant can be found in Yehoshafat Harkabi, *The Palestinian Covenant and Its Meaning* (London: Vallentine Mitchell, 1979).

40. See Gregory Mahler, *Constitutionalism and Palestinian Constitutional Development* (Jerusalem: Palestinian Academic Society for the Study of International Affairs, 1996).

41. William Korey, "The PLO's Conquest of the U.N.," *Midstream* 25, no. 9 (1979): 10–15, and Hazem Nusibeh, *Palestine and the United Nations* (New York: Quartet, 1982).

42. See, for example, A. Shiblak, "Palestinians in Lebanon and the PLO," *Journal of Refugee Studies* 10, no. 3 (1997): 261–88.

43. For a historical approach to this topic, see Fuad Jabber, "The Palestinian Resistance and Inter-Arab Politics," in *The Politics of Palestinian Nationalism*, ed. William B. Quandt, Fuad Jabber, and Ann M. Lesch (Berkeley: University of California Press, 1973), pp. 155–216. See also Aaron David Miller, *The Arab States and the Palestine Question: Between Ideology and Self-Interest* (New York: Praeger, 1986).

44. See Gregory Mahler, "The Palestinian Election of January, 1996," *Electoral Studies* 15, no. 3 (1996): 414–22. See also "Arafat Opens PNA Council," *Facts on File*, March 7, 1996, accession number: 1996063278.

45. "International Observers," *Jerusalem Times* (January 19, 1996): 7.

46. Center for Palestine Research and Studies, "Results of Public Opinion Poll #20" (Nablus: CPRS, October 1995), pp. 20–21.

47. Jerusalem Media and Communication Center, "Public Opinion Poll No. 11: On Palestinian Elections" (East Jerusalem: JMCC, December 1995), pp. 5, 13.

48. In the Oslo 2 Accords, the term *Ra'is* was used because the Israelis did not want to accord the newly elected Palestinian executive the legitimacy of the title of president, while the Palestinians wanted the legitimacy that would come with that title. The Arabic term *Ra'is* can be translated as either "chairman" or "president." The Israelis consistently use the former when referring to Mr. Arafat, and the Palestinians consistently use the latter.

49. Salwa Kanaana, "First Elections Called Success," *Palestine Report* 1, no. 35 (January 24, 1996): 1; "Will of the People Expressed," *Palestine Report* 1, no. 35 (January 24, 1996): 18.

50. "How Fair Was the Election?" *Palestine Report* 1, no. 37 (February 9, 1996): 6–7.

51. Stephanie Nolen, "Election No Step Forward for Women," *Palestine Report* 1, no. 36 (February 2, 1996): 6.

52. Ghassan Khatib, "The Value of the Vote," *Palestine Report* 1, no. 36 (February 2, 1996): 12–13. See Jonathan Schanzer, *Hamas vs. Fatah: The Struggle for Palestine* (New York: Palgrave Macmillan, 2008).

53. For results of the election, see Central Elections Commission, Palestine, "The Final Results of the Second PLC Elections," January 29, 2006, www.elections .ps/template.aspx?id=291, last accessed May 2010. See the map in the *New York Times* that explains voting and districts in this election. See "Palestinian Elections," January 26, 2006, www.nytimes.com/imagepages/2006/01/25/international/20060125 _palestinianELECTION_GRAPHIC.html.

54. See Scott Wilson, "Hamas Sweeps Palestinian Elections, Complicating Peace Efforts in Mideast" *Washington Post*, January 27, 2006, online edition, www .washingtonpost.com/wp-dyn/content/article/2006/01/26/AR2006012600372 .html, last accessed May 2010.

55. See Hillel Frisch, *Countdown to Statehood: Palestinian State Formation in the West Bank and Gaza* (Albany: State University of New York Press, 1998); and Yazid

Sayigh, *Armed Struggle and the Search for State: The Palestinian National Movement, 1949–1993* (New York: Oxford University Press, 1997).

56. For examples of this body of literature, see Issa Al-Shuaibi, "The Development of a Palestinian Entity-Consciousness, Part I," *Journal of Palestine Studies* 9, no. 1 (1979): 67–84; "Part II," 9, no. 2 (1980): 50–70; and "Part III," 9, no. 3 (1980): 99–124. See also Schanzer, *Hamas vs. Fatah*.

57. Metzger, Orth, Sterling, *This Land*, p. 244.

58. Emile Sahliyeh, *The Lebanon War: Implications for the PLO* (Boulder, Colo.: Westview, 1985).

59. See "Other Persian Gulf News: Area States End Jordan, PLO Aid," *Facts on File*, October 30, 1991, accession number: 1991046130.

60. On Friday, December 14, 2001, the cabinet officially voted to declare Yasser Arafat "irrelevant" and indicated that "it will no longer have anything to do with him." See Herb Keinon, "Cabinet Declares Arafat 'Irrelevant.' IAF Strikes Palestinian Targets in West Bank and Gaza Strip," *Jerusalem Post* (December 14, 2001): 1A.

61. Michael Akehurst, "The Place of the Palestinians in an Arab-Israeli Peace Settlement," *Round Table* (October 1980): 443–50.

62. See, among other sources, the following: Akram Hanieh, "The Camp David Papers," *Journal of Palestine Studies* 30, no. 2 (2001): 75–98; *The Camp David Accords and Related Documents* (Beer-Sheva, Israel: Chaim Herzog Center for Middle East Studies and Diplomacy, 1998); Shibley Telhami, "From Camp David to Wye: Changing Assumptions in Arab-Israeli Negotiations," *Middle East Journal* 53, no. 3 (1999): 379–93; and Kristen Schulze, "Camp David and the Al-Aqsa Intifada: An Assessment of the State of the Israeli-Palestinian Peace Process," *Studies in Conflict and Terrorism* 24, no. 3 (2001): 215–33.

63. See the chronological guide to agreements assembled by the Ministry of Foreign Affairs on their Web page, "The Peace Process: Reference Documents," www .mfa.gov.il/mfa/go.asp?MFAH00pq0, accessed October 2003.

64. Arie Bregman, *The Economy of the Administered Areas, 1968–1973* (Jerusalem: Bank of Israel, 1975).

65. *Facts about Israel* (Jerusalem: Ministry of Foreign Affairs, 1985), pp. 44–45.

66. See Avram Bornstein, *Crossing the Green Line between the West Bank and Israel* (Philadelphia: University of Pennsylvania Press, 2002).

67. See essays by Sasson Levi, "Local Government in the Administered Territories," and by Avraham Lavine, "Social Services in the Administered Territories," in *Judea, Samaria, and Gaza: Views on the Present and Future*, ed. Daniel J. Elazar (Washington, D.C.: American Enterprise Institute for Public Policy Research, 1982); Faisal Azaiza and Jenny Brodsky, "Changes in the Arab World and Development of Services for the Arab Elderly in Israel during the Last Decade," *Journal of Gerontological Social Work* 27, nos. 1–2 (1996): 37–55; and R. Savaya, "Political Attitudes, Economic Distress, and the Utilization of Welfare Services by Arab Women in Israel," *Journal of Applied Social Sciences* 21, no. 2 (1997): 111–19.

68. *Facts about Israel* (1985), p. 45. See Ilan Gur-Ze'ev, *Conflicting Philosophies of Education in Israel/Palestine* (Boston: Kluwer Academic, 2000).

69. See, for example, Margot Dudkevitch and Mohammed Najib, "Israel Denies Keeping Gazans from W. Bank Universities," *Jerusalem Post* (September 3, 1998):

2; see also "Foreign Protesters Clash with Troops," *Jerusalem Post* (December 30, 2001): 3.

70. See Sela and Ma'oz, *The PLO and Israel*.

71. Eetta Prince Gibson, "The Fiber of Our Society Is Being Destroyed," *Jerusalem Post Magazine* (September 14, 2001): 18. See Nasser Abufarha, *The Making of a Human Bomb: The Ethnography of Palestinian Resistance* (Durham, N.C.: Duke University Press, 2009).

72. Gibson, "The Fiber of Our Society," p. 18.

73. Ephraim Sneh, as quoted in Gary Wolf, ed., *Israel Press Highlights* (New York: Institute of Human Relations, American Jewish Committee, December 12, 1988), pp. 1–2.

74. See Reuven Kaminer, *The Politics of Protest: The Israeli Peace Movement and the Palestinian Intifada* (Portland, Ore.: Sussex Academic Press, 1996). See also Ruth Linn, "Where Have All the Critics Gone? Moral Psychology and the Question of Selective Resistance to War: From Vietnam to an Israeli Vietnam to the Intifada," *Journal of Psychology and Judaism* 23, no. 3 (1999): 125–40, and "When the Individual Soldier Says 'No' to War: A Look at Selective Refusal During the Intifada," *Journal of Peace Research* 33, no. 4 (1996): 421–33; Yechezkel Dar et al., "The Imprint of the Intifada: Response of Kibbutz-Born Soldiers to Military Service in the West Bank and Gaza," *Armed Forces and Society* 26, no. 2 (2000): 285–313. See also Lev Luis Grinberg, *Politics and Violence in Israel/Palestine: Democracy versus Military Rule* (New York: Routledge, 2010).

75. J. Hiss and T. Kahana, "Suicide Bombers in Israel," *American Journal of Forensic Medicine and Pathology* 19, no. 1 (1998): 63–68; Fiamma Nirenstein, "How Suicide Bombers Are Made," *Commentary* 112, no. 2 (2001): 53–56. See also Moises F. Salinas, *Planting Hatred, Sowing Pain: The Psychology of the Israeli-Palestinian Conflict* (Westport, Conn.: Praeger, 2007).

76. See Ifat Maoz, "The Violent Asymmetrical Encounter with the Other in an Army-Civilian Clash: The Case of the Intifada," *Peace and Conflict* 7, no. 3 (2001): 243–63; Amnesty International, *Israel and the Occupied Territories: Excessive Use of Lethal Force* (London: Amnesty International, 2000), and *Israel and the Occupied Territories: Mass Arrests and Police Brutality* (London: Amnesty International, 2000); and Yuval Ginbar and Zvi Shulman, *Demolishing Peace: Israel's Policy of Mass Demolition of Palestinian Houses in the West Bank* (Jerusalem: B'Tselem, 1997).

77. See "Officials: Hamas and Fatah Agree to Ceasefire," *CNN World Online*, December 16, 2006, www.cnn.com/2006/WORLD/meast/12/17/mideast.gaza/index.html, accessed May 2010.

78. One of the best studies of Israeli policy and the nature of Arab life in Israel is Ian Lustick's *Arabs in the Jewish State* (Austin: University of Texas Press, 1980). See also Marwan Bishara, *Palestine/Israel: Peace or Apartheid—Prospects for Resolving the Conflict* (New York: Zed, 2001); Alexander Bligh, "The Intifada and the New Political Role of the Israeli Arab Leadership," *Middle Eastern Studies* 35, no. 1 (1999): 134–65; Edgar O'Ballance, *The Palestinian Intifada* (New York: St. Martin's, 1998); Roane Carey, ed., *The New Intifada: Resisting Israel's Apartheid* (New York: Verso, 2001); and Penny Johnson and Eileen Kuttab, "Where Have All the Women (and Men) Gone? Reflections on Gender and the Second Palestinian Intifada," *Feminist Review* 69, no. 1 (2001): 21–43.

79. One of the most frequently cited sources in this area is the report of the National Lawyers Guild 1977 Middle East Delegation, *Treatment of Palestinians in Israeli-Occupied West Bank and Gaza* (New York: National Lawyers Guild, 1978).

80. See, for instance, Michael Adams, "Israel's Treatment of the Arabs in the Occupied Territories," *Journal of Palestine Studies* 6, no. 2 (1977): 19–40.

81. See Sabri Jiryis, "The Legal Structure for the Expropriation and Absorption of Arab Lands in Israel," *Journal of Palestine Studies* 2, no. 4 (1973): 82–104. See the article "U.S. Scores New Settlements," *Facts on File*, April 29, 1999, accession number: 1999134650: "The U.S. April 14 stepped up its criticism of the Netanyahu government's construction of Jewish settlements. The Israeli daily newspaper Haaretz that day reported that U.S. satellite photographs had disclosed the establishment of 18 new settlements on West Bank hilltops. Twelve of the new settlements had been set up since Netanyahu and Arafat had signed the Wye River accord, adopted under the Oslo peace framework, in October 1998. Under the Oslo accords, Israel and the Palestinians had both promised to desist from unilateral actions that could prejudice final-status peace arrangements."

82. Ann Lesch, "Israeli Deportation of Palestinians from the West Bank and the Gaza Strip, 1967–1978," *Journal of Palestine Studies* 8, no. 3 (1979): 81–107. See also "Middle East: Israel Probes Palestinian Civilian Deaths; Other Developments," *Facts on File*, September 1, 2002, accession number: 2002260190; see especially the section "Militants' Families Expelled." This theme is further developed in Saree Makdisi, *Palestine Inside Out: An Everyday Occupation* (New York: W.W. Norton, 2008).

83. "Document: Amnesty International, Administrative Detention in Israeli Occupied Territories," *Middle East Journal* 32, no. 3 (1978): 337–40. See also "Israeli Troops in the Raids Confiscated Hundreds of Arms and Destroyed an Unknown Number of Palestinian Homes and Shops," *Facts on File*, March 7, 2002, accession number: 2002244240.

84. See, for example, the full text of the UN Security Council Resolution on Israeli Actions in the Occupied Territories passed December 29, 1987, by a vote of fourteen in favor, none against, with the United States abstaining, published in *American-Arab Affairs* 23 (1987–1988): 145–47. See also Esther Cohen, *Human Rights in the Israeli-Occupied Territories, 1967–1982* (Manchester, U.K.: Manchester University Press, 1986); Lisa Hajjar, "Human Rights in Israel/Palestine: The History and Politics of a Movement," *Journal of Palestine Studies* 30, no. 4 (2001): 21–38; Ruchama Marton, "A View from Within: Problems Confronting Human Rights Organizations in Israel and the Occupied Territories," *Arab Studies Quarterly* 22, no. 1 (2000): 39–51; and the text of the U.S. Department of State, "Country Reports on Human Rights Practices for 1992: Israel and the Occupied Territories," *Journal of Palestine Studies* 23 (Fall 1993): 125.

85. See Rephael Vardi, "The Administered Territories and the Internal Security of Israel," in *Judea, Samaria, and Gaza: Views on the Present and Future*, ed. Daniel J. Elazar (Washington, D.C.: American Enterprise Institute for Public Policy Research, 1982), pp. 171–90. A very good perspective is offered by Yaacov Bar-Siman-Tov, *Israel and the Intifada: Adaptation and Learning* (Jerusalem: Hebrew University of Jerusalem, 2000).

86. Teddy Kollek, "Introduction: Jerusalem—Today and Tomorrow," in *Jerusalem: Problems and Prospects*, ed. Joel Kraemer (New York: Praeger, 1980), p. l.

87. Saul B. Cohen, *Jerusalem: Bridging the Four Walls; A Geopolitical Perspective* (New York: Herzl, 1977), p. 11.

88. Cohen, *Jerusalem*, p. 11.

89. Colin Williams, *Jerusalem: A Universal Cultural and Historical Resource* (Palo Alto, Calif.: Aspen Program on Communications & Society, 1975), as cited in Cohen, *Jerusalem*, p. 23. See also Ira Sharkansky, "Religion and Politics in Israel and Jerusalem," *Judaism* 44, no. 3 (1995): 328–41; Karen Armstrong, *Jerusalem: One City, Three Faiths* (New York: Ballantine, 1997); or Marshall Breger and Thomas Idinopulos, *Jerusalem's Holy Places and the Peace Process* (Washington, D.C.: Washington Institute for Near East Policy, 1998).

90. See Joel Kraemer, "The Jerusalem Question," in *Jerusalem: Problems and Prospects*, ed. Joel Kraemer (New York: Praeger, 1980), esp. pp. 24–35; see also Bernard Wasserstein, *Divided Jerusalem.*

91. Cohen, *Jerusalem*, p. 12. See also Mosheh Amirav, *Jerusalem Syndrome: The Palestinian-Israeli Battle for the Holy City* (Portland, Ore.: Sussex Academic Press, 2009).

92. Kollek, "Introduction," p. 1.

93. See the discussion of this in Alisa Ginio, "Plans for the Solution of the Jerusalem Problem," in *Jerusalem: Problems and Prospects*, ed. Joel Kraemer (New York: Praeger, 1980), pp. 41–71.

94. Peretz, *The West Bank*, p. 45. See Ian Lustick, "Has Israel Annexed East Jerusalem?" *Middle East Policy* 5, no. 1 (1997): 34–44.

95. Uzi Benziman, "Israeli Policy in East Jerusalem after Reunification," in Kraemer, *Jerusalem*, p. 101. Benziman discusses a wide range of actions by the Israeli government in response to the needs of the Arab population in the annexed area, in such policy areas as education, culture, language, the press, consulates, the United Nations, tax law, the economic system, and religious autonomy.

96. Cohen, *Jerusalem*, p. 33; the five geopolitical imperatives that follow are derived from more detailed discussion by Cohen, *Jerusalem*, pp. 33–34. See also Ira Sharkansky, *Governing Jerusalem: Again on the World's Agenda* (Detroit, Mich.: Wayne State University Press, 1996).

97. A full discussion of the kinds of issues that surface in this context can be found in the essay by Emanuel Gutmann and Claude Klein, "The Institutional Structure of Heterogeneous Cities: Brussels, Montreal, and Belfast," in *Jerusalem: Problems and Prospects*, ed. Joel Kraemer (New York: Praeger, 1980), pp. 178–207. At the end of their comparative essay, they discuss the lessons that the political leadership of Jerusalem can learn from the experiences of these three cities. See also Meron Benvenisti, *City of Stone: The Hidden History of Jerusalem* (Berkeley: University of California Press, 1996); and Ruth Kark and Michal Oren-Nordheim, *Jerusalem and Its Environs: Quarters, Neighborhoods, Villages, 1800–1948* (Jerusalem: Hebrew University Press, 2001).

98. A good essay addressing many of these questions is Daniel Elazar's "Local Government for Heterogeneous Populations: Some Options for Jerusalem," in *Jerusalem: Problems and Prospects*, ed. Joel Kraemer (New York: Praeger, 1980), pp. 208–28.

99. For examples of this kind of study and criticism, see Abdul-Illah Abu-Ayyash, "Israeli Regional Planning Policy in the Occupied Arab Territories," *Journal of Palestine Studies* 5 (1976): 83–108; Abdul-Illah Abu-Ayyash, "Israeli Planning Policy in the Occupied Arab Territories," *Journal of Palestine Studies* 11, no. 1 (1981):

111–23; and Bakir Abu-Kishk, "Arab Land and Israeli Policy," *Journal of Palestine Studies* 11, no. 1 (1981): 124–35.

100. See, for example, Avner Yaniv and Fabian Pascal, "Doves, Hawks, and Other Birds of a Feather: The Distribution of Israel Parliamentary Opinion on the Future of the Occupied Territories, 1967–1977," *British Journal of Political Science* 10, no. 3 (1980): 260–66.

101. The problem with this position is that many years before his death King Hussein announced that he was giving up any claim to the Occupied Territories and supporting the PLO. See "Jordan's West Bank Move Upsetting Daily Life," *New York Times* (October 18, 1988): 1.

102. Peretz, *The West Bank*, pp. 50–51. A lengthy discussion of the bureaucratic processes governing these settlements, how they are established, plans for future settlements, and domestic Israeli opposition to these settlements can be found in Peretz's chapter 5, "Jewish Settlement in the West Bank," pp. 59–77. See also Alwyn Rouyer, *Turning Water into Politics: The Water Issue in the Palestinian-Israeli Conflict* (New York: St. Martin's, 2000).

103. Yehuda Lukacs, *Israel, Jordan, and the Peace Process* (Syracuse, N.Y.: Syracuse University Press, 1997).

104. See Ian Lustick, "Israel and the West Bank after Elon Moreh: The Mechanics of De Facto Annexation," *Middle East Journal* 35, no. 4 (1981): 557–77.

105. See Efraim Ben-Zadok, "The Limits to the Politics of Planning," in *The Impact of Gush Emunim: Politics and Settlement in the West Bank*, ed. David Newman (New York: St. Martin's Press, 1985), p. 141.

106. Cohen, *Jerusalem*, pp. 109–70.

107. Ben-Zadok, "Limits," p. 150.

108. For examples of this kind of criticism, see Abu-Ayyash, "Israeli Regional Planning Policy"; Salah El-Din Amer, "The Problem of Settlements in Occupied Territories," *Revue Egyptienne de Droit Internationale* 35 (1979): 11–44; and Ann Lesch, "Israeli Settlements in the Occupied Territories," *Journal of Palestine Studies* 8, no. 1 (1978): 100–20.

109. Moshe Drori, "The Israeli Settlements in Judea and Samaria: Legal Aspects," in *Judea, Samaria, and Gaza: Views on the Present and Future*, ed. Daniel J. Elazar (Washington, D.C.: American Enterprise Institute for Public Policy Research, 1982), pp. 44–80.

110. Peretz, *The West Bank*, p. 46.

111. Peretz, *The West Bank*, p. 47.

112. Meron Benvenisti, with Ziad Abu-Zayad and Danny Rubenstein, *The West Bank Data Base Project 1986: Demographic, Economic, Legal, Social, and Political Developments in the West Bank* (Boulder, Colo.: Westview, 1986), p. 46.

113. Foundation for Middle East Peace, "Settlements in the West Bank," www.fmep .org/settlement_info/settlement-info-and-tables/stats-data/settlements-in-the-west-bank-1/?searchterm=None, accessed May 2010. It should be noted that these data come from the Israeli Central Bureau of Statistics. See also Sean McMahon, *The Discourse of Palestinian-Israeli Relations: Persistent Analytics and Practices* (New York: Routledge, 2010).

114. UN Security Council, Resolution 465 (1980), at unispal.un.org/UNISPAL.N SF/0/5AA254A1C8F8B1CB852560E50075D7D5, accessed March 2010.

115. UN Security Council, Resolution 465 (1980).

116. For an example of this kind of statement, see the story in *Ha'aretz* by Barak Ravid, "Netanyahu Extends Benefits to Isolated West Bank Settlements," *Ha'aretz* online, December 9, 2009, www.haaretz.com/news/netanyahu-extends-benefits-to-isolated-west-bank-settlements-1.2471, accessed May 2010.

117. See Israel Ministry of Foreign Affairs, "Israeli Settlements and International Law, May 2001," May 20, 2001, www.mfa.gov.il/mfa/go.asp?MFAH0jyz0, accessed May 2010.

118. See Avner Yaniv and Yael Yishai, "Israeli Settlements in the West Bank: The Politics of Intransigence," *Journal of Politics* 43, no. 4 (1981): 1105–28; William Harris, *Taking Root: Israeli Settlement in the West Bank, the Golan, and Gaza-Sinai, 1967–1980* (New York: Research Studies Press, 1980); Gershon Baskin and Zakaria Qaq, *The Future of the Israeli Settlements in Final Status Negotiations* (Jerusalem: Israel/Palestine Center for Research and Information, 1997); Yehezkel Lein, *Builders of Zion: Human Rights Violations of Palestinians from the Occupied Territories Working in Israel and the Settlements* (Jerusalem: B'Tselem, 1999); Yuval Ginbar, Yael Stein, and Zvi Shulman, *Israeli Settlement in the Occupied Territories as a Violation of Human Rights: Legal and Conceptual Aspects* (Jerusalem: B'Tselem, 1997); and Ann Lesch, "Israeli Settlements."

119. Author's interview with Menachem Begin, May 30, 1980, in the Knesset, in Jerusalem.

120. For discussion of this philosophy and its empirical validity, see Benvenisti, *The West Bank*. See also Seth Tillman, "The West Bank Hearings: Israel's Colonization of Occupied Territory," *Journal of Palestine Studies* 7 (1978): 71–87.

121. David Weisburd and Elin Waring, "Settlement Motivations in the Gush Emunim Movement: Comparing Bonds of Altruism and Self Interest," in *The Impact of Gush Emunim: Politics and Settlement in the West Bank,* ed. David Newman (New York: St. Martin's Press, 1985), pp. 183–99.

122. One recent fascinating study of this phenomenon is Ian Lustick's *For the Land and the Lord: Jewish Fundamentalism in Israel* (New York: Council on Foreign Relations, 1988). The book is a study of Jewish fundamentalism, tracing its evolution and impact, focusing upon *Gush Emunim,* contemporary Israeli policy, and the issue of settlements in the Occupied Territories.

123. See Yosseph Shilhav's essay "Interpretation and Misinterpretation of Jewish Territorialism," in *The Impact of Gush Emunim: Politics and Settlement in the West Bank,* ed. David Newman (New York: St. Martin's Press, 1985), pp. 111–24.

124. Gershon Shafir, "Institutional and Spontaneous Settlement Drives: Did Gush Emunim Make a Difference?" in *The Impact of Gush Emunim: Politics and Settlement in the West Bank,* ed. David Newman (New York: St. Martin's Press, 1985), p. 153.

125. See Shlomo Swirski, Etty Konor-Attias, and Alon Etkin, *Government Funding of the Israeli Settlements in the West Bank, Gaza Strip and Golan Heights in the 1990s* (Tel Aviv: Adva Center, 2002).

126. Benvenisti, *The West Bank,* pp. 46–47, 53.

127. One of the best discussions of this is to be found in Abraham Becker, *Israel and the Palestinian Occupied Territories: Military-Political Issues in the Debate.* (Santa Monica, Calif.: Rand, 1971). See also David Kretzmer, *The Occupation of Justice: The Supreme Court of Israel and the Occupied Territories* (Albany: State University of New York Press, 2002); Raja Shehadeh, *From Occupation to Interim Accords: Israel and the Palestinian Territories* (Boston: Kluwer Law International, 1997).

128. A discussion of the mechanics of the military government administration can be found in Peretz, *The West Bank*, pp. 79–87.

11 THE PEACE PROCESS

1. See the Israel Ministry of Foreign Affairs, "The State of Israel," *Facts about Israel*, online edition, www.mfa.gov.il/MFA/Facts%20About%20Israel/History/HISTORY-%20The%20State%20of%20Israel, accessed May 2010.

2. Ilan Peleg, ed., *The Middle East Peace Process: Interdisciplinary Perspectives* (Albany: State University of New York Press, 1998); Jerry W. Wright, ed., *Structural Flaws in the Middle East Peace Process: Historical Contexts* (New York: Palgrave, 2002); Avi Shlaim, *War and Peace in the Middle East: A Concise History* (New York: Penguin, 1995).

3. See Reuven Hazan, "Intraparty Politics and Peacemaking in Democratic Societies: Israel's Labor Party and the Middle East Peace Process, 1992–1996," *Peace Research Abstracts* 38, no. 4 (2001): 451–600; Robert O. Freedman, "New Challenges to the Middle East Peace Process," *Midstream* 42, no. 7 (1996): 2; Efraim Karsh, "Peace, Despite Everything," in *Israel's Troubled Agenda*, ed. Efraim Karsh (Portland, Ore.: Frank Cass, 1997).

4. Jerome Segal, "Peace Process, R.I.P. Clearing Up the Right-of-Return Confusion," *Middle East Policy* 8, no. 2 (2001): 23–32.

5. Marshall J. Berger and Ora Ahimeir, eds., *Jerusalem: A City and Its Future* (Syracuse, N.Y.: Syracuse University Press, 2002).

6. D. Bar-Tal and Y. Y. I. Vertzberger, "Between Hope and Fear: A Dialogue on the Peace Process in the Middle East and the Polarized Israeli Society," *Political Psychology* 18, no. 3 (1997): 667–81; Stuart Cohen, "The Peace Process and Societal-Military Relations in Israel," in *The Middle East Peace Process: Interdisciplinary Perspectives*, ed. Ilan Peleg (Albany: State University of New York Press, 1998).

7. Zeev Maoz, *Regional Security in the Middle East: Past, Present, and Future* (Portland, Ore.: Frank Cass, 1997).

8. William B. Quandt, *Peace Process: American Diplomacy and the Arab-Israeli Conflict Since 1967* (Washington, D.C.: Brookings Institution Press, 2001); Center for Policy Analysis on Palestine, *Honest Broker? U.S. Policy and the Middle East Peace Process* (Washington, D.C.: Center for Policy Analysis on Palestine, 1997). See also Aaron David Miller, *The Much Too Promised Land: America's Elusive Search for Arab-Israeli Peace* (New York: Bantam, 2008).

9. See "The Armistice Agreements," in Israel Ministry of Foreign Affairs, "Israel-Egyptian Armistice Agreement," February 24, 1949, www.mfa.gov.il/MFA/Foreign+Relations/Israels+Foreign+Relations+since+1947/1947-1974/Israel-Egypt+Armistice+Agreement.htm, accessed May 2010. See Number 4, "Israel-Egypt Armistice Agreement, 24 February 1949"; Number 5, "Israel-Lebanon Armistice Agreement, 23 March 1949"; Number 6, "Israel-Jordan Armistice Agreement, 3 April 1949"; and Number 7, "Israel-Syria Armistice Agreement, 20 July 1949."

10. Mark Tessler, *A History of the Israeli-Palestinian Conflict* (Bloomington: Indiana University Press, 1994), p. 273.

11. See Israel Ministry of Foreign Affairs, "History: The State of Israel," *Facts about Israel*, online edition, www.mfa.gov.il/MFA/Facts+About+Israel/History/HISTORY -+The+State+of+Israel.htm, accessed May 2010.

12. See Israel Ministry of Foreign Affairs, "History: State of Israel."

13. The full text of UN Resolution 242 can be found on the Ministry of Foreign Affairs Web page: "UN Security Council Resolution 242," www.mfa.gov.il/MFA/ Peace+Process/Guide+to+the+Peace+Process/UN+Security+Council+Resolution+24 2.htm, accessed May 2010.

14. The text of the Khartoum Resolution can be found on the Ministry of Foreign Affairs Web page: "The Khartoum Resolutions," www.mfa.gov.il/MFA/ Peace+Process/Guide+to+the+Peace+Process/The+Khartoum+Resolutions.htm, accessed May 2010.

15. The full text of UN Resolution 338 can be found on the Israel Ministry of Foreign Affairs Web page: "UN Security Council Resolution 338," www.mfa.gov.il/ MFA/Peace+Process/Guide+to+the+Peace+Process/UN+Security+Council+Resoluti on+338.htm, accessed May 2010.

16. There has been much discussion over what caused Sadat to undertake this momentous journey. One interesting account is to be found in Uri Dan and Sidney Zion, "Untold Story of Mideast Talks," *New York Times Magazine* (January 21, 1979): 20–22, and (January 28, 1979): 32–38, 42–43.

17. C. Paul Bradley, *The Camp David Peace Process: A Study of Carter Administration Policies (1977–1980)* (Grantham, N.H.: Thompson and Rutter, 1981), p. 19.

18. Analyses of the long-term peace process can be found in, inter alia, Melvin Friedlander, *Sadat and Begin: The Domestic Politics of Peacemaking* (Boulder, Colo.: Westview, 1983); and Lester Sobel, ed., *Peace-Making in the Middle East* (New York: Facts on File, 1980).

19. Bradley, *The Camp David Peace Process*, pp. 4–17. See Jimmy Carter's *Palestine Peace Not Apartheid* (New York: Simon and Schuster, 2006).

20. For some interesting perspectives on the personal dynamics of this period, see Ezer Weizman, *The Battle for Peace* (New York: Bantam, 1981), especially chapter 25, "Of Squirrels and Presidents"; Moshe Dayan, *Breakthrough: A Personal Account of the Egypt-Israel Peace Negotiations* (New York: Knopf, 1981), pp. 152–59; and William Quandt, *Camp David: Peacemaking and Politics* (Washington, D.C.: Brookings Institution, 1986), pp. 168–259.

21. For the text of the agreements, see "A Framework for Peace in the Middle East Agreed at Camp David," and "Framework for the Conclusion of a Peace Treaty between Egypt and Israel," *Middle East Journal* 32, no. 4 (1978): 471–94. The text is available online on the Israel Ministry of Foreign Affairs Web page, "Camp David Accords," September 17, 1978, www.mfa.gov.il/MFA/Peace+Process/ Guide+to+the+Peace+Process/Camp+David+Accords.htm, accessed May 2010.

22. This was an important issue, since in 1967 President Nasser had unilaterally told the UN Peacekeeping Forces in the Sinai to leave their positions, and they were obligated to obey, thus precipitating the start of the fighting in 1967. See "Egypt-Israel: Protocol Establishing the Sinai Multinational Forces and Observers," *International Legal Materials* 20, no. 5 (1981): 1190–97.

23. An example of reaction can be found in "Egyptian-Israeli Treaty: An Appraisal," *Pakistan Horizon* 32, no. 3 (1979), pp. 15–29.

24. See Israel Ministry of Foreign Relations, "Israel among the Nations: Middle East and North Africa," section "Egypt," *Facts about Israel,* www.mfa.gov.il/MFA/Facts+About+Israel/Among+the+Nations/ISRAEL+AMONG+THE+NATIONS-+Middle+East+-+North+Afri.htm, accessed May 2010.

25. Typical of this literature is the contribution of Fayez Sayegh, "The Camp David Agreement and the Palestine Problem," *Journal of Palestine Studies* 8, no. 2 (1979): 3–54.

26. For a detailed chronology of the progress made in the period between Camp David and the eventual signing of the treaties, see Clete Hinton, *Camp David Accords* (Los Alamitos, Calif.: Hwong, 1980). The full text of the Israeli-Egyptian peace treaty can be found on the Israel Ministry of Foreign Affairs Web page: "Israel-Egypt Peace Treaty," March 26, 1979, www.mfa.gov.il/MFA/Peace+Process/Guide+to+the+Peace+Process/Israel-Egypt+Peace+Treaty.htm, accessed May 2010.

27. An analysis of stages of the return of Sinai to Egypt appeared in "Sinai Returns to Egypt," *New York Times* (April 26, 1982): 1.

28. "Conflict Resolved," *New York Times* (September 30, 1988): 1.

29. See "Sadat of Egypt Is Assassinated at Military Parade," *Facts on File,* October 6, 1971, accession number: 1981033590.

30. See Israel Ministry of Foreign Affairs, "History: The State of Israel."

31. See the America.gov Web page supported by the U.S. Department of State: "Middle East Peace Chronology," www.america.gov/st/peacesec-english/2007/December/20071221154042IHecuoR5.682009e-02.html, accessed May 2010. Much of the chronology that follows in this chapter is based upon the chronology found here.

32. See "Palestinians Slain in Lebanese Refugee Camps; Storm over Israeli Role; Israel Bars Inquiry," *Facts on File,* September 16, 1982, accession number: 1982031430; later in the process more information emerged as shown in the article "Massacre Inquiry Warns Top Israeli Leaders," *Facts on File,* November 24, 1982, accession number: 1982039880.

33. The charges against Sharon were that he permitted a Christian militia to enter two Palestinian refugee camps in Beirut and that he must have known that the Christians would kill the Muslim refugees. Hundreds of Palestinians were killed in the event.

34. See America.gov, "Middle East Peace Chronology." The full text of the Israeli Peace Initiative can be found on the Israel Ministry of Foreign Affairs Web page: "Israel's Peace Initiative, May 14, 1989," www.mfa.gov.il/MFA/Peace+Process/Guide+to+the+Peace+Process/Israel-s+Peace+Initiative+-+May+14-+1989.htm, accessed May 2010.

35. See "Middle East: Egypt Approves Baker Plan on Talks; Other Developments," *Facts on File,* December 6, 1989, accession number: 1989036930.

36. "Israel: Cabinet Crisis Ends," *Facts on File,* January 2, 1990, accession number: 1990041521.

37. "Shamir Loses Confidence Vote, Israeli Government Falls," *Facts on File,* March 16, 1990, accession number: 1990042205.

38. See America.gov, "Middle East Peace Chronology."

39. The full text of the invitation to the Madrid Peace Conference can be found on the Israel Ministry of Foreign Affairs Web page: "Invitation to Ma-

drid Peace Conference, October 30, 1991," www.mfa.gov.il/MFA/Peace+Process/ Guide+to+the+Peace+Process/Madrid+Letter+of+Invitation.htm, accessed May 2010.

40. See America.gov, "Middle East Peace Chronology."

41. See the Israel Ministry of Foreign Affairs Web page, "The Madrid Framework: Guide to the Mideast Peace Process," www.mfa.gov.il/mfa/go.asp?MFAH00ig0, accessed May 2010. All of the opening and closing speeches from the conference itself can be found at Israel Ministry of Foreign Affairs, "The Madrid Conference Speeches, October–November 1991," www.mfa.gov.il/mfa/go.asp?MFAH0dg10, accessed May 2010.

42. Detailed notes on each of the working groups and the progress they have made to date can be found on the Israel Ministry of Foreign Affairs Web page, "The Multilateral Negotiations," www.mfa.gov.il/mfa/go.asp?MFAH00ii0, accessed May 2010.

43. See America.gov, "Middle East Peace Chronology."

44. See Dan Izenberg, "Knesset Repeals Ban on Meetings with Terror Groups," *Jerusalem Post* (January 20, 1993): 1.

45. Uri Savir, *The Process: 1,100 Days That Changed the Middle East* (New York: Random House, 1998); Robert O. Freedman, *The Middle East and the Peace Process: The Impact of the Oslo Accords* (Gainesville: University Press of Florida, 1998); Robert Rothstein, Moshe Ma'oz, and Khalil Shiqaqi, eds., *The Israeli-Palestinian Peace Process: Oslo and the Lessons of Failure; Perspectives, Predicaments, and Prospects* (Brighton, U.K.: Sussex Academic Press, 2002).

46. The full text of the Israel-PLO recognition documents can be found on the Israel Ministry of Foreign Affairs Web page: "Ministry of Foreign Affairs," > "Peace Process," > "Reference Documents," > "Israel-PLO Recognition, September 9–10, 1993," at www.mfa.gov.il/mfa/go.asp?MFAH00pz0, accessed May 2010.

47. See America.gov, "Middle East Peace Chronology."

48. See "Rabin, Arafat Hold Talks in Cairo on Palestinian Self-Rule," *Facts on File*, October 6, 1993, accession number: 1993054942. The full text of the Israel-Palestinian Declaration of Principles documents can be found on the Israel Ministry of Foreign Affairs Web page: "Israel-Palestinian Declaration of Principles, September 13, 1993," www.mfa.gov.il/MFA/Peace+Process/Guide+to+the+Peace+Process/ Declaration+of+Principles.htm, accessed May 2010. The full text of the Israel-Jordan Common Agenda documents can be found on the Israel Ministry of Foreign Affairs Web page: "Israel-Jordan Common Agenda, September 14, 1993," www.mfa.gov.il/ MFA/Peace+Process/Guide+to+the+Peace+Process/Israel-Jordan+Common+Agenda .htm, accessed May 2010. See also Dona Stewart, *Good Neighbourly Relations: Jordan, Israel and the 1994–2004 Peace Process* (London: Tauris, 2007).

49. The full text of the Treaty of Peace between Israel and Jordan documents can be found on the Israel Ministry of Foreign Affairs Web page: "Treaty of Peace between Israel and Jordan, October 26, 1994," www.mfa.gov.il/MFA/Peace+Process/ Guide+to+the+Peace+Process/Israel-Jordan+Peace+Treaty.htm, accessed May 2010. See also Avi Shlaim, *Lion of Jordan: The Life of King Hussein in War and Peace* (New York: Knopf, 2008); and Marwan Muasher, *The Arab Center: The Promise of Moderation* (New Haven, Conn.: Yale University Press, 2008).

50. The full text of the Agreement on the Preparatory Transfer of Powers and Responsibilities (Israel-PLO), August 29, 1994, documents can be found on the Israel Ministry of Foreign Affairs Web page: "Agreement on Preparatory Transfer of Powers

and Responsibilities, August 29, 1994," www.mfa.gov.il/mfa/go.asp?MFAH00q90, accessed May 2010.

51. See Israel Ministry of Foreign Relations, "Israel among the Nations: Middle East and North Africa," section "Jordan."

52. The full text of the Israeli-Palestinian Interim Agreement on the West Bank and the Gaza Strip documents can be found on the Israel Ministry of Foreign Affairs Web page: "Interim Agreement between Israel and the Palestinians, September 28, 1995," www.mfa.gov.il/MFA/Peace+Process/Guide+to+the+Peace+Process/ THE+ISRAELI-PALESTINIAN+INTERIM+AGREEMENT.htm, accessed May 2010.

53. "Israel, Palestinians Sign Land-for-Peace Deal, Interim Accord Breaks 19-Month Stalemate in Talks," *Facts on File*, October 23, 1998, accession number: 1998114830.

54. "Israel, Palestinians Sign," *Facts on File*.

55. There is a literature on the role of Europe in the Wye progress. See Commission of the European Communities, "The Role of the European Union in the Peace Process and Its Future Assistance to the Middle East," *Journal of Palestine Studies* 27, no. 3 (1998): 148–51; Philip H. Gordon, *The Transatlantic Allies and the Changing Middle East* (New York: Oxford University Press, 1998); and Alicia Martin-Diaz, "Middle East Peace Process and the European Union: A Working Paper" (Luxembourg: European Parliament, 1999).

56. The full text of the Wye River Memorandum documents can be found on the Irael Ministry of Foreign Affairs Web page: "The Wye River Memorandum, October 23, 1998," www.mfa.gov.il/MFA/Peace+Process/Reference+Documents/ The+Wye+River+Memorandum.htm, accessed May 2010.

57. Don Peretz and Gideon Doron, "Sectarian Politics and the Peace Process: The 1999 Israeli Elections," *Middle East Journal* 54, no. 2 (2000): 259–74. See also Gilead Sher, *The Israeli-Palestinian Peace Negotiations, 1999–2001* (New York: Routledge, 2006).

58. "Palestinian-Israeli Violence Erupts, Killing Nearly 70," *Facts on File*, September 28, 2000, accession number: 2000188160.

59. "Palestinian-Israeli Violence," *Facts on File*.

60. "Barak Resigns, Forcing New Election within 60 Days," *Facts on File*, December 9, 2000, accession number: 2000195460.

61. "Middle East: Sharon Declares Oslo Accord Dead; Other Developments," *Facts on File*, January 10, 2001, accession number: 2001200670.

62. "Likud Leader Sharon Elected Israel's Prime Minister," *Facts on File*, February 6, 2001, accession number: 2001203210.

63. The site includes a wide range of reference materials, including answers to frequently asked questions; Palestinian violence and terrorism; the international war against terrorism; special reports by a wide range of government agencies (last update November 1, 2002); graphs and statistics authored by the IDF spokesman of recent terrorist attacks; a list of victims of Palestinian violence and terrorism since September 2000; the Tenet Cease-Fire Document; the report of the Sharm el-Sheikh Fact-Finding Committee; a list of suicide bombings; a report on the Arab summit in Cairo (October 21–22); the Sharm el-Sheikh summit (October 16–17); documentation on the participation of Palestinian children in violence; copies of the legal indictments of terrorists; background of events; statements, briefings, and interviews

(by Israelis and non-Israelis); official position papers by Israel and the UN (speeches and documents); and other government communiqués. The site is at the Israel Ministry of Foreign Affairs, "Palestinian Violence and Terrorism since 2000," www .mfa.gov.il/MFA/Terrorism-%20Obstacle%20to%20Peace/Palestinian%20 terror%20since%202000/Palestinian%20violence%20and%20terrorism%20 since%20September, accessed May 2010.

64. The final report of the Sharm el-Sheikh Fact Finding Committee can be found on the Israel Ministry of Foreign Affairs Web site, "Sharm el-Sheikh Memorandum on Implementation Timeline of Outstanding Commitments of Agreements Signed and the Resumption of Permanent Status Negotiations," www.mfa.gov.il/MFA/ MFAArchive/1990_1999/1999/9/Sharm+el-Sheikh+Memorandum+on+Implement ation+Timel.htm, accessed May 2010.

65. "Sharm el-Sheikh Memorandum," p. 5.

66. "Saudi Peace Plan Linking Arab Recognition of Israel to Withdrawal from Occupied Lands Gains Support," *Facts on File*, February 17, 2002, accession number: 2002242540.

67. Much of the material in the next two pages comes from Gregory Mahler and Alden Mahler, *The Arab-Israeli Conflict: An Introduction and Documentary Reader* (New York: Routledge, 2010), pp. 29-31. See also on American diplomacy in the Middle East Martin Indyk, *Innocent Abroad: An Intimate Account of American Peace Diplomacy in the Middle East* (New York: Simon and Schuster, 2009), and William Quandt, *Peace Process: American Diplomacy and the Arab-Israeli Conflict Since 1967* (Washington, D.C.: Brookings, 2005).

68. Nationmaster, "Suicide Bombers," www.nationmaster.com/encyclopedia/ Suicide-bombers, accessed May 2010.

69. The full text of the Roadmap can be found at the Israel Ministry of Foreign Affairs Web page, "A Performance Based Roadmap to a Permanent Two-State Solution to the Israeli-Palestinian Conflict,"www.mfa .gov.il/MFA/Peace+Process/Guide+to+the+Peace+Process/A+Performance -Based+Roadmap+to+a+Permanent+Two-Sta.htm, accessed May 2010. As well, the European Union has continued to encourage a peaceful outcome in the Middle East. Their Web page, European Union External Action, "The EU and the Middle East Peace Process," can be found at http://ec.europa.eu/external_relations/mepp/ index_en.htm, last accessed May 2010. See, for a critical approach, Tanya Reinhart, *The Road Map to Nowhere: Israel/Palestine Since 2003* (New York: Verso, 2006).

70. See "Prime Minister Ariel Sharon's Address to the Knesset—the Vote on the Disengagement Plan (October 25, 2004)," as reprinted in *The Arab-Israeli Conflict: An Introduction and Documentary Reader*, by Gregory Mahler and Alden Mahler (London: Routledge, 2010).

71. As'ad Ganim, *Palestinian Politics After Arafat: A Failed National Movement* (Bloomington: Indiana University Press, 2010).

72. BBC News, "U.N. Says Gaza Crisis 'Intolerable'," *BBC News Online*, September 26, 2006, http://news.bbc.co.uk/2/hi/middle_east/5382976.stm, accessed July, 2010.

73. BBC News, "U.N. Says Gaza Crisis 'Intolerable,'" *BBC News Online*, September 26, 2006, http://news.bbc.co.uk/2/hi/middle_east/5382976.stm, accessed July 2010.

74. The text for the Common Agenda can be found at the Israel Ministry of Foreign Affairs Web page: "Israel-Jordan Common Agenda," www.mfa.gov.il/MFA/Peace%20 Process/Guide%20to%20the%20Peace%20Process/Israel-Jordan%20Common%20 Agenda, accessed May 2010. See also Madiha Rashid Al-Madfai and Efraim Karsh, "Jordan, the United States and the Middle East Peace Process, 1974–1991," *Political Studies* 44, no. 4 (1996): 778–80; Adnan Abu Odeh, *Jordanians, Palestinians, and the Hashemite Kingdom in the Middle East Peace Process* (Washington, D.C.: United States Institute of Peace Press, 1999); and Curtis R. Ryan, "Jordan in the Middle East Peace Process: From War to Peace with Israel," in *The Middle East Peace Process: Interdisciplinary Perspectives*, ed. Ilan Peleg (Albany: State University of New York Press, 1998).

75. See the Israel Ministry of Foreign Affairs Web page: "Israel-Jordan Negotiations: The Bilateral Negotiations," www.mfa.gov.il/MFA/Peace%20Process/ Guide%20to%20the%20Peace%20Process/Israel-Jordan%20Negotiations, accessed May 2010.

76. Further discussion of these areas of cooperation can be found on the Israel Ministry of Foreign Affairs Web page: "Israel-Jordan Negotiations."

77. Documents related to Operation Grapes of Wrath can be found on the Israel Ministry of Foreign Affiars Web page: "IDF Operation in Lebanon—Grapes of Wrath," www.mfa.gov.il/MFA/MFAArchive/2000_2009/2003/12/IDF%20Operation%20 in%20Lebanon%20-%20Grapes%20of%20Wrath, accessed May 2010.

78. See the Ministry of Foreign Affairs Web page: "Israel-Lebanon Negotiations: The Bilateral Negotiations," www.mfa.gov.il/MFA/Peace%20Process/Guide%20to%20 the%20Peace%20Process/Israel-Lebanon%20Negotiations, accessed May 2010.

79. Israel Ministry of Foreign Affairs, "Israel-Lebanon Negotiations."

80. Israel Ministry of Foreign Affairs Web page: "Israel-Syria Negotiations: The Bilateral Negotiations," www.mfa.gov.il/MFA/Peace%20Process/Guide%20to%20 the%20Peace%20Process/Israel-Syria%20Negotiations, accessed May 2010.

81. Israel Ministry of Foreign Affairs, "Israel-Syria Negotiations."

82. "Israel Suspends Middle East Peace Process; Barak Takes 'Time Out' for Assessment, Seeks Coalition Government," *Facts on File* 60, no. 3125 (2000): 797.

83. Ilana Kass, Bard O'Neill, and Sheila Katz, "The Deadly Embrace: The Impact of Israeli and Palestinian Rejectionism on the Peace Process," *Middle East Journal* 51, no. 4 (1997): 611–17. See also Yaacov Bar-Siman-Tov, "Israel's Peace-Making with the Palestinians: Change and Legitimacy," in *Israel's Troubled Agenda*, ed. Efraim Karsh (Portland, Ore.: Frank Cass, 1997).

84. Israel Ministry of Foreign Affairs, "Israel-Palestinian Negotiations." See also Indyk, *Innocent Abroad*.

85. See Israel Ministry of Foreign Affairs Web page: "Declaration of Principles on Interim Self-Government Arrangements September 13, 1993," www.mfa .gov.il/MFA/Peace%20Process/Guide%20to%20the%20Peace%20Process/ Declaration%20of%20Principles, accessed May 2010.

86. Israel Ministry of Foreign Affairs, *Facts about Israel*, online edition, at www. mfa.gov.il/MFA/Peace%20Process/Guide%20to%20the%20Peace%20Process/ Declaration%20of%20Principles, accessed May 2010.

87. The Interim Agreement created three different types of areas in the Occupied Territories, according to the Israeli Ministry of Foreign Relations, Israel Ministry of Foreign Affairs Web page, "The Israel-Palestinian Negotiations," www

.mfa.gov.il/MFA/Peace%20Process/Guide%20to%20the%20Peace%20Process/Israel-Palestinian%20Negotiations, accessed May 2010:

"Area A—comprising the main cities of the West Bank: full Palestinian Council responsibility for internal security and public order, as well as full responsibility for civil affairs. (The city of Hebron was subject to special arrangements set out in the Interim Agreement; the Protocol concerning the redeployment in Hebron was signed in January 1997.)

"Area B—comprising small towns and villages in the West Bank: Palestinian Council responsibility for civil affairs (as in Area A) and maintenance of public order, while Israel retained overriding security responsibility to safeguard its citizens and to combat terrorism.

"Area C—comprising all Jewish settlements, areas of strategic importance to Israel and largely unpopulated areas of the West Bank: full Israeli responsibility for security and public order, as well as civil responsibilities related to territory (planning and zoning, archeology, etc.). The Palestinian Council assumes responsibility with regard to all other civil spheres of the Palestinian population."

88. Mr. Per Stig Møller at an interview in Copenhagen, Denmark, May 9, 2003.

89. References to the Road Map come from documents provided by Danish foreign minister Per Stig Møller.

90. Foreign Minister Møller, May 9, 2003.

91. Foreign Minister Møller, May 9, 2003.

Index

About the Author

Gregory S. Mahler was educated at Oberlin College and Duke University, and has studied and taught about Israeli politics for over three decades. He has lived in Jerusalem on several occasions and has been a visiting professor at both the Hebrew University of Jerusalem and Tel Aviv University. He is the author or editor of more than two dozen books and numerous articles, and he has served as president of the Association for Israel Studies. He is currently professor of politics and academic dean and vice president for academic affairs at Earlham College in Richmond, Indiana. His most recent volume on Israeli politics is *The Arab-Israeli Conflict: An Introduction and Documentary Reader* (2010), coedited with his daughter, Alden R. W. Mahler.